Human Rights and the Northern Ireland Conflict

This interdisciplinary book explores the Northern Ireland conflict through a human rights framework.

The book examines the conflict from the creation of the Northern Ireland state in 1921 to 2014. This timeframe allows an analysis of how human rights impacted upon the conflict in its broadest understanding (i.e. the pre-violent conflict, the violent conflict and the post-violent conflict phases). Furthermore, it allows for a better understanding of how the various stages of the conflict impacted upon how human rights are understood in Northern Ireland today. The study's main findings are that: (i) human rights had a significant impact on the development of the conflict; (ii) human rights violations were both underlying causes and direct causes of the descent into violence; (iii) the conflict coloured the view of human rights held by the main political actors; and (iv) human rights continue to be partially understood through the prism of the conflict. More generally, this interdisciplinary work explores the relationship between law, politics and conflict.

This book will be of much interest to students of human rights, conflict resolution, British politics, law and security studies.

Omar Grech is a lecturer at the University of Malta, and has a PhD in politics from the University of Limerick, Ireland.

Law, Conflict and International Relations

Series Editors:

Chandra Lekha Sriram

SOAS

Julie Mertus

American University

Karin Aggestam

University of Lund

and

Lorraine Elliott

Australian National University

This series will bring together cutting-edge, interdisciplinary scholarship on law, conflict, and international politics, encompassing the fields of international criminal law, international human rights law, and international humanitarian law, and law relating to the use of force, and conflict prevention, resolution, peacemaking, and peacebuilding, and resort to the use of force.

International Law, Politics and Inhumane Weapons
The Effectiveness of Global Landmine Regimes
Alan Bryden

Transitional Justice and Peacebuilding on the Ground
Victims and Ex-combatants
Edited by Chandra Lekha Sriram, Jemima Garcia-Godos, Johanna Herman and Olga Martin-Ortega

International Law and Civil Wars
Intervention and Conflict
Eliav Lieblich

Human Rights and the Northern Ireland Conflict
Law, Politics and Conflict 1921–2014
Omar Grech

Human Rights and the Northern Ireland Conflict

Law, Politics and Conflict 1921–2014

Omar Grech

Routledge
Taylor & Francis Group
LONDON AND NEW YORK

First published 2017 by Routledge

2 Park Square, Milton Park, Abingdon, Oxon, OX14 4RN
605 Third Avenue, New York, NY 10017

Routledge is an imprint of the Taylor & Francis Group, an informa business

First issued in paperback 2020

British Library Cataloguing in Publication Data
A catalogue record for this book is available from the British Library

Library of Congress Cataloging in Publication Data
A catalog record for this book has been requested

ISBN: 978-1-138-70471-8 (hbk)
ISBN: 978-0-367-78722-6 (pbk)

Typeset in Bembo
by Wearset Ltd, Boldon, Tyne and Wear

This book is dedicated to my late father Tony and to my nephew Adam Albert.

Contents

Acknowledgements

My initial expression of appreciation is due to Professor Tom Lodge, who supervised the doctorate upon which this book is based. He agreed, without hesitation, to supervise a Maltese lawyer who intended to add to the already voluminous literature on Northern Ireland. His precise and erudite commentary was of inestimable help throughout. Furthermore, I thank Dr Rory Costello and Dr Andrew Shorten who commented in detail on the various chapters incisively and very helpfully. This work has been greatly improved by the comments of Professor Brice Dickson, Professor of International and Comparative Law at Queens University, Belfast.

It is a pleasure to record my gratitude to Dr Colm Regan who read through successive drafts of the dissertation providing advice, encouragement and support. His wife, Hilda Maguire, was always equally supportive and in my visits to Ireland organised beds, transport and meals. In this context, my thanks are due to Ciara Regan and Tony Daly, Aife and Graham Cowap, as well as Anna and John Daly. They all proved, beyond reasonable doubt, that Irish hospitality cannot be surpassed.

Thanks are also due to the Director of the Mediterranean Academy of Diplomatic Studies, Professor Stephen Calleya, who read through the manuscript and provided timely advice and encouragement. I would also like to express my appreciation to the Chancellor of the University of Malta and Judge at the International Tribunal for the Law of the Sea, Professor David J. Attard for his guidance in all matters pertaining to international law. I also thank Professor Juanito Camilleri and Professor Alfred Vella, former and current Rector respectively of the University of Malta, for their support.

In the early phase of my research I was assisted by the Embassy of the USA to Malta with a Fulbright award which allowed me to spend a semester at the School of Conflict Analysis and Resolution, George Mason University. In this respect my thanks to former US Ambassador to Malta, Professor Douglas Kmiec as well as to my good friends Professor Richard Rubenstein, Professor Kevin Avruch, Professor Susan Hirsch, Professor Karina Korostelina and Dr Michael English who all helped make my stay in the USA both productive and pleasurable. Thanks also to my friend Dr Tony Axisa for his support.

I also wish to record my gratitude to the staff of the Linen Hall Library in Belfast for their courteous and punctual assistance. A sincere note of thanks is due to Mr Peter Calleya for casting his meticulous eye on the final text to detect any linguistic errors. My heartfelt appreciation to everyone who agreed to be interviewed by me in the course of my research: Mr Jonathan Bell MLA, Professor Brice Dickson, Ms. Judith Gillespie CBE, Mr Will Kerr, Ms. Emma Little, the Right Honourable Paul Murphy MP, Mr Dermot Nesbitt, Ms Catriona Ruane MLA and Professor Chris Sidoti. It has been a pleasure to work with Hannah Ferguson and Andrew Humphrys at Routledge: their courteous and timely assistance made a difference.

While recording my gratitude to everyone who offered insights and advice during my research, I must stress that any errors or omissions are my own.

Finally, my biggest debt of gratitude is to my family: my brother Marcello, his wife Melanie and my nephew Adam but, above everyone else, my late father Tony and my mother Agnes who always encouraged, assisted and promoted all my academic endeavours.

Abbreviations

CAIN	Conflict Archive on the Internet
CAJ	Committee on the Administration of Justice
CRM	civil rights movement
CSJ	Campaign for Social Justice
DHAC	Derry Housing Action Committee
DUP	Democratic Unionist Party
ECHR	European Convention on Human Rights
HCL	Homeless Citizens League
HET	Historical Enquiries Team
HMIC	Her Majesty's Inspector of Constabulary
HRC	Human Rights Commission
ICCPR	International Covenant on Civil and Political Rights
ICESCR	International Covenant on Economic, Social and Cultural Rights
IRA	Irish Republican Army
MLA	Member of the Legislative Assembly
MP	Member of Parliament
NGO	non-governmental organisation
NICRA	Northern Ireland Civil Rights Association
NIHRC	Northern Ireland Human Rights Commission
NILP	Northern Ireland Labour Party
NIO	Northern Ireland Office
NIPC	Northern Ireland Political Collection
OSCE	Organisation of Security and Cooperation in Europe
PD	People's Democracy
PSNI	Police Service of Northern Ireland
RUC	Royal Ulster Constabulary
SACHR	Standing Advisory Committee on Human Rights
SDLP	Social Democratic and Labour Party
UDHR	Universal Declaration of Human Rights
UUP	Ulster Unionist Party
UUUC	United Ulster Unionist Council
UVF	Ulster Volunteer Force

1 Introduction

Human rights: key issues for Northern Ireland

This study focuses on the human rights agenda in the context of the Northern Ireland conflict in all its phases (pre-violent conflict, violent conflict and post-violent conflict). The development of a human rights lexicon and legislation has been a slow and arduous process in all contexts (local, regional and international) but the process has been more fraught in divided societies which by their very nature render decision making and governance more complex. Northern Ireland is no exception. The development of the human rights agenda in Northern Ireland has faced numerous, strenuous challenges revolving especially around a few key human rights concepts. This introductory section seeks to explain the nature of the research questions posed in this study. It then supplies a succinct overview of the academic treatment of the Northern Irish conflict to clarify how this study will be adding fresh insights and to explicate how this study fits in with the existing literature on the conflict in Northern Ireland. This Introduction concludes with a brief methodological note setting out the methods through which the research questions are explored and answered.

This study will be addressing two related research questions:

1 the extent to which, and ways in which, human rights influenced the Northern Ireland conflict in its various phases (pre-conflict, during conflict and post-conflict); and
2 how the conflict in Northern Ireland influenced the understanding of human rights within Northern Ireland with specific reference to the two main political traditions (i.e. unionism and nationalism).

At the outset, it is important to highlight that this study focuses primarily on the political institutions, processes and players with more limited attention devoted to the manifold activities of civil society. In fact, the role of civil society will only be examined to the extent that it impacted on political institutions, processes and players: most evidently in the civil rights period. This is not to deny the continuing relevance of civil society to the development of human rights in Northern Ireland but rather a recognition that a comprehensive treatment of the role of civil society requires a separate in-depth study. Anything less would not render justice to the complex role played by civil society in Northern Ireland in the field of human rights.

The timeframe adopted for the analysis of these questions and the response to them spans from 1921 with the creation of Northern Ireland until 2014. The essential disagreement that has coloured the history of Northern Ireland – and indeed its right to exist as a separate state – revolves around who has the right to decide its constitutional status. This question falls within the discussion on the right of self-determination in international law. In practice the right of self-determination has two distinct elements: namely, who has the right to exercise it and what can the persons who possess this right decide. Thus, one may formulate the right to self-determination as two distinct questions: who is the "self" in self-determination and what may the "self" determine? The first part of this chapter will seek to answer these two questions.

The political history of Northern Ireland from its creation until the imposition of direct rule in 1973 was a history of one-party rule based on a majoritarian democratic principle. Given the above-cited nature of Northern Ireland as a divided society where elections are about ethnic and sectarian politics, as a result all the elections (which were broadly free and fair) resulted in a majority for the Ulster Unionist Party (UUP) which ruled, virtually unchallenged, for 50 years. This fact, coupled with a generalised feeling of grievance which could not be channelled effectively through the existing political structures, lay at the heart of the decision taken by the nationalist/republican community to take to the streets in the 1960s. The nationalist/republican community perceived that the existing system of parliamentary democracy offered them no prospect of providing them with an effective political voice. As a result a segment of the nationalist and republican community took politics to the streets, with the end result being a slide into violence from which it took 30 years to emerge. Intrinsic to this series of events was a further fundamental disagreement between the two communities, namely a disagreement on the nature of a democratic society. In simple terms the unionist community considered that democratic principles were being abided by in the Northern Ireland political system, with the government being entrusted to the party obtaining the majority of seats in Parliament (and incidentally the majority of votes) in free and fair elections. The nationalist/republican community considered that the characteristic of alternation in government (which characterises most democracies) was absent from Northern Ireland politics and that the majority party ignored the rights and aspirations of the minority community, which was thus denied a voice in shaping its own future.

The sense of grievance held by the nationalist/republican community will be explored fully in the subsequent chapters. At this stage, it suffices to say that a widespread feeling existed within the minority community that the government representing the majority party discriminated against them in issues such as employment, housing, policing, etc. This sense of being discriminated against because of their belonging to the minority community brings to the fore of the debate the issue of minority rights. The issue of minority rights is clearly and strongly linked with the issues of self-determination and of democracy. Minority rights constitute a guarantee for those citizens of the state whose views on self-determination are not prevalent and whose democratic rights consist in voting in elections where their political views do not have a realistic possibility of ever being implemented.

As the nationalist/republican community perceived this denial of their minority rights as being perpetrated by the governing unionist party, one of the issues with which the nationalist/republican community had to contend was the means through which they could advance their legitimate rights. In this context, a fracture existed within the same minority community as to what were legitimate avenues through which they could achieve their aims. Broadly speaking nationalists advocated peaceful, non-violent methods (including peaceful street protests) whereas republicans accepted that violence was also a legitimate means through which what they considered to be their rights could be sought. Fundamentally what this republican perspective meant in human rights terms was that certain rights (in this case the republican conception of self-determination and of minority protection) trumped the rights of those who were the victims of violence. Thus, in this context, it is important to examine the relevant debates on the interdependence and indivisibility of human rights as well as when (if ever) and to what extent some rights may take precedence over other rights.

However, before exploring each of these key human rights issues in turn, a brief introduction to the practice and theory of human rights will contextualise the subsequent and more focused discussion. In particular, the general legal and political framework in which human rights emerged as a force in world and domestic affairs will be described and briefly examined.

Why human rights in Northern Ireland?

The Northern Ireland conflict has been explored and examined through numerous perspectives. In 1990 John Whyte commented that since 1968 there "has been an explosion of research on the area" and that "it is quite possible that in proportion to size Northern Ireland is the most heavily researched area on earth".[1] Since 1990 the amount of research on Northern Ireland has undoubtedly multiplied. The 1998 Peace Agreement itself provided an extended scope for examination of how peace was achieved and the inevitable reflections on lessons learned from the Northern Irish experience in peace making. The basic premise of this study is that notwithstanding the plethora of literature on the Northern Ireland conflict, there has been no sustained study of the conflict, conflict resolution and post-conflict phase from a human rights perspective.

Whyte's study examines the literature on Northern Ireland from a number of perspectives. In the first part he analyses the literature on the community divide in Northern Ireland from religious, economic, political and psychological perspectives; while in the second part Whyte identifies four strands of literature on the nature of the conflict: (i) nationalist interpretations; (ii) unionist interpretations; (iii) Marxist interpretations; and (iv) internal conflict interpretations. Throughout these various strands of interpretation of the community divide and conflict, human rights perspectives feature in numerous ways. Studies that offer economic interpretations, for instance, draw heavily on issues of discrimination. Likewise, religious interpretations also include references to discrimination and religious rights. However, the conflict is not interpreted, examined and explored from a primarily human rights perspective.

The CAIN (Conflict Archive on the Internet) Ulster website recommended reading bibliography,[2] lists 169 books under 14 categories. None of these publications deals exclusively with an exclusive human rights perspective except for a Committee on the Administration of Justice (CAJ) publication entitled *Civil Liberties in Northern Ireland: The CAJ Handbook*. This publication provides "advice and information on a wide variety of common legal problems encountered by people living in Northern Ireland".[3] Therefore, this publication is intended as a guide to citizens and other persons living in Northern Ireland on their legal rights and obligations and on the mechanisms available to them to implement such rights. It does not examine the development of human rights in the context of the conflict and the impact of the conflict on human rights in Northern Ireland.

In fact, the key difference of this study in comparison to other studies of the conflict is that it adopts a human rights framework of analysis. In practice, this means that the study utilises international and regional human rights law for analysing political developments (particularly the various developments related to the conflict) in Northern Ireland in the period 1921–2014.[4]

The fundamental questions it seeks to answer are to what extent have human rights impacted on the conflict, conflict resolution and post-conflict situation in Northern Ireland and to what extent have human rights in Northern Ireland been shaped by the conflict? These are questions that have not been addressed before as comprehensively as they will be treated in this study. A further difference of this study from existing literature on the Northern Ireland conflict with respect to human rights relates to the timeframe adopted in this study (1921–2014). Existing literature on the Northern Ireland conflict traditionally explores human rights issues in Northern Ireland in the context of the civil rights period.

In contrast, this study examines the impact human rights had on the conflict as well as the effect of the conflict on the human rights agenda in Northern Ireland during all the various phases of the conflict. This broader discussion of the relationship between human rights and conflict in Northern Ireland is part of the originality of this study. Although it is sometimes assumed that human rights did not exist until the adoption of the Universal Declaration on Human Rights in 1948, the story and history of human rights is of much longer standing. Ideas of natural rights and natural law, the rule of habeas corpus, the struggle against discrimination and slavery, the rhetoric of Magna Carta, the Glorious Revolution, the French Declaration of the Rights of Man and of the Citizen and the American Declaration of Independence, religious and secular ideals of social justice, as well as numerous other social and legal developments predated, the Universal Declaration of Human Rights (UDHR). While it is true that a sustained effort at the international legal protection of human rights only occurred after 1945, it is essential to recognise the important historical antecedents which allowed the creation of an international legal architecture for the promotion and protection of human rights.

In the context of this study the adoption of a human rights framework of analysis of the Northern Irish conflict is important to assess the extent to which even prior to the descent into violent conflict – and indeed from the inception of the Northern Irish state – the language of discrimination and rights permeated political discourse. The early part of the study will, in fact, throw light on the adoption of human rights discourse by both communities. As will transpire in subsequent chapters the adoption of stringent measures relating to law and order were defended by the Unionists as necessary to protect the ancient liberties enjoyed by the people of the United Kingdom. Conversely, the security measures were denounced by the minority nationalist community as an attack on their freedoms while the economic disadvantage they suffered was described within the context of the language of discrimination.

John Whyte's 1990 seminal work *Interpreting Northern Ireland*[5] divided the literature up to the period into four main schools: Traditional Unionist, Traditional nationalist, Marxist (of diverse hues) and Internal-Conflict. This distinction is still a valid and useful one in terms of categorising the literature on the Northern Ireland conflict. Since the publication of Whyte's *Interpreting Northern Ireland* a large amount of literature on Northern Ireland has been published. Among the key studies that examine and seek to explain the development of the conflict since Whyte are: Bowyer Bell's *The Irish Troubles: A Generation of Violence 1967–1992*[6] published in 1993; McGarry and O'Leary's *Explaining Northern Ireland*[7] published in 1995; Bew, Gibbon and Patterson's *Northern Ireland, 1921–2001: Political Forces and Social Classes*[8] published in 2002; Bew's *Ireland: The Politics of Enmity*[9] published in 2007; and Cochrane's *Northern Ireland: The Reluctant Peace*[10] published in 2013.

Of these publications, Bowyer Bell's work adopts a broadly Internal-Conflict type of analysis which emphasises the political and the paramilitary perspectives. This does not mean he fails to consider the roles played by the UK and Irish governments, but altogether the focus of the book is on the Northern Irish political and paramilitary protagonists. The study is limited to the period of 1967 to 1992 which means that the study does not delve sufficiently into the root causes of the conflict which clearly preceded 1967. Bowyer Bell's evidently intimate knowledge of republican paramilitary circles is not matched with a similar knowledge and understanding of loyalist paramilitary circles. This may be viewed as skewing the balance of the book.

In *Explaining Northern Ireland*, McGarry and O'Leary perform two tasks: they review the literature on the Northern Ireland conflict and then they provide their own analysis of the conflict and suggest possible solutions. In reviewing the literature of the conflict they depart slightly from Whyte's classification by extending the categories through which they classify the literature. Apart from nationalist and Unionist interpretations, they refer also to interpretations based on Green Political Economy; and interpretations based on Revisionist Marxism. These classifications are broadly in line with Whyte's (with the addition of Green Political Economy). However, under the general rubric of Internal Explanations of the conflict McGarry and O'Leary identify three categories of interpretation: interpretations based on religious divides; interpretations based on cultural divides and, finally, interpretations based on Liberal Economics. In their own explanation of the conflict they adopt an ethno-national conflict approach which in itself can be classified as an essentially internal explanation of the conflict (not without external influences).

Bew *et al.*'s *Northern Ireland: 1921–2001 Political Forces and Social Classes* is essentially a Revisionist Marxist approach to explaining the descent into violence in Northern Ireland giving weight to the economic factors behind the civil rights movement and highlighting the growing divide between the Protestant elite and the broader Protestant population. In fact, the authors effectively ascribe the dissolution of the Protestant rule in Northern Ireland to this rift between elites and the proletariat. In his more recent publication *Ireland: The Politics of Enmity* (2007) Bew provides a survey of Irish history (north and south) which moves away from the Marxist Revisionist approach and instead develops a primarily political narrative based on Irish and UK political actors. The parts dealing with the conflict in Northern Ireland present the conflict as essentially an internal one (internal understood as encompassing the islands of Ireland and Britain) and one characterised by internal politics. For instance, he characterises the failure by the British government to dissolve Stormont upon taking over the security of Northern Ireland in 1969 as an error which facilitated the deepening violence. Thus, Bew presents a predominantly internal political narrative that weaves together British, Irish and Northern Irish perspectives.

One of the most recent explorations of the Northern Ireland conflict is Feargal Cochrane's *Northern Ireland: The Reluctant Peace* (2013). Cochrane examines the conflict from the late 1960s onwards and argues that the Peace Process has not yet delivered its full promise for the people of Northern Ireland. In describing how divisions between Protestants and Catholics were exacerbated by the violent conflict, Cochrane adopts a primarily internal explanation while not ignoring external influences and factors that have aided the Peace Process to develop. Cochrane like other authors considers some of the human rights aspects of the conflict from the civil rights period onwards.

Whyte's categorisation of the Northern Ireland conflict literature is not without difficulties. For example, this categorisation includes in the Internal-Conflict category works which give significant attention and weight to external explanations of the conflict such as Adrian Guelke's *Northern Ireland: The International Perspective* or Frank Wright's *Northern Ireland: A Comparative Perspective* which, as Whyte concedes, is "interested in the interaction of internal and external forces" that shape the conflict.[11] This approach which adopts a combined internal/external interaction focus has been increasingly important as the Peace Process developed and took shape. Indeed it is probably more precise to classify such publications under the rubric of "Internal Dynamics and External Factors Interaction".

The increasing role of UK–Republic of Ireland negotiations, the role of the USA and, more limitedly, the role of European institutions in the run-up to and the immediate aftermath of the Peace Agreement has naturally increased academic attention towards the international perspective. Adrian Guelke has contributed significantly to the literature on the role of the USA in the Northern Ireland peace process.[12] On the European dimension, of special interest is the work of Brice Dickson whose book on the role of the European Convention on Human Rights (ECHR) in the conflict demonstrates the gradual impact the Convention had on certain aspects of the conflict while at the same time acknowledging its limitations in dealing with crisis situations.[13] Dickson's analysis is framed within the specific confines of the European Convention which focuses on a specific set of rights (Articles 2 to 14 and other rights protected under the various Protocols). In this sense, it is different from the more comprehensive approach to human rights adopted in this study.[14] Moreover, while Dickson's timeframe extends from 1968, this study, as already highlighted, adopts a longer timeframe commencing from the formation of the Northern Irish state. The literature that adopts an internal-external interaction approach is especially relevant given that this study also adopts this approach. In examining the relevance of human rights to the development of the conflict this study also hypothesises that some of the root causes of the conflict as well as some of its developments have been impacted upon by externally derived norms.

There is a branch of the Northern Ireland conflict literature that focuses more closely on the role of human rights in the conflict. The previously cited book on the European Convention by Brice Dickson is an eminent example. This publication has a very precise focus with the ECHR being the dominant framework of analysis. Other relevant literature is the CAJ publication edited by Brice Dickson and Brian Gormally entitled *Human Rights in Northern Ireland: The Committee on the Administration of Justice Handbook* which provides detailed information on a wide range of specific rights with explanations of existing laws and case-law for each right. As the title to the handbook implies this publication provides a clear and relatively exhaustive exposition of the applicable legal norms protecting human rights in Northern Ireland as well as the existing interpretations of such norms.

Two other major contributors to the human rights literature in Northern Ireland are Christine Bell and Colin Harvey. Christine Bell's *Peace Agreements and Human Rights*[15] published in 2000 examines the relationship between human rights and peace agreements not limited to Northern Ireland, although Northern Ireland features substantially in the argument as one of the four key case studies. Bell's approach focuses on the role of human rights in the peace processes and particularly in the peace agreement with a rigorous legal approach but without engaging significantly in explaining the causes of the conflict from a historical perspective. Colin Harvey has also brought a wealth of human rights legal expertise to bear on the issue of human rights in Northern Ireland. The 2009 article *Designing a Bill of Rights for Northern Ireland* examines the complexity of delivering a Bill of Rights for Northern Ireland as envisaged in the Agreement from a constitutional and political point of view while arguing that such a delivery could transform Northern Ireland into a model human rights jurisdiction. Harvey, as editor of *Human Rights, Equality and Democratic Renewal in Northern Ireland* published in 2001, examines the complexity which the Peace Agreement presents in terms of the constitutional set up of the United Kingdom with a strong focus on human rights and equality perspectives. The key premise of the book is that the delivery of all the elements of the Peace Agreement presents a "significant challenge which impacts upon the constitutional set-up of the UK" and which will necessitate a "re-think of the orthodox understandings of constitutional law and politics in the United Kingdom".[16]

In comparison, this study bridges the historical approaches (adopted by Bew, Bowyer Bell, McGarry and O'Leary, as well as others) which contribute different interpretations of the conflict with the human rights thematic approach adopted, inter alia, by Dickson, Bell and Harvey. It bridges the gap between essentially political or economic narratives and legal interpretations. Similar to the historical narratives, this study adopts a broadly historical chronology which, however, is interpreted using a human rights framework of analysis. This human rights framework of analysis, while rooted in international, regional and domestic human rights standards, is adopted to interpret key events that shaped the conflict in Northern Ireland which is viewed as a predominantly Northern Irish conflict revolving, at least partially, around competing interpretations of rights. Thus, the study with its human rights perspective applied to Northern Ireland's internal dynamics places itself in the Internal Dynamics and External Factors Interaction literature. Most importantly, viewing the history of Northern Ireland through a human rights prism supplies a different understanding of the causes of key developments. As will be evidenced in the Conclusion, a human rights prism contributes a significant added value to the understanding of the impact of human rights on the conflict, the politics and the current situation in Northern Ireland.

The questions posed by a human rights framework of analysis are anchored in international human rights standards that have evolved over the past 100 years but which have even more remote antecedents. In particular, the human rights framework that will be utilised in this study is based on the UN Universal Declaration of Human Rights, UN human rights treaties and the European Convention on Human Rights. This framework is thus clearly founded on the international and regional standards which have been accepted by the United Kingdom, Ireland and the rest of the European continent. Most importantly, these rights are taken to be applicable *as a whole* and situations where rights are singled out for unique application or exception will be highlighted. The universality, indivisibility and interdependence of human rights, as emphasised by the relevant United Nations resolutions and declarations, will also form part of the human rights framework that this study adopts as its point of departure.[17] This is particularly relevant in the context of human rights since, as will be argued in this study, the conflicting communities have (at times) sought to apply human rights selectively depending on which rights suited their cause.

The study will suggest that this selective approach to human rights has been both a partial cause of the conflict as well as a root cause for the still unsurmounted obstacles in implementing the human rights dimension of the Northern Ireland Peace Agreement. This has also resulted in a more general failure to achieve positive peace or, in the language of the Universal Declaration of Human Rights, a failure to construct a community where people "act towards one another in a spirit of brotherhood".[18]

Methodology

This study adopts a qualitative research methodology with a focus on the identification, collection and interpretation of primary documentary sources. The choice of primary sources – with respect to documents – was influenced by the main question which this study seeks to explore and answer, i.e. the impact of human rights doctrines on political decision making and programmatic thinking. This meant that the main concern of the study was to identify ways in which conceptions of human rights surface in the more formalised language of politics – when it is addressed to a public constituency. Thus, the choice of evidence tends to focus on the level of "high politics" – parliamentary debates, expressions of formal political commitment such as manifestos and programmes, and agreements.

The primary sources which have been identified and collected fall into five broad categories. The first category refers to documents produced by United Kingdom (UK) and Northern Irish governmental authorities and agencies including: correspondence to and from Ministers, civil servants and politicians; public and confidential reports with a special emphasis on confidential reports that have been released as per the 30-year rule operated by the UK government; and legislation enacted by the UK Parliament, the Northern Irish Parliament and the Northern Irish Executive.

The second category of primary source materials can be described as documents produced by the international and regional governmental and non-governmental organisations such as the United Nations, the United Nations High Commission for Human Rights, Amnesty International. These documents were identified and collected from the websites of the relevant organisations. A third category of materials refers to legal materials, composed of international, regional and domestic legal instruments and court decisions emanating from courts in the UK, Northern Ireland and the European Court of Human Rights. These were identified and collected on the relevant UK legal databases and the website of the European Court of Human Rights.

The fourth category relates to documents produced by UK and Northern Irish political parties including electoral manifestos, policy documents as well as politically significant correspondence of representatives of political parties. The final category of primary source materials consists of interviews with Northern Irish politicians (and former politicians), individuals who played a key role in human rights work in Northern Ireland and also interviews with current and former high-ranking members of the Police Service of Northern Ireland (PSNI). The Northern Irish politicians were identified with two main criteria in mind: that they were involved (or are still involved) in the Northern Irish political process and that they represent the two major political traditions in Northern Ireland. Given that the Northern Irish conflict, as will be argued, revolves on the conflict between the two main traditions, representation of the two major political traditions was essential. The interviewees who played a key role in the evolving human rights agenda in Northern Ireland are the first Chair of the Northern Ireland Human Rights Commission (NIHRC) as well as the Chair of the Bill of Rights Forum. The choice of members of the Police Service of Northern Ireland relates to the transformation of the policing system in Northern Ireland into a police system with a high focus on human rights, which has been one of the major legacies of the Peace Agreement.

Thus, the interviewing focuses on informants who could speak with authority about fairly recent developments. Unlike historians who work with oral testimony, the study is not interested in retrospective recollection because of the obvious danger that participants in events occurring decades ago might explain their actions with ex post facto rationalisations.

The study examines and interprets these primary source materials to provide answers to the two research questions posed in this study. Furthermore, the study also utilises secondary source materials such as books, journal and newspaper articles and other similar materials to complement the primary source materials. Such secondary sources provide alternative views and interpretations of the facts examined throughout this study. Some of the secondary source materials, such as memoirs written by political protagonists as well as newspaper articles recording specific events and occurrences, also complement the primary sources which have been utilised.

Chapter outline

The next chapter provides the human rights framework which anchors the study; it explains the human rights concepts that are utilised throughout the study and outlines the chronology of the rise of human rights on the international plane. Chapter 3 then explores how language on discrimination and equality developed in Northern Ireland during the period starting from the founding of the state until after World War II. The chapter argues that the language of discrimination and equality, which lies at the heart of the concept of human rights, played an important role in the political discourse of the early years of the Northern Irish state. This argument is an important one to understand later attitudes to human rights within Northern Ireland and to establish that rights-based discourse has a longer pedigree within Northern Ireland than usually recognised.

Within this context, Chapter 4 examines how the civil rights period brought an unprecedented level of engagement with rights language and ideas in Northern Ireland. It also explores how the events of the period changed perceptions about rights in Northern Ireland. The chapter establishes that the emphasis on rights language during this period created a trajectory which in later decades would be continuously returned to in Northern Ireland's political discourse and influenced to some extent the Northern Irish political actors. The longer-term impact of the civil rights movement's focus on rights also contributed a strong rights agenda becoming virtually inevitable as the political peace process developed.

Building on the previous chapter, the main argument in Chapter 5 is that in the 1970s and 1980s two important strands developed in Northern Ireland with respect to human rights. The first strand highlighted in this chapter refers to the extent to which the descent into violence was fuelled by human rights violations and how violence exacerbated human rights abuses. This descent into violence brought the debate on self-determination to the fore at the expense of a focus on rights. The second strand developed in this chapter relates to how in parallel with, and notwithstanding, the above-mentioned strand human rights language maintained a role in the Northern Irish political landscape. This chapter argues both that human rights violations impacted on the conflict in significant ways and that the continuing concern with rights in Northern Ireland led to human rights becoming an important part of the peace process and the eventual peace agreement. Fundamentally, the chapter holds that the growing international respectability of human rights helped maintain some focus on rights even as violent conflict raged with self-determination as the key political question. Chapter 6 covers a crucial period when political actors in Northern Ireland engaged more deeply with rights language and the Peace Agreement with a strong human rights dimension was adopted. The chapter argues that human rights shaped to some degree the political choices of Northern Irish political parties as well as decisions taken by the UK and Irish governments. Furthermore, it is contended that as globally accepted human rights norms became ever more influential internationally, they also played a role in achieving a political settlement in Northern Ireland.

Chapter 7 examines how the human rights agenda has developed in the post-conflict phase with a focus on the extent to which the human rights dimension of the Peace Agreement has been implemented. This chapter assesses the success and failures of the human rights agenda while reflecting on why there have been these successes and failures. It also explores how and why in today's Northern Ireland the main political traditions continue to use the language of rights extensively. The chapter demonstrates that the use of rights language in Northern Ireland increased during this period, mirroring the growing role of human rights standards both regionally and internationally.

The concluding chapter outlines how the language of human rights and ideas about rights evolved in Northern Ireland, pointing out that they have a longer history than usually acknowledged. The chapter also establishes that human rights concepts have both influenced the conflict to a significant degree and that human rights understandings in Northern Ireland were themselves influenced by the conflict.

Notes

1 John Henry Whyte, *Interpreting Northern Ireland* (Oxford: Clarendon Press, 1990), viii.
2 Martin Melaugh, "The Troubles – Suggested Reading", 1 November 2007, http://cain.ulst.ac.uk/bibdbs/bibliography/index.html.
3 Brice Dickson, ed., *Civil Liberties in Northern Ireland: The CAJ Handbook*, 2nd edn. (The Committee on the Administration of Justice, 1993), 6.
4 A human rights framework of analysis is an accepted academic analytical framework; see, for example, Rory O'Connell, Aoife Nolan, Colin Harvey, Mira Dutschke and Eoin Rooney, *Applying an International Human Rights Framework to State Budget Allocations: Rights and Resources* (Routledge, 2014).
5 Whyte, *Interpreting Northern Ireland.*
6 J. Bowyer Bell, *The Irish Troubles: A Generation of Violence 1967–1992* (New York: St. Martin's Press, 1993).
7 John McGarry and Brendan O'Leary, *Explaining Northern Ireland: Broken Images* (Oxford and Massachusetts: Blackwell Publishers, 1995).
8 Paul Bew, Peter Gibbon and Henry Patterson, *Northern Ireland 1921–2001: Political Forces and Social Classes* (London: Serif, 2001).
9 Paul Bew, *Ireland: The Politics of Enmity 1789–2006* (Oxford: Oxford University Press, 2007).
10 Feargal Cochrane, *Northern Ireland: The Reluctant Peace* (New Haven: Yale University Press, 2013).
11 Whyte, *Interpreting Northern Ireland*, 201.
12 See, for example, Adrian Guelke, "The United States and the Peace Process", in *The Northern Ireland Question: The Peace Process and the Belfast Agreement*, ed. Brian Barton and Patrick J. Roche (London: Palgrave Macmillan, 2009); and Adrian Guelke, "The USA and the Northern Ireland Peace Process", *Ethnopolitics* 4, no. 4 (November 2012): 424–38.
13 Brice Dickson, *The European Convention on Human Rights and the Conflict in Northern Ireland* (New York: Oxford University Press, 2012).
14 The fundamental difference of this study from Dickson's is that while Dickson's book focuses on the contribution made during the conflict by the European Convention on Human Rights, this study focuses on the impact of human rights as a whole on the conflict. Dickson's key questions are summarised by the author as follows:

> Has the European Convention, through its adjudication and enforcement organs, satisfactorily protected people's human rights during the conflict? Has

> it helped to bring the conflict to an end, or has it in any way facilitated its prolongation? Whatever the answers to these questions, they lead to two further lines of inquiry: how has the European Convention itself been affected by the issues arising out of the conflict in Northern Ireland, and can the Convention now make a positive contribution to the regulation of conflicts elsewhere in Europe on the basis of what has been learned from dealing with the conflict in Northern Ireland?

These are substantially different questions from the ones posed in this study.

15 Christine Bell, *Peace Agreements and Human Rights* (Oxford: Oxford University Press, 2000).

16 Colin J. Harvey, ed., *Human Rights, Equality and Democratic Renewal in Northern Ireland* (Oxford: Hart Publishing, 2001), 1.

17 The 1993 UN World Conference on Human Rights stated: "All human rights are universal, indivisible and interdependent and interrelated. The international community must treat human rights globally in a fair and equal manner, on the same footing, and with the same emphasis." United Nations World Conference on Human Rights, *Vienna Declaration and Programme of Action.*

18 United Nations General Assembly, *The Universal Declaration of Human Rights*, Article 1.

2 Human rights

Key notions

Human rights: an introduction

The concept of human rights is a revolutionary one when considered in the context of the nation state. Ever since the Westphalian model of the state emerged in the late seventeenth century the notion of state sovereignty and non-interference in the internal affairs of other states evolved into a fundamental rule of international relations. The concept of state sovereignty (where a state owes no allegiance to any superior authority) when translated into practice meant that states were not accountable to anyone when they acted within their territorial borders.[1] Effectively the way in which a state treated its own citizens within its borders was a matter for that state only.

This notion of absolute sovereignty of states was gradually eroded because of a series of campaigns that sought to place some limits on the way in which states acted within their borders. The initial campaign waged from the middle of the nineteenth century revolved around the abolition of slavery and the slave trade. The campaign was successful to the extent that by the end of the century slavery and the slave trade became effectively illegal under international law and slavery could no longer be allowed by states within their borders. Thus, the sovereignty of states was limited (in however miniscule a manner) by the fact they could not allow slavery and the slave trade to be practiced within their territory.

A second movement which sought to limit the sovereignty of states was that which developed as a result of the end of World War I. This referred to the protection of minorities within certain states following the redrawing of numerous national borders in the wake of the Great War.[2] As a result of this movement certain states were prevented from taking measures prejudicing a number of rights of minority groups and this limited their sovereignty to a small degree.[3] During the same period the International Labour Organisation also embarked on a campaign to secure certain basic rights for workers, which states would have to guarantee.

Between 1919 and 1936 the International Labour Organisation sponsored 44 conventions[4] which came into force and covered a wide array of workers' rights from hours of work to safety provisions and holidays with pay. Thus, states which became parties to these conventions were obliged to ensure that workers within their jurisdiction enjoyed the rights set forth in the various conventions. Again, the sovereignty of states (in this case within the ambit of employment legislation) was being slightly restricted through the operation of international law.

The well documented atrocities of the World War II period forced the international community to reflect on necessary interventions to avoid such atrocities in the future with action being agreed on two fronts – human rights and human responsibilities. At the Nuremberg Tribunals of 1945/1946, set up to try Nazi war criminals, a key principle was established – individuals have responsibilities and obligations under international law. Therefore, individuals who commit grave breaches of human rights are responsible under international law for such breaches and are liable for them.

The human rights side of the coin was immediately evident in the Preamble to the Charter of the United Nations (1945) which points out that one of the aims of the UN is that of "encouraging respect for human rights and for fundamental freedoms". The Charter contains numerous references to the term human rights but there is no definition or description of the term – the task of definition fell to the Commission on Human Rights established by the General Assembly of the UN and led to the formulation of the Universal Declaration on Human Rights, adopted on 10 December 1948. This Declaration was eventually followed by two conventions (the International Covenant on Civil and Political Rights and the International Covenant on Economic, Social and Cultural Rights) which came into force vis-à-vis state parties in 1976.

Essentially, the net effect of these initiatives was to restrict further the sovereignty of states in terms of the treatment of their own nationals. The Nuremberg principles sought to achieve this aim by holding individuals (including responsible officials and political and military leaders) liable for grave human rights breaches. On the other hand, the Declaration and the two Covenants required states to protect fundamental rights and freedoms that are essential to ensure the dignity of the human person. Apart from these universal and general human rights covenants, the international community also saw the adoption of numerous thematic human rights treaties in areas such as racial discrimination, women's rights, torture and children's rights amongst others. Furthermore, regional organisations have also adopted conventions which establish human rights protection mechanisms in Africa, the Americas as well as Europe.[5]

The proliferation of human rights conventions as well as the increasing adoption of the human rights agenda in all its facets by governmental and non-governmental organisations at the local, regional and international levels has transformed human rights into a key component of domestic and international politics. It has been argued that "the idea of human right has wings. It has its way around the globe, and we are reminded often of its importance."[6] All told, human rights have had a dramatic impact on a range of state (and organisational) behaviours, activities and policies. Hardly any area of political life is immune from the influence of human rights. A raft of domestic policies dealing with housing, employment, and even tax may be viewed from the perspective of social and economic rights. The behaviour of states in the field of justice and security is increasingly assessed with reference to international human rights standards[7] while foreign policy is also being influenced by human rights concerns. It is clear that the absolute sovereignty of states established in the Treaty of Westphalia has been very gradually, but persistently, eroded by the rise of human rights. As Richard Falk has argued,

> there is a clear trend away from the idea of unconditional sovereignty and toward a conception of responsible sovereignty, namely, that governmental legitimacy depends upon adherence to minimum humanitarian norms and on a capacity to act effectively to protect citizens from acute threats to their security and well-being.[8]

Self-determination: for whom?

One of the problems associated with the rise of the Westphalian nation state refers to the stability of the state as a political unit enjoying a well defined territorial integrity. This stability and territorial integrity of the state is challenged when a certain group, within the population of a state, sharing a common language, religion, ethnicity or other characteristic claims the right to secede from the state in order to form a separate and sovereign political unit.

According to Thomas Franck there have been three major historic waves of state formation, dissolution and transformation which have impacted heavily on the development of international relations and international law. In particular, he highlights "the disintegration of the Spanish-American Empire, the defeat of Imperial Germany, Austro-Hungary and the Sublime-Porte, and the rise of anti-colonialism and nationalism in Africa, Asia and the Caribbean"[9] as key moments when territorial integrity and political stability were severely challenged. The defeat of Imperial Germany, Austro-Hungary and the Sublime-Porte coincided with the development of the concept of self-determination in international relations and in international law that would pose a continuing and present danger to state stability and territorial integrity. The principle was proposed separately and with different nuances by Woodrow Wilson and Vladimir Lenin.

The Wilsonian right of self-determination was meant to apply to the post-war European context with the prospect of its application to other continents at some future, indeterminate date. In fact, nowhere in the Fourteen Points does one find an unequivocal proclamation of the right of peoples to determine their own destiny autonomously. Point Five advocates:

> A free, open-minded, and absolutely impartial adjustment of all colonial claims, based upon a strict observance of the principle that in determining all such questions of sovereignty the interests of the populations

> concerned must have equal weight with the equitable claims of the government whose title is to be determined.[10]

This in no way implied an absolute right to self-determination for colonial peoples. Conversely, the Leninist conception of self-determination was a radical one "and he intended it to apply unconditionally to the non-European peoples being held in the grasp of the colonial order".[11]

There is no doubt that in the short term Wilson's formulation was applied in preference to Lenin's, although it is equally clear that the Leninist approach found its application in the context of the anti-colonial movement of the 1950s and 1960s. Nevertheless, both formulations were essentially political ones which were difficult to translate into precise legal norms. The essentially political nature of the concept of self-determination and its various contrasting interpretations constitute both its enduring appeal as well as its central weakness. Even at the very inception of the concept, the definition of what a unit entitled to self-determination could determine was unclear. Falk, for example, mentions that Wilson's Secretary of State had clarified the Wilsonian right to self-determination as consisting of self-government within existing colonial structures.[12]

This interpretation was maintained vis-à-vis the colonial territories of Africa and Asia with the establishment of the Mandate system administered by the League of Nations. However, within the European context this was disregarded with respect for example to the constituent states of the Austro-Hungarian Empire. Thus, from the very beginning the notion of self-determination was pulled in different directions by the forces of political convenience, morality and law.

The UN Charter failed to clarify the concept of self-determination although it is mentioned twice in the text of the Charter. Article 1(2) states that one of the aims of the UN is "[t]o develop friendly relations among nations based on respect for the principle of equal rights and self-determination of peoples, and to take other appropriate measures to strengthen universal peace".

Equally unenlightening is the reference in Article 55 which holds that relations among nations should be based on respect for the principle of equal rights and self-determination of peoples. One may suggest that these two mentions only served to expedite the move of self-determination from a political principle to the realm of international law and to emphasise that self-determination belonged to peoples. At the same time it has been argued that self-determination, in contrast to sovereignty and all that flows from it, was not originally perceived as an operative principle of the Charter, "it was one of the desiderata of the Charter rather than a legal right that could be invoked as such".[13] While this may have been the case at the time the Charter was adopted, the dual reference to self-determination in the constituent treaty of the leading international organisation was bound in the medium term to glaze the concept of self-determination with a patina of legality which soon deepened. Whatever the legal effect of the inclusion of the concept of self-determination in the Charter, questions about the content of the principle remained. In particular, issues relating to who qualified as a people, how the self could be identified and what such self could determine remained open questions.

Crawford interprets the references to self-determination in the Charter by providing two possible alternatives. He explains that

> the term can refer to the sovereign equality of existing States, and, in particular, the right of the people of a State to choose its own form of government without external intervention. It can also mean the right of a specific territory (or more correctly its peoples) to choose their own form of government irrespective of the wishes of the rest of the State of which that territory is a part.[14]

Once again the uncertainty around the exact content of self-determination is apparent.

The UN again returned to the concept of self-determination in the 1960s, initially with an important General Assembly Resolution adopted in 1960 and then also in the texts of the two Human Rights Covenants adopted in 1966. General Assembly Resolution 1514 of December 1960 adopted the Declaration on the Granting of Independence to Colonial Countries and Peoples which, inter alia, declared that: "All peoples have the right to self-determination; by virtue of that right they freely determine their political status and freely pursue their economic, social and cultural development." This formulation reiterates the point that self-determination pertains to peoples but, in this case, it is clear from the preamble (and the title) that it particularly referred to peoples who are under colonial rule. Furthermore, the concept of self-determination is clearly moved from a purely political concept to a legal one with the reference to the "right" to self-determination. The formulation adopted in this resolution also attempts to answer the question relating to the content of this right. It indicates that what the self can determine is its political status and matters relating to their economic, cultural and social development. Although within the context of this resolution (clearly advocating for an end to colonial rule) the right to self-determination was clearly associated with the creation of new post-colonial states, the right to determine one's political status does not in itself imply a right to secession. Political status may also refer to diverse systems of government such as republicanism, monarchical systems (of various kinds), federalism, etc.

In the 1960s the anti-colonial sentiment was at its highest and the concept of self-determination proved to be a useful tool to break colonial rule in Asia, Africa and other parts of the world. To this day there is no doubt that the peoples of territories under colonial rule or under foreign occupation have in international law a right to self-determination that may be expressed in three ways:

1 by emerging as a sovereign independent state;
2 through free association with an independent state;
3 via integration with an independent state.[15]

However, by the 1970s the number of peoples living under colonial rule (as traditionally understood) or under foreign domination had dwindled to a handful of territories. At the same time, a more difficult and potentially destabilising question arose, which went beyond the applicability of the right to self-determination to colonial territories. The question referred to the right to self-determination of groups linked by ethnicity, language or religion (or a combination of these factors) that lived within states which were not of a clearly colonial nature. This mainly referred to minorities which inhabited existing states where borders had been drawn (usually by colonial powers or by victorious powers in post-war scenarios or as compromises to avoid wars).[16]

These situations where minorities exist within established states (as for example the Basque minority within Spain) raise the question as to whether the right to self-determination is applicable to them or whether it is applicable but to a lesser extent or not applicable at all. Guidance on this matter may be derived from several UN sources. The two 1966 Human Rights Covenants[17] both commence in their common Article 1 with a statement of the right to self-determination:

> 1 All peoples have the right of self-determination. By virtue of that right they freely determine their political status and freely pursue their economic, social and cultural development.
> 2 All peoples may, for their own ends, freely dispose of their natural wealth and resources without prejudice to any obligations arising out of international economic co-operation, based upon the principle of mutual benefit, and international law. In no case may a people be deprived of its own means of subsistence.
> 3 The States Parties to the present Covenant, including those having responsibility for the administration of Non-Self-Governing and Trust Territories, shall promote the realization of the right of self-determination, and shall respect that right, in conformity with the provisions of the Charter of the United Nations.

The two Covenants, although adopted within the anti-colonial milieu, were not dealing specifically with the issue of colonialism (unlike the previously cited UN GA Resolutions 1514 and 1541). Thus, the inclusion of the right to self-determination may be interpreted in a wider manner than the two resolutions. The crucial points in this context are (1) the definition of the term "peoples" and (2) the definition of the phrase "freely determine their political status".

Brownlie describes peoples as "cohesive national groups"[18] which seems to connote that the essential requirement for a group to qualify as a people is a bond of nationality, which in the context of a group seeking a new nationality seems rather perplexing. In a different context Brownlie explains that the right to self-determination pertains to a "community which has a distinct character", which is a wide characterisation that may include bonds of race, ethnicity, language, religion etc. According to Cassese, self-determination is only clearly established as a matter of international law as "anti-colonial standard, as a ban on foreign occupation, and as a requirement that all racial groups be given full access to government".[19] Thus, beyond the clear confines of colonial rule, foreign occupation and apartheid there seems to be a vista of uncertainty and doubt. This doubt continues to be reflected in the academic treatment of nationhood.

It has been suggested that the content of the right to self-determination should be understood in two distinct scenarios: that of external self-determination and that of internal self-determination. External self-determination refers to the right to self-determination including the right to the formation of a separate state, whereas internal self-determination refers to the "pursuit of its political, economic, social and cultural development within the framework of an existing state".[20] Higgins seems to concur with this view, as she argues that self-determination refers to the right of the majority within a generally accepted political unit to the exercise of power. In other words, it is necessary to start with stable boundaries and to permit the political change within them. That the right of self-determination operates within generally accepted political units is an essential premise.[21]

Within this context, it is apparent that international law is attempting to balance two conflicting desiderata: the territorial integrity, sovereignty and stability of existing states; and the right of certain groups existing within these states to some form of political autonomy. One of the most recent constructions of the right to self-determination by the UN was formulated in 1993 within the context of the UN World Conference of Human Rights. Once again the UN attempted to balance these conflicting concepts and stated that self-determination

> shall not be constructed as authorizing or encouraging any action which would dismember or impair, totally or in part, the territorial integrity or political unity of sovereign and independent states conducting themselves in compliance with the principle of equal rights and self-determination of peoples and thus possessed of a Government representing the whole people belonging to the territory without distinction of any kind.[22]

This construction makes it clear that secession is not an option outside colonial contexts. However, there seems to be a caveat that territorial integrity may be jeopardised by a state not complying with the duty of ensuring equal rights and internal self-determination. In particular, there seems to be a duty that the government of the state be representative of the whole people living in the state's territory. The question remains of what "a government representing the whole people" means. The threshold of non-compliance required to trigger off a right to secession seems to be rather high. The Canadian Supreme Court in the Quebec Secession Case highlights the notion that the right to external self-determination only arose in "the most extreme cases and, even then, under carefully defined circumstances",[23] having regard to the parallel need for respect for the territorial integrity of states.

Thus, what if a state does not comply with this requirement, such as is the case if a certain group is denied participation in government or denied, in a systematic manner, fundamental rights? Crawford claims that in such cases "international law allows (in extreme cases of oppression) remedial secession to discrete people within a state". The situation arising in Kosovo seems to validate Crawford's view. Although the International Court of Justice's Advisory Opinion on the legality of Kosovo's unilateral declaration of independence did not enter the merits of this issue, the emergence of Kosovo as a state recognised by numerous other states seems to suggest that "remedial secession" may be successful in law and practice. The Court in the Kosovo case did however indicate that this matter was susceptible to disagreement and one may not give a conclusive answer to the question of whether remedial secession is a right under international law. The Court in fact stated that:

> Whether outside the context of non-self-governing territories and peoples subject to alien subjugation, domination and exploitation, the international law of self-determination confers upon part of the population of an existing State, a right to separate is, however, a subject on which radically different views were expressed.... Similar differences existed regarding whether international law provides for a right of "remedial secession", and, if so, in what circumstances.

The emphasis on the strong differences expressed with respect to the applicability of the right to self-determination in non-colonial situations lead one to suggest that whereas it is impossible to state that a right of remedial secession exists, remedial secession may in certain circumstances be successful and allowed by international law. One may also add that the success or otherwise of such remedial secession will be determined by de facto political considerations and criteria of effectiveness rather than by strictly legal ones.

Rights of representation and models of democracy

One of the matters which were referred to in the discussion on self-determination was the issue of representative government and rights of representation more generally. In assessing the scope of the right to self-determination the question of what "a government representing the whole people" means was left open. Does this requirement imply that a government must include representatives from the different sectors of society? Or does this simply mean that all adults, without distinction, should have a right to vote, propose themselves for office and maintain political activity without hindrance? This is not the right forum for an extended debate on the nature and extent of the right of political representation or democratic models. However, a few reflections on these issues may help to clarify the complexities inherent in these issues and their relevance to the conflict in Northern Ireland.

The nature of representative government is difficult to define precisely and the relation between such government and democracy is a complex one. This complexity around democracy is well elucidated by David Held who suggests that "Not only is the history of democracy marked by conflicting interpretations, but also ancient and modern notions intermingle to produce ambiguous and inconsistent accounts of the key terms of democracy".[24] The Universal Declaration of Human Rights seems to imply that all that is required in terms of representational rights is for all citizens to have the "right to take part in the government of his country, directly or through freely chosen representatives".[25] In terms of democracy it states that

> the will of the people shall be the basis of the authority of government; this will shall be expressed in periodic and genuine elections which shall be by universal and equal suffrage and shall be held by secret vote or by equivalent free voting procedures.

Article 25 of the International Covenant on Civil and Political Rights (ICCPR) essentially reiterates the right to take part in public life and the right to vote and to be elected in elections. The basic requisites for these elections according to this provision are that they be genuine, periodic, based on universal and equal suffrage and also that they be held by secret ballot. These rights to political participation and to political representation are held, like all the rights included in the ICCPR (except for self-determination), by individuals. Thus, neither minorities – of whatever configuration – nor indeed other collectivities have political rights in terms of the Universal Declaration or the ICCPR. It is only the individual members of a minority or collectivity that possess these rights while evidently membership of such a minority should in no way impede the exercise of these rights. Hence, if a state allows all its adult citizens, without distinction of any kind, full and unfettered exercise of the right to vote in free elections and the right to stand for office in such elections, that state would be fulfilling the requirements of the Universal Declaration and the ICCPR.

Thus, there seems to be no clearly established right in international law to a minority having a representation in government or even in legislative assemblies, although in discussions on the nature of democracy it has been argued that it is important for different sectors of society to have adequate political representation. In terms of the nature of democratic models of governance the most often assumed paradigm is that of majority rule. This has been the case since the earliest manifestations of democracy in ancient Greece. Decisions in democratic Greek city-states were taken on the basis that each citizen had one vote and that the will of the majority should prevail. In describing (unflatteringly) the democratic model Aristotle stated that whatever the majority decides is final and constitutes justice.[26] This conception of democratic decision making clearly leaves the minority unprotected from the excesses of the majority. This risk is higher in polarised societies where tension or animosities exist between the majority and minority groups. And it is a risk which has long been recognised. The Roman Republic for instance recognised the importance of institutions which were inclusive of all the main sectors of society; in particular, republican Rome was concerned with its two major constituencies: the common people (plebeians) and the aristocracy (patricians) and eventually fashioned its institutions to accommodate the interests of both.

David Held in his comprehensive overview of democratic models refers to a number of concerns raised by different thinkers on the potential risks posed by the majoritarian basis of democratic rule. In this vein, Held refers to Madison's critique of what he terms "pure democracy" (as practised in ancient Greece) and its propensity to be "intolerant, unjust and unstable".[27] In pure democracies, according to Madison, "a common passion or interest, felt by the majority of citizens generally shapes political judgments, policies and actions" and furthermore the immediate nature of pure democracy means that there was no check on the sufferings that can be imposed on weaker parties.[28] Madison suggested that a large electoral body and representational politics as opposed to direct democracy were tools that would overcome the dangers of the tyranny of the majority.

The great advocate of liberal democracy John Stuart Mill also recognised the potential dangers of the tyrannous majority operating within a democratic context and thus he conceived of several basic liberties pertaining to individuals which could not be denied or overridden by majority rule. Particularly, Mill considered freedom of speech, freedom of the press and freedom of assembly as important protections for the individuals and minorities against the excesses of the majority. Mill believed that these freedoms together with representative democracy[29] that controlled and monitored a competent bureaucracy would guarantee the benefits of democratic governance while avoiding its excesses.

Admittedly, Mill's conception of fundamental freedoms was limited to a few liberties (of property, expression and association). However, his emphasis on liberties which could not be overridden by government provides an essential requirement for democratic governance that does not prejudice the basic rights of individuals who do not form part of the majority. In this context, it could be argued that Mill was essentially following Locke's general conception of "legitimate government based on consent, in which the majority rules but may not violate people's fundamental rights".[30] The fundamental rights Locke was referring to were the right to life, liberty and property. It is worth highlighting that Locke's and Mill's rights even when amplified by the advent of the International Bill of Rights were not intended to provide political representation in government or in the legislative to minority groupings.

The political representation of minority groups remained a matter for states to regulate. In some jurisdictions, different minorities are given quotas in Parliament while in others, due to the concentration of a minority in a certain area, it acquired parliamentary representation in competition with other groups. For instance, Jordan has reserved seats in Parliament for Christian, Circassian and Bedouin minorities, while in Spain the Basque community through being prevalent in one geographical area obtains representation in the Spanish Parliament without any quota system being in place. The problem of minorities and political representation is of special salience where political parties are organised around ethnic, religious or linguistic lines. In such scenarios citizens vote their caste rather than casting their vote.[31] This means that unless there are significant demographic shifts the likelihood is that a political party representing the majority ethnic/linguistic/religious group will maintain a permanent monopoly over government. Thus, one-party rule may come about as a result of democratic governance.

The limits of majoritarian democratic systems in terms of the danger of a tyrannous majority were dealt with, to an extent, by classical pluralism. This school of thought claims that in democracies decision making is based on the mediation of different interests pursued by different groups rather than on majority decision making. The key aspects of this school of thought focuses on the following characteristics of democratic states, namely that there "exist multiple power-centres, diverse and fragmented interests, the marked propensity of one group to offset the power of another, a transcendent consensus which bounds state and society, the state as judge and arbitrator between factions".[32] The idea of the pluralist democratic state is that in any given society there exist multiple interest groups which vie with each other to shape public policy and that governments have to mediate these different interests. Furthermore, individuals usually "enjoy multiple memberships among groups with diverse – and even incompatible – interests" which means that each group will normally remain too weak and divided to possess excessive power.[33]

Nevertheless, in states where there is a strong ethnic/religious/linguistic-based identity the normal patterns of democratic governance described by pluralists disintegrate. The power centres solidify around majority and minority identities and individuals tend to think in items of monochromatic identities rather than multiple ones. In such states (Northern Ireland or Lebanon are examples) decision making does not conform to the pluralist conception of democratic governance.

In the context of states deeply divided along ethnic/religious/linguistic lines the importance of guarding against the "tyrannous majority" is even more salient as the minority is likely to interpret all decisions taken by the majority from a sectarian perspective. Thus, all decisions taken by the majority representatives (in Parliament and in government) are usually interpreted as "attacks" on the minority communities even where no sectarian motivation animated the majority decision makers. Within such a scenario attempts at mitigating the impact of a "tyrannous majority" has attracted two major approaches; one revolves around an involvement of the minority in government while the other maintains the simple majoritarian democratic model with strong minority guarantees in the form of constitutionally protected rights. The latter will be discussed in the next section while at this stage the former will be discussed briefly.

The concept of involving, in a structured manner, minorities in governance through the proportional allocation of seats in Parliament and in government is referred to in contemporary democratic discourse as consociationalism and is particularly associated with the work of Arend Lijphart.[34] In consociational systems, power is shared among the various groups that obtain parliamentary representation and government is not conducted on the basis of a simple parliamentary majority. Lijphart argues that while most people associate democracy with majoritarian systems there are other systems which he refers to as consensus democracies.[35] In fact, Lijphart suggests that in heterogeneous societies, especially those within which there are deep fissures along ethnic, religious, linguistic or other lines, majoritarian rule is likely to be dangerous. Within such societies

> majority rule is not only undemocratic but also dangerous, because minorities that are continually denied access to power will feel excluded and discriminated against and they may lose allegiance to the regime. … In the most deeply divided societies, like Northern Ireland, majority rule spells majority dictatorship and civil strife rather than democracy.[36]

The consensus or consociational model attempts to avoid the dangers that majoritarianism poses in deeply divided societies by focusing on inclusiveness. In the consensus model executive power is not concentrated in the hands of the majority but is instead shared and dispersed. The most evident feature of the consensus model is that the executive is formed not by the majority but by all or most of the important parties in a broad coalition. This consensus model is adopted in a number of jurisdictions both via informal agreements (such as the case in Switzerland) as well as through formal constitutional arrangements (such as is the case in Belgium and Northern Ireland). In the context of minority protection, the consensus model offers not only a passive protection of their key interests by the state but an active involvement by the minority in shaping the policies by which they are to be governed and in this sense a role in shaping their own future.[37] Conversely, divided societies adopting the majoritarian system may offer the minority rights and guarantees as protection against any encroachment upon the minority's most fundamental needs and interests.

Minority rights and guarantees

As highlighted in the context of the discussion on self-determination, groups which have a separate ethnic, linguistic or religious identity do not possess a clear right to external self-determination. They may in appropriate circumstances, if they qualify as "a people" in international law, have a right to internal self-determination. However, the concept of "a people" in international law is somewhat nebulous and, in practice, seems to be clearly applicable to very few groupings. Beyond the category of indigenous peoples the two foremost examples in international legal practice seem to be the Palestinians and the Kurds. A much wider concept is the concept of a minority. This concept includes within its meaning groups that do not necessarily fall within the purview of the concept of "a people". Numerous definitions of minorities may be found in the literature but a definition which has been widely used is the definition drafted by the UN Special-Rapporteur Capotorti who defines minorities as:

> a group numerically inferior to the rest of the population of a State, in a non-dominant position, whose members – being nationals of the State – possess ethnic, religious or linguistic characteristics differing from those of the rest of the population and show, if only implicitly, a sense of solidarity, directed towards preserving their culture, traditions, religion or language.[38]

Such minorities are, and have been, an inevitable characteristic of most states. States are rarely constituted of mono-ethnic, mono-religious and mono-linguistic communities. While a few states may be so constituted, most states contain within their borders minorities as defined by Capotorti. From an international law point of view, the concern with such minorities was one of the earliest indicators of a shift in international law from a purely state-centric legal system to a legal system concerned with entities other than states. Most legal scholars identify the post-World War I creation of a minorities regime as prefiguring the human rights era that was eventually ushered in by the end of World War II.[39]

The essential characteristics of the legal framework for the protection of minorities that was put in place in the aftermath of World War I was constructed based on a series of treaties between the victorious powers and a number of European states which contained within their borders numerically significant minorities. The post-war minorities regime, however, was confined to Europe (except for the inclusion of Iraq) and focused essentially on central and eastern Europe (including the Balkans).[40] The system for the protection of minorities was predicated on two principles: that of ensuring equality and that of protecting peculiarities. This was confirmed by the Permanent Court of International Justice in the Minority Schools in Albania case of 1935 which stated that the purpose of the system was to secure for minorities "the possibility of living peaceably … while at the same time preserving the characteristics which distinguish them from the majority". The Court then proceeded to explain that in order for this purpose to be achieved what was required was:

> first … to ensure that nationals belonging to racial, religious or linguistic minorities shall be placed in every respect on a footing of perfect equality with the other nationals of the State … second … to ensure for the minority elements suitable means for the preservation of their racial peculiarities, their traditions, and their national characteristics.[41]

The system for the protection of minorities disintegrated with the advent of World War II and in the post-war era the attention of international law shifted onto the broader concept of individual human rights. This is evidenced in the UN Charter where human rights are referred to abundantly whereas the concept of minority is absent. The Charter however does refer to the principles of equality and non-discrimination which were highlighted above as an essential element of minority protection. Equally there is no reference to minority rights within the Universal Declaration of Human Rights and it has been suggested that this omission is unsurprising in the post-war context given that "to a majority of States, individualistic human rights without any special concession to particular groups of society seemed a sensible, modern, and democratic programme".[42] The only concession to minority rights in the early history of the UN was a call, made in a General Assembly Resolution adopted together with the Universal Declaration, for the "thorough study of the problem of minorities".[43]

The emphasis on individual rights as opposed to group rights seemed to be the right way forward given the perceived failure of the minority rights regimes established in the wake of World War I. While it may be argued that a basic "right to existence" for national, ethnic, racial and religious groups was affirmed through the 1948 Genocide Convention, the same convention did not protect such groups from "cultural destruction" but only from "physical destruction". Thus, the post-war legal infrastructure, while guaranteeing physical existence for certain groups, did not protect their right to cultural existence or more broadly their "right to identity". The emphasis was on equal treatment and non-discrimination; the protection of peculiarities went on the backburner within the international community.

Eventually though there was a reappraisal of this position and the necessity for both individual rights as well as group rights became apparent. This reappraisal is evidenced in the inclusion of a minority rights clause in the International Covenant on Civil and Political Rights. In this context, Article 27 of the Covenant is the relevant provision which is "the conventional and customary law recognising" the rights of minorities in international law:

> In those States in which ethnic, religious or linguistic minorities exist, persons belonging to such minorities shall not be denied the right, in community with the other members of their group, to enjoy their own culture, to profess and practise their own religion, or to use their own language.

This provision seeks to protect the cultural life of ethnic, religious and linguistic minorities which even in democratic states may be at risk of assimilation into the majority culture. It also attempts to realise the "right to identity" which John Burton identifies, in its human needs form, as an essential need which, when denied, may lead to violent conflict. The importance of identity in fuelling conflict is clearly stated by Burton:

> needs that are frustrated by institutions and norms require satisfaction. They will be pursued in one way or another. These needs would seem to be even more fundamental than food and shelter.... Denial by society of recognition and identity would lead, at all social levels, to alternative behaviors designed to satisfy such needs, be it ethnic wars, street gangs or domestic violence.[44]

The issue of minority protection is, in fact, linked to both self-determination and political representation. In states where minorities participate in government through consensus models of democracy or are allowed a degree of internal self-determination through federal structures or other forms of decentralisation, minorities may have a modicum of decision making powers and control over aspects of governance. Nevertheless, minorities in centralised states, where societies are sharply divided along ethnic, linguistic or religious fissures, may lack any form of effective political representation that translates into some form of decision making powers. In the latter scenario, the adoption of national democratic and electoral models based on a winner-takes-all concept may permanently exclude a minority from participation in government. An excellent example of such a state was pre-direct rule Northern Ireland where the Unionist Party governed uninterruptedly for five decades while the minority community remained in opposition throughout. Minorities, barred from exercising internal self-determination, within a centralised state and excluded from decision making processes are likely to interpret this exclusion as an attack on their identity. In these societies, which follow a majoritarian electoral system where citizens vote along sectarian lines the decisions of the elected government are likely to be interpreted (rightly or wrongly) through a prism of discrimination. Furthermore, once a democratic model is being maintained and followed the governments in these societies can claim a certain moral legitimacy. In these cases, minority rights in the form of equality legislation and protection of peculiarities are the essential and unique guarantees to ensure they retain their identity and are not subject to discrimination at the state or local level.

Human rights: is there a hierarchy of rights?

Even a cursory look at a very few human rights issues illustrates the kaleidoscopic nature of the human rights agenda. The issues of self-determination, political representation and minority rights, highlighted above, are just the tip of the human rights iceberg. Human rights law and practice covers, inter alia, the rights to liberty, health, property, family life, education, fair trial and fair conditions of employment. Furthermore, the human rights agenda also provides for a number of freedoms such as freedom of expression, conscience, peaceful assembly and association.

This panoply of rights was evident in the Universal Declaration of Human Rights itself which brought together, for the first time, rights of different kinds: economic, social, cultural, political and civil. The Declaration itself makes no distinction, and marks no hierarchy between the different rights. In fact, it has been suggested that:

> When read as it was meant to be, namely as a whole, it is an integrated document that rests on a concept of the dignity of the human person within the human family. In substance, as well as in form, it is a declaration of interdependence of people, nations, and rights.[45]

The two covenants mentioned above, while separating civil and political rights from social, economic and cultural rights, did not explicitly refute the notion that the two sets of rights are interdependent. Soon after the adoption of the Covenants the indivisibility of human rights was proclaimed as an essential element of the human rights edifice. The Final Act of the 1968 UN Teheran Conference on Human Rights stated that "human rights and fundamental freedoms are indivisible, the full realization of civil and political rights without the enjoyment of economic, social and cultural rights is impossible".[46]

The importance of the indivisibility and interdependence of human rights re-emerged forcefully in the wake of the end of the Cold War. The 1993 UN World Conference on Human Rights articulated this principle clearly and concisely: "All human rights are universal, indivisible and interdependent and interrelated. The international community must treat human rights globally in a fair and equal manner, on the same footing, and with the same emphasis."[47] This emphasis on indivisibility and interdependence in the aftermath of the Cold War was understandable as the divisions between civil and political rights, on the one hand, and social, economic and cultural rights, on the other, had been conceived, at least partially, as ideological divisions between West and East. The end of the Cold War seemed to project a new world order in which old ideological divisions would be overcome and thus the human rights agenda also sought to reap the benefits of this new world order.

The debate around the interdependence and indivisibility of human rights has, nevertheless, persisted as new challenges to these principles have arisen in different contexts. Scenarios in which these challenges have arisen refer to situations where two or more rights have come into collision or where decisions must be taken which gives precedence to one right over another. The idea of human rights that conflict with each other is, in fact, not an unusual one.

Situations where rights clash with one another or where a right must be prioritised over another are common enough. In fact, it has been argued that "it is unlikely that conflicts between established rights will ever be eliminated".[48]

One such scenario of human rights in conflict with each other, which has risen to prominence in recent years, involves the doctrine of humanitarian intervention or what Geoffrey Robertson refers to as "The Guernica Paradox: Bombing for Humanity".[49] Essentially, the paradox refers to humanitarian intervention in utilising armed force is breaching fundamental rights (such as the right to life) in order to protect human rights (usually protecting communities from egregious human rights abuses such as genocide, crimes against humanity, etc.) The question of the use of force to achieve or protect particular human rights is a quintessentially difficult one. The conflicting rights in, for example, the Kosovo conflict were the right to life of people killed in Belgrade by aerial bombings as against the right to life, or not to be ethnically cleansed, of Kosovar Albanians.

This conflict between rights arises in other circumstances apart from those related to formal cases of humanitarian intervention where communities are protected by outside forces, such as when communities themselves resort to the use of force to protect themselves from human rights abuses. One can illustrate this latter scenario in the light of the preceding discussion of the right to self-determination, the right to political representation and minority rights. If a minority community is denied any form of self-determination, has no – or limited – rights to political representation and is not guaranteed certain basic minority rights, is such a minority entitled to use armed force to achieve its objectives?

The use of armed force to achieve human rights is a complex and challenging issue since at the heart of it is the crucial question if certain rights (such as self-determination) are more important than other rights (such as the right to life). In the context of minority communities struggling for their rights, as outlined above, the question may also be framed as to whether the rights to self-determination, political representation or minority protection of one group (the minority) take precedence over the rights to life and physical integrity of another group (all those who are victims of the armed struggle).

The Universal Declaration of Human Rights, which remains the single most authoritative (if only because most often referred to) document in human rights history, does not provide a direct answer to these questions. However, in its Preamble the Declaration does prefigure the probability of a resort to rebellion where human rights are abused: "Whereas it is essential, if man is not to be compelled to have recourse, as a last resort, to rebellion against tyranny and oppression, that human rights should be protected by the rule of law." The Declaration, however, does not stipulate at what stage is such rebellion justified. Both the words "tyranny" and "oppression" are open to various interpretations. In this context, the Preambular reference to tyranny, oppression and rebellion is not sufficiently clear to provide precise guidance in practice. Nor does the reference to rebellion specify whether such rebellion may be violent armed rebellion as opposed to a Gandhian rebellion consisting of civil disobedience and other pacifist methods.

Thus, in international human rights law we do not find a precise answer to the question of whether violence is ever justified in pursuing human rights aims. However international humanitarian law may provide some guidance as to what kind of violence is never permissible whatever the justness of the cause that is being pursued. Thus, if one accepts the hypothesis that violent rebellion is permissible when serious and systematic human rights violations occur through tyranny and oppression, one is still faced by the question of the kind and extent of violence that is permissible.

International humanitarian law which applies in situations of armed conflict is clear that individuals who are hors de combat (for example, civilians) may never be the targets of violence in situations of international and non-international armed conflict. The requirement to protect civilian life from violence is a key, non-derogable, principle of international humanitarian law. Even if a given situation of rebellion does not qualify as an internal conflict for the purposes of international humanitarian law, the principle of the sanctity of civilian life would seem to be equally applicable in such a situation. This point of view is sustained also by reference to a hierarchy of human rights that is implicit in certain human rights treaties.

Article 4 of the International Covenant on Civil and Political Rights states that

> 1 In time of public emergency which threatens the life of the nation and the existence of which is officially proclaimed, the States Parties to the present Covenant may take measures derogating from their obligations under the present Covenant to the extent strictly required by the exigencies of the situation, provided that such measures are not inconsistent with their other obligations under international law and do not involve discrimination solely on the ground of race, colour, sex, language, religion or social origin.
> 2 No derogation from articles 6, 7, 8 (paragraphs 1 and 2), 11, 15, 16 and 18 may be made under this provision.

Thus, sub-article 2 of this article renders certain rights absolute, even in times of emergency. These rights include the right to life, freedom from torture, freedom from slavery or servitude, freedom from criminal guilt unless determined by law, as well as the freedoms of thought, conscience and religion. The implication is clear that the right to life is an absolute, non-derogable right in times of peace (as per the Universal Declaration, the ICCPR and other instruments), in times of emergency falling short of an armed conflict (as per Article 4(2) of the UDHR[50]) and also in times of armed conflict (according to the Geneva Conventions 1949 and the Additional Protocols of 1977). In view of these legal considerations it may be concluded that (1) it is unclear whether the use of violence is permissible to achieve human rights objectives and (2) the use of violence in pursuit of human rights objectives, even if legally permissible, may never target civilians.

Notes

1 The only exception being when a state mistreated a citizen of another state, in which case the state of nationality of the mistreated person could make a complaint against the offending state under the principle of the diplomatic protection of nationals.
2 The protection of minorities in international law was also prefigured in the late nineteenth century in the Final Act of the Congress of Berlin (13 June 1887–13 July 1887) which accorded special legal status to some religious groupings in the concerned states.
3 The issue of minority protection will be discussed more fully in subsequent sections of this chapter. See Chapter 1.
4 The total number of conventions that were adopted was 67; however 23 of these were shelved and never came into force. See International Labour Organization, Conventions, 2012, accessed 24 January 2012, www.ilo.org/dyn/normlex/en/f?p=NORMLEXPUB:12000:0::NO:::.
5 *African (Banjul) Charter of Human and Peoples' Rights*, 1981; *American Convention on Human Rights*, 1969; Council of Europe, *Convention for the Protection of Human Rights and Fundamental Freedoms as Amended by Protocols No. 11 and No. 14*, 1950.
6 Richard P. Claude and Burns H. Weston, *Human Rights in the World Community*, 2nd edn. (Philadelphia: University of Pennsylvania Press, 1992), 2.
7 Security forces in situations of armed conflict are regulated by international humanitarian law, which is a branch of law closely allied to international human rights law.
8 Richard. A. Falk, *Human Rights Horizons* (London: Routledge, 2000), 69.
9 Thomas M. Franck, *Fairness in International Law and Institutions* (Oxford: Clarendon Press, 1998), 147.
10 Woodrow Wilson, *President Wilson's Fourteen Points*, 1918, accessed 24 January 2012, http://wwi.lib.byu.edu/index.php/President_Wilson's_Fourteen_Points.
11 Falk, *Human Rights Horizons*, 104.
12 Ibid., 105.
13 Michla Pomerance, *Self-Determination in Law and Practice: The New Doctrine in the United Nations* (The Hague: Martinus Nijhoff Publishers, 1982), 9.
14 James R. Crawford, *The Creation of States in International Law*, 2nd edn. (Oxford University Press, 2007), 114.
15 These were established in United Nations General Assembly, *Principles Which Should Guide Members in Determining Whether or Not an Obligation Exists to Transmit the Information Called for under Article 73 E of the Charter of the United Nations, United Nations General Assembly Resolution*, vol. 1541, 1960. This same resolution provided for the ways in which the people of such colonial territories should decide on such matters. For example, one requirement was that a decision to enter a free association with an independent state "should be the result of a free and voluntary choice by the peoples of the territory concerned expressed through informed and democratic processes". Furthermore a decision to opt for integration should be based on "the freely expressed wishes of the territory's peoples acting with full knowledge of the change in their status" and then only after the attainment of "an advanced stage of self-government with free political institutions".
16 It may argued that the Anglo-Irish Treaty, 1921, was one such instance.
17 International Covenant on Civil and Political Rights, 1966, and International Covenant on Economic, Social and Cultural Rights, 1966.
18 Ian Brownlie, *Principles of Public International Law*, 5th edn. (Oxford: Oxford University Press, 1998), 599.
19 Antonio Cassese, *International Law*, 2nd edn. (Oxford: Oxford University Press, 2005), 60.

20 Reference re Secession of Quebec, [1998] 2 SCR 217 (Supreme Court of Canada 1998).
21 Rosalyn Higgins, *International Law and the Avoidance, Containment and Resolution of Disputes*, General Course on Public International Law, Recueil Des Cours, Vol. 230 (The Hague: MartinusNijhoff, 1991), 165.
22 United Nations World Conference on Human Rights, *Vienna Declaration and Programme of Action*, 25 June 1993, accessed 15 June 2014, www.ohchr.org/EN/ProfessionalInterest/Pages/Vienna.aspx.
23 Reference re Secession of Quebec, [1998] 2 SCR 217 (Supreme Court of Canada 1998).
24 David Held, *Models of Democracy*, 2nd edn. (Cambridge: Polity Press, 1996), x.
25 United Nations General Assembly, *The Universal Declaration of Human Rights*, 1948, Article 21.
26 Aristotle, *Politics*, trans. T. A. Sinclair (Harmondsworth: Penguin Books, 1983), 362.
27 Held, *Models of Democracy*, 89.
28 Ibid.
29 Held explores the limits of Mill's representative government which is, however, not immediately relevant for this study.
30 Michael Sandel, ed., *Justice: A Reader* (New York: Oxford University Press, 2007), 83.
31 John. P. Darby, *Scorpions in a Bottle: Conflicting Cultures in Northern Ireland* (London: Minority Rights Publications, 1997), 58.
32 Held, *Models of Democracy*, 204.
33 Ibid.
34 Lijphart himself states that he merely described systems which political practitioners had developed over the years. See Arend Lijphart, "Constitutional Design for Divided Societies", *Journal of Democracy* 15, no. 2 (April 2004).
35 Arend Lijphart, *Patterns of Democracy* (New Haven: Yale University Press, 1999), 31.
36 Ibid., 32–3.
37 Incidentally such a politically active citizen is what the ancient Athenian democracy required of its citizens.
38 Monograph 23 prepared by Special Rapporteur Francesco Capotorti towards his *Study on the Rights of Persons Belonging to Ethnic, Religious and Linguistic Minorities* (Geneva: UN Center for Human Rights, n.d.) for the UN Sub-Commission on the Prevention of Discrimination and Protection of Minorities, UN Doc E/CN.4/Sub.2/384/Add.1–7.
39 Antonio Cassese refers to the rights of minorities that developed after World War I as one of the "normative innovations [that] were indicative of the new tendency to pay greater attention to the interests of human beings, who until then had had no say whatsoever in the international community". Antonio Cassese, *International Law* (Oxford: Oxford Universty Press, 2005), 39. Malcolm Shaw argues that the minorities regime developed during the interwar period "paved the way for later concern to secure human rights". Malcolm Shaw, *International Law* (Cambridge: Cambridge University Press, 2003), 31.
40 The states which were included in the League of Nations minority protection system were: Albania, Austria, Bulgaria, Czechoslovakia, Estonia, the Free City of Danzig, Greece, Hungary, Iraq, Lithuania, Latvia, the territory of Memel, Poland, Romania, Turkey, the territory of Upper Silesia and Yugoslavia.
41 Minority School in Albania, Advisory Opinion 26 (Permanent Court of International Justice 1935).
42 Patrick Thornberry, *International Law and the Rights of Minorities* (Oxford: Clarendon Press, 1991), 137.

43 International Bill of Human Rights, 217, vol. III, 1948.
44 John W. Burton, "Conflict Resolution: The Human Dimension", *International Journal of Peace Studies* 3, no. 1 (January 1998), accessed 15 June 2014, www.gmu.edu/programs/icar/ijps/vol.3_1/burton.htm.
45 Mary Ann Glendon, *A World Made New: Eleanor Roosevelt and the Universal Declaration of Human Rights* (New York: Random House, 2001), 174.
46 The International Conference on Human Rights, *Proclamation of Teheran, Final Act of the International Conference on Human Rights*, U.N. Doc. A/CONF. 32/41, vol. 3, 1968, www1.umn.edu/humanrts/instree/l2ptichr.htm.
47 *Vienna Declaration and Programme of Action*, A/Conf.157/23, 12 June 1993, accessed 12 October 2014, www.ohchr.org/EN/ProfessionalInterest/Pages/Vienna.aspx.
48 Xiaobing Xu and George Wilson, "On Conflict of Human Rights", *Pierce Law Review* 5, no. 1 (December 2006), 40.
49 Geoffrey Robertson, *Crimes against Humanity: The Struggle for Global Justice* (Harmondsworth: Penguin Books, 2006), 468.
50 United Nations General Assembly, The Universal Declaration of Human Rights, 1948, Article 4.

3 Human rights in Northern Ireland, 1921–1964

Developments, issues and perceptions

Introduction

Any attempt to chart a historic outline of political developments in Northern Ireland is a fraught one. Historical accounts always court controversy but in the context of Ireland there is certainly no agreed history, and in the case of Northern Ireland this is particularly so. Versions of history compete with one another and stretch far back into the mists of time. Competing histories range from the comparatively recent events surrounding Bloody Sunday, to the details of the Anglo-Irish Treaty and ensuing Civil War, to the Easter Rising of 1916 and the Home Rule debates of the 1870s and further back in time to the 1689 Battle of the Boyne and the immigration from Great Britain of the 1600s referred to as the Plantation of Ulster. Different attitudes exist to history even further into the mythical past of Cuchulain celebrated by the Protestant republican W. B. Yeats.

Each of these landmark events, and countless others, have their own versions of history through which communities construct an imagined past that is often used as an instrument to vindicate present positions. There is, in fact, a body of literature (by writers such as Conor Cruise O'Brien, Joe Lee, Ruth Dudley Edwards and others) which offers an explanation of contemporary politics with reference to historical episodes.[1] It has been noted that the Good Friday Agreement is in fact an agreement to disagree about the future of Northern Ireland[2] and certainly about its past too.[3] The impossibility of imagining a common future is, one may argue, inextricably linked to the impossibility of constructing an agreed past or even to accept that there may be other, equally valid, interpretations of history.

Given this reality it is especially difficult to frame a discussion of what happened in terms of rights and freedoms in the early years of the existence of Northern Ireland. This chapter is intended as a brief, non-exhaustive historical overview of Northern Ireland viewed with a human rights lens. Such an overview will serve as a background to the main argument of this study that revolves around the role of human rights values, principles and processes in Northern Ireland post-1998. The objectives of this overview are twofold: to determine the role played by the human rights agenda in the development of the Northern Ireland conflict; and to assess how the two main communities viewed the role and content of the human rights agenda in the years leading to the sustained violent conflict that characterised Northern Ireland from 1969 to 1998.

This chapter is divided into two major sections: (1) one section dealing with the situation prevailing in Northern Ireland from its birth as a separate political entity and a constituent state of the United Kingdom (1921) to the end of World War II (1945); and (2) a subsequent section that examines the increasing role of human rights in Northern Ireland's sociopolitical context from the end of World War II until the early 1960s. This latter section also places the human rights developments in Northern Ireland within a broader international context.

The birth of Northern Ireland: 1921–1945

Ireland formally became an integral part of the United Kingdom in 1801 after the passing of the Act of Union (Ireland) in the Irish Parliament and the Union with Ireland Act in the British Parliament in 1800. This meant that the existing Irish Parliament which had over the years obtained a significant measure of autonomy was dissolved and Ireland started sending Members of Parliament to Westminster.

The circumstances under which the Irish Parliament voted in favour of the Act of Union is another of the contested episodes of Irish history, with some historians claiming that the British authorities bribed a number of Irish Members of Parliament to secure the passage of the Act.[4] Whatever the merits of this claim a movement demanding Home Rule for Ireland soon evolved. The basic request of the Home Rule movement was the creation of an Irish Parliament which would deliver self-government for Ireland in the sphere of domestic affairs with the Imperial Parliament in Westminster retaining power over imperial affairs, namely defence and foreign affairs.

There were successive attempts at achieving a Home Rule solution for Ireland as Irish requests became more vocal and as more radical groups requesting a complete break with the United Kingdom and total independence for Ireland also emerged. Liberal Prime Minister William Gladstone sought to resolve the Irish issue by granting Home Rule to Ireland, although twice his attempts at passing Irish Home Rule Bills in the United Kingdom Parliament were thwarted by negative votes. The first attempt in 1885 was rejected in the House of Commons while in 1893 the second Home Rule Bill was defeated in the House of Lords.

The Liberal government of Prime Minister H. H. Asquith made another attempt at enacting an Irish Home Rule Bill in 1914. The Bill received the Royal Assent as the Government of Ireland Act in 1914 but the effective operation of the Act was suspended due to the outbreak of World War I. Developments in Ireland eventually meant that this Act never came into force, as the Easter Rising of 1916 and the 1918 conscription crisis meant that a different kind of Irish nationalist movement had emerged which requested a sovereign, independent Ireland. In fact, in the 1918 elections to the United Kingdom Parliament, the Irish Parliamentary Party which had become the main Irish political party under the leadership of Charles Stewart Parnell and then John Redmond lost almost all its seats. Sinn Féin, the republican party, won 73 seats, the Irish Parliamentary Party six seats and the Ulster Unionist Party 22 seats.

Sinn Féin Members of Parliament refused to take up their seats in Westminster and set up an Irish Parliament (Dáil Éireann), while also declaring Irish independence. This was deemed illegal by the British authorities and a guerrilla style military campaign between the Irish Republican Army (IRA)/ Sinn Féin and British troops took place between 1919 and 1921 when a truce was agreed to by both sides. The truce was followed by a negotiation between the representatives of the IRA/Sinn Féin and the British government. These negotiations resulted in the Anglo-Irish Treaty which provided for the establishment of an Irish Free State with the option for the six north-eastern counties to remain part of the United Kingdom if the Northern Ireland Parliament so wished. The Anglo-Irish Treaty in itself led to civil war within the Irish Free State between the parties which were in favour of the Treaty and those who were against because of the partition. Violence was also rife in Northern Ireland as republicans opposing partition fought against loyalist forces who wished to retain the union with the United Kingdom.

In this context of instability and violence the United Kingdom's Parliament had enacted the Government of Ireland Act of 1920 which provided for the establishment of two Home Rule Parliaments in Ireland: one for Northern Ireland and one for Southern Ireland. The Act provided for the establishment of two sets of political institutions on the island of Ireland. Essentially, it sought to establish two Parliaments: one for Northern Ireland (being the six counties of Antrim, Armagh, Down, Fermanagh, Londonderry and Tyrone) and another Parliament for the remaining 26 counties. This was originally done to placate the threats of revolt of the majority Protestant community in the north-eastern counties who refused to be governed by, as they saw it, Catholic Irish nationalists. Eventually, following the Anglo-Irish Treaty the Northern Ireland Parliament was allowed to opt out of the Irish Free State in terms of the Treaty itself and of the Irish Free State Constitution Act of 1922 which was enacted by the UK Parliament in December of 1922 to give effect to the provisions of the Treaty. The Parliament of Northern Ireland duly voted to opt out of the Irish Free State and to retain the union with the United Kingdom which then became the United Kingdom of Great Britain and Northern Ireland.

The eventual victory of the pro-Treaty forces within the Irish Free State did not altogether obliterate the view held by a considerable section of the population of the Irish Free State and by almost all of the non-unionist (primarily Catholic) community in Northern Ireland that partition was an illegal act that violated the territorial integrity of Ireland as a unitary political entity. This meant that a considerable minority within the new state of Northern

Ireland viewed Northern Ireland as an illegitimate entity and considered it to be only a matter of time before the six counties reunited with the rest of Ireland as part of Ireland (as the Irish Free State became known in 1937).

Self-determination: for whom?

The constitutional status of Northern Ireland is perhaps the first human rights issue that arises in the context of the establishment of Northern Ireland as a separate political entity. In human rights terms this issue is addressed under the rubric of the right to self-determination. Human rights principles had not yet been formulated in terms of international conventions and a human rights language not yet articulated. However, this right to self-determination gradually became a foundation stone of international human rights law, with the right being listed as the first article of both the International Covenant on Civil and Political Rights and the International Covenant on Economic, Social and Cultural Rights. Hence, its inclusion as the first human rights issue within the Northern Ireland question.

The right to self-determination was first articulated in different ways by President Woodrow Wilson in his Fourteen Points and also by Vladimir Ilyich Lenin in *The Right of Nations to Self-Determination*. The Wilsonian right to self-determination[5] which he intended to be read as an organic component of his Fourteen Points gradually transformed itself into a stand-alone principle that would have dramatic repercussions in world history. In this early phase of its exposition and implementation it was used with a certain discretion balancing it against other competing principles. This balancing act was visible in the redrawing of boundaries in Europe following World War I where self-determination was one of several principles which were considered in the exercise of boundary demarcation.

The situation in Ireland was based on a double claim of self-determination. Irish republicans and nationalists claimed that Ireland and the Irish population had the right to self-determination to be exercised through an Irish Parliament (for nationalists) and through a sovereign Irish republic (for republicans). Unionists in the north-eastern counties claimed they had the right to self-determination as a minority in Ireland to retain the union with the United Kingdom. Kevin Boyle and Tom Hadden have suggested that the Northern Ireland context "presents, in a particular stark form, opposing and equally attractive principles of self-determination and national independence".[6]

The question that the UK government had to resolve was which unit has the right to self-determination? This is a question which, to this day, elicits considerable debate and disagreement in international law and in international practice.[7] The UK government, under pressure from both Irish republicans (through the IRA's military campaign) and Irish unionists (who since 1912 had vowed to use all necessary means, including force, to retain their constitutional status as part of the United Kingdom), decided to allow both communities to exercise their right to self-determination. The result was the creation of the Irish Free State and of Northern Ireland as two separate political entities with different constitutional status.

The definition of the scope of the right to self-determination is not only the first human rights question that arose within the Northern Ireland context but it is also the one which still remains an open question to the extent that the two main communities in Northern Ireland still have different preferences on how to exercise this right, with unionists adhering to the link with the United Kingdom and republicans arguing for union with Ireland. The Good Friday Agreement resolved the issue by effectively providing that Northern Ireland as a political unit and, more specifically, the people of Northern Ireland have the right to determine how to exercise this right. This is an important departure from republican (specifically Sinn Féin) orthodoxy which held and, in some ways still argues, that the proper political unit that should exercise the right is the people of the island of Ireland as a whole.[8]

The dispute as to the proper exercise of this human right (as we would now refer to it) manifested itself intensely upon the birth of Northern Ireland. One can argue that the manifestation took three principal forms: (1) the resolution adopted by the Parliament of Northern Ireland to exercise its right under the Irish Free State Constitution Act to "opt out" of the Free State; (2) an eruption of violence between the Protestant and Catholic communities (which in the counties of Northern Ireland was a preceding and recurring phenomenon); and (3) a widespread feeling amongst the Catholic nationalist community that the nascent Northern Ireland state was an illegitimate and transient political entity, which feeling translated into a number of Catholics refusing to serve as public servants within the new Northern Irish state.

On the 7 December 1922 the Parliament of Northern Ireland, which had been established under the terms of the Government of Ireland Act 1920, exercised its right to opt out of the Irish Free State in terms of Articles 11 and 12 of the Irish Free State (Agreement) Act 1922. The Prime Minister of Northern Ireland presented the resolution of the Northern Ireland Parliament to King George V through the Lord Chamberlain.

Ever since Britain became directly involved in the government of Ireland in the twelfth century "there has been intermittent strife and warfare",[9] and this conflict was given a further edge since the Plantation of Ulster in the sixteenth century, when in the north-eastern counties of Ireland Protestant (especially Presbyterian) settlers from the United Kingdom (specifically Scotland) made their home within Ulster and became the majority faith community therein. Their faith-based link with the United Kingdom was cemented by increasing commercial and, later on, industrial links with towns in the north-western UK (Glasgow and Liverpool being two key examples).[10] These Protestant communities were considered as tools of the British colonial power and as such viewed with suspicion, distrust and dislike by the Catholic population as historically "The servitors, soldiers and settlers who flooded into Ulster, [were] continually criticised as usurpers and interlopers in the contemporary Gaelic literature."[11]

Relations between the two communities were tense and sectarian violence often flared. Nolan states that "Local feuds between Catholics and non-Catholics were of long-standing in the counties of Ulster."[12] The Home Rule debates of the 1870s and 1910s exacerbated the already tense situation. The Protestant community was largely against home rule and insisted on its right to remain part of the UK. It was, in fact, in the period of the First Home Rule Bill that the term "unionists" gained currency as the word to describe those who opposed Home Rule for Ireland because they favoured union with Great Britain. Unionist leaders described Home Rule as "Rome Rule", claiming that an Irish Parliament would be effectively a tool in the hands of the Catholic Church. As the prospect of Home Rule for Ireland became ever more likely, with the passage of the Parliament Act of 1910 which limited severely the veto powers of the House of Lords, unionist opposition to Home Rule intensified. Led by figures such as Edward Carson, unionists pledged to oppose Home Rule with every possible means. This indicated to the UK government that they were prepared to use force to sustain their right to remain part of the United Kingdom.

The situation deteriorated in the wake of the partition with civil war raging in the Irish Free State and violence being widespread in Northern Ireland.[13] In this context one can identify the violence throughout Ireland at the time as typical of violent conflict that erupts regularly in disputes concerned with self-determination.

The third aspect of the manifestation of competing concepts of self-determination was evidenced by the Catholic community's reaction to the establishment of Northern Ireland. Apart from the violence outlined above, a section of the Catholic community in Northern Ireland remained unreconciled to the establishment of Northern Ireland as a separate political entity and viewed it as an illegitimate entity that could not survive. In order to display their objection to the Northern Irish state a significant number of Catholics refused to acknowledge the state and to serve in its fledgling institutions. McKittrick and McVea summarise the attitude and approach of a portion of the Catholic community: "They often resorted to boycotting the new institutions, both political leaders and Catholic bishops making no secret of their hope that Northern Ireland would not last."[14] This attitude would also have an impact on subsequent debates on the reasons why Catholics were under-represented in the institutions of Northern Ireland. Unionists claimed that any inequality in the representation of Catholics in Northern Ireland's institutions was, inter alia, due to Catholics refusing to serve. Another effect of this abstentionist attitude was that it was perceived by Unionists as evidence that Catholics were intent on destabilising the state and would work for its disappearance. As a result, the feeling grew that Catholics could not be trusted to exercise public functions loyally and in the best interest of the Northern Irish state. One may also note that the Catholic boycott approach also remained an important element in republican politics for many years, with Sinn Féin maintaining an abstentionist policy in the Westminster Parliament to signify its lack of acceptance of partition.

As a result of the violence and instability that ensued following the partition, other human rights issues (as they would be termed in the human rights era post-1945) soon emerged within Northern Ireland itself. These issues were arguably a direct result of the exercise in "dual" self-determination that the Anglo-Irish Treaty had sanctioned, since they relate to measures undertaken by the first Northern Irish executive and legislature to bring order and stability to the state.

At this stage, it is worth mentioning that elections to a Northern Ireland Parliament were held in 1921 and the elections returned 40 Ulster Unionist Members of Parliament, six Sinn Féin Members of Parliament and another six Nationalist Party Members of Parliament.[15]

The overwhelming majority which the Unionist Party obtained coupled with the absentionist policy of Sinn Féin and the Nationalist Party meant that the unionists faced no opposition in Parliament. The Unionist Party thus formed a government led by Sir James Craig. One of the first and most pressing issues that the Northern Ireland executive had to deal with was to assert the authority of the state over its territory and bring an end to the violence and instability that partition had given rise to. The urgency of this issue was highlighted in the House of Commons debate in the Motion to the Address following the opening of the Northern Ireland Parliament in 1922. The Address proposed the introduction of a Bill which, according to the Prime Minister, would provide the civil authorities with the power to deal with the situation.[16]

The Special Powers Act

The instrument through which the Northern Irish government sought to establish order and stability was the Civil Authorities (Special Powers) Act (Northern Ireland) 1922 (hereinafter referred to as "the Act"). The stated purpose of the Act was to "empower certain authorities of the Government of Northern Ireland to take steps for preserving the peace and maintaining order in Northern Ireland, and for purposes connected therewith."[17]

The Act in itself was far-reaching (as is typical of such emergency laws) and critics would describe it as draconian in terms of the powers given to the Minister responsible.[18] Although at the time of its enactment there were no international human rights instruments against which to measure the Act, even when measured against the then prevailing UK legislation and practice, it appears that the Act overrode certain rights and liberties which existed under United Kingdom legislation at the time.[19] In particular, the ability to impose detention without trial (referred to as internment) was clearly against the most ancient civil liberty enshrined in the laws of the United Kingdom: habeas corpus. Nevertheless, one may note that even in the "human rights world" post-1945 – including in the contemporary developed world – we still witness internment or similar types of detention in circumstances where states claim emergency situations.

Laura Donohue has carried out one of the few academic evaluations of the impact of the Act.[20] She argues that the Act became a major component of the grievance held by the Catholic minority due to the arbitrary and discriminatory way the powers under the Act were exercised, particularly after the immediate emergency of 1922 was over. The parliamentary debates in the Northern Ireland House of Commons show that the general lawlessness and violence in Northern Ireland was a very serious concern. In introducing the Bill the Parliamentary Secretary to the Ministry of Home Affairs stated that "This is an exceptional time and requires exceptional measures."[21] This view was echoed by Mr Robert J. Lynn, Member of Parliament for Belfast West, when he claimed that "We are living not in normal, but in very abnormal times."[22]

Sir Robert Anderson MP (Member of Parliament) framed the discussion on the Bill – in an earlier debate on the Motion to the Address – around the notion of rights and freedoms. While accepting that the various measures that would be included in the Act could be interpreted "as coercive and as being vindictive" the motivation behind such measures was "to secure the liberties and rights of the citizens of this community".[23] Furthermore, he made a point of stating that in these matters there was and should be no distinctions between different religions. This indirect expression of concern before the Bill was given a first reading in Parliament, that the resultant Act would be perceived as being anti-Catholic, proved to be well founded. This matter was addressed directly in the debate on the second reading of the Bill where the Unionist MP Mr. M'Guffin anticipated the criticisms that would be levelled at the Act by the Catholic community:

> The Bill is not directed against any particular section or denomination. That is one thing sure. A great deal of capital will, in all probability, be made out of it, and we have seen it suggested even in certain quarters that the Bill is directed to the discomfiture of Roman Catholics, and to inflict signal injustice upon them. No such purpose is in the view of the Government, and no such suspicion may be entertained with respect to it. It is introduced to bring peace and the restoration of order which appertains to the interests of all, to the whole body politic. That is the purpose of this Bill.[24]

Considering that no-one really disputes that Northern Ireland, at this point in time, was both unstable and violent[25] there seems to be a case for accepting the views expressed by the supporters of the Act upon its introduction. However, Donohue suggests that once the violence engendered by the partition subsided, the act was used by the unionist controlled government as a tool "to prevent the expression of republican ideals". Furthermore, she also argues that unionists considered the Act "as necessary to maintain the constitutional structure of the North". Linking this to the preceding discussion on self-determination, it appears that unionists found the Act a useful mechanism to protect their right to self-determination. This attitude is evidenced in some of the correspondence quoted by Donohue with representatives of unionist associations stating that the Act was an important tool to protect their rights. The sentiment that the measures undertaken in terms of the Act were necessary for the protection of liberties is well articulated in the following letter to the Minister for Home Affairs: "We are extremely proud to know that we have such a loyal advocate of our liberties that no encroachment can come without being noticed."[26]

In her detailed examination of how the Act was applied Donohue demonstrates that the regulations issued under the Act and especially the orders issued pursuant to these regulations were overwhelmingly impacting on the nationalist and republican communities. This was so in terms of the banning of public events, gatherings and marches, where unionist/Protestant events were only banned rarely and then only incidentally; in censorship as applied to publications the censored or banned publications or films targeted by governmental orders were a mixture of republican and communist materials, while unionist/Protestant publications seem to have been immune from such censorship or banning. The anti-republican ethos of the Act was further strengthened with the adoption of a regulation under the Act prohibiting the display of the Irish flag. The fact that the police were authorised to remove such flags even where there was no evidence of a risk of disorder through such display (such as in staunchly Catholic areas) exemplified the political objective of the regulation rather than its public order nature. The analysis of the implementation of the Act led Donohue to conclude that:

> the government failed to distinguish between violent and non-violent challenges to the government. Thus although the emergency legislation was targeted at a small slice of the minority population, in fact its oppressive nature affected the whole minority community, establishing a sense of injustice that exploded with the civil rights marches.[27]

In summary, there is no doubt that the nationalist community felt targeted and abused by the Act and its implementation. Donohue claims that they had good reason to feel targeted, especially after the violence had subsided. John Darby emphasises this perception held by the nationalist community: "In the administration of justice Catholics have long believed that the Special Powers Act, which placed considerable emergency powers in the hands of the Minister of Home Affairs, was aimed exclusively against the nationalist minority."[28]

At the same time as noting the nationalist perceptions, it is important to also view the Act from a unionist and Protestant viewpoint. As noted in the parliamentary debates around the introduction of the Act, unionists considered the Act as an important mechanism through which their rights and liberties could be protected. This points to a clear divide, with unionists viewing the Act as an instrument to maintain their rights and liberties (as well as public order) and nationalists and republicans (and thus most of the Catholic population) viewing the Act as an instrument of oppression that denied their basic rights of expression, association and political organisation. This may serve to illustrate that both communities had a strong sense of rights-based approaches.

However, it also evidences that the two communities had very divergent views on what right and liberty are. This disagreement on the definition of human rights is, as shall be seen, a constant theme in the Northern Irish political discourse.

Electoral systems and processes

Apart from enacting the Special Powers Act, early Northern Irish Parliaments and administrations also dealt with another matter that would be at the core of the nationalist grievances that erupted in the 1960s: electoral systems and processes. The first two Northern Irish Parliaments were elected on the basis of proportional representation. The results of the first election have already been alluded to. The 1921 election using proportional representation resulted in the Ulster Unionist Party obtaining 66.95 per cent of the popular vote which translated into 76.92 per cent of the seats in Parliament. Thus the system rewarded the Ulster Unionists with a "bonus" of 10 per cent more seats than they got votes. The non-unionist vote was split between Sinn Féin and the Nationalist Party. Sinn Féin obtained 20 per cent of the vote but only 11.5 per cent of the seats. However, the Nationalist Party's results were almost perfectly proportional 11.8 per cent of the vote returning 11.5 per cent of the seats.

The 1925 elections (the last held under the proportional representation system) saw a decline in the Ulster Unionist Party's vote with 55 per cent of the popular vote translating into 61 per cent of the Stormont seats. This decline may be ascribed to the presence of Independent Unionist candidates who obtained 9 per cent of the votes and 7.6 per cent of the seats. In the absence of Sinn Féin, the Nationalists polled 23.7 per cent of the vote and obtained 19.2 per cent of seats. This breakdown of the results indicates that the main differences in performance were attributable to whether the unionist and nationalist vote was split or not. Nevertheless, a bias in favour of the Ulster Unionists is evident even under the proportional representation system with the party obtaining more seats than votes in both elections. This must have been due to the way in which electoral boundaries were drawn and also partly due to the existence of a University vote and a second vote for owners of business premises.

In 1928 the Northern Irish Parliament voted to change the voting system to the first-past-the-post model used for Westminster elections. It has been a common nationalist complaint that this change was intended to work against the nationalist community. However, studies quoted by John Whyte in his balanced and scrupulous examination of discrimination in electoral practices[29] show that this complaint was exaggerated. In fact, the 1929 elections resulted in the Ulster Unionists gaining 71 per cent of the seats although they only obtained 50.8 per cent of the vote: a difference in their favour of just over 20 per cent. At the same time the Nationalist Party obtained 21.5 per cent of the seats although it gathered 11.6 per cent of the vote: a difference in their favour of just under 10 per cent. The main losers under the new system were the Independent Unionists, the Ulster Liberals and the Labour Party. The former had only 5.7 per cent of the seats although it had polled 14 per cent of the vote while Labour with 8 per cent of the popular vote had 1.9 per cent of the seats. The Ulster Liberals obtained no seats notwithstanding having won over 6 per cent of the vote. This loss by the minor parties is highlighted by Whyte:

> Osborne, Pringle and Buckland focus their criticisms, not on what the 1929 reapportionment did to nationalists, but on its other effects. The abolition of PR generally weakens small parties, and the main losers in Northern Ireland were Labour, independent unionists, and other groups, who fell from eight seats in 1925 to four in 1929, although their share of the vote increased.[30]

All told it seems that the system adopted by the Northern Ireland Parliament for its elections as from 1929 onwards did not unduly discriminate against nationalists, although it did benefit considerably the governing party. The reasons for the change do not appear to have been discriminatory in their intent although self-serving motives of the governing party are evident. The Northern Irish Prime Minister addressing the issue in the Northern Ireland Parliament claimed that his interest was that of creating a Parliament where it was clear who was in favour of the union with Great Britain and who was against with no parties that entertained other issues apart from the constitutional one:

> What I want to get in this House, and what I believe we will get very much better in this House under the old-fashioned plain and simple system, are men who are for the Union on the one hand or who are against it and want to go into a Dublin Parliament on the other.[31]

He also claimed that the first-past-the-post system created strong and stable government. This, given the circumstances of Northern Ireland, meant strong unionist government. Apart from a desire to strengthen the Unionist Party's position at the expense of the smaller parties (though perhaps not the nationalists per se), a further consideration that is relevant in this context is that it brought the electoral system for Northern Ireland's party in line with the electoral system of the United Kingdom Parliament, which served to further emphasise the union between Northern Ireland and the United Kingdom.[32] The parliamentary debates in the Northern Irish House of Commons however, do reflect a significant concern by the nationalist party representatives that the abolition of proportional representation would be prejudicial to the minorities. The leader of the Nationalist Party at Stormont Joe Devlin expressed this concern in one of the debates on proportional representation:

> I think this [abolition of proportional representation] is a mean, contemptible and a callous attempt by the majority which you now rob the minority not of the safeguard which they asked for but of the safeguard which was incorporated in this Measure by a Tory British government, who thought it an essential feature of their Measure in the task of national pacification that Proportional Representation should be introduced.[33]

The debates also demonstrate that "rights language" was also used to attack the abolition of the proportional system. Sam Kyle, a Northern Ireland Labour Party MP, in the same debate quoted above, stated that:

> I would warn those sections of the citizens whose rights are protected and governed by the Act of 1920 that a change of the character announced by the Prime Minister [i.e. abolition of proportional representation] … is very dangerous to their rights.[34]

Numerous similar concerns were expressed in a number of debates in the House of Commons which dealt with this matter. Whatever the ultimate net effect of the change from the proportional system to the first-past-the-post system, it is clear from the parliamentary debates that nationalists (as well as smaller parties) perceived the change negatively and as prejudicial to their interests and – as evidenced above – their rights. This perception would doubtless have been shared by the nationalist community and served to further their sense of grievance against the unionist government.

The nationalist complaints concerning electoral practices concerned, even more acutely, the electoral practices adopted for local authority elections. The electoral system for local elections was changed from proportional representation to first-past-the-post early on in the history of the Northern Ireland Parliament. The changes in electoral practices for local and municipal elections were also severely criticised by the nationalist community for being based on gerrymandered boundaries that delivered distorted results. Although at the time of the abolition of proportional representation for local elections the nationalist Members of Parliament were not taking their seats in Stormont their sense of grievance at this decision was expressed in later debates. In his criticism of the effects of the abolition of proportional representation for the House of Commons, Joe Devlin referred specifically to the effect that the same change had had in local government:

> The Nationalists constitute roughly a good third of the population, and therefore should control the same proportion of public bodies. They did so before the setting up of the Northern Parliament. But no sooner did the members of the Government feel themselves secure in Parliamentary

> power than they began to put into operation a well-thought-out plan to gerrymander the local government electoral areas for the specific purpose of controlling the public bodies.... There are in Northern Ireland two Corporations, Belfast and Derry; six county councils, 32 urban district councils, and 32 rural district councils, or 72 in all. To those are to be added at least a dozen other public bodies with various responsibilities, making a total of 84 in the Six Counties. But out of the 84 the Nationalists control only two. Proportional Representation was abolished in the rural areas of the Province and the result was that those of us who constitute forty per cent, of the population of the Province rule four of the councils out of 84.[35]

In the previously cited work by Whyte, the evidence provided shows a case of abuse in the local elections, thus substantiating the nationalist viewpoint in this regard. Of particular weight in this context are references to official papers quoted by Buckland, where cooperation (some would say collusion) between unionist activists and government officials in drawing local authority boundaries is evidenced. Whyte concludes that whereas most nationalist complaints over electoral practices are exaggerated or unfounded,

> when it comes to gerrymandering of local government boundaries, criticism is much more firmly based. Nationalists were manipulated out of control in a number of councils where they had a majority of electors. This is one of the clearest areas of discrimination in the whole field of controversy.[36]

The unionist viewpoint on the issue of local government gerrymandering revolves largely around the economic argument that since unionists, in general, paid more rates they were entitled to more representation. This argument finds little support in contemporary human rights and democratic principles and was largely being discarded at the time. In fact, the trend in the United Kingdom ever since the Great Reform Act of 1832 was to move away from such notions of franchise to a more egalitarian notion.

In conclusion, one may argue that the electoral practices as developed in the early life of Northern Ireland certainly created a sense in the minority nationalist population of electoral discrimination both at the parliamentary level (where the balance of probability seems against such discrimination having occurred) and especially at the local government level. In the latter case, the perception of discrimination appears borne out in fact as well. The unionist-led 1922 alteration of the local government voting system and boundary delineation may partly have been motivated by a wish to redress unionist grievance since as has been claimed "[m]aybe it was the pre-1920 situation that was unfair [to the unionists]". This motivation loses validity when the effects of the local government electoral practices post-1922 are viewed in the round. One may contend that the unionist experience in this sphere was, as in the case of the Special Powers Act, derived from a desire to preserve the Union and the rights and liberties they perceived the Union to provide them with, at all costs. Even at the cost of discriminating against the minority population in terms of electoral fairness. One also notices that even in the pre-human rights era examined here, the language of rights and liberties figures considerably in the arguments put forward by the leaders of both communities. Once again though, as with the Special Powers Act, the two communities had divergent views of what these rights and liberties were and to whom they appertained.

The participation of the minority community in public institutions

The nationalist community and, more so, the republican strand of it, were initially intent on boycotting the institutions of the Northern Irish state. This is nowhere more evident than in the attitude towards the main public institution of the state: Parliament. Between 1921 and 1925 the Members of Parliament elected on behalf of Sinn Féin and of the Nationalist Party pursued a policy of abstention by not taking up their seats at Stormont. Furthermore, when the Nationalist Party did take up the seats it won in the 1925 parliamentary election it refused to assume the role of official opposition.

This attitude by the Nationalist Party was an expression of the belief that the partition of Ireland was an illegal act and that the Northern Irish state was thus illegitimate. One may argue that this attitude and its expression coloured to some degree unionist behaviour towards nationalists in the early years of Northern Ireland's existence. In fact, it lent credence to, if it did not create, the unionist belief that the nationalist community was not to be trusted with the execution of the functions of the state since they were inherently disloyal. This early decision by the Nationalist Party was also reflected in the attitude of the nationalist community at large, where few members of the community chose to serve in the civil service. This attitude is especially evident with respect to the Royal Ulster Constabulary (RUC) where, although a third of the places in the force were reserved for Catholics, the number of Catholics in the Northern Ireland police force was always limited.[37]

Following this early boycotting of public institutions, the attitude of the nationalist community towards serving in the Northern Irish public institutions (as expressed by their political representatives) gradually shifted. This shift is noticeable in relatively early claims that the Northern Irish public service was discriminating against the Catholic community in recruitment. Joe Devlin as leader of the Nationalist Party at Stormont articulated these claims on several occasions in parliamentary debates concerning the civil service: "There is a grave suspicion amongst many members of the public that certain people are kept out of these [civil service] appointments because of their religion."[38]

Nationalist Party MPs also criticised the control of the selection processes by unionist Members of Parliament and called for a review of these mechanisms which would involve at least one Nationalist MP in the process:

> You cannot expect a substantial minority of the people to have confidence in any body which has sway over so much of material interest to them when they have absolutely no representative upon that Committee. I would urge the Government as a matter of justice and fair play, and if they wish to transform their verbal gestures into something practical, to adopt the suggestion I have made and appoint on that Committee someone who will carry the confidence not only of the public representatives who sit on these benches but of the whole community whom we represent in Northern Ireland. I think it is perfectly indefensible to say that out of six members three should be selected from one side of the House.[39]

One notes in both these parliamentary interventions the references to suspicion, confidence, fair play and justice which seem to confirm that in the case of public employment the issue of perception is once again of paramount importance. The clear implication of both these statements is that the perception held by the Catholic community was that selection processes were biased against Catholics, or put another way favoured Protestants, and that in order to allay such perceptions the minority should be represented and involved in the selection process.

It is also appropriate to present the unionist view on this matter as in direct response to the intervention just quoted, a unionist MP responded by referring to the fact that the nationalist MPs had refused to take up their seats in Parliament and thus could not have been included in the committee concerned.[40] The clear implication was that the nationalist parliamentarians had only themselves to blame for the lack of representation accorded to their community.

The debates surrounding discrimination in employment in Northern Ireland gradually developed into a major bone of contention between the communities and this contention was articulated in Parliament (both at Stormont and at Westminster), in the media as well as in academic publications. In fact, as an issue it continued to bedevil Northern Ireland throughout the conflict, and even in the post-conflict years when most civil rights matters had been resolved through legislative enactments or policy changes.[41] It has even been suggested that discrimination in employment practices was one of the two most important factors that led to the Northern Irish civil rights movement of the 1960s.[42] The parliamentary debates referred to above indicate that the seeds of this debate on discrimination in employment practices had been laid early on in the life of Northern Ireland. The perception of discrimination accumulated within the nationalist community (inter alia as a result of unionist control of civil service recruitment and also of Protestant firms preferring to recruit Protestant workers) and was robustly denied by unionists who claimed that any differentials in public and private employment were due to various factors not related to direct discrimination.[43]

In conclusion, it is suggested that the birth of Northern Ireland was accompanied by the emergence (or crystallisation) of a number of issues related to human rights principles and norms. These issues include: self-determination; political representation and electoral practices; emergency legislation and the administration of justice more generally; as well as employment discrimination, which matters would, in the next two decades:

1 be categorised under the developing category of human rights;
2 continue to intensify the division between the two communities; and
3 culminate in the civil rights movement of the late 1960s which, in itself, is considered to be a turning point in the Northern Ireland conflict.

Human rights come to the fore: 1945–1964

The 1930s were a period of consolidation in Northern Ireland. The problems outlined in the section above, solidified but without any major shocks to the political system, although sporadic violence did erupt in 1931 and 1932.[44] The UUP continued its domination of the Northern Ireland Parliament and of government while violence subsided and the IRA campaigns were in remission. The appearance of stability was reinforced by the virtually unchanging government where James Craig served as Prime Minister from 1921 to 1940. On the nationalist side, the political outlook also remained stable with the Nationalist Party retaining its position as the parliamentary voice of the nationalist community with an average of ten seats. The Nationalist Party had limited impact in Parliament due to the overwhelming UUP majority and also due to its somewhat disorganised structure. Nevertheless, the Nationalist MPs continued to express the grievances of the nationalist community relating to the issues presented in the section above. The outbreak of war probably hardened unionist perceptions of Catholic disloyalty as a result of the Irish Republic's decision to remain neutral during World War II while Northern Ireland joined the United Kingdom's efforts with determination and a strong sense of pride insofar as the unionist community was concerned.

The major argument presented in this section will be that World War II, or more precisely its aftermath, would have a momentous effect on the history of Northern Ireland viewed from a human rights perspective. The history of Northern Ireland in the period post-1945 requires a broadening of the scope of vision when examined through a human rights lens. International developments in the context of the United Nations and later on in the Council of Europe established human rights principles and legal norms as part of the common legal, political and social language throughout the world and in western Europe in particular. Northern Ireland forming part of western Europe was thus also impacted in this vein. Internal developments within the United Kingdom also require consideration as the Labour Party government of 1945–1951 introduced fundamental social and economic changes that also influenced Northern Ireland. Thus it is suggested that the Northern Irish human rights history of 1945–1968 necessitates an analysis at three levels:

1 the international level of analysis;
2 the European or continental level of analysis; and
3 the United Kingdom level of analysis (including Northern Ireland itself).

The international and regional human rights context

Whereas human rights values and principles have a long history in various cultures and philosophical traditions[45] and a few initial tentative steps towards establishing international human rights standards were taken in the inter-war period,[46] there is no doubt that the term "human rights" fully entered international law and politics as a result of the founding of the United Nations. The UN Charter clearly established the protection and promotion of human rights as one of the aims of the organisation both in its Preamble as well as in Article 1(3).

The decision by the UN to create a specific Human Rights Commission to formulate a definition of human rights would change the history of human rights. The Commission drafted the Universal Declaration of Human Rights (UDHR) which was approved by the General Assembly of the UN on 10 December 1948. Apart from its intrinsic value as a declaration that explains what human rights consist of, the Declaration over a short period assumed the character of an inspirational document referred to by peoples of all cultures, religions and races. Mary Anne Glendon argues that following the adoption of the Declaration:

> To the astonishment of many, human rights would become a political factor that not even the most hardshelled realist could ignore. The Universal Declaration would become an instrument, as well as the most prominent symbol, of changes that would amplify the voice of the weak in the corridors of power. It challenged the long-standing view that a sovereign state's treatment of its own citizens was that nation's business and no one else's.... Its thirty concise articles inspired or influenced scores of postwar and postcolonial constitutions and treaties.... It became the polestar of an army of international human rights activists, who pressure governments to live up to their pledges and train the searchlight of publicity on abuses that would remain hidden in former times.[47]

Thus, the Declaration acted as a mechanism that internationalised human rights issues. This meant that human rights language became part of the political discourse world-wide. This internationalisation process occurred at a variety of levels. Increasingly, newly independent states incorporated human rights principles in their constitutions,[48] domestic courts gradually started referring to the Declaration and human rights in their decisions, politicians and societal leaders also frequently quoted from the Declaration and alluded to human rights in their speeches in national legislatures and elsewhere, while a growing body of human rights focused civil society also developed both domestically and internationally. The cumulative effect of these factors, whatever the motivation for them, resulted in human rights values, principles and legislation becoming one of the features in domestic politics and international relations in the decades following World War II. Glendon's references to the power of inspiration and mobilisation of the Declaration are particularly relevant in the context of Northern Ireland.

It is difficult to assess the direct impact of the Declaration on the human rights context of Northern Ireland. There seems little evidence of changes made to the Northern Ireland legislative framework for the promotion of human rights in the immediate period following the adoption of the Declaration. Nevertheless, it is possible to discern a measure of impact of the Declaration in the growing debate around human rights issues in the Northern Ireland Parliament. For instance, in a debate concerning powers of internment in 1959, MP Harry Diamond referred to the Declaration and to the fact that the United Kingdom had supported the adoption of the Declaration.[49] In introducing her Private Members' Human Rights Bill, MP Sheelagh Murnaghan also referred to the Declaration, as did MP Tom Boyd in the same debate.[50] While these and other references in the Northern Irish Parliament cannot be said to be evidence of a substantial impact of the Declaration in Northern Ireland, they do indicate an awareness of how the Declaration could contribute to the human rights agenda. In summary, it may be suggested that the Declaration's impact may be articulated in the following terms:

1. it created the dynamic that would lead to the establishment of international human rights law which in itself became an important measure against which Northern Ireland's human rights issues could be measured;
2. it was a direct source of inspiration for the creation of the European Convention on Human Rights which would eventually be one of the legal battlefields in which the Northern Ireland conflict would be fought;[51]
3. it inspired the American civil rights movement which in its turn was adopted as a model by the Northern Irish civil rights activists; and
4. it was in itself a source of reference for some politicians and activists in Northern Ireland.

The Council of Europe, which was founded in 1949, adopted the European Convention on Human Rights in 1950 with the aim of creating a judicial system for the enforcement of certain human rights within the member states of the Council of Europe. The rights protected in the Convention and thus susceptible to the jurisdiction of the European Court of Human Rights are essentially civil and political rights. The Convention has been amended on a regular basis to include more rights and to render the Court more efficient. The United Kingdom was one of the founding members of the Council of Europe and became a party to the Convention in 1951. The Convention also extended to Northern Ireland as part of the United Kingdom and thus, in principle, human rights were afforded an additional layer of protection in Northern Ireland as from 1953, the date on which the Convention came into force. This additional layer of protection remained somewhat ineffectual until 1966 when the United Kingdom granted its citizens the right of individual petition under the Convention. Interestingly the Republic of Ireland allowed its citizens the right of individual petition in 1953 upon ratification. The first case dealt with by the European Court of Human Rights was *Lawless* v. *Ireland*, decided on 1 July 1961. It concerned the Republic of Ireland's internment legislation adopted to counter the activities of the IRA (especially during its Border Campaign).[52]

Brice Dickson provides a detailed analysis of the Convention's impact on Northern Ireland and in so doing describes its limitations and possibilities.[53] Of particular interest, for the purposes of this study, is the impact that the Convention had on bringing human rights to the fore of the conflict in Northern Ireland. Dickson suggests that the Lawless case referred to above and which was filed by Lawless in 1957, "brought home to people *throughout* [emphasis added] Ireland that the European Convention on Human rights could be a tool worth resorting to in order to vindicate a human rights claim".[54] Furthermore, he indicates that the nascent Campaign for Social justice looked to the Court as a vehicle for redressing grievances within Northern Ireland. In the period covered in this Chapter (1945–1964) the Convention and Court were in their infancy with the Court still conservative in its approach, especially when defining the margin of appreciation allowed to states in determining what is acceptable in a democratic society.

Whatever the effectiveness or otherwise of the Convention in dealing with hard cases there are other indications of the impact that the Convention and its parent body, the Council of Europe, had in these early years. Within the context of this study it is certainly of interest and worth alluding to is an early reference to human rights issues within the Northern Ireland House of Commons. Indeed, from an examination of the parliamentary debates from 1945 onwards the first direct reference to human rights at Stormont[55] was on 7 October 1952. The reference bears to be quoted in full:

> Mr. Diamond asked the Prime Minister if his attention has been drawn to the statement made at the Council of Europe Conference at Strasbourg "that human rights are being violated in Northern Ireland every day"; and whether he will take steps to restore these human rights to all sections of the population.[56]

The brief exchange that followed this question featured Nationalist Party MPs condemning the Northern Ireland government for failing to protect the human rights of the minority community while the unionist response emphasised that human rights in Northern Ireland were highly respected. In the years immediately following the adoption of the Convention there was limited attention paid to it in Northern Ireland. However, there are further references within the Northern Ireland Parliament to the Council of Europe or the Convention in the years following 1952. Moreover, the references were on both sides of the House of Commons with, for example, opposition politicians stating that the special powers assigned to the Minister of Home Affairs in Northern Ireland were the subject of strong condemnation at the Council of Europe. In response, the relevant government Minister used the Convention to support the government's stance on internment without trial:[57]

> The Hon. Member for Falls referred to the European Convention on Human Rights drawn up some six years ago.... He quite rightly stressed the Article dealing with liberty, but even this widely accepted Convention recognizes there are times when to preserve what I have described as the fight for freedom for their people a government are entitled to restrict the liberty of the individual without recourse to the ordinary processes of law.

As in the case of the references to the Universal Declaration of Human Rights, one cannot read too much in the above-mentioned parliamentary references to the Council of Europe and the Convention. Nevertheless, they are indications that the human rights language was taking root in Northern Ireland and that this process was being influenced to some degree by the Council of Europe's activity and by the Convention itself.

As already indicated the relationship between the Convention and the Troubles in Northern Ireland has been subjected to careful analysis by Dickson. The overall conclusion arrived at by Dickson is that the Convention had a limited impact on the conflict in Northern Ireland. The Court's reticence in intruding upon states' "margin of appreciation", as well as the inherent limitations in the Convention (such as the powers of derogation), restricted the applicability of the Convention in Northern Ireland. Nevertheless, the history of the Northern Ireland Civil Rights Association (NICRA) and the Campaign for Social Justice (CSJ) do show that its leaders were, to some extent, inspired and influenced by the Convention.[58] One may suggest that the Convention, although limited in its direct application to the circumstances of Northern Ireland, was one of several mechanisms whereby the civil rights movement attempted to: (1) internationalise the situation in Northern Ireland and (2) push the Northern Ireland (and later the British) government to redress their grievances. In this context one may describe the Convention as one of many instruments of mobilisation (internally in Northern Ireland, within the United Kingdom as a whole and internationally) which brought human rights into centre stage in Northern Ireland.

Developments in the United Kingdom and Northern Ireland

The period from 1945 to 1951 was one of profound social and political change in the United Kingdom. The 1945 election of a Labour government under Prime Minister Clement Attlee ushered in an era of reform in a number of spheres. The most far-reaching and enduring reform was arguably the creation of the Welfare State, with the creation of a National Health Service (NHS), a programme of public housing and educational reform[59] being some of the central tenets of the new system. From a human rights perspective, the Welfare State, in fact, attempted to realise some of the economic and social rights that are included within the Declaration. In particular, the creation of the NHS aimed at realising the right to health,[60] while educational reforms were intended to guarantee the right to education for all children.[61] The housing programme was, in turn, attempting to alleviate the problem of lack of affordable housing thus securing for more people their right to housing.[62]

Gradually these reforms also took root in Northern Ireland with a National Health Service for Northern Ireland, a programme for public housing and educational reform through the Education (Northern Ireland) Act of 1947. The traditional understanding of the causes for the rise of a human rights-based movement in Northern Ireland places considerable importance on the emergence of a more articulate and educated Catholic population. It is part of the broadly accepted narrative of the human rights history in Northern Ireland that the civil rights movement (CRM) which emerged in the 1960s was a result of an expanding Catholic middle class and that such expansion was a result of the introduction of welfare state reforms, particularly in education.

This understanding of the civil rights movement, understood as a consequence of an expanding middle class was expressed by the Cameron Commission in its report:

> A much larger Catholic middle-class has emerged, which is less ready to acquiesce in the acceptance of a situation of assumed (or established) inferiority and discrimination than was the case in the past. This is, we think, an important and new element in the political and social climate of Northern Ireland and has played its part in the events which led to the setting up of this Enquiry. We were impressed by the number of well-educated and responsible people who were and are concerned in, and have taken an active part in, the Civil Rights movement, and by the depth and extent of the investigations which they have made, or caused to be made, to produce evidence to vouch their grievances and support their claims for remedy.[63]

John Darby has suggested that the Education (Northern Ireland) Act of 1947 was of importance in this context.[64] This Act mirrored closely the UK Education Act of 1944 introduced by the wartime coalition government which, inter alia, extended free education to secondary schools. The attribution of the rise of the Catholic middle class to educational reform is based on the premise that Catholics, being generally less well-off than Protestants, the reform allowed more Catholic children from poorer backgrounds to access education at the secondary and eventually also tertiary level. These educated young men and women with better educational backgrounds were thus able to articulate the grievances of their community more effectively and also, to an extent, more academically.

This narrative of the growth of the Catholic middle-class is not without its critics. It has been argued that this narrative is "part of an elitist approach to the Civil Rights Movement".[65] An alternative approach eschews the hypothesis that the Catholic middle class was the principal actor and force in the movement and instead focuses on a bottom-up, "popular" approach which views the civil rights movement as "a largely disorganized and spontaneous popular protest movement".[66] The reason for this popular movement according to this view was not educational reform but an increased interaction between the Catholic population and the Northern Irish state apparatus as a result of the establishment of the welfare state. This perspective locates the rise of the civil rights movement in post-war state expansion whereby the State became the provider of services such as health, housing, education etc:

> As local government became the chief interface between the Catholic community and the newly enlarged state machine so also it became an area of bitter political conflict and protest. Nearly all early civil-rights protests in fact, arose just in this particular context.[67]

This is an interesting argument which, however, was not supported in its formulation by adequate research. Nevertheless, there is certainly relevance to the fact that as the state, through local authorities, became a supplier of public goods such as housing the possibility for discrimination in this area was also created. Since before the advent of the welfare state the amount of public housing in Northern Ireland was negligible it is axiomatic that there was little scope for discriminating in its allocation and likewise little scope for the Catholic community to perceive, rightly or wrongly, such discrimination.

One may also contend that educational reforms had a threefold effect:

1. expanding the middle class which Cameron and others argue played some role – whatever its precise dimension – in the civil rights movement;
2. making the Catholic population at large more aware of their disadvantage and less likely to accept such disadvantage (whether real or perceived) without resorting to the kind of political protest which was expanding in Europe and especially the USA; and
3. expanding the consciousness of rights and of the consciousness of the definition of human rights with a consequent rise in aspirations.

All told, it seems clear that the creation of the welfare state in the United Kingdom and its adoption in Northern Ireland was one of the factors which contributed to the rise of the civil rights movement in Northern Ireland. This factor together with the emergence of human rights as an important aspect of world politics (through the UN, its specialised agencies and international human rights non-governmental organisations (NGOs)) and of regional politics (through the work of the Council of Europe and civil society) created the opportunity for human rights to become such an important part of Northern Irish political life. It may be argued that the international human rights efforts, chiefly the UN Universal Declaration of Human Rights, crystallised the concept of human rights and crafted its language while the European Convention contributed towards an understanding of human rights as law. On the other hand, the introduction of the welfare state in the United Kingdom and Northern Ireland was a factor in shaping an environment where there was a more aware, articulate and ambitious community seeking to break away from its social, economic and political disadvantage which it perceived to be a result of discrimination by the ruling majority community.

Having considered briefly some of the broad international and regional contexts within which human rights emerged as an important political, social and legal phenomenon in Northern Ireland it is necessary to assess some of the concrete human rights issues that prevailed in Northern Ireland from 1945 until the rise of the civil rights movement in the mid-1960s. As in the previous sections this is done with reference to the political developments in Northern Ireland during this period.

Human rights issues in post-war Northern Ireland: continuity and change

The major human rights issues highlighted in the earlier part of this chapter, which covered the period from 1921 to the outbreak of World War II, revolved around self-determination, the Special Powers Acts, electoral practices and the access to public employment. Most of these issues remained relevant in the post-war period although employment and electoral practices appeared to gain in importance while the access to public housing emerged as another key feature of the human rights debate. Furthermore, the human rights agenda under the rubric of the civil rights movement emerged as a powerful mobilising concept within the minority community. This movement challenged severely the political establishment and ultimately (in conjunction with other factors) led to division and dissent within the Unionist Party as well as the decline and eventual disappearance of the Nationalist Party as the major political representative of the minority.

Self-determination

In the period under investigation the Catholic community in Northern Ireland continued to support the Nationalist Party with a section of the community supporting the Northern Ireland Labour Party, although Catholic support for the Labour Party decreased following its decision to formally position itself in favour of union with the United Kingdom in 1949. In the period covered in this section electoral support from the Catholic community also went to a more limited extent to the Liberal Party as well as the Socialist Republican Party and Irish Labour Party.[68] The Protestant community's electoral support went overwhelmingly to the Unionist Party (sometimes referred to as the Official Unionist Party) for most of the period covered in this section, although some Independent Unionists did gather support in electoral contests. Towards the end of this period the Unionist Party was challenged by the rise of the Protestant Unionist Party (forerunner of the Democratic Unionist Party) as well as by divisions within its ranks.

The issue of self-determination therefore crystallised around the respective positions of the Unionist Party in defence of the union with the United Kingdom and of the Nationalist Party with its insistence that it would seek to argue for a united Ireland through constitutional means. These positions were challenged by occasional IRA military initiatives to push for Irish unity through the use of force, most notably the Border Campaign which went on intermittently between 1956 and 1961 although the height of this campaign was reached in the period of 1956–1958. This campaign was relevant from a human rights perspective since it resulted in a revival of internment without trial both in Northern Ireland and in the Republic of Ireland. The period from 1945 to 1968, however, can be classified as one where human rights concerns with equality took precedence over constitutional issues relating to the status of Northern Ireland.

The Special Powers Act of 1922 was initially renewed annually but it became permanent in 1933. As highlighted earlier the Act provided the Minister for Home Affairs with a range of considerable powers in order to maintain order and security within Northern Ireland. One may argue that the most serious power held by the Minister was that of ordering internment without trial since such power offended the principle of individual freedom and went against the principle of due process.

This point was made consistently by Nationalist Party politicians as well as other political representatives of the minority community such as Harry Diamond. These politicians insisted that internment was used more than was strictly necessary by the exigencies of the situation, that it continued to be used when the situation had calmed down and that it was used not only against individuals known to be involved in IRA activity but also as "revenge against them [the internees] for what he [the Minister for Home Affairs] considers their sympathy and support for those who have caused all this trouble [referring to the Border Campaign]".[69] On the other hand the unionist politicians continued to view the Act in general and the power of internment without trial in particular as a legitimate and essential tool in the fight against terrorism. This attitude was summed up by the then Minister of Home Affairs:

> It is a fact that in any community of people individual rights must always be in the common interest, subject to certain exceptions and restrictions. Of course this, in turn, means that in a time of emergency it may lead to a restriction of the freedom of movement or the rights of the individual, and it follows that it is the primary duty of a Government to take such steps as will secure the preservation of peace and the maintenance of order. In other words, if I might put it this way, when emergency measures are taken it is for the purpose of the protection of the rights of the individual and not in any way to interfere with them.[70]

On balance, it may be argued that whatever the merits of this attitude in practice, the activities of the IRA in its Border Campaign allowed for such an attitude to be expressed with a measure of credibility. The operation of the Act continued to be a source of grievance for the minority community as evidenced by the views expressed, at regular intervals, by political representatives in the Northern Irish House of Commons. Apart from internment, the banning of public manifestations as well as publications and the perceived lack of impartiality by the Ministry of Home Affairs and the police in applying the Act were recurring issues which the minority community (or at least part of it) resented. The literature on the Act ranges from outright condemnations of the Act[71] to more balanced views[72] which, at least, acknowledge the context in which the Act was adopted. Others commented on how the Republic of Ireland itself adopted similar emergency legislation to counter IRA activity and indeed went further than Northern Ireland in punishing IRA personnel.

Nevertheless, Whyte's conclusion that overall "even when the circumstances are explained, the Act appears to have been unduly severe"[73] seems to be correct. It cannot be doubted that whatever the motivation for the Act and however the Act was applied throughout the existence of the Stormont Parliament, it continued to present a point of divergence from a human rights perspective. The majority community viewed it as an important tool in preserving their rights and freedoms against terrorism while the minority community viewed it as a repressive tool applied in a partial manner against their interests.

Electoral practices and processes

The problems with electoral practices outlined previously in the context of the period 1921 to 1945 continued in the period under review. Once again, the major disagreement concerned insistent claims by Nationalist representatives of gerrymandering conducted by the unionist government in local elections. As was highlighted in the previous section dealing with electoral practices the evidence of gerrymandering at local government level appears to be quite conclusive and unionists did draw the local government boundaries to favour their party. The leader of the Nationalist Party in the Northern Ireland Parliament in 1957 drew attention to this as had been the case with previous and successive Nationalist parliamentarians. The local authorities which were highlighted by James McSparran were Derry City, Omagh, County Tyrone and County Fermanagh, all of which according to McSparran had a substantial majority of nationalist (by which one presumes he meant Catholic) residents but a minority of nationalist representation in local government.

The Nationalist Party leader in drawing attention to these issues made a point of emphasising the possible consequences of this situation where the minority community felt that their political aspirations and rights were not being properly respected. In fact, McSparran, having reeled off the list of local authorities where gerrymandering was alleged, stated that:

> These facts can be verified in any way any impartial observer wants to look at them, and I appeal to Hon. Members on the other side of the House as reasonable men who are aware of these facts to say if they think that the sort of situation created by them … in the course of time will not lead to such a condition of resentment and dissatisfaction as will provide proper feeding ground for a policy of physical force.[74]

Clearly the implication being suggested here is that unless these grievances were addressed by the unionist government, a growing number of members in the minority community would resort to violence.

The importance of local government electoral practices can be described as twofold. First, and most obviously, there is the relevance of political representation and the notion that the elections should reflect the wishes of the majority community. Second, the control of local authorities was of special importance in the context of Northern Ireland where local government was both a source of employment and the provider of public housing and other public services. All told, the effect of gerrymandering in local elections was to create strong resentment within the minority community that the unionist government was not willing to act in a fair manner. This in turn engendered in the minority community stronger suspicions against the government in all other areas of public life.

A rising tide of discrimination?

In the period under examination, which led to the emergence of the civil rights movement, the notion of discrimination became the major focus in Northern Ireland political discourse. As Mitchell points out:

> It is even possible to make a case … that the issues on the Irish conflict changed radically enough between 1921 and 1966 from issues of

establishing an independent, united Irish republic to those of civil rights for the minority in the North.[75]

One may suggest that this transformation is due to the fact that discrimination became the key organising concept for the nationalist community. This, in itself, was a result of numerous factors some of which have already been alluded to. The long, unbroken history of one-party rule; the sense that the Special Powers Act was applied unfairly against the minority community; the frustration at gerrymandered local authority boundaries and the feeling that employment (both public and private) was more difficult to acquire for members of the minority community – all contributed to an accumulation of a sense of victimhood over the years for Catholics in Northern Ireland.

In the ten years following the end of World War II Northern Ireland witnessed a steady growth in the availability of public housing and "as public housing became more plentiful, so complaints about its allocation multiplied".[76] The allocation of housing became another field of contention where claims of discrimination surfaced from the mid-1950s onwards. Two examples from the Northern Ireland Parliament of how this issue was a recurring theme. Nationalist MP Cahir Healy referred to the fact that this was an issue which had been raised in the House before:

> It is a shame that houses should be allocated on grounds other than need. I am making a statement that has been made here before and also in another place that certain estates are reserved for people of a certain religious point of view, of a certain political point of view.[77]

Nor were the claims of discrimination only against unionist controlled councils. Claims that nationalist controlled councils also engaged in discrimination in housing allocation were also made at Stormont. Labour Party MP Tom Boyd in one of the parliamentary debates alleged that the nationalist controlled Omagh council discriminated against Labour Party activists in the provision of public housing.[78]

As in all other fields of contention questions as to whether in fact there was any discrimination in the allocation of public housing and, if so to what extent, have received very different responses. The Cameron Report on the outbreak of the disturbances in Northern Ireland published in 1969 gave due importance to the issue of fairness in the allocation of public housing. It found that the "the Civil Rights march in Dungannon on 24th August … occurred because of the feelings aroused by the much publicised Caledon incident and was intended mainly as a protest against housing policy in the area."[79] Its overall conclusion on whether public housing was subject to discrimination indicated that the allocation of housing policy was "distorted" for political ends in certain unionist controlled local authorities.[80] Whyte on the other hand, after examining the various claims and counter-claims,[81] concludes that "discrimination seems to have been less widespread in housing than in, say, public employment."[82] Be that as it may, it is difficult not to conclude that discrimination in the allocation of public housing did exist to some extent and that the publicity afforded to *causes célèbres* such as the Caledon incident magnified the issue and consolidated the view that discrimination was practiced and that action against it was not being taken.

The issue of employment where, according to Whyte, discrimination existed to a greater extent than in housing presents very much the same scenario. Nationalists claimed that discrimination was practiced against the minority community in public employment[83] while the unionists claimed that either no discrimination was practiced and/or that any differences in public employment were due to Catholics not applying or accepting certain positions[84] or else that certain civil service positions could not be entrusted to persons with nationalist sympathies in order to protect the state. The then Prime Minister of Northern Ireland, Viscount Brookeborough articulated the latter point as follows:

> We are being fair. Those people who are represented by hon. Members opposite are getting their proportion of appointments according to the population, but what country is going to fill the Civil Service and other bodies by people who are being induced by hon. Gentleman opposite to destroy the country? We should be lunatics to do so, and we are not lunatics.[85]

The situation thus was one where nationalists increasingly claimed discrimination in public employment while unionists refuted such claims basing themselves on a variety of factors but frequently referring to the specific circumstances of Northern Ireland. Thus, even at times when the issues of discrimination and human rights were on the rise within the political discourse of Northern Ireland, the constitutional question continuously cast its long shadow. The following response by a unionist MP to a nationalist claim of discrimination illustrates this fact:

> I would remind the hon. Member that so far as I know there is no other country in the world where the main aim of the principal Opposition Party is to overthrow the Constitution of the country.[86]

In the mid to late 1960s the conflation between human rights issues and constitutional questions was to assume a far greater and more sinister connotation. The late 1950s saw the first signals of an emerging civil rights movement while the first years of the 1960s witnessed the growth of a full-fledged civil rights movement in Northern Ireland. The movement, although attracting republican support, was expressly concerned with discrimination in housing allocation, employment and local electoral processes.[87] This same movement, however, was deemed by parts of the unionist community as a thinly veiled attempt at destabilising the Northern Irish state through the language and processes of human rights.[88] The tensions created by these competing visions and ideas eventually erupted into violence thus aiding the perception of conflation between human rights, constitutional matters and violence. With the eventual descent into violence human rights concerns became at once both more urgent and fundamental as well as more prone to being used and abused for partisan reasons.

Summary

Throughout this chapter an attempt has been made to map some of the human rights issues that arose from the birth of Northern Ireland to the early 1960s. This has been done in the following manner:

1 by reviewing, primarily from a political point of view, how the political parties in Northern Ireland have adopted human rights discourse (whether or not they adopted human rights values is more open to interpretation) and how they have reacted to human rights matters in the early history of the Northern Irish state; and
2 by exploring how human rights language and concerns developed in Northern Ireland prior to and following World War II. In the latter case, this also was done also by taking into account how progress at the international, regional and UK level influenced such developments in Northern Ireland.

This attempt at charting some of the human rights milestones on the political terrain of Northern Ireland was principally conducted through a review of statements made by political representatives in the Northern Irish Parliament as the main forum for political expression in the period under examination. One may suggest that several elements have emerged from this exercise which may be summarised as follows:

1 Human rights issues and concerns, broadly understood, have lain at the heart of the Northern Ireland conflict. First, self-determination and the scope for its exercise which is the ultimate basis for the conflict is also a human rights issue. In fact, both the International Covenant on Civil and Political Rights (ICCPR) and the International Covenant on Economic, Social and Cultural Rights (ICESCR) commence with a statement proclaiming self-determination. This is even more relevant in the context of Northern Ireland where the majority community considered that its human rights (typically referred to by unionists as "civil and religious rights") could only be secured through the continuing union with the United Kingdom. Conversely, the minority community considered that the right to self-determination of the people of Ireland was prejudiced by partition and later came to view the Northern Irish state as one which discriminated against them and deprived them of their human rights.

Thus, a portion of the minority community adopted the opposite view to the unionist community and held that their human rights would only be fully protected through union with the Republic of Ireland.

2 Within the minority community, which *ab initio* was suspicious and resentful of the Northern Irish government, there grew a gradual and increasing feeling (as articulated by its political representatives) that they were being discriminated against in a number of areas including political participation, the operation of emergency legislation, employment and housing. With the growth of the international human rights movement globally and with the social changes[89] that occurred within the United Kingdom and Northern Ireland the feeling of discrimination came to be expressed more forcefully and effectively by the minority. This expression saw the adoption by the minority of broadly accepted human rights language and references to international human rights instruments as a lever to achieve change.

3 The majority community, to some extent, was slower in responding to the growth and broadening of the international human rights movement. Their language remained more tied to the traditional views of civil and political rights as articulated in the Glorious Revolution. In a sense, Unionism retained a Lockean language of rights while the Nationalists adopted, relatively swiftly, the broader and more universal discourse of the Universal Declaration of Human Rights. There was also a feeling amongst some unionist politicians, usually expressed in Parliament through accusations of hypocrisy against Nationalists, that the adoption of human rights language by the same Nationalists was merely instrumental to their real objective of a united Ireland. Finally, one cannot discount the view as expressed by Viscount Brookeborough in the statement quoted above, that the protection of Northern Ireland's constitutional status and the legitimate rights of the majority could only be fully secured by some limited breaches of the rights of the minority. This appeared to be accompanied by the implication that this approach was inevitable given the disloyalty towards the state and state institutions by a portion of the minority community.

All told, the evolution of a human rights agenda in Northern Ireland's first 40 years appears to have been inextricably linked with the constitutional question (or to put it in human rights language, with the right to self-determination). The relationship between human rights and the constitutional question became even more intricate with the rise of the civil rights movement in the 1960s. Nationalist adoption of human rights language and practices became more marked and more public. At the same time, Unionism seemed divided on how to react to this new movement with some counselling reform while others advocated resistance. The ultimate result of these centrifugal forces was a breakdown in peace and security with a descent into violence which ultimately led to a period in which human rights suffered its worst and most egregious abuses in Northern Ireland.[90]

One of the striking aspects of the post-war period is how traditional ideas of political liberties broaden to embrace socioeconomic perspectives and ideas of fairness in, for example, public provision of accommodation and employment. This broadening of the human rights idea emerges both from international and domestic developments. At the international level the adoption of the Universal Declaration of Human Rights clarifies that human rights have a socioeconomic content as well as civil and political content. On the domestic front the emergence of the welfare state in the UK with its emphasis on the state as a guarantor of socioeconomic well-being expanded the concept of what citizens could rightfully expect from the state as a matter of law and policy. These developments had an impact on the consciousness of rights and human rights in Northern Ireland for the minority community.

These matters, together with the traditional nationalist complaints around discrimination (which have been abundantly referred to above), provide an explanation of why civil rights began to eclipse self-determination in the public consciousness of an increasing number of nationalists in Northern Ireland. This chapter provides an examination of the story of human rights and politics in Northern Ireland further back than other treatments. In essence it suggests that the concepts and language of equality and discrimination, which predated the rights language of the post-war period, were concepts that were rooted in Northern Irish political life prior to the civil rights movement. Thus, the civil rights movement grew out of a historically quite well entrenched public discourse about rights (although initially couched in a language of discrimination and equality rather than rights) and that rights discourse did not enter the Northern Irish political debate in the 1960s.

The next chapter will examine, once again from a human rights perspective, the events from 1965 (approaching the height of the civil rights movement) until 1972, which was the year which registered the greatest number of deaths in the conflict and also the year in which direct rule from London replaced the Northern Ireland Parliament.

Notes

1 See, for example, Conor Cruise O'Brien, *States of Ireland* (London: Hutchinson, 1972); Ruth Dudley Edwards, *The Faithful Tribe: An Intimate Portrait of the Loyal Institutions* (London: Harper Collins, 1999); and Joseph J. Lee, *Ireland 1912–1985: Politics and Society* (Cambridge University Press, 1989).

2 This point is made, amongst others, by Michelle Parlevliet who states that the Good Friday Agreement "means different things to different groups. … The absence of a strong common vision of the future among unionists and nationalists is both a cause and consequence of the different meanings the agreement holds." Michelle Parlevliet, "Icebergs and the Impossible: Human Rights and Conflict Resolution in Post-Settlement Peace Building", in *Human Rights and Conflict Resolution in Context*, ed. Eileen F. Babbett and Ellen L. Lutz (New York: Syracuse University Press, 2009).

3 This is evidenced by the references to parity of esteem for the culture and traditions of the two communities. Vide, inter alia, Article 1(v) of the Constitutional

Issues section of the Agreement. The Northern Ireland Peace Agreement, accessed 16 June 2014, http://peacemaker.un.org/sites/peacemaker.un.org/files/IE%20GB_980410_Northern%20Ireland%20Agreement.pdf.

4 See, for example, Patrick M Geoghegan, *The Irish Act of Union: A Study in High Politics* (London: Palgrave Macmillan, 2000) who argues that there was corruption on a grand scale in securing the Act of Union, as well as one of the earlier historians of the Act of Union, William E. H. Lecky who in his *Historical and Political Essays* of 1908 argues that there was a lavish distribution of peerages to secure the passage of the Act. William E. H. Lecky, *Historical and Political Essays* (London: Longmans, Green and Co., 1908).

5 Incidentally it has been suggested by Martin Mensargh that in Ireland "The backdrop to the war of independence had been the doctrine of self-determination proclaimed by President Wilson." Martin Mensargh, "The Background to the Irish Peace Process", in *A Farewell to Arms? From "Long War" to Long Peace*, ed. Michael Cox, Adrian Guelke and Fiona Stephen (Manchester: Manchester University Press, 2000), 10.

6 Kevin Boyle and Tom Hadden, *Ireland: A Positive Proposal* (Harmondsworth: Penguin Books, 1985), 12.

7 For a comprehensive account of the development and application of the principle of self-determination in international law, see James Summers, *Peoples and International Law: How Nationalism and Self-Determination Shape a Contemporary Law of Nations* (The Hague: Martinus Nijhoff Publishers, 2007).

8 Gerry Adams, *The New Ireland: A Vision for the Future* (Dublin: Brandon Books, 2005).

9 Boyle and Hadden, *Ireland:A Positive Proposal*, 11.

10 David McKittrick and David McVea have commented that "This north-eastern region was very much part of the British industrial economy, Belfast having closer ties and economic similarities with Glasgow and Liverpool than with Dublin." David McKittrick and David McVea, *Making Sense of the Troubles: The Story of the Conflict in Northern Ireland* (Chicago: New Amsterdam Books, 2002), 3.

11 Éamonn Ó Ciardha and Micheál Ó Siochrú, "A Laboratory for Empire", *History Today* 17, no. 6 (December 2009), 11.

12 James T. Nolan, *The Status of the Catholic Minority in Northern Ireland 1920–1939* (Unpublished Doctoral Thesis, Fordham University, 1953), 70.

13 The situation was described by James Craig, the Northern Irish Prime Minister as "a cause of grave anxiety and alarm". Northern Ireland House of Commons, *The Parliamentary Debates: Official Report*, 14 March 1922, col. 12, http://stormontpapers.ahds.ac.uk/stormontpapers/pageview.html?volumeno=2&pageno=.

14 McKittrick and McVea, *Making Sense of the Troubles*, 6.

15 Sydney Elliott, *Northern Ireland Parliamentary Election Results, 1921–72* (Chichester: Political Reference Publications, 1973).

16 Northern Ireland House of Commons, *The Parliamentary Debates: Official Report*, 14 March 1922.

17 Preamble to the Great Britain Parliament, Civil Authorities (Special Powers) Act (Northern Ireland), 1922, accessed 18 January 2011, http://cain.ulst.ac.uk/hmso/spa1922.htm.

18 In this case the Minister of Home Affairs in terms of Article 1(2) of the Act although the Minister could delegate any of his powers to a police officer.

19 Such as freedom of assembly and trial by jury.

20 Laura K. Donohue, "Regulating Northern Ireland: The Special Powers Acts, 1922–1972", *The Historical Journal* 41, no. 4 (1998): 1089–120.

21 Northern Ireland House of Commons, *The Parliamentary Debates: Official Report*, 21 March 1922, col. 91, http://stormontpapers.ahds.ac.uk/stormontpapers/pageview.html?volumeno=2&pageno=85.

22 Ibid.
23 Northern Ireland House of Commons, *The Parliamentary Debates: Official Report*, 15 March 1922, col. 41, http://stormontpapers.ahds.ac.uk/stormontpapers/pageview.html?volumeno=2&pageno=29.
24 Northern Ireland House of Commons, *The Parliamentary Debates: Official Report*, 21 March 1922, col. 95.
25 The causes for such violence and instability as well as its perpetrators, were however, a matter that was – and is – very much disputed by both sides.
26 Quoted in Donohue, "Regulating Northern Ireland", 1100.
27 Ibid.
28 Darby, *Scorpions in a Bottle*, 29.
29 John Whyte, "How Much Discrimination Was There under the Unionist Regime, 1921–68?", in *Contemporary Irish Studies*, ed. Tom Gallagher and James O'Connell (Manchester: Manchester University Press, 1983).
30 Ibid.
31 Northern Ireland House of Commons, *The Parliamentary Debates: Official Report*, 25 October 1927, col. 2276, http://stormontpapers.ahds.ac.uk/stormontpapers/pageview.html?volumeno=8&pageno=2239.
32 The Prime Minister, Viscount Craigavon, said in Parliament in 1927: "what is good enough for her [Great Britain] is good enough for us here in Ulster." Ibid., col. 2273.
33 Ibid., col. 2280.
34 Ibid., col. 2254.
35 Ibid., col. 2282.
36 Whyte, "How Much Discrimination Was There under the Unionist Regime, 1921–68?".
37 John Darby states that as late as the 1960s Catholics in the police force amounted to only 12 per cent of the force. Darby, *Scorpions in a Bottle*, 28.
38 Northern Ireland House of Commons, *The Parliamentary Debates: Official Report*, 22 April 1926, http://stormontpapers.ahds.ac.uk/stormontpapers/pageview.html?volumeno=7&pageno=671. See also Northern Ireland House of Commons, *The Parliamentary Debates: Official Report*, 3 May 1927, http://stormontpapers.ahds.ac.uk/stormontpapers/pageview.html?volumeno=8&pageno=1033, amongst others.
39 Jim McAllister, Northern Ireland House of Commons, *The Parliamentary Debates: Official Report*, 5 April 1927, col. 671, http://stormontpapers.ahds.ac.uk/stormontpapers/pageview.html?volumeno=8&pageno=597.
40 Dehra Chichester, Northern Ireland House of Commons, *The Parliamentary Debates: Official Report*, 5 April 1927, col. 672.
41 Although the employment debate later in the 1980s and 1990s shifted to the differentials between Catholic and Protestant unemployment and underemployment.
42 This will be discussed in the next section of this chapter. Kassian Kovalchek argues the crucial importance of employment issues in Kassian A. Kovalcheck, "Catholic Grievances in Northern Ireland: Appraisal and Judgment", *The British Journal of Sociology* 38, no. 1 (March 1987): 77–87.
43 Factors such as different attitudes to work, geographical differences and employment being offered mainly through word of mouth and direct recommendation have been variously been suggested as explanations of employment differentials. A fuller discussion of the issue will be provided in the next section.
44 Darby, *Scorpions in a Bottle*.
45 See inter alia Micheline R. Ishay, *The History of Human Rights: From Ancient Times to the Globalization Era* (Oakland: University of California Press, 2008).
46 For example, the establishment of the International Labour Organisation which promoted a number of international conventions purporting to provide some minimum protection for certain workers.

47 Mary Ann Glendon, *A World Made New: Eleanor Roosevelt and the Universal Declaration of Human Rights* (New York: Random House, 2001), xvi.
48 Almost all the newly independent states that resulted from the decolonisation process in the 1950s and 1960s incorporated some human rights principles in their constitutions, with a number of these constitutions using the UDHR as a direct source.
49 Northern Ireland House of Commons, *The Parliamentary Debates: Official Report*, 16 June 1959, col. 1825, http://stormontpapers.ahds.ac.uk/stormontpapers/pageview.html?volumeno=44&pageno=1900#fwd-44-1805.
50 Northern Ireland House of Commons, *The Parliamentary Debates: Official Report*, 16 June 1964, col. 1993, http://stormontpapers.ahds.ac.uk/stormontpapers/pageview.html?volumeno=57&pageno=1963.
51 The Preamble of the Convention states unambiguously that it was being adopted while "Considering the Universal Declaration of Human Rights proclaimed by the General Assembly of the United Nations on 10th December 1948" and "Considering that this Declaration aims at securing the universal and effective recognition and observance of the Rights therein declared". Furthermore the aim of the Convention was defined as being "to take the first steps for the collective enforcement of certain of the rights stated in the Universal Declaration". The relevance of the Convention to Northern Ireland will be elaborated upon in the following pages.
52 The petition was ultimately unsuccessful and the Court unanimously decided that Ireland was not in breach of the Convention.
53 Brice Dickson, *The European Convention on Human Rights and the Conflict in Northern Ireland* (New York: Oxford University Press, 2012).
54 Ibid., 42.
55 This is other than references to pensioner's rights and the civic rights of teachers which occur intermittently in the mid to late 1940s. These references are not however references to broad human rights issues but specific problems relating to the status of teachers and pensioners. In both cases the term "human rights" was not employed.
56 Northern Ireland House of Commons, *The Parliamentary Debates: Official Report*, 7 October 1952, col. 1305, http://stormontpapers.ahds.ac.uk/stormontpapers/pageview.html?volumeno=36&pageno=1301.
57 Walter Topping MP, Northern Ireland House of Commons, *The Parliamentary Debates: Official Report*, 16 June 1959, col. 1848.
58 In fact NICRA itself was involved in filing cases at the European Court of Human Rights: see in this respect Dickson, *The European Convention on Human Rights and the Conflict in Northern Ireland*, 47.
59 Although one should note that the educational reforms in the United Kingdom (excluding Northern Ireland) were first introduced by the wartime coalition government through the Education Act of 1944.
60 United Nations General Assembly, *The Universal Declaration of Human Rights*, Article 25.
61 Ibid., Article 26.
62 Ibid., Article 25.
63 The Honourable Lord Cameron, *Cameron Report – Disturbances in Northern Ireland* (Belfast: Her Majesty's Stationery Office, September 1969), para. 11.
64 Darby, *Scorpions in a Bottle*, 30.
65 Michael Morgan, "Post-War Social Change and the Catholic Community in Northern Ireland", *Studies: An Irish Quarterly Review* 77, no. 308 (December 1988), 431.
66 Ibid.
67 Ibid., 432.

68 In effect the Liberal Party only ever won one seat in the Queen's University constituency, which was held by Sheelagh Murnaghan between 1961 and 1969, while Harry Diamond was the sole representative of the Socialist Republican Party between 1945 and 1969 (Belfast, Falls constituency). The Irish Labour Party was represented by Gerry Fitt from to 1962 to 1972 (Dock constituency). Gerry Fitt and Harry Diamond joined forces to form the Republican Labour Party in 1964.
69 Harry Diamond MP, Northern Ireland House of Commons, *The Parliamentary Debates: Official Report*, 16 June 1959, col. 1828.
70 Walter Topping MP, ibid., col. 1846.
71 John Whyte refers to inter alia Frank Gallagher, *The Invisible Island: The Story of the Partition of Ireland* (London: Victor Gollancz, 1957) and National Council for Civil Liberties, *Report of a Commission of Inquiry Appointed to Examine the Purpose and Effect of the Civil Authorities (Special Powers) Acts (Northern Ireland) 1922 and 1933* (London: NCCL, 1972). John Whyte, "How Much Discrimination was There under the Unionist Regime, 1921-68?".
72 An example of such balanced view is John Whyte's study itself. John Whyte, "How Much Discrimination Was There under the Unionist Regime, 1921-68?".
73 Ibid.
74 Northern Ireland House of Commons, *The Parliamentary Debates: Official Report*, 5 February 1957, col. 26, http://stormontpapers.ahds.ac.uk/stormontpapers/pageview.html?volumeno=41&pageno=1.
75 Christopher Mitchell, "Beyond Resolution: What does Conflict Transformation Actually Transform?", *Peace and Conflict Studies* 9, no. 1 (May 2002), 4.
76 John Whyte, "How Much Discrimination Was There under the Unionist Regime, 1921–68?".
77 Cahir Healy MP, Northern Ireland House of Commons, *The Parliamentary Debates: Official Report*, 5 June 1957, col. 1458, http://stormontpapers.ahds.ac.uk/stormontpapers/pageview.html?volumeno=41&pageno. Another example of a Nationalist MP alleging discrimination in housing (and public appointments) is Joseph Francis Stewart MP, Northern Ireland House of Commons, *The Parliamentary Debates: Official Report*, 2 April 1958, col. 61, http://stormontpapers.ahds.ac.uk/stormontpapers/pageview.html?volumeno=42&pageno=43.
78 Tom Boyd MP, Northern Ireland House of Commons, *The Parliamentary Debates: Official Report*, 16 June 1964, cols 1997–8.
79 The Honourable Lord Cameron, *Cameron Report – Disturbances in Northern Ireland*, para. 29. The Caledon incident referred to the action by Nationalist MP Austin Currie, who squatted in a house that had been allocated to a young, unmarried unionist woman in preference to a Catholic family. The squatting MP was removed forcibly by the police. The decision to allocate the house to the young woman was criticised by the Cameron Report which stated that "By no stretch of the imagination could Miss Beanie be regarded as a priority tenant." See para. 28.
80 Ibid., para. 141.
81 Chiefly by Liam O'Dowd, "Shaping and Reshaping the Orange State: An Introductory Analysis", in *Northern Ireland: Between Civil Rights and Civil War*, by Liam O'Dowd, Bill Rolston and Mike Tomlinson (CSE Books, 1980); Denis P. Barritt, and Charles F. Carter, *The Northern Ireland Problem: A Study in Group Relations*, 2nd edn. (New York: Oxford University Press, 1972); Derek Birrell, "Relative Deprivation as a Factor in Conflict in Northern Ireland", *The Sociological Review* 20, no. 3 (1 August 1972): 317–43; and Frank Gallagher, *The Invisible Island: The Story of the Partition of Ireland* (London: Victor Gollancz, 1957).
82 Whyte, "How Much Discrimination Was There under the Unionist Regime, 1921–68?".

83 For instance, see Francis Hanna MP, Northern Ireland House of Commons, *The Parliamentary Debates: Official Report*, 30 March 1954, col. 1579, http://stormontpapers.ahds.ac.uk/stormontpapers/pageview.html?volumeno=38&pageno=1541; Harry Diamond MP, Northern Ireland House of Commons, *The Parliamentary Debates: Official Report*, 7 May 1958, col. 580, http://stormontpapers.ahds.ac.uk/stormontpapers/pageview.html?volumeno=42&pageno=561; Joseph Connellan MP, Northern Ireland House of Commons, *The Parliamentary Debates: Official Report*, 15 March 1960, col. 811.

84 See Brian McConnell MP, Northern Ireland House of Commons, *The Parliamentary Debates: Official Report*, 30 March 1954, col. 1589.

85 Northern Ireland House of Commons, *The Parliamentary Debates: Official Report*, 30 March 1954, col. 1582.

86 Brian Faulkner MP, Northern Ireland House of Commons, *The Parliamentary Debates: Official Report*, 8 June 1960, col. 1902.

87 This is largely the conclusion of the Cameron Report quoted above.

87 This suspicion continued in parts of unionist thought even after 1998. Arthur Aughey argues that some unionists conceived "Arrangements for the internal governance of Northern Ireland, along with the Sinn Féin 'rights agenda', would it was believed transform the character of public life in a manner conducive to republican purpose." Arthur Aughey, "The 1998 Agreement: Unionist Responses", in *A Farewell to Arms? From "Long War" to Long Peace*, ed. Michael Cox, Adrian Guelke and Fiona Stephen (Manchester University Press, 2000), 69.

88 Including educational reforms and the greater provision of public services.

90 The exact reasons for the outbreak of violence remain, like almost everything else in Northern Irish history, disputed. However, the Cameron Report refers to numerous general and particular causes for the outbreak of violence in 1969 including disorganised leadership of the civil rights movement, infiltration of marches by "revolutionary elements", the role of People's Democracy, the "interventions by followers of Major Bunting and the Rev. Dr. Paisley" as well as the inept handling of the police including the unnecessary use of force.

4 The impact of the civil rights movement on human rights in Northern Ireland

Introduction

As highlighted in the introduction to the previous chapter, Northern Ireland has many histories and there are numerous episodes that are considered to be turning points in its histories. The civil rights period is certainly one such phase in the history of Northern Ireland. Its real inspirations, aims, significance and effects are still disputed. Bew, Gibbon and Patterson provide a socioeconomic interpretation of the origins of the movement, arguing against the commonly held assumption that the civil rights movement arose from a newly radicalised middle class as claimed by the Cameron Report.[1] The situation they argue was "rather one in which the social basis, the political space and impetus for a middle-class reform movement all coincided".[2] Authors such as Christopher Hewett argue that the civil rights movement was essentially a nationalist tool through which the reunification of Ireland could be achieved and that "the nationalists who predominated in the movement were not really interested in [civil rights] reforms."[3] Hewett also argues that Catholic grievance was exaggerated. A contrary view espoused by Richard English is that there was a genuine Catholic grievance that lay at the heart of the movement and that while there was a strand of radical nationalism within the movement, "the civil rights movement comprised, for the most part, … people for whom the thrust of the campaign was the entirely reasonable demand for fair treatment within a state which hitherto had not provided it."[4] Bob Purdie, who provides the most comprehensive treatment of the movement, depicts the movement as a mosaic composed of different constituent parts, each having its own ideas and intentions within the movement.[5] This view, which is a very persuasive one, allows the attribution of different intents to the movement.

In their history of the Northern Ireland conflict McKittrick and McVea essentially adopt this same viewpoint when they hold that the movement was an amorphous one "in the sense that it had no coherent central leadership and no formal membership."[6] They also hold that the Northern Ireland Civil Rights Association (NICRA) was unable to exercise effective control on the movement as a whole which emphasises that there cannot be a single intent or coherent plan attributable to the civil rights movement as a whole.

This amorphous nature of the movement allowed people to hold such disparate views about it. Thus, Ian Paisley speaking in a British Broadcasting Corporation (BBC) interview stated that the "Civil Rights Movement was actually a United Ireland Movement."[7] From the opposite side of the political divide Gerry Adams stated that the

> civil rights movement sought elementary rights which were taken for granted in Britain and Western Europe. The movement had not demanded the abolition of the state, nor a united Ireland, but the reaction of unionism, supported by British intervention, brought the constitutional question to the fore and the existence of the Six County state into question.[8]

The contrasting views which the civil rights movement has excited are, in themselves, an indicator of the importance of this period for contemporary Northern Ireland. In a study which explores the impact of human rights concepts, principles and processes on the Northern Ireland conflict, the civil rights period assumes an ever greater salience. One ought also to state at the outset that for the purposes of this study the critical issues relate to the views and perceptions on human rights held by the different communities in Northern Ireland as a result of the civil rights period rather than the exact details of what happened from a chronological and historical viewpoint. The main arguments presented in this chapter are that: (1) the various communities in Northern Ireland emerged from the civil rights period with a partial or incomplete understanding of human rights; and (2) rights language became even more strongly rooted in the political discourse of Northern Ireland. The importance of this argument rests on the theses that such understandings continue to colour human rights language and practice in Northern Ireland.

In the previous chapter an attempt was made to provide an overview of how human rights concepts and discourse developed in Northern Ireland from the inception of the state in 1921 to the early 1960s. The 1960s was throughout the world an era of rapid change. Departure from tradition and history was the order of the day. In Northern Ireland this sense of change was expressed vividly in the rhetoric of the new Prime Minister, Terence O'Neill, who took over the premiership from Lord Brookeborough in 1962. In 1965 this sense of transformation and visions of new beginnings was expressed by O'Neill in a speech: "We want to build an opportunity state in which no man will be imprisoned by his environment and in which every individual will have the chance to realize his full potential."[9]

The language opportunity and individual potential articulated by O'Neill was not far from the language of human rights which, as evidenced in the previous chapter, was flourishing in the world at large and increasingly in Northern Ireland too. By the end of the period that will be examined in this chapter (1972), Northern Ireland had indeed changed drastically but not in the vein suggested by O'Neill nor in the spirit of the civil rights movement

(CRM). Northern Ireland did not transform itself into an opportunity state nor into a state governed by civil rights concerns. Instead it transformed into a state torn by violent conflict, ruled directly from Westminster and with British troops patrolling its streets. The rise of the civil rights movement and the reactions towards it by the various actors in Northern Ireland played a part in this transformation.

This chapter seeks to explore the dynamics which led to this transformation in the years from 1964 to 1972 with a focus on human rights. Particularly, this chapter attempts to understand the relevance of this period to the development (positively and negatively) of human rights concepts and practices in Northern Ireland. It also seeks to develop an understanding of how the events of this period changed perceptions about human rights in Northern Ireland. The questions to which answers will be sought are the following:

1 In what ways did the notion and practice of human rights change in Northern Ireland as a result of the civil rights movement?
2 In what ways and to what extent did the civil rights movement shape the views on human rights held by the different communities of Northern Ireland?
3 In what ways and to what extent did the civil rights movement contribute to political change in Northern Ireland?

This exploration will be conducted in light of the discussion in the previous chapter around how human rights discourse and practice developed in Northern Ireland since the creation of the state in 1921.

The civil rights movement: early developments

The disparate views on the civil rights movement in Northern Ireland may be explained not only by the wearing of sectarian lenses but also by the more objective difficulty of assessing the history of a movement made up of a number of different groups of varying size and with overlapping but not identical aims and objectives. The individuals involved in these various groupings came from different backgrounds: some nationalist, others republican; most were Catholics but, early on, a few were Protestants; some had socialist leanings, others markedly Marxist; some were university students, others were professionals; some were genuinely committed to the idea of civil rights, while others viewed civil rights as a tactic. How does one make sense of such an array of groupings, political affiliations, intellectual backgrounds and beliefs?

One may suggest that one way of understanding the period referred to as the civil rights era is by viewing the period as one marked by change but also by continuity. This view is not widely held. Bob Purdie in his comprehensive study of the origins of the civil rights movement remarked that in the 1960s "peace seemed secure enough for new departures and new experiments. The civil rights movement was one of these new departures."[10]

It is certainly true that the civil rights movement's tactics of direct action and peaceful civil protest were novel approaches in Northern Ireland politics[11] and to this extent it eventually managed to shake the complacency of all political parties at Stormont. It is likewise true that the movement was an unprecedented effort to bring civil rights issues to the very centre of political attention and discourse without reference to the issue of partition. The fact that the movement made a strenuous effort to avoid the constitutional issue was a further new departure.

However, as highlighted in the previous chapter, human rights concerns, usually articulated in terms of discrimination, formed part of the political debate in Northern Ireland since the creation of the state. The principal human rights concerns of the period 1921–1964 revolved around the franchise, the Special Powers Act, employment, housing and self-determination.[12] These were the same issues (except for self-determination) that were raised, admittedly in sharper relief than ever before, by the civil rights movement. This should serve as a reminder that the civil rights movement was characterised by continuity as well as change. The first attempt at enacting a Human Rights Act, which would have included a Human Rights Commission for Northern Ireland, was made in 1964 (by the Ulster Liberal MP, Sheelagh Murnaghan) the same year that the Campaign for Social Justice (CSJ) was established. This coincidence further emphasises both aspects of continuity and change. The continuity refers to the futile parliamentary efforts at dealing with human rights issues while the change refers to the formation of the CSJ as a non-governmental, non-partisan organisation devoted to "bringing the light of publicity to bear on the discrimination which exists in our community against the Catholic section of that community representing more than one-third of the total population".[13]

Bob Purdie in his previously cited work stated that

> Northern Irish nationalists … had often made the propaganda point that Catholics in Northern Ireland were denied equal rights as citizens of the United Kingdom, but this had never been more than a means of exposing the Unionists in front of British public opinion; the solution was still a united Ireland.[14]

The insistence by Northern Irish nationalists that Northern Ireland was an illegitimate entity, the early boycotts and abstentionism and the Nationalist Party's refusal to take up the role of Official Opposition at Stormont all seemed to substantiate this view. The view that the Nationalist Party was ineffectual in securing any progress on rights and only used old-fashioned nationalist flag-waving was also held by significant sections of the Catholic community. This is evident in the election results obtained by the party when challenged by figures emerging from the civil rights movement. John Hume, for example, won election to Stormont in 1969 against the leader of the Nationalist Party Eddie McAteer, claiming that

> it was no longer enough simply "to raise the flag of Ireland once every five years by using it as a political emblem ... while doing nothing about the basic problems of the people". It was evident that people had been forced onto the streets because of their "disillusionment with the existing political attitudes to the problems of social justice" and the abject "failure of existing opposition to force the Unionist Government to abandon their policies which offend."[15]

What is also interesting in this context is that the Nationalist Party was generally inward looking. It failed to build alliances with Westminster-based politicians or parties who could have been helpful to its interests. Partly this was a result of its traditional opposition to partition which translated into a wariness of dealing with Westminster politics. It also was not significantly influenced by international developments in terms of rights language and concepts of fairness. The civil rights movement, as will become apparent later in this chapter, was more attuned to international developments and sought to use them to its advantage. It also made a determined effort (especially in its early phase) to attract support from sympathetic figures in UK politics.

O'Neillism, the prospect of reform and human rights

Lord Brookeborough's 20-year premiership is sometimes considered, especially in the light of hindsight and with the knowledge of what came after, as an unbroken period of stability and tranquillity in the history of Northern Ireland. However, it is worth noting that this view of Brookeborough's period in office is somewhat misleading. Apart from the IRA Border campaign which was eventually defeated, the 1950s saw a period of industrial decline in Northern Ireland which resulted in growing unemployment even among the Protestant working-class. The result of this economic decline was both an increasing focus on economic issues (as opposed to constitutional matters) and an increase in support mainly (although not exclusively) from the Protestant working-class for the Northern Ireland Labour Party (NILP), which, with its natural focus on socioeconomic matters and its pro-union stand, appeared an attractive proposition to more voters in Northern Ireland, especially in the unionist working class.[16] This economic decline impacted, mainly, on the working classes in all communities including the Protestant one. This may also have nurtured a sense of insecurity and threat within sections of the Protestant working class, rendering them more likely to adopt a negative attitude to the CRM.

This increased support for parties of the left (such as Republican Labour, Independent Labour, Irish Labour or the Northern Ireland Labour Party) was evident in the elections from 1953 onwards. By the 1963 elections the Northern Ireland Labour Party's vote had risen to 25 per cent. This in itself was alarming enough for the Unionist Party, which in the 1963 election lost three seats albeit with a higher share of the vote. Soon after the election Lord

Brookeborough was persuaded to resign as Prime Minister to be replaced by Terence O'Neill.

O'Neill's accession to the premiership was not universally popular. His desire to appear to be a reforming prime minister appealed to those within the Unionist Party who favoured economic and political reform. However, a strong section of the party was opposed to reform which they anticipated would weaken the unionist hold on political power. For O'Neill advocated reform both in economic terms as well as in political terms. In particular, he favoured efforts at reconciliation with the Republic of Ireland and also within Northern Ireland between Protestants and Catholics. These efforts at reconciliation were advocated through rhetoric and symbolism. His speeches and interviews called for better conditions for Catholics in Northern Ireland as well as better relations with the Republic of Ireland. The symbolism of his meetings with the Irish Taoiseach Sean Lemass and his visit to a Catholic convent reinforced his rhetoric.

For those unionists who were opposed to reforms this rhetoric and symbolism fuelled their opposition to O'Neill and his reforms. However, at the same time neither O'Neill's rhetoric nor the symbolism of his acts were sufficient for those Catholics whose expectations were heightened by both O'Neill's words and his symbolic actions. While in the short term O'Neill's policies and actions were applauded by numerous commentators along most of the political spectrum (but by no means by all), the medium- to long-term effects of his policies was to create unfulfilled expectations within the minority community and to harden the attitude of those unionists who were antipathetic to change.

What then were the reforms that O'Neill planned and in some cases implemented? It has been argued that O'Neill's strategy was essentially an assimilatory one. Marc Mulholland has characterised O'Neill's plan as one which intended to "draw in Catholics into the Unionist alliance, even at the expense of alienating some Protestant traditionalists".[17] The tools with which to implement his assimilationist strategy included economic regeneration through the attraction of new industry and the improvement of public infrastructure. The focus on economic planning and industrial investment as a theme of the O'Neill premiership was clearly established in the first Queen's Speech presented soon after he became Prime Minister. The tone of O'Neill's comments in the Debate on the Address is best described as Wilsonian.[18] He emphasised technological innovation, industrial training and economic planning within a framework of a rapidly changing society. In the early parts of his comments he sought to create this aura of change as being driven not only by government but more broadly:

> Many bodies outside the Government have applied their minds to our basic problems and there has been a more spectacular flow of ideas and advice than ever before in our history. Not all of those ideas may be practicable, but the new vigour which they demonstrate is an essential part of our revitalisation.[19]

The new society which O'Neill was aiming to create was based on a belief in the primacy of economic factors: thus, the emphasis in the Queen's Speech on education, training and job creation. There is no mention in the Queen's Speech, nor in the speeches by the MPs proposing and seconding the motion on the Queen's speech (both delivered by unionist MPs), of issues related to discrimination or civil rights. However, the subtext of the speeches as well as the Prime Minister's own response seems to have been that if the economy improves and if more houses are built and more jobs are created the whole population of Northern Ireland would benefit. "Better education, better training, better management" were the points of the trident with which the Prime Minister proposed to kill the ills of Northern Ireland.

As an illustration of the new Ulster which O'Neill was proposing he sanctioned the building of the new model town of Craigavon following in the footsteps of Milton Keynes in England, as an example of a modern Ulster.[20] Yet even in this "model" the traditional sectarian divides could not be avoided.[21] The name of Craigavon in itself was perceived by the Catholic community as a sectarian symbol commemorating the first Prime Minister of Northern Ireland who in the memory of Catholics was a symbol of the discrimination they felt that they had suffered. The difficulty in moving beyond the sectarian divide was highlighted in the same debate by the Nationalist MP Cahir Healy. Healy commenting on the push for industrial revitalisation warned that "No leader of industry wants to come to a locality where discrimination is being practised in housing or employment."[22]

Another difficulty with O'Neill's reforms was that they were essentially paternalistic when paternalistic rhetoric and styles of government were out of favour. His comment that

> It is frightfully hard to explain to Protestants that if you give Roman Catholics a good job and a good house they will live like Protestants because they will see neighbours with cars and television sets; they will refuse to have eighteen children. But if a Roman Catholic is jobless, and lives in the most ghastly hovel, he will rear eighteen children on National Assistance. If you treat Roman Catholics with due consider and kindness, they will live like Protestants in spite of the authoritative nature of their Church.[23]

exemplifies this approach and his beliefs which were well intentioned but offensive to Catholics. What is instructive in this comment apart from the stereotyping of Catholics is the articulation of a certain unease which O'Neill had in dealing with Protestants. This twin difficulty of persuading Protestants and alienating Catholics would eventually bring down O'Neill's premiership.

Apart from the early promises of economic renewal and industrial innovation what were the steps taken by the O'Neill government in the field of human rights? In particular, did the O'Neill administration respond to the concerns of the Catholic community vis-à-vis the Special Powers Act, the franchise, employment and housing? With respect to the latter two issues the O'Neill government sought to include house-building and investment-attraction projects as key parts of its programme. These projects were not directly aimed at addressing the grievances, real or perceived, of the minority but were presented as necessary for the well-being of the community as a whole. However, O'Neill was clear that Catholics should be included in the new economic dispensation. How far this was the case is, as a matter of course, disputed.

In the spheres of franchise and the Special Powers Act, the debate was sharper and there was little room for ambiguity. The nationalists claimed that the franchise should be reformed and reflect the principle of "one person one vote" at all levels, national and local. The unionist rank and file was unenthusiastic on this point. Likewise, as discussed in the previous chapter, the Special Powers Act was considered to be an instrument of oppression that should be removed by the nationalists and a tool to preserve law and order that should be maintained by the unionists. There was no easy way of balancing these clearly conflicting views and expectations.

O'Neill had to tread carefully so as not to alienate too many of his unionist MPs while the impatience of the nationalist community grew. If one sticks with raw facts one notes that the franchise issue was dealt with by the O'Neill Cabinet in 1968 through the Electoral Law Amendment Act which ended the business vote and the university vote for Stormont elections.

The thornier issue of the franchise for local authority elections was the subject of much debate and dissent, in particular vis-à-vis the business vote and ratepayer suffrage which, on the one hand, gave multiple votes to company directors and, on the other, disenfranchised a considerable part of the adult population. O'Neill's government did not manage to resolve this matter and it was only finally resolved after the Macrory Report was published in 1970. The Special Powers Act was semi-retired in November 1968 when Cabinet decided that it should be laid aside for use only in case of an extreme emergency – the irony being that the extreme emergency in this case would materialise sooner than thought. At the same time the Cabinet decided a points system for the allocation of public housing as well as an ombudsman for Northern Ireland. If one keeps to the bare facts, one notices that the major complaints of the minority community were either dealt with very late in the O'Neill premiership or not at all. As will be seen later on, the civil rights movement claimed that these late reforms were only achieved as a result of the pressure exerted by the movement.

The Nationalist Party at Stormont did not significantly change its positions during O'Neill's tenure as Prime Minister. It took over the role of Official Opposition between February 1965 and October 1968 but it essentially continued to repeat grievances as it had done in the previous 20 years. The more imaginative opposition came from the Northern Ireland Labour Party and Gerry Fitt (representing the Republican Labour Party). In terms of human rights issues the contribution of the Ulster Liberal MP Sheelagh Murnaghan needs to be highlighted as she battled to introduce a Human Rights Act for Northern Ireland on four separate occasions between 1964 and 1968.

In March 1964, William Boyd of the Northern Ireland Labour Party presented a Racial Discrimination Bill which intended to render illegal and punishable by law discrimination (and incitement to discrimination) based on race, colour or religion. Without entering into the details of the debate on this Bill it is important to note that the governmental response was to reject the Bill on the grounds that:

> this Bill does not and, indeed, cannot achieve its objects and, therefore, should not be accepted. I doubt very much whether any additional legislation can improve the situation. What we must strive for is a better understanding between all sections of the community based on mutual respect.[24]

This reasoning (or excuse, depending on your viewpoint) would be repeated on numerous occasions in the period to reject Human Rights Bills presented by Sheelagh Murnaghan. The efforts by Ms. Murnaghan in this respect merit some consideration for two reasons: first, the Bills she presented outlined for the first time the prospect of a Human Rights Commission for Northern Ireland; and second, they were debated at a time when the civil rights movement outside Parliament was in its infancy.

The first attempt at enacting a Human Rights Bill was made by Ms. Murnaghan in June 1964. The Bill presented by the Ulster Liberal MP was intended to outlaw discrimination and provide a remedy to victims of discrimination. The Bill proposed the establishment of a Human Rights Commission with semi-judicial functions and also with the possibility of making recommendations to Governmental agencies and departments. The O'Neill government rejected the Bill overwhelmingly with the Attorney General echoing the Home Affairs Minister quoted above stating: "In short it is not a matter for legislation."[25] He also stated that any discrimination that existed in Northern Ireland was less than in most other countries and criticised the judicial functions assigned to the Human Rights Commission.

The year 1964 also saw the Campaign for Social Justice established, and can be described as the year when the civil rights movement started taking shape. It seems significant that in the same year two separate Bills dealing with anti-discrimination measures were debated (and rejected) in Parliament. The history of the decade might have been somewhat different if the O'Neill administration had enacted the legislation proposed by these MPs, which would have provided aggrieved individuals a legitimate vehicle through which their grievances could be adjudicated in a fair manner.

The subsequent attempts from 1964 to 1968 by Murnaghan to pass a Human Rights Act at Stormont were all roundly rejected by the Unionist Party. The reasons for rejecting the Bills were always articulated in terms of discrimination not being an area which one could legislate against even as many parts of the world enacted legislation that did precisely this.[26] Thus, Stormont lost several opportunities to act in some manner to assuage the feeling of grievance held by the Catholic community. This lack of progress in the parliamentary sphere must account to some extent to the growth of the extra-parliamentary civil rights movement.

It was only in late 1968, after the 5 October Londonderry March of that year that the unionist government announced a number of measures that dealt with some of the grievances advanced by the civil rights movement. The reforms envisaged by O'Neill at the beginning of his premiership never bore fruit. The economic situation did not improve as promised nor did the great infrastructural projects result in greater opportunity for all. In this respect the fate of Craigavon, where only half of the planned buildings were completed, could be a metaphor for the O'Neill years. These failures were certainly not intentional, quite the reverse. Perhaps, in part, the failures were a result of O'Neill being "too full of vague good intentions" as his Cabinet Secretary, Sir Kenneth Bloomfield remarked retrospectively.[27] Part of the failure may also be attributable to the fact that not everyone was as well-intentioned as he was, both within the community he represented as well as in the minority community.

Housing and direct action

Housing allocation, as highlighted earlier, continued to be a major issue of discord in Northern Ireland throughout the 1960s. The debates on housing at Stormont were frequent, long and acrimonious. The dialogue was well rehearsed, with the government claiming that more houses were being built and that their allocation was essentially fair while the nationalist opposition accused the Unionist Party of favouring house building programmes in Protestant areas and of discrimination in housing allocation (through unionist controlled local authorities).

For example, in a debate on the Supply Vote held on 27 February 1964, the Minister for Health and Local Government (responsible for Housing) stated that:

> By the end of December, 1963, there were 3,346 houses completed in Londonderry City since 1944. There were 303 under construction and 121 approved but not started. The houses immediately planned by the Corporation total 325 and the Housing Trust, in addition to its major redevelopment scheme in Londonderry City, is also building 324 between the verge of the city and just outside the city.... That is the type of drive which is going on in housing.[28]

In a Motion on the Allocation of Houses presented by the Nationalist MP Thomas Gormley in 1964 the same MP presented the nationalist claim which, in one form or another, was the standard complaint expressed by the nationalist opposition for many years:

> It is notorious that in the Six Counties public representatives on certain councils have for years deliberately denied houses to those desperately in need of them. The basis of the denial, I am sorry to say, was very often religious and political. When we have tried to spotlight that fact we have found that various people in authority have all seemed to dodge the issue.[29]

These two excerpts illustrate the respective positions of the two main parties at Stormont, which with varying emphases were made over the years. The repetitiveness of the debates was summed up by a unionist parliamentarian who in response to this Motion stated that "this same Motion has been before the House in three other occasions. This is the fourth in this Parliament. It is true that the words of the Motions have been different, but in substance they have been the same."[30] The latter phrase may be applied to the positions expressed by the parties at Stormont with respect to housing allocation in the various debates: the words may have changed from one debate to another but the substance remained the same.

This stasis may explain, at least partially, the rise in extra-parliamentary activity around the issue of housing allocation. However, as Purdie has pertinently noted, the issue of housing allocation was not a generalised one in Northern Ireland but rather a localised one in certain specific areas. Purdie points out that the fact that the house-building programme in Northern Ireland was creditable, as continuously claimed by unionist ministers,

> did not mean that there was no scope for grievances. In fact, it heightened them by making it possible for those who were not benefiting to compare themselves with those who were.... Needless to say, these dissatisfied groups were mainly Catholics in the lower income brackets.[31]

The main localities where this dissatisfaction was evident were those west of the Bann and in particular in those localities where the balance between the two communities was fine and the allocation of housing could alter this balance from an electoral point of view.

One such locality was Dungannon, which would become a household name in the early history of the civil rights movement. It was in Dungannon that the Homeless Citizens League (HCL) was founded in 1963 by Angela McCrystal as well as Conn and Patricia McCluskey, later famous for founding the Campaign for Social Justice. The HCL merits attention, not so much for its efforts to articulate the grievances felt by Catholics but for the way in which they attempted to do so which included direct action. The first of this direct action took the form of assisting homeless families to squat in prefabricated housing owned by the local council. The local council threatened legal action but the general sympathy was with the squatters. The matter attracted considerable attention and eventually an HCL delegation met with the responsible Minister who managed to persuade the unionist controlled local council to reach an acceptable compromise. This was more than the local nationalist politicians or the nationalist MPs managed to secure. Here then was a form of political action which, unlike speechifying at Stormont or gesture politics in the town hall, seemed to get some results. What is interesting to note about the HCL is that its creation was attributable to a number of women who were directly affected by the housing problem. Conn McCluskey in his memoir describes the creation of the HCL as follows:

> The strain on young mothers trying to maintain order and a degree of quiet, where most facilities had to be shared, was very great. Men on night shift work found it impossible to sleep.... Something had to be done. A few married women called a meeting chaired by a local curate. Banded together as the Homeless Citizens League, a committee was formed....[32]

This form of direct action arose at a time when it was getting worldwide publicity in the USA with the efforts of the black civil rights movement. Purdie refers to numerous episodes which illustrated how the events in the American south were inspiring HCL members in Dungannon. The parallels with the black civil rights movement will be discussed later, nevertheless at this stage it suffices to point out that the events in Alabama were noted and may have served to embolden the homeless citizens of Dungannon. It has been suggested that the very significant media coverage afforded to the Washington marches in the USA emboldened the HCL to take more decisive action.[33] Housing in Dungannon would return to the centre of the Northern Ireland civil rights movement in 1968 when the young Nationalist MP Austin Currie squatted in a house to protest against a specific housing allocation by the local council.[34]

The relative success of the HCL in winning concessions from the unionists encouraged the HCL leadership to take this extra-parliamentary route further. Conn and Patricia McCluskey, reflecting on their decision to form the Campaign for Social Justice (CSJ), admitted that the impetus came from the perceived success of the HCL which contrasted with the futility of nationalist opposition and the appetite for mobilisation of the Catholic community. Vincent Feeney commented that as a result of the reaction to HCL action the McCluskeys "quickly realised that there was a tremendous yearning among the Catholic people for organisation and leadership. There and then they decided to establish a group of educated people who would articulate the frustrations of the minority."[35] A number of points emerge from the above:

1 The Catholic community was increasingly frustrated by the ineffectiveness of their elected politicians.
2 The cadre of educated Catholics wishing to contribute to the betterment of their community had enlarged as a result of educational reforms discussed in the previous Chapter.

3 The CSJ was a middle-class Catholic organisation and self-consciously so as is evident from its originators and composition.[36]
4 Rather than take forward the direct-action tactic tentatively developed by the HCL, the CSJ would focus on information gathering and publicity.

The CSJ, in its statement of aims, highlighted its mission as data collection on discrimination in jobs and housing and the circulation of such data as widely as possible in order to ensure "equality for all". In order to emphasise its non-sectarian nature, it consciously avoided the border question and explicitly stated it had no interest in ending partition. Through this position, it sought to appeal to Protestants who were disturbed by claims of discrimination but who would not wish to cooperate with an ant-partitionist organisation.

Another factor worth mentioning in the context of the formation of the CSJ is its effort to attract the attention of the Westminster politicians and the UK public generally to issues of discrimination in Northern Ireland. The leadership of the CSJ felt that if the public in the UK was educated on the situation prevailing in Northern Ireland they would insist on reforms as would the politicians at Westminster. The CSJ was in particular keen to mobilise the UK Labour Party to support its activities. In fact, the front page of the CSJ *Newsletter* always bore two quotations by the Labour leader Harold Wilson where he expressed his support for the CSJ. One of the quotations read as follows:

> I agree with you as to the importance of the issues with which your Campaign is concerned and can assure you that a Labour government would do everything in its power to see that the infringements of justice to which you are so rightly drawing attention are effectively dealt with. – Harold Wilson writing to the Campaign of Social Justice in September 1964.[37]

This tactic of arousing the support of the UK public and its political representatives sought to put pressure on the unionist government from the outside. One can see a parallel with the American civil rights movement's efforts at using the Federal government to force the southern states to acquiesce to their demands.[38] Incidentally, the Republican Labour Party politician Gerry Fitt also sought to use his links with the UK Labour Party and individual Labour MPs at Westminster to involve the UK government in Northern Irish politics. This tactic is worth reflecting upon given that it may be construed as a tacit acceptance of the union by the nationalists within the CSJ. An appeal to the central government for protection does imply a de facto acceptance of that government. This tactic is, in effect, taking at least some within the nationalist community to a different place vis-à-vis their relationship with the United Kingdom. This tactic is moving them away from simply denying the legitimacy of the UK government and of Northern Ireland's place within the UK to acknowledging the UK government's factual sovereignty and also recognising the legal consequences that flow therefrom.

What then were the activities in which the CSJ engaged? Essentially the major efforts of the CSJ were directed at publishing pamphlets which sought to illustrate the unfairness that prevailed in Northern Ireland in certain sectors of public life. In its first pamphlet, *Why Justice Cannot Be Done*, the CSJ argued that the legislation under which Northern Ireland was operating (the Government of Ireland Act 1920) did not provide any means whereby claims of discrimination could be addressed and, if verified, redressed. Other pamphlets addressed the issues of the franchise for local government (*Londonderry. One Man, No Vote*), the need to involve British public opinion in the Northern Ireland situation (*What the Papers Say*), the non-availability of legal aid for discrimination cases (*Legal Aid to Oppose Discrimination – Not Likely!*) and generally discrimination in housing, employment and voting (*The Plain Truth*). All of these pamphlets were intended to create consciousness within Northern Ireland and the United Kingdom as a whole as to discriminatory practices which the CSJ held were pursued by the unionist government both at Stormont and in local authorities under unionist control. All of this underscores the point made above vis-à-vis the shift within a part of the nationalist community of its attitude towards the United Kingdom government.

Apart from the above-mentioned pamphlets the CSJ also issued a *Campaign Newsletter* which was circulated initially to UK Labour Party MPs and other UK politicians but later extended to an international audience. The *Campaign Newsletter* of 5 September 1967 emphasised this broadening of circulation:

> Those of you who received our earlier communications must regard these recent ones as very formal and detailed. The reason is that the Newsletters now circulate very widely, not only to all United Nations delegations, but to politicians and important people in practically every country.[39]

The references to the United Nations and to the global reach of the lobbying efforts signal the increasing importance of the international dimension to the civil rights campaigners. The efforts to internationalise the Northern Ireland civil rights situation is also evident in subsequent *Campaign Newsletters*. For instance, the *Newsletter* of 15 August 1970 highlights press cuttings that relate to Northern Ireland in Russia, France, Spain, the USA as well as the Vatican.[40] As early as 1968 the *Newsletter* was also highlighting the possible role of the European Court of Human Rights in Northern Ireland.[41] All of this is clear evidence that the international rise in interest for human rights issues was being utilised by the civil rights campaigners in seeking to achieve their aims.

It is difficult to ascertain to what extent the aims of the CSJ were met. The UK government did not indicate any major shift in its policy on Northern Ireland (which was basically to leave the province to its own devices) in the period 1964 to 1966 at the height of the CSJ's activities. Some members of the UK Labour Party did voice concern over human rights issues in Northern Ireland[42] but there was no substantial change in the policy of the UK government until the events of 1968 forced Wilson's hand.

The Labour government elected in 1964 with Harold Wilson as Prime Minister showed continuity rather than change in its policy towards Northern Ireland. This change from a Conservative government to a Labour government was, optimistically, expected to result in a stronger interest in the claims of the Catholic community by the UK government. Nevertheless, the status quo was effectively maintained. One can claim that the CSJ's efforts did not achieve immediate and direct results even when a theoretically more sympathetic government was installed at Westminster. On the other hand, the CSJ did manage to achieve a modicum of media visibility in the UK as a whole and particularly in Northern Ireland. The visibility it attracted in Northern Ireland was entirely extra-parliamentary since the only direct mention of the CSJ in the Stormont parliamentary debates was a fleeting one, made in 1969, in the context of the Cameron Report.

From a human rights perspective, there may be a criticism to be levelled at the approach taken by the CSJ. This does not relate mainly to the fact that the CSJ was a Catholic-dominated organisation. After all it is to be expected that those who perceive themselves to be at the receiving end of discrimination should be most vociferous and active in protesting. Criticising the CSJ or the civil rights movement more generally for its strong Catholic links would be like criticising the US civil rights movement for having a black leadership. The criticism that may be made from a human rights perspective is that the CSJ failed to place its mission of highlighting discrimination against Catholics within a broader human rights context. This could have been done by reaching out to other discriminated groups in the province and by highlighting the universality and indivisibility of human rights. For instance, the movement was criticised for not reaching out to Protestants by condemning discrimination practiced by Catholic councils.[43] A further powerful point made by Brice Dickson in this context is the exclusive focus by most of the movement on human rights violations committed by the state while never considering breaches of rights committed by non-governmental entities.[44] Whether this would have persuaded the majority of unionists that the CSJ was not a nationalist or republican front is doubtful. In divided societies, such as Northern Ireland, the validity of ideas and initiatives are most often determined by who proposes them rather than by their intrinsic value. Nevertheless, a broader and more universalist approach by the CSJ, and *multo magis* by NICRA, as we shall see might have benefited the subsequent history of civil rights in Northern Ireland.

The birth of NICRA

The Northern Ireland Civil Rights Association (NICRA) is widely considered to have been the primary, though not exclusive, promoter of the civil rights movement.[45] In this context it is worth highlighting the birth of NICRA since this was the first Northern Ireland organisation to deal explicitly and exclusively with civil rights, as opposed to social justice or partition or socialism, and because the role of NICRA in shaping the history of the idea of human rights in Northern Ireland is an important one.

Ten years after its formation NICRA itself attempted to write a history of itself and while so doing accepted the difficulty of the venture owing to the fact that "no one person knows all the events yet and no two people agree exactly on how those events should be interpreted."[46] The disagreements on the interpretation of the events surrounding NICRA is still evident today and perhaps continue to shape ideas on human rights held by some of the people of Northern Ireland. The disagreements around NICRA (as evidenced by the organisation's own acknowledgment that no one knows all the events surrounding its formation and that even within it there were disagreements as to interpretation) are also evident from the extremely contradictory statements made by Northern Irish politicians from opposing sides. For instance, the former Ulster Unionist MP John Taylor told the Saville Inquiry into Bloody Sunday that NICRA "was used as a cover for terrorists".[47] Conversely, Gerry Adams, commemorating the establishment of NICRA, stated that it was "the beginning of a long and difficult struggle for basic civil and human rights, including the right to vote".[48] Insofar as academic commentators are concerned, the movement in general and thus also NICRA are mostly considered as complex and multi-faceted, which accounts for such a diversity of views. NICRA was certainly a very broad coalition of interests and ideas and this shall be further explored hereunder.

Apart from issues of interpretation of events there is also a difficulty in ascertaining how NICRA was born and the precise circumstances of its formation remain elusive. Such questions turned out to be more than academic exercises since, as we shall see the individuals and groups who attacked and defended NICRA referred to its origins in doing so. This failure to identify the exact birth of NICRA is due, according to the organization itself, to the fact that "NICRA did not begin at a precise time in a definite place."[49]

Nevertheless, there appears to be agreement on the main protagonists in the formation of NICRA with the Wolfe Tone Societies, the Trades Union movement, left wing parties (from Labour to Communist), the students of Queen's University and the CSJ being the primary players in the birth of NICRA. The political allegiances and motivations of these various actors in creating NICRA would in due course prove to be a source of challenge and dispute that never completely dissipated from Northern Irish society.[50]

The aims of NICRA as articulated in their founding document were strongly based in human rights discourse: the defence of the basic freedoms of all citizens; the protection of the rights of all individuals; highlighting all possible abuses of power; demanding guarantees of freedom of speech; assembly and association; and informing the public of their rights. From a human rights perspective, these aims were unobjectionable. They highlighted the rights of all individuals and the importance of monitoring state institutions in order to protect rights. However, these aims are striking both for what they specifically include as well as for what they specifically exclude. There is no specific mention of socioeconomic rights, in particular access to housing and employment, two of the traditional key demands of nationalists. Conversely, there is a specific mention of the right to free speech and association. The inclusion of these rights may be interpreted as a win for the republican strand within the CRM which saw NICRA as a vehicle through which they could mobilise support for the lifting of the ban on republican clubs in Northern Ireland.

Initially, the activities sponsored by NICRA remained grounded in the CSJ's approach of documenting grievances and attempting to win support for its objectives from as many people as possible within Northern Ireland, the Republic and the UK more broadly. It is worth noting that in its early phase NICRA was involved in lobbying on behalf of a group of travellers in Belfast.[51] This reaching out beyond the issue of discrimination against Catholics indicated the comprehensive understanding of human rights which was, regrettably, to remain underdeveloped in the years to come.

The first 18 months or so of NICRA's existence were not marked by vigorous activity and new approaches but rather by continuity and moderation. This continuity and moderation (perhaps inevitably) did not capture the imagination of the public at large and as a result more dynamic voices in the movement began to emerge. The Cameron Report remarked that until the march of 24 August 1968 NICRA's "activities had so far been limited and attracted little publicity".[52] It seems clear that this points to two strands within the Catholic community through their participation in the movement. One section of the Catholic community involved in NICRA, and in the CRM in general, adopted an incremental, cautious approach focusing on research, on documenting abuses and on using such detailed documentation to lobby UK politicians and wider public opinion. Another section was more radical, influenced by the direct action of the US civil rights movement (and later by the student revolts around Europe), which pushed for a greater stress on taking their cause to the streets. The lack of progress made by the more cautious strand eventually led to the adoption of more militant action pushed by the more radical sections of the CRM. Had the documentary and lobbying efforts been more successful, the history of the CRM and of Northern Ireland might have been different.

Civil rights: marching to where?

It has been argued that the change in direction which was to bring NICRA unprecedented attention and support came about as a result of the soul-searching going on within NICRA, as well as the increasing impact of Martin

Luther King's marches within the US civil rights movement.[53] The effectiveness of these marches in gathering and expressing support for the US civil rights movement must have struck some members of the NICRA leadership as a potentially useful route for NICRA to take.[54] Nevertheless, the direct impetus for NICRA to move towards street protest emerged from the action of Austin Currie, the Nationalist MP who campaigned vigorously, in Parliament and outside Parliament, against Dungannon Rural District Council's decision to allocate a new house in Caledon to an unmarried Protestant woman in preference to Catholic families who needed rehousing. Once Currie's protests went unheeded he occupied the house allocated to Miss Beanie together with a Catholic family. Immediately following this occupation, they were evicted by a group of policemen (one of whom was Miss Beanie's brother). In the words of the Cameron Report, "[q]uite apart from the real merits of Mr. Currie's case against the allocation, he scored thereby a major propaganda success."[55]

This propaganda success appealed to the more dynamic elements in the NICRA leadership and although there were some doubters, who were unenthusiastic about involving NICRA in direct action, NICRA eventually decided to stage a march in Dungannon to ride the wave of Currie's success. At a meeting held on 27 July 1968 NICRA decided to organise a march from Coalisland to Dungannon's Market Square on 24 August. This decision to hold the march was thus taken in the month following the Currie Caledon incident and was thus clearly connected to it as the Cameron Report confirmed.

The link between the first march and the Caledon incident is relevant in that it seems to indicate that NICRA's resort to marches was not a premeditated tactic but one that was resorted to in a specific context and with some reticence. The relative success of the first march was to encourage NICRA to adopt marches as their preferred tactic in promoting their cause. However, within NICRA doubts as to the effectiveness of marches in achieving its objectives remained throughout. It has been suggested that once violence reared its head on 5 October 1968 the continuation and expansion of the marches was done more in anger than in the belief it would achieve its civil rights aims.[56] From the Cameron Report and from Purdie's exhaustive study it emerges that the decision to hold the marches was not always initiated by NICRA (the 5 October march being a key example of a march initiated by local groups) and that NICRA did not always have effective control of the marches through the stewards.[57] In essence, it appears that taking to the streets was originally a contextual decision (inspired by Caledon) and that the Dungannon march was followed by a number of other marches "requested" by local groups (with varying objectives) and that these were not always well organised and coordinated. Ultimately, a reading of the marching period of the CRM seems to suggest that it was never entirely clear where the marches would lead to and that different organisations and individuals expected them to lead in different directions.

Success in the street?

The intricate history and chronology of the CRM following the first civil rights march in Dungannon is beyond the scope of this study. What is attempted here is a sketch of the impact which these marches had in the immediate term. One may argue that the events in Londonderry of 5 October 1968 were critical in terms of giving unprecedented attention to the CRM and in creating a wave of public support both within Northern Ireland and also externally (particularly in the UK as a whole and the USA). In brief, what occurred was that the Derry Housing Action Committee (DHAC) invited NICRA to hold a march in Derry on the lines of the first civil rights march in Dungannon. The Derry march was however immediately fraught with difficulties, including the eventual decision by the Minister of Home Affairs to ban part of the route.[58] Eventually, the organisers decided to proceed with the march and the end result was that the RUC used their batons against the marchers and used water wagons to disperse them.[59] The impact of these events was a wave of public support that swelled the ranks of the CRM and also put the Northern Ireland government on the defensive vis-à-vis the media and the UK Parliament and government.

The Northern Ireland government was clearly concerned with the amount of negative press comment which started to gather momentum following 5 October. In a memorandum to the Cabinet dated 14 October 1968 the Prime Minister stated:

> Londonderry has dramatically altered this situation [support from the UK government] to our great disadvantage. Whether the Press and TV coverage was fair is immaterial. We have now become the focus of world opinion; indeed we know through official channels that the Embassy and B.I.S. [British Information Service] in America have been under intense pressure from the American press.[60]

The Conclusions of the Cabinet Meeting held on the same date[61] include three references to the press in a document barely two pages long. In the first item entitled "Chief Whip's Appearance on David Frost's Television Programme" the minutes reported that "The Prime Minister congratulated the Chief Whip on his excellent performance in Friday's programme on the Londonderry situation." Minute 3 referred to "the need for consideration of the criticisms of Government policy which had been voiced on television and the Press over the past week" and further down "in this situation it was most unfortunate that Northern Ireland's political problems should be highlighted by a hostile press." Regarding the continuing negative press commentary, a decision was taken at the Cabinet meeting of 5 December "that a Police Public Relations Officer should be appointed to deal with the Press and Television media".[62]

This negative media commentary was problematic for the Northern Ireland government both in itself and, perhaps more importantly, for the effect it had on the attitude of the UK government. The UK government and Parliament had traditionally sought not to involve themselves in Northern Ireland. In this context, a practice had developed at Westminster where discussion on the domestic affairs of Northern Ireland (i.e. those matters not being "reserved matters" under the 1920 Act) was not allowed. Over the years, a number of Labour MPs sympathetic to the nationalist cause had tried unsuccessfully to circumvent this practice. However, with the increasingly negative public opinion vis-à-vis the Northern Ireland government rendered this position increasingly untenable. The Labour Prime Minister Harold Wilson faced increasing pressure from his own Members of Parliament as to the situation in Northern Ireland following the events of 5 October. As a result, the UK government put pressure on the Northern Ireland government to accelerate reforms aimed at meeting the demands of the CRM, mainly with respect to housing allocation and local government franchise.

The nature of the pressure exerted by the UK government on the Northern Irish executive may be gauged by an examination of several confidential documents relative to this period. This is of interest given that, according to research carried out, these documents have not been referred to by authors such as Purdie, English, Hewett or Dickson. The minutes of a meeting held on 4 November 1968 at 10 Downing Street (official residence of the UK Prime Minister) between the UK Prime Minister and Home Secretary with the Northern Ireland Prime Minister, Minister of Commerce and Minister of Home Affairs provide interesting insights in this respect. Prime Minister Wilson commenced the meeting by referring to the fact that while Northern Ireland's executive was responsible for internal matter, ultimate responsibility rested with the United Kingdom. He added that "There was now great concern at Westminster over many aspects of the Northern Ireland scene and this embraced not only Members of Parliament but himself and his colleagues."[63] This statement was followed by the not-so-veiled threat that if reforms did not materialise on the local franchise and on the Special Powers Act amongst other things, the UK government would reduce the financial assistance provided to Northern Ireland. The UK Home Secretary further commented that "He did not see how the Prime Minister could defend at Westminster such things as the company vote and the failure to grant the local government vote to all over 21 years of age."[64]

The impact of this pressure on the UK government is evident in the minutes of the Northern Ireland Cabinet meetings held on 7 and 20 November 1968, when the Cabinet discussed how to react to the pressure exerted by the UK government.[65] The minutes reveal dissension within the Cabinet between those advocating reform led by the Prime Minister (Captain O'Neill) and those resistant to reform led chiefly by the Minister for Home Affairs (William Craig). The net results of these meetings was the eventual adoption of a programme of reform announced on 22 November which included the appointment of a Development Commission for the Londonderry area; demonstrably fair methods for the allocation of public authority houses; the appointment of an Ombudsman and consideration of the need for other machinery to consider citizens' grievances outside the central government field; the abolition of the company vote in local government elections; and a review of the special powers as soon as circumstances allowed. Thus, the Northern Ireland government attempted to satisfy most of what it perceived to be the key demands of the CRM. The one key demand clearly omitted from this programme of reforms was the demand for "one person one vote" for the local government elections.[66]

It is worth noting that pressure from the UK government played an important role in bringing forth these changes. In his famous "Ulster at a Crossroads" speech Terence O'Neill expressly stated that "I knew full well that Britain's financial and other support for Ulster so laboriously built up could no longer be guaranteed if we failed to press on with such a programme [of reform]."[67] While this was probably welcomed by the nationalist community, it will have alienated some unionists as an imposition from outside (indeed a number of ministers referred to "duress" when discussing this matter in Cabinet). This may further have created a perception amongst unionists that civil rights and human rights were an outside imposition and thus alien to them.

Another critical moment in the escalation of the conflict was the Belfast to Derry march of 1 to 4 January 1969 organised by the People's Democracy. This march was intended to proceed over a number of days, on the example of the US civil rights marches, but was not endorsed by NICRA who advised against holding the march. Initially the march set off from Belfast with a limited number of people which grew over the course of the march to a few hundred. There was some minor violence before the final day of the march with the marchers attacked by loyalists but nothing serious occurred. On the final day of the march, the marchers were ambushed by a loyalist group of around 200 people at Burnotollet bridge around seven miles from Derry. The attack which had clearly been planned in advance resulted in 13 marchers being injured and requiring hospital treatment. The RUC contingent (of about 80 constables), which had been accompanying the marchers, were deemed to have done nothing to protect the group from the attack while the nationalists were further incensed by the subsequent decision by the RUC to break up the rally in Derry (which was to have been the climax of the whole march) and also by the entry of the RUC in the Catholic Bogside area of Derry.

This series of events resulted in serious rioting in Derry which lasted for a few days. The seriousness of the events of 4 January were also evidenced by the statement issued by the Prime Minister Terence O'Neill on 5 January where he warned that further public order measures would be taken if the marches were not terminated while also predicting (with considerable accuracy) that if the situation did not return to normal, deaths could soon ensue. The effect of the events surrounding the Belfast to Derry march served to reiterate the view held by nationalists that the RUC was their enemy not their protector and that the state in general was prejudiced against their views and interests. These events also consolidated the unionist view that nationalist elements were striving to destabilise the state. In the words of Terence O'Neill those who planned the march at best "were careless of the effects it would have [while] at worst, they embraced with enthusiasm the prospect of adverse publicity causing further damage to the interests of Northern Ireland".

Nevertheless, within the context outlined above it is at least arguable that the CRM achieved a degree of success in fulfilling a number of its aims. The fact that this success did not satisfy completely the CRM (or parts of the movement) may be attributable to a number of reasons; including the increasing disagreements within the CRM itself.

The civil rights movement, attitudes to human rights and dissent

The CRM was inherently prone to internal disagreements, being formed of a number of entities, associations and individuals. As already indicated even within NICRA itself there were various strands of opinion represented: republicans, nationalists, Labour politicians including those from the Northern Ireland Labour Party who had broadly unionist leanings, as well as representatives of the CSJ and DHAC amongst others. Even at the outset it was likely that the objectives of these different groups would not be identical and likewise the strategies they would be willing to adopt. In the run-up to the 5 October Londonderry march there was an example of this disagreement when the Minister of Home Affairs banned part of the route to be followed by the civil rights marchers. The NICRA Committee had to consider whether to proceed with the march or not and there was division over this with the CSJ's Conn McCluskey arguing against proceeding and the DHAC representatives being adamant for the march to proceed.[68] Following the events of 5 October the disagreements within the CRM increased and it has been suggested that in the year following the Londonderry march "the civil rights movement was riven by bitter disputes as irreconcilable differences emerged." This is confirmed by the Chairman of NICRA in 1969 who stated that "We in the Civil Rights Movement have in the past been riven by internal dissensions – by jealousies and uncharitable suspicions."[69]

A key protagonist in accentuating these differences was the People's Democracy (PD) organisation emerging from Queen's University in Belfast but soon attracting support from various quarters including the militant and radical left, popular throughout Europe, particularly students, at the time. The initial impetus for establishing the PD were the events of 5 October following which a group of students at Queen's University organised a meeting, on 9 October, to protest at what they considered police brutality towards the marchers during the Londonderry march. The list of demands submitted by the students on 9 October was broadly aligned with the demands of NICRA and included a demand that the government agree to enact the already mentioned Human Rights Bill repeatedly proposed in Parliament by Sheelagh Murnaghan.

However, the evolution of the students' organisation that became PD was such that it remained an "un-structured" grouping with an "amorphous character"[70] which resulted in an organisation which housed individuals with very different orientations including genuine civil rights reformists but also radicals who were ready to resort to militant and potentially violent tactics. The Cameron Report was critical of the actions of PD and held that the ideas of the major leaders of PD were "far more politically extreme than the objects for which the Civil Rights Association has campaigned" and also that they represented "a threat to the stability and existence of the Northern Ireland Constitution".[71] The tension between NICRA and PD may also be seen through the insistence by the PD on continuing the marches while NICRA had decided on a truce on all civil rights marches.[72] Although subsequent to this there was a short period within which NICRA and PD cooperated closely, the paths of the two organisations diverged in terms of their objectives and tactics. PD had a revolutionary streak which NICRA never really possessed and it eventually transformed into a staunch left-wing party with structures and membership, thus moving away from its unstructured, civil rights student movement origins.

A speech delivered at a PD meeting in late 1968 gives a flavour of how PD viewed itself to be different from other strands working within the CRM. In advocating continued militancy, the speaker stated that "a new danger, and from within the movement itself must be recognised. This comes from those who appeal for moderation.... They, like the Unionists, fear change most for what it means to their privileges."[73] In the same speech a campaign of civil disobedience was proposed which was to be modelled to some extent on "the Negro resistance in the United States". Evidence of the influence of the American civil rights campaign may be discerned in the advocacy of a disruption of public transport by a "total boycott as was done in one city in America with the result that the local Transport Company, brought to near bankruptcy, was forced to yield to the demand of the protesting negro population".[74]

The move of the PD to more radical socialist positions can be evinced from the PD political programme adopted in 1970. The opening line of the PD programme stated the aim of PD as "the establishment of a socialist system of society in Ireland and throughout the world. The first step towards that objective is the establishment of a Workers' and Small Farmers' Republic in the 32 counties of Ireland." The programme goes on to explain that Ireland needed to be freed from both imperialism and capitalism and that the latter was both tinged with green and orange. In describing how this programme was to be achieved PD did not rule out the use of force arguing that "a certain degree of counter force may be necessary to carry out the wishes of the people".[75]

One may suggest that because of its militancy and revolutionary tendencies PD fanned the flames of suspicion of even moderate unionists towards the CRM. PD's actions also intensified the climate of impending violence that hung over Northern Ireland in late 1968 and afterwards. Thus, PD must share some of the responsibility for the increasing distrust towards civil rights by the unionist community and for the escalation of violence within Northern Ireland.

The tensions within NICRA between those coming from the CSJ camp and those espousing PD or even republican ideals was clearly expressed by the former group. In February 1970 Brid Rogers, John Donaghy and Conn McCluskey (members of the NICRA Executive and key CSJ persons) wrote a memorandum addressed to the other NICRA Executive members explaining their disagreements. Their complaints focused on a number of issues. Their first point concerned what they considered to be the exploitation of NICRA as from June 1969 "to suit one political movement, that of International Revolutionary Socialism".[76] A second issue centred on the links of NICRA to the IRA, especially through the activities of the American-based National Association for Irish Justice.[77] They also criticised NICRA's decision to take over *The Citizen Press* magazine from the Citizens Defence Committee (CDC) of the Falls Road.

Tellingly, Rogers, Donaghy and McCluskey argued that the magazine as inherited from the CDC "associated NICRA too closely with one sectional group" and that "The tone of the first two issues had nothing to appeal to the socially conscious Protestants whom we must attract in large numbers if our movement is to progress."[78] This view was also echoed by others. James McSparran writing in January 1969 in the *Irish News* commented that the movement should focus on rights issues, be inclusive, act legally and with restraint:

> The Civil Rights Movement has to adopt the words of Sir Winston Churchill "Reached the end of the beginning". If they continue their lawful protests, particularly in Britain and abroad, with dignity and restraint and charity towards all in this area, rigorously excluding from the ranks those who have any aims other than those of the movement, they should soon see their dedicated campaign arriving at the "beginning of the end".[79]

At this stage, it is useful to reflect on the divergent attitudes towards human rights within the nationalist/republican community. The official history of NICRA indicates that the tensions within the organisation were very real. One of the tensions that emerged within the leadership of NICRA was related to disagreement between those arguing for the primacy of "Catholic rights" as opposed to those arguing in favour of "socialist rights".[80] The latter were identified with the PD strand of NICRA. The essence of the disagreement is clearly articulated by NICRA: "It was the old problem of determining who should have political priority in demanding both the type of rights and in making pre-conditions as to whom those rights should benefit most."[81]

That such an issue should arise in a civil rights movement is an indication that the various groups within NICRA had a limited understanding of human rights. Essentially, they each viewed human rights within the narrow lens of their interests. This partial or incomplete conception of human rights was also evident from the choice of rights which NICRA focused upon. The list of aims was as follows:

- to defend the basic freedoms of all citizens;
- to protect the rights of the individual;
- to highlight all possible abuses of power;
- to demand guarantees for freedom of speech, assembly and association;
- to inform the public of their lawful rights.

The list is fascinating in its mix of the very general and the very specific. Basic freedoms, rights of the individual, abuse of power, lawful rights are very generic terms, especially when not qualified by some specific standard (such qualification, for example, could have been drafted as follows: the basic freedoms as enunciated in the Universal Declaration of Human Rights). Conversely, the demand for freedom of speech, assembly and association is calling for very specific human rights. Why was NICRA so generic in four instances and extremely specific vis-à-vis three rights?

This emphasis on very specific rights is also witnessed in the 1973 NICRA publication entitled *Proposals for Peace, Democracy and Community Relations*. This publication was a response to the UK government's 1973 White Paper entitled *Northern Ireland Constitutional Proposals*. The NICRA response emphasised the right to organise politically for republicans including the rights to advocate peacefully for republicanism. It also emphasised, in the proposed Bill of Rights, the necessity of ending the oath of allegiance to assume any public office, the right to display flags freely and the right to a fair trial.[82] No specific references were made to a host of other rights such women's rights, children's rights, employment rights, access to education etc.

The Social Democratic and Labour Party (SDLP) had also endorsed these particular rights as being the most important ones in 1972 soon after its formation. In its 1972 proposals for resolving the Northern Ireland political impasse and the violent conflict, the SDLP outlined, inter alia, the human rights perspective. In the section entitled "Individual Rights" it stated:

> The Treaty shall guarantee the normal and accepted civil liberties already accepted by the Joint Sovereigns. Such rights as the right to free speech, publication and peaceful assembly, equality before the law, freedom from arbitrary arrest, freedom from imprisonment or other form of punishment without trial, freedom from cruel and unusual punishments shall be protected by the courts of law.[83]

This emphasis on these specific human rights seems to echo the specific interests of the republican section of the minority community. In one of his publications Gerry Adams recognised that a leading interest of the republican movement in NICRA was the possibility to agitate in favour of the right of republicans to organise politically. Adams stated unequivocally that "to succeed we needed to win the right to organize politically".[84]

Overall, it is clear that a considerable section of the nationalist/republican community had an instrumental view of human rights. NICRA's official history seems to suggest that it was not only republicans such as Gerry Adams who viewed civil rights as an instrument for party political ends. In fact, NICRA's history implies that even the SDLP used civil rights in a similar manner:

> Like the PD before them the SDLP were to use the popular cause of civil rights to gain political support and then attempt to swing a mass movement behind them on the basis that only their political philosophy could guarantee such rights.[85]

As mentioned in Chapter 3, sections of the nationalist community in Northern Ireland viewed the civil rights campaign as a relief from the impossibility of achieving change through the normal political processes. They viewed the emphasis on human rights as a way of ending the discrimination they felt they were subjected to since the nationalist politicians had signally failed to register any achievement in this respect. This may be seen in some of the comments made by John Hume in the Northern Ireland House of Commons soon after his election to Parliament in the wake of his leading role in the civil rights movement.

In various instances Hume referred to the need for equality between the citizens of Northern Ireland and identified the civil rights movement and marches as a mechanism for claiming that equality. The fundamental issue articulated by Hume was that the civil rights movement was simply a reaction to discrimination and second class citizenship for the nationalist community.

On one occasion Hume referred specifically to the issue of minority rights and accused the majority of trampling on the rights of the minority.[86] This particular reference illustrates that at least part of the minority community did conceive civil rights as very largely an issue of minority rights and relief for the minority. On another occasion when discussing the situation in Derry John Hume stated that:

> I have always believed that the future of the city of Derry depends not on a continuation of a tale of two cities but the removal of the roots of community division, which have been injustice in the past. It is the removal of these injustices and the basing of community relations on a proper basis, a basis of justice, which hold out the only prospect for a viable future.[87]

The reference to the injustices suffered by the minority community was made in the context of the Derry street marches and Hume made clear that the protests were a result of the injustices which the minority community felt that they had been subjected to. Whatever the subjective merits or demerits of such an attitude, it meant that for a section of the nationalist community human rights were approached simply as relief from discrimination for the minority. While relief from discrimination and minority rights are part of the human rights concept, it is certainly not a complete picture of human rights.

In the majority community, the conflict within the unionist cabinet following the events of 5 October and the increasing internal and external pressures for civil rights reforms has already been alluded to. The dissent within unionist ranks may be described as one characterised by disagreement on the nature of the reaction to the CRM with the liberal wing led by O'Neill advocating reform but the more "conservative" wing advocating a strong and relatively uncompromising response. The more conservative Cabinet members such as William Craig emphasised that the Cabinet should not agree to reforms under duress while the more liberal ones claimed that the only way to safeguard Northern Ireland's constitutional and political system was by agreeing to reforms. Prime Minister O'Neill in a secret Cabinet Memorandum went so far as to state that the minority did have a legitimate grievance which needed to be addressed.[88] This fracture between liberals and conservatives was also reflected in the Unionist Party as a whole. Some unionist Members of Parliament at Stormont and at Westminster were critical of reforms and were deemed by the more liberal unionists as too defensive and old-fashioned. In responding to a letter of criticism by Sir Knox Cunningham MP, O'Neill expressed his disagreement with such a conservative and defensive position:

> You may wish to remain in what you consider to be a strong defensive position established over the years, but I would ask you to recall what happened to the Maginot line and to remember that in politics, as in warfare, one does not win today's battles with yesterday's tactics or yesterday's weapons.[89]

This dissension within Cabinet and the parliamentary party was also evident in more vivid form in the unionist community at large. A key characteristic of the civil rights era was the emergence of the Reverend Ian Paisley as a charismatic leader of the more conservative unionist community. His emergence as a staunch opponent of the CRM was symbiotic with the CRM itself as he emerged as a practitioner of politics in the streets. His campaign was based on a drive to galvanise unionist anti-CRM sentiment by leading them to counter-marches and counter-demonstrations, both against NICRA-sponsored marches as well as against the Queen's University students' marches (the People's Democracy). Paisley and the movement that he gradually developed were an expression of dissent from the mainstream Unionist Party policies and, while the movement was not numerous in its early days, it did represent a growing sentiment in the unionist community. The essential thrust of the Ulster Defence Committee of which Ian Paisley was a chairman and of the Ulster Protestant Volunteers led by his associate Major Bunting was that Northern Ireland needed to be defended against the Catholic/nationalist/republican attempts at destabilising it. They saw the CRM simply and solely as a tactic designed to achieve the end of partition with the consequent absorption of Northern Ireland into a Catholic Irish Republic. Thus, the Paisleyite approach was to mobilise unionist sentiment against what it perceived to be the enemies of a unionist, Protestant Northern Ireland which included Catholics, nationalist and republicans but also liberal unionists and Protestants who were aligning themselves with the ecumenical movement.

The Northern Irish Cabinet was evidently concerned by the activities of the Paisleyite movement to the extent that there was, at least for a period of time, a monthly report of these activities drawn up for the government.[90] The concern may also be evinced from references to the risk posed by "extremist Protestant elements" who "arranged parades and meetings for obstructive purposes".[91] This was a clear reference to the counter-marches organised by the Paisleyite movement in order either to persuade the Minister of Home Affairs to ban the marches on public order grounds or to ensure that the civil rights marchers would be confronted by the ant-civil rights marchers led by the Reverend Paisley.[92]

Within this context two issues stand out from a human rights perspective:

1 the generally suspicious approach to the CRM by the unionist community was taken to another level by Ian Paisley and his followers. The Paisleyites were not merely suspicious or generally distrustful of the CRM but positively antagonistic. They were also willing to express this antagonism in the streets as a counter to the taking to the streets by the CRM. This must have contributed to create in that section of the unionist community that followed the Paisleyite approach a genuine resentment towards the CRM and very possibly towards civil rights and human rights more generally;
2 the taking to the streets by the Paisleyite movement in the obstructive manner already referred to contributed (at least according to the Cameron Report) to the escalation of violence during the period from 5 October 1968.[93]

Northern Ireland and human rights in the aftermath of the civil rights era

There is no doubting the fact that the civil rights era saw a reconfiguration of the party-political scene in Northern Ireland both within the unionist and the nationalist camp. The Unionist Party, which had monopolised the Protestant vote since the creation of the state, witnessed a fracturing in its internal cohesion as a direct result of the response to the CRM. A section of the party was unhappy with O'Neill's response and advocated a more uncompromising and harsher response than that pursued by O'Neill. The differences between O'Neill and Craig on the handling of the CRM were symptomatic of the divisions within the party. This internal dissension was to lead to the secession of a part of the Unionist Party into the Vanguard Unionist Party led by Craig himself. The resignation of O'Neill in 1969 may be interpreted as a victory for the more hard-line approach within the Unionist Party. The victory of the hardliners may also have been due, in some measure, to the Rev. Ian Paisely's challenge to traditional unionism. Within this context, the emergence of the Democratic Unionist Party as an alternative unionist voice was another factor that emerged from the civil rights era and one which had an enduring impact on Northern Irish politics.

The most dramatic change in terms of party political transformation was the demise of the Nationalist Party and the rise of the SDLP as a party based on constitutionalism and civil rights. It may be argued that the rise of the SDLP was a direct result of the civil rights era and of the confluence of: (1) the more direct and dynamic action style nationalism practiced by younger nationalists such as Austin Currie; (2) the political effectiveness and working-class appeal of Gerry Fitt as a republican labour politician and (3) the strong, dignified rights-based and constitutional doctrine expounded by John Hume. It is worth noting that these three political approaches all contributed to the CRM. The SDLP was to become the major party representing the nationalist community in Northern Ireland but also marked a departure in the nationalist political approach. This departure was marked by an acceptance of the constitutional reality of the border and by a more markedly left of centre ideology with a strong, continuing emphasis on the centrality of human rights in their political agenda.

A further change in the Northern Irish political landscape was the (re-)emergence of political violence and of paramilitary organisations linked, directly or indirectly, to political parties. The IRA and Sinn Féin had, of course, been a feature in Northern Irish politics since 1921. However, the post-CRM period saw IRA re-enter the scene in a strong way and gather a level of popular support which it had not enjoyed for many decades.

Violence and militarisation

By far the most dramatic change in Northern Ireland in the years of the CRM was the descent into a sustained period of sectarian violence which characterised the province for at least 25 years. This period referred to, euphemistically, as "The Troubles" may be categorised according to international systems of classification as an armed conflict of a non-international character.[94] From 1970 to 1994 (both years inclusive) the annual number of battle-related deaths in Northern Ireland was over 25, which is the widely accepted threshold to categorise a situation as an armed conflict.[95] It may also be worth noting that in October 1970 in a confidential letter from the Prime Minister of Northern Ireland to the General Commanding Officer of Northern Ireland, the Prime Minister remarked that Northern Ireland was "far removed" from times of peace.[96]

The descent into a situation of armed conflict had numerous effects on Northern Ireland. Generally, Northern Ireland became a more militarised society with three interconnected episodes: (1) the arrival of British troops in the province; (2) the rise of the IRA; and (3) the proliferation of unionist paramilitary groups. One ought also to mention that the introduction of internment in August 1971 further contributed to the movement towards emergency and militarisation. This militarisation may be seen both as a consequence of the sectarian violence but also as a phenomenon that provoked further violence. While the arrival of the British troops was originally intended to restore order, the British military presence soon became for republicans a further impetus towards violence. The IRA managed to recruit significant numbers of young Catholics into its fold as Catholics felt they needed protection from the violence perpetrated against them by the police and the loyalist paramilitaries. The introduction of internment also contributed to swelling IRA ranks. Recruitment was strengthened by the perception that the British army instead of protecting the Catholic communities was, in fact, persecuting them. On the other hand, the loyalist paramilitaries sought to protect not only their communities from IRA violence but the border itself which they felt was challenged by the changes advocated by the CRM allied to the widely held belief (amongst unionists) that the CRM was a republican front. These three interrelated factors soon became absorbed into a vicious cycle of violence which created other forms of cultural and structural violence.

Human rights: progress and regress

When examined from a human rights perspective the CRM presents a number of difficult issues both in terms of its proponents and supporters as well its opponents and detractors. One may suggest that the issues can be categorised as issues of substance and issues of perception. The issue of substance refers to the involvement of individuals in the creation and operation of NICRA (and other organisations active in the CRM) who were also active within the IRA and who, as such, were committed to the use of physical violence for political purposes. This raises the matter of the compatibility (or lack thereof) between an involvement in a human rights organisation and a commitment to the use of violence. The Universal Declaration of Human Rights, the European Convention on Human Rights, the International Covenant on Civil and Political Rights and numerous other human rights instruments affirm the right to life and physical integrity of every human being. Support of, or involvement in, physical violence for political (or other) purposes appears to be incompatible with this human right. Furthermore, it is widely acknowledged by human rights instruments and declarations that human rights are universal, indivisible and interdependent.[97] The notions of indivisibility and interdependence are of particular salience in this context. If one applies these notions to the case in point one would have to conclude that a commitment to, or support of, violence would be a denial of the indivisibility and interdependence of human rights. This is not to say that the involvement of IRA activists in the CRM invalidates the movement's aims, strategies and actions but it does render the work of the CRM more difficult to assess.

Within this context one notes that the second difficult issue (of the interpretation and perception of the CRM) is closely related to the first. Opponents of the CRM regularly attempted to challenge the legitimacy of the movement by pointing to the inconsistency of a movement which was explicitly committed to the advancement of civil rights through peaceful means but which included individuals who had a parallel commitment to the use of violence for political purposes. The involvement of IRA supporters in the CRM was thus a perfect vehicle through which its opponents could present the CRM as being one weapon in the arsenal of the IRA. Through this "guilt by association" the opponents of the CRM managed, to some extent, to solidify the perception in unionist circles that the CRM was intrinsically republican. What is even more unfortunate for human rights and the history of human rights in Northern Ireland is that civil rights (and human rights) became characterised as a nationalist/republican concept and the language of human rights became associated in the always delicate Northern Irish lexicon with nationalist/republican aspirations. The universality, indivisibility and interdependence of human rights were thus fundamentally challenged in the province.

With respect to individuals who were using human rights principles and language but held a parallel commitment to violence, one can note that their engagement with human rights failed to shift their political position in terms of violence. However, this is not to say that human rights did not impact on the republican political movement or even nationalist politics. One can note that ever since the civil rights period republicanism sought to engage with human rights in a sustained fashion. It was, one may argue, an incomplete understanding of human rights but it had an impact nonetheless on future political action and language. As will become apparent in subsequent chapters, the republican movement (chiefly through Sinn Féin) continued to refer to human rights in their political struggle and political manifestos. In a wider political sense, human rights proved to be a strong mobilising factor for the minority community. It proved to be a broader, more attractive and more acceptable political idea than republicanism given its association with violence or even than the ineffective, traditional nationalist politics. The birth of the SDLP with a very strong human rights emphasis and its replacing the old Nationalist Party is also evidence of this. Moreover, for the minority community the civil rights period crystallised a clearer sense of having suffered abuse of rights they ought to have as a matter of law and policy.

On the other hand, the opponents and detractors of the CRM went further than challenging the CRM's association with the IRA (which from a human rights perspective was a legitimate challenge to present given the IRA's commitment to violence). The detractors, who were naturally unionist in political complexion, also attempted to invalidate the CRM by associating it with republicanism and nationalism. As highlighted above nationalist and republican associations and individuals were prominent in the formation and operation of the CRM. However, the freedom to associate and to express views and opinions belongs to every individual as long as the individual does not abuse these rights. The unionist opponents of the CRM, by harping on the nationalist or republican background of individuals involved in the CRM, were coming perilously close to arguing that republicans and nationalists could not legitimately be involved in the promotion and protection of human rights and that their involvement in such endeavours was automatically suspect. If one takes a dispassionate view of the debate, one would point out that it is natural for individuals coming from a minority community (be it ethnic, political, socioeconomic or religious) to be more vocal and involved in pushing forward the human rights agenda.

Irrespective of the wrongs or rights of the debate surrounding the CRM (which ultimately may never be resolved) human rights as a concept suffered grievously in the aftermath of the CRM. The already referred to association of human rights with nationalism and republicanism rendered the majority community suspect towards human rights language (though not necessarily towards its practice). The questioning of the sincerity of the commitment to human rights as a principle rather than as a strategy or tactic to end partition remained prevalent in unionist communities. Thus, rather than an affirmation of universality and common humanity, human rights – in effect – became another dividing line between the two communities in Northern Ireland. The diversity of views on human rights is still evident in the post-conflict era, not least in the continuing difficulties in agreeing a Bill of Rights for Northern Ireland as was mandated by the Good Friday Agreement.

From a human rights perspective, the most serious negative repercussion of the events which surrounded the CRM was the descent into violent sectarianism. Physical violence had featured intermittently in the history of Northern Ireland[98] but the intensity and spread of the violence which emerged in the 1970s was of an altogether different scale. The direct and indirect impact of this violence on individuals, families and communities of all religious and political beliefs was immense.[99] The impact of violence on the human rights of the people of Northern Ireland was extensive, enduring and operated at several levels. The most obvious level at which violence impacted on human rights in Northern Ireland was the physical violence which deprived human beings of their right to life through bombings, shootings and other forms of killings. It impacted on the right to privacy and enjoyment of family life and their right to property, with families having their homes attacked and damaged. It also impacted on the right not to be subject to arbitrary detention, with internment being widely used following its introduction in 1971. The paramilitary punishment beatings that evolved, in lieu of policing, in certain parts of Northern Ireland abused the right to be free from torture and inhuman and degrading treatment and on occasion the right to life. Beyond these and other forms of direct violence, other indirect forms of violence developed as part of the climate of violence. It has been argued that direct violence and structural violence are highly interdependent.[100] This interdependence is usually expressed in terms of the capacity of structural violence to produce direct violence. However, direct violence may also create and contribute to structural violence. It seems reasonable to argue that this was the case in Northern Ireland.

Notwithstanding the difficulties highlighted above, there were significant improvements in the practice of human rights within Northern Ireland during the civil rights period or in its immediate aftermath. This is especially the case in the context of measures to combat discrimination. The changes in the franchise for local government elections have already been mentioned. Within the long-standing and very vexed question of housing, progress was also registered with the creation of the Northern Ireland Housing Executive in 1971 which achieved some success in building better housing and in awarding housing based on clearer and equitable criteria. Less success was registered in dealing with the other main area of grievance, that of employment. Given the continuing economic difficulties faced by Northern Ireland, unemployment levels remained relatively high. It appeared to the Catholic community that such unemployment fell disproportionately on them. The major efforts in dealing with discrimination in employment practices were to come later in the mid-1970s[101] although one cannot exclude that the demands made by the CRM contributed to the adoption of these measures. The civil rights era also witnessed the adoption, as already mentioned, of the Commissioner for Complaints Act (Northern Ireland) of 1969 which created an ombudsman-style system of redress for maladministration and injustices which had not existed before. Thus, in the civil rights era a number of specific measures were enacted aimed at dealing with the issue of discrimination which had long bedevilled the political life of Northern Ireland. While the measures in themselves did not resolve the issues they sought to address they were initial steps in enacting human rights legislation in Northern Ireland. Later legislation would increase the quantity and quality of human rights law in the province. One should not overstate the case for human rights legislation. After all there is some truth in Oliver Goldsmith's view when he wrote: "How small, of all that human hearts endure, that part which laws or kings can cause or cure." However, that small part which laws can remedy or address is relevant not only in itself but for the signal it sends to society.

Having considered both the positive and negative elements emerging from the civil rights era one may suggest that the concept, discourse and practice of human rights in Northern Ireland was shaped in significant ways during this period:

1 Human rights moved to centre stage in Northern Ireland, upstaging the border, albeit momentarily, as the main political issue in the province. Although the border, terror and security as well as the search for peace crowded into the centre of Northern Irish political life, human rights continued to maintain an important role in the province.[102] The movement of human rights to centre stage in Northern Irish political life was attributable to numerous factors. The rise of an educated, rights-aware Catholic middle-class, exemplified by the Campaign for Social Justice, has already been discussed.[103] The taking up of the civil rights cause by the student movement at Queens University that became the People's Democracy was another factor that has been raised in this context.[104] Richard English has pointed out that for a time in the mid-1960s, even the IRA itself and the broader republican movement became seriously interested in civil rights, especially through the influence of socialist republican intellectuals such as Roy Johnston, Anthony Coughlan and Desmond Greaves. Admittedly, these republicans all aspired towards a united Ireland but they considered that their aspiration could be achieved also through a civil rights campaign.[105] Thus, middle-class Catholics, university students, republicans and even liberal Protestants helped bring civil rights to centre stage. Above all, the media attention that the civil rights marches attracted, sometimes because of the violence that accompanied them, brought rights to the attention, even if only superficially, of all sectors of Northern Irish society. The extent to which civil rights became a prominent part of Northern Ireland can be assessed by the numerous references to civil rights issues in Northern Irish newspapers. Apart from reporting on individual marches and so on, commentary was plentiful, as well as numerous reports featuring British groups and individuals supporting the Northern Ireland civil rights campaign.[106]

2 Human rights in Northern Ireland were internationalised to an extent hitherto unknown, particularly through explicit references to the US civil rights movement. It is however relevant to note that this link was never fully explored and elaborated upon by NICRA and other associated organisations. The internationalisation of human rights issues was also assisted, to a more limited extent, through the global protest youth movement of the late 1960s. Reference has already been made, inter alia, to PD being inspired in their militancy by the American civil rights movement[107] and to the CSJ's increasing efforts to attract international attention (including an increasing awareness of the possibilities afforded by the European Court of Human Rights).[108] There was also more international awareness of Northern Ireland in international human rights circuits. For instance, in 1969 the respected International Commission of Jurists included the human rights situation in Northern Ireland in its Review.[109] Northern Irish newspapers also increasingly reported on how foreign governments and press reflected on the situation in Northern Ireland.[110] Clearly, interest in Northern Ireland abroad grew during this period while Northern Irish awareness of this fact also increased.

3 Human rights as an issue became a polarising factor within Northern Ireland. Some of the reasons for this polarisation have already been referred to and whichever factors contributed most to this polarising process the important fact is that the process occurred. By the end of the CRM, rights language was firmly fixed in the nationalist/republican orbit whereas rights-talk was clearly perceived by unionists as a tool in the republican strategy to achieve a united Ireland and to undermine the Northern Irish state.

4 Human rights practice was boosted from the legislative point of view through the adoption of a number of measures and laws (dealing with franchise, housing, ombudsman etc). The building of a framework of human rights laws and processes commenced during the civil rights period, continued ever since, culminating in the Bill of Rights envisaged as a possibility in the Good Friday Agreement but which has, as yet, not been enacted.

5 Human rights were seriously undermined at the height of the CRM with episodes of physical violence, such as during the marches in Armagh, Newry and the Belfast to Derry march.[111] These episodes eventually escalated (not with the inevitability of a Greek tragedy but through specific decisions made) into a spiral of violence that left many dead and injured over a 30-year period. Consequently, the most basic of rights, the right to life, was denied to all of the victims of the conflict.

6 Human rights did not change the beliefs and practices of those committed to physical violence as a political option even though they were involved in the CRM; but human rights did impact on the politics of Northern Ireland by providing a key organisational concept to the SDLP which arose as the main nationalist party, and on Sinn Féin which adopted significant human rights discourse and policies over time. In terms of broader political feeling in the minority community human rights became, and remained, an important aspect of their political identity.

7 Attitudes towards human rights by the various communities developed and hardened during the civil rights period. As human rights took centre stage in the public life of Northern Ireland, the various communities had to engage with, and develop attitudes towards, the concept of human rights. From the description of O'Neill's attempts to reform Northern Ireland one may conclude that the moderate wing of Unionism (typified by O'Neill) looked at human rights reforms as essentially assimilationist policies through which nationalists would be drawn into an acceptance of Northern Ireland politically and socially. Thus, moderate unionists' approach to human rights language and reforms may be summarised as *human rights as assimilation*. This contrasted with the attitude to human rights within the less moderate unionist community led by figures such as William Craig and Ian Paisley. This hard-line unionist community viewed human rights language negatively as a purely republican ploy and as a threat to the Northern Irish state. It is an attitude that may be defined

as *human rights as threat*. On the nationalist/republican side there also developed two different conceptions of human rights. Amongst the moderate nationalist community, human rights during the civil rights period became a form of relief from discrimination that had been ongoing since the creation of the state. Human rights within this section of the community were viewed chiefly as an antidote to the discrimination they suffered as members of a particular community. This attitude to human rights may best be described with the epithet of *human rights as relief*. Finally, there was a strand within the republican movement that conceived of human rights during the period as an instrument through which the state could be destabilised and rendered ungovernable. These four different conceptions of human rights are all either partial or mistaken and to varying degrees continued to colour views on human rights in Northern Ireland for decades. This is a matter that will be returned to in the following chapters.

Finally, it is evident that the civil rights movement was a seminal moment in the human rights history of Northern Ireland. As has been highlighted, the movement developed because of numerous factors. The rise of the Catholic professional class was one such factor, while the rising sense of entitlements produced by the welfare state was another factor. As the state became a dispenser of housing, health and education, the minority community became especially perceptive to such entitlements being dispensed fairly. Thus, perception of unfairness mobilised even the poorer segments of the minority who most depended on public entitlements. Another factor that aided the rise of the civil rights movement was the rise in tertiary education, with a greater number of Catholics at Queen's University and also the rise of left-wing sentiment throughout the 1960s in Europe. This was a factor that contributed to the establishment of PD. The rise of human rights within the UK, Europe and in the USA also influenced the rise of the movement.

All of these factors influenced the rise of the civil rights movement but in its turn the movement sought to influence the political situation as a result of these factors. For example, the movement sought to lobby the UK government directly as well as indirectly through international lobbying. It did so by using rights language and notions of fairness which had risen significantly in profile internationally. Because human rights language and practice was growing internationally, pressure around the issues of discrimination and rights became a greater concern for the UK government. Rights and discrimination became more effective tools to leverage the UK government, which in turn then pressured the Northern Ireland devolved government.

Within Northern Ireland, the civil rights movement impacted on minority politics with the eclipse of the Nationalist Party and the rise of the SDLP, a party with a strong emphasis on rights and with a commitment to engage with the Northern Irish state much more than the Nationalist Party ever did. The republican political discourse also adopted a strong rights language to forward its agenda. With respect to the politics of the majority community the Democratic Unionist Party (DUP) was created as a more combative unionist party, partially as a response to the civil rights movement. All told, this emphasis on rights language established a trajectory which in later decades would be regularly referred to and revived within Northern Ireland's political discourse. In the longer term the impact of the civil rights movement's emphasis on rights in Northern Ireland made a strong rights agenda inescapable when the political peace process developed.

Notes

1 The Honourable Lord Cameron, *Cameron Report – Disturbances in Northern Ireland* (Belfast: Her Majesty's Stationery Office, September 1969).
2 Paul Bew, Peter Gibbon and Henry Patterson, *Northern Ireland 1921–2001: Political Forces and Social Classes* (London: Serif, 2001), 146.
3 Christopher Hewett, "Catholic Grievances, Catholic Nationalism and Violence in Northern Ireland during the Civil Rights Period: A Reconsideration", *The British Journal Of Sociology* 32, No. 3 (September 1981), 377.
4 Richard English, *Armed Struggle: The History of the IRA* (London: Pan Books, 2003), 98.
5 Bob Purdie, *Politics in the Streets: The Origins of the Civil Rights Movement in Northern Ireland* (Belfast: Blackstaff Press, 1990).
6 David McKittrick and David McVea, *Making Sense of the Troubles: The Story of the Conflict in Northern Ireland* (Chicago: New Amsterdam Books, 2002), 44.
7 Ian Paisley interviewed by Eamonn Mallie, aired on BBC One, 13 January 2014.
8 Gerry Adams, *Before the Dawn: An Autobiography* (Dingle, Ireland: Brandon Books, 1996), 92.
9 Quoted in the *Irish Weekly*, 29 May 1965.
10 Purdie, *Politics in the Streets*, 1.
11 Although one ought to highlight that taking to the streets is a favourite occupation in Northern Ireland with public commemorations and parades (be they for St. Patrick's Day, the Twelfth (Orangemen's Day, 12 July), the 1916 Easter Rising or Armistice Day).
12 See the preceding chapter.
13 The Campaign for Social Justice in Northern Ireland, "Northern Ireland: Why Justice Cannot Be Done", 1964, accessed 9 February 2012, http://cain.ulst.ac.uk/events/crights/pdfs/csj85.pdf.
14 Purdie, *Politics in the Streets*, 2.
15 Brendan Lynn, *Holding the Ground: The Nationalist Party in Northern Ireland, 1945–1972* (Aldershot: Ashgate, 1997).
16 For an in-depth discussion of the NILP, see Aron Edwards, *A History of the Northern Ireland Labour Party: Democratic Socialism and Sectarianism* (Manchester: Manchester University Press, 2009).
17 Marc Mulholland, "Assimilation versus Segregation: Unionist Strategy in the 1960s", *Twentieth Century British History* 11, no. 3 (2000), 284.
18 Indeed there is a touch of Harold Wilson's "white heat of the technological revolution" rhetoric in O'Neill's early pronouncements as Prime Minister.
19 Captain Terence O'Neill, Northern Ireland House of Commons, *The Parliamentary Debates: Official Report*, 22 October 1963, col. 29.
20 BBC, Craigavon Town Planning: British Modernism 50 Years on, 24 October 2014, www.bbc.com/news/uk-northern-ireland-29728971.

21 It has recently been argued that "The Craigavon brand was fundamentally and fatally flawed from the outset. Naming it after the first unionist prime minister was perhaps an unwise opening move in terms of achieving crosscommunity buy-in." Ibid.
22 Mr. Cahir Healy MP, Northern Ireland House of Commons, *The Parliamentary Debates: Official Report*, 23 October 1963, col. 52, http://stormontpapers.ahds.ac.uk/stormontpapers/pageview.html?volumeno=55&pageno=45.
23 Interview with Terence O'Neill, *Belfast Telegraph*, 10 May 1969.
24 Minister of Home Affairs, William Craig MP, Northern Ireland House of Commons, *The Parliamentary Debates: Official Report*, 3 March 1964, col. 1434, http://stormontpapers.ahds.ac.uk/stormontpapers/pageview.html?volumeno=56&pageno=1359.
25 Attorney General, Edward Warburton Jones MP, Northern Ireland House of Commons, *The Parliamentary Debates: Official Report*, 16 June 1964, col. 2023.
26 Including in the United Kingdom where Westminster passed the first Race Relations Act in 1965.
27 Interview with Sir Kenneth Bloomfield, *BBC Radio Ulster*, 7 December 2007.
28 Minister for Health and Local Government, Northern Ireland House of Commons, *The Parliamentary Debates: Official Report*, 27 February 1964, col. 27, http://stormontpapers.ahds.ac.uk/stormontpapers/pageview.html?volumeno=56&pageno=1281.
29 Thomas Gormley MP, Northern Ireland House of Commons, *The Parliamentary Debates: Official Report*, 12 May 1964, col. 811, http://stormontpapers.ahds.ac.uk/stormontpapers/pageview.html?volumeno=57&pageno=791.
30 Joseph Burns MP, Northern Ireland House of Commons, *The Parliamentary Debates: Official Report*, 12 May 1964, col. 824.
31 Purdie, *Politics in the Streets.*
32 Conn McCluskey, *Up off Their Knees: A Commentary on the Civil Rights Movement in Northern Ireland* (Conn McCluskey and Associates, 1989), 10.
33 Catherine B. Shannon, "From House Rights to Civil Rights 1936–1968", in *The Field Day Anthology of Irish Writing*, ed. Angela Bourke (Cork: Cork University Press, 2002), 380.
34 As mentioned at the close of the preceding chapter the Cameron Commission identified this action as a key moment in its findings.
35 Vincent E. Feeney, "Westminster and the Early Civil Rights Struggle in Northern Ireland", *Eire-Ireland* 11, no. 4 (1976), 4–5.
36 As mentioned in the introduction to this chapter Bew, Gibbon and Patterson reject the view that the civil rights movement was simply a middle-class phenomenon and provide interesting evidence in this respect. Nevertheless it is clear from the composition of the CSJ that this particular organisation was very much a middle-class organisation. The two key founders, Patricia and Conn McCluskey, were a teacher and a doctor respectively. The Committee as listed in their publications included a dentist (Maurice Byrne), an architect (Brian Gregory) as well as two fellows of the Royal College of Surgeons (Peter Gormley and Connor Gilligan).
37 *Campaign Newsletter*, 5 September 1967, vol. 4 (Castlefields, Dungannon: Campaign For Social Justice in Northern Ireland, 1967).
38 The parallel from a constitutional point of view was imprecise as the respective constitutional positions of the part to the whole were significantly different.
39 Ibid.
40 *Campaign Newsletter*, 15 August 1970, vol. 11.
41 *Campaign Newsletter*, 27 December 1968, vol. 8.
42 Harold Wilson, in his history of the 1964 Labour government, *A Personal Record: The Labour Government, 1964–1970* (New York: Little, Brown, 1971), refers to

the growing interest from Labour MPs in human rights issues (including human rights in Northern Ireland), specifically those entering Parliament in 1964 and 1966. This pressure became formalised in 1965 with the establishment by a number of Labour Party MPs of the Campaign for Democracy in Ulster (CDU).

43 This point is made in Patrick J. Roche and Brian Barton (editors), *The Northern Ireland Question: Myth and Reality* (Tonbridge: Wordzworth Publishing, 2013), 54.

44 Brice Dickson, *The European Convention on Human Rights and the Conflict in Northern Ireland* (Oxford: Oxford University Press, 2010).

45 Bob Purdie, in *Politics in the Streets*, gives an exhaustive history of the movement and it is beyond the aims of this work to write another such history or even reconsider Purdie's examination.

46 Northern Ireland Civil Rights Association, *"We Shall Overcome"…. The History of the Struggle for Civil Rights in Northern Ireland 1968–1978* (Belfast: Northern Ireland Civil Rights Association (NICRA), 1978).

47 BBC Report, 15 March 2002, http://news.bbc.co.uk/2/hi/uk_news/northern_ireland/1874598.stm.

48 Irish Republican News, 31 January 2008, http://republicannews.org/current/news/2008/01/civil_rights_movement_remember.html#.VZO6nvmqqko.

49 Ibid.

50 This matter is elaborated upon below.

51 Purdie, *Politics in the Streets*, 134.

52 The Honourable Lord Cameron, *Cameron Report – Disturbances in Northern Ireland*, para. 30.

53 Ann Hope, "From Civil Rights to Guerrilla War: The Northern Ireland Civil Rights Association's Struggle for Democracy 1969–1972" (Labour Studies Diploma Thesis, Ruskin College, 1976), 33.

54 It may be worth pointing out that NICRA however did not have within the ranks of its leadership an individual with Martin Luther King's charisma and authority.

55 The Honourable Lord Cameron, *Cameron Report – Disturbances in Northern Ireland*, para. 28.

56 Purdie, *Politics in the Streets*, 3.

57 This was perhaps inevitable given NICRA's somewhat loose structure.

58 The difficulties also included the highly charged atmosphere in Derry where historical Protestant defence against Catholic King James is a matter of pride for the Protestant community and where the walled city was considered a no-go area for Catholic marchers.

59 The Cameron Report gives an account of what happened and concluded that "the police broke ranks and used their batons indiscriminately on people in Duke Street" and also criticised the use of water cannons by the police: "there was no justification for use of the water wagons on the bridge, while the evidence which we heard and saw on film did not convince us of the necessity of their use in Duke Street." See The Honourable Lord Cameron, *Cameron Report – Disturbances in Northern Ireland*, para. 51.

60 Public Records Office, Northern Ireland, *Memorandum by the Prime Minister*, 14 October 1968, CAB/4/1406.

61 Public Records Office, Northern Ireland, *Conclusions of a Meeting of the Cabinet Held at Stormont Castle*, 14 October 1968 at 10.00, CAB/4/1406/16.

62 Public Records Office, Northern Ireland, *Conclusions of a Meeting of the Cabinet Held at Stormont Castle*, 5 October 1968 at 11.15, CAB/4/1423/18.

63 Public Records Office, Northern Ireland, *Meeting at 10 Downing Street*, 4 November 1968, CAB/4/1413/9.

64 Ibid.

65 Public Records Office, Northern Ireland, *Conclusions of a Meeting of the Cabinet Held at Stormont Castle*, 7 November 1968, at 11.15, CAB/4/1413/22; and Public Records Office, Northern Ireland, *Conclusions of a Meeting of the Cabinet Held at Stormont Castle*, 20 November 1968 at 10.30, CAB/4/1418/11.

66 The Conclusions of the Cabinet meeting of Wednesday 15 January 1969 show that resistance to "one person one vote" for local elections was particularly strong and there was a belief expressed by some Ministers that reform of the local government franchise was "most unlikely to be acceptable to their Party in view of the recent pledges given to them". Public Records Office, Northern Ireland, *Conclusions of a Meeting of the Cabinet Held at Stormont Castle*, 15 January 1969 at 10.00, CAB/4/1427/24.

67 Captain Terence O'Neill, *Television Broadcast by Captain Terence O'Neill, Prime Minister of Northern Ireland on B.B.C. (Northern Ireland) and Ulster Television* (Public Records Office of Northern Ireland, 9 December 1968), CAB/9/B/205/8.

68 Purdie, *Politics in the Streets*, 140.

69 Frank Gogarty, *Speech by Dr. Frank Gogarty, Chairman of NICRA to the First National Conference of the National Association for Irish Justice* (New York: City center, November 1969).

70 The Honourable Lord Cameron, *Cameron Report – Disturbances in Northern Ireland*, para. 195.

71 Ibid., para. 203.

72 Purdie disagrees that this indicated a profound difference between NICRA and PD and views the respective decisions as purely tactical. However, while within NICRA there was some willingness to test the veracity of O'Neill's reform programme, this clearly was not the case with PD.

73 Text of a speech made on 21 December 1968 advocating campaign of civil disobedience. Speaker unknown, Speech, 21 December 1968, Northern Ireland Political Collection, Linen Hall Library, Belfast, P1063.

74 Ibid.

75 People's Democracy, *Peoples Democracy: What It Stands For, Its Attitudes*, February 1972.

76 Communication to Civil Rights Association Members from Mrs Brid Rodgers, John Donaghy and Conn McCluskey, 1 February 1970, 1.

77 Ibid., 2.

78 Ibid.

79 James McSparran, "Reformers and Reforms", *Irish News*, 29 January 1969.

80 Northern Ireland Civil Rights Association, *"We Shall Overcome".... The History of the Struggle for Civil Rights in Northern Ireland 1968–1978*.

81 Ibid.

82 NICRA, "Proposals for Peace, Democracy and Community Relations" (NICRA, Belfast, March 1973), accessed 18 February 2012, http://cain.ulst.ac.uk/events/crights/nicra/nicra73.htm.

83 The Social Democratic and Labour Party, "Towards a New Ireland: Proposals by the Social Democratic and Labour Party" (The Social Democratic and Labour Party, 1972), accessed 18 February 2012, http://cain.ulst.ac.uk/events/crights/sdlp1972.htm.

84 Gerry Adams, *The New Ireland: A Vision for the Future* (Dublin: Brandon Books, 2005), 29.

85 Northern Ireland Civil Rights Association, *"We Shall Overcome".... The History of the Struggle for Civil Rights in Northern Ireland 1968–1978*.

86 John Hume, Northern Ireland House of Commons, *The Parliamentary Debates: Official Report*, 20 May 1970, col. 618, http://stormontpapers.ahds.ac.uk/stormontpapers/pageview.html?volumeno=76&pageno=559.

87 John Hume, Northern Ireland House of Commons, *The Parliamentary Debates: Official Report*, 5 November 1969, col. 971, http://stormontpapers.ahds.ac.uk/stormontpapers/pageview.html?volumeno=74&pageno=951.
88 O'Neill wrote: "Of course there are anti-partition agitators prominently at work, but can any of us truthfully say in the confines of this room that the minority has no grievance calling for a remedy?" Public Records Office, Northern Ireland, *Memorandum by the Prime Minister*, 14 October 1968, CAB/4/1406.
89 Letter from Captain Terence O'Neill to Sir Knox Cunningham (Public Records Office of Northern Ireland, 13 March 1968), CAB/9/U/5/2.
90 See for example: *List of Principal Meetings and Other Events Connected with the Free Presbyterian Church during the Month of September 1968* (Public Records Office of Northern Ireland, 1968); and *List of Principal Meetings and Other Events Connected with the Paisleyite Movement during the Month of October 1968* (Public Records Office of Northern Ireland, 1968), CAB/9/B/300/3.
91 Public Records Office, Northern Ireland, *Conclusions of a Meeting of the Cabinet Held at Stormont Castle*, 14 October 1968.
92 The Cameron Report was very critical of the Paisleyite movement in this context. See The Honourable Lord Cameron, *Cameron Report – Disturbances in Northern Ireland*, paras 216–26.
93 See ibid., para. 226:

> Both these gentlemen and the organisations with which they are so closely and authoritatively concerned must, in our opinion, bear a heavy share of direct responsibility for the disorders in Armagh and at Burntollet Bridge and also for inflaming passions and engineering opposition to lawful, and what would in all probability otherwise have been peaceful, demonstrations or at least have attracted only modified and easily controlled opposition.

94 Major peace and conflict studies institutions categorise as armed conflict those situations of conflict which produce more than 25 battle-related deaths a year. For example, see such as Department of Conflict and Peace Research at the University of Uppsala which defines armed conflict as "a contested incompatibility which concerns government and/or territory where the use of armed force between two parties, of which at least one is the government of a state, results in at least 25 battle-related deaths". Department of Peace and Conflict Research, Uppsala University, "Definition of Armed Conflict", n.d., www.pcr.uu.se/research/ucdp/definitions/definition_of_armed_conflict.
95 Ibid.
96 CAB/9/G/89/3, Public Records Office of Northern Ireland.
97 For instance, the World Conference on Human Rights' Vienna Declaration and Programme of Action at article 5 states that "All human rights are universal, indivisible and interdependent and interrelated." United Nations World Conference on Human Rights, *Vienna Declaration and Programme of Action*, 25 June 1993.
98 This point has already been referred to in the previous chapter and in the decade prior to the CRM Northern Ireland had witnessed the IRA Border Campaign.
99 See in this context Susan McKay, *Bear in Mind These Dead* (London: Faber & Faber, 2008).
100 Johan Galtung first developed the theory of structural violence and argued its relationship with direct violence in "Violence, Peace, and Peace Research", *Journal of Peace Research* 6, no. 3 (1 January 1969): 167–91.
101 This matter as well as other human rights measures enacted in the period from the mid-1970s to the mid-1990s will be addressed in the next chapter.
102 The continuing importance of human rights in Northern Ireland may be evidenced from the fact that human rights provisions were included in the The Sunningdale Agreement, 1973, para. 11, Anglo-Irish Treaty, 1921, Art. 5–6,

John Major and Albert Reynolds, *Joint Declaration on Peace: The Downing Street Declaration*, 15 December 1993, para. 5; and, of course, The Northern Ireland Peace Agreement (The Belfast Agreement), accessed 16 June 1998, http://peacemaker.un.org/sites/peacemaker.un.org/files/IE%20GB_980410_Northern%20Ireland%20Agreement.pdf.

103 See Chapter 1.

104 See Chapter 1.

105 Richard English, *Armed Struggle: The History of the IRA* (London: Pan Books, 2004), 85–8.

106 See, for example: "Offences of Genocide in North", *Irish News*, 5 March 1969; "400,000 Students Back North's CR Movement", *Irish News*, 30 November 1968; "Social Justice March in England", *Belfast Telegraph*, December 1968; and "Rights: Baptist Pledges Support", *Belfast Telegraph*, 21 November 1968.

107 See Chapter 1.

108 See Chapter 1.

109 ICP, *Human Rights in Northern Ireland* (International Commission of Jurists, 1969).

110 See, for example, in January 1969: "How the Russians See Us", *Belfast Telegraph*, 22 January 1969; "Sorrow over NI: Vatican Newspaper", *The Irish Times*, 8 January 1969; "Le Monde Asks How Long Can Britain Stay Aloof?", *Irish News*, 14 January 1969; "US Sees Mirror in Ulster", *Belfast Telegraph*, 8 January 1969.

111 "Bloody Sunday" refers to an incident that happened on 30 January 1972 in Derry when, during a protest against internment organised by NICRA, the British Army shot dead 14 civilians taking part in the protest. These facts were ascertained by the Report of the Bloody Sunday Inquiry chaired by Lord Saville. See http://webarchive.nationalarchives.gov.uk/20101017060814/http://report.bloody-sunday-inquiry.org, accessed 23 January 2015.

5 Rights, violence and negotiations, 1971–1984

Introduction

The period covered in this chapter is a long one but from a human rights point of view it was dominated by a limited number of concerns. The first concern was the introduction of internment which was to have a catastrophic effect on the relationship between the Catholic community and the Northern Ireland (and British) governments. This issue is intimately connected with the rise in violence throughout the Province, which was in itself a matter of grave concern from a human rights perspective. A related concern was the treatment and status of detainees and prisoners. This latter issue would have a deep practical and symbolic importance that would lead to the electoral rise of Sinn Féin as well as a sustained attack on the British government by the IRA. A third relevant issue in terms of human rights refers to the efforts made at reaching a political settlement in Northern Ireland from the early 1970s to the mid-1990s. These efforts, as will be seen, all sought to deal with human rights concerns including issues of political representation and democracy. Finally, the period in question also witnessed continuing efforts at improving the socioeconomic situation in Northern Ireland.

One of the fundamental points addressed in this chapter relates to how in Northern Ireland two distinct trajectories were created with respect to human rights because of the descent into violent conflict. One trajectory saw rights language and concern lose momentum as a result of violence, internment and other aspects of the conflict. Radicalisation of important segments of the minority community (and then also of segments in the majority community) led to a narrowing of the human rights focus. Essentially, we witness a return to the primacy of the right to self-determination at the expense of other rights as one trajectory. The other trajectory sees rights language maintaining its role in the political discourse of Northern Ireland and gradually buttressed by the impact of the expanding corpus of international human rights norms. By the end of the period this latter trajectory is once more ascending and provides a solid space upon which the Peace Agreement with its abundant human rights language can gain widespread acceptance.

This chapter essentially demonstrates two important strands in Northern Ireland vis-à-vis human rights. In the first instance, it emphasises how human rights violations assisted the descent into violence and how this descent into violence in its turn exacerbated human rights violations. Hence, it is argued that human rights breaches, in effect, helped alter significantly the political scenario in Northern Ireland. It did so both in terms of a shift in the political discourse with the return to the primacy of self-determination and in terms of introduction of direct rule with its attendant political consequences. The analysis of specific instances of serious human rights violations by state and non-state actors is of importance given that abuses by state actors were used to justify violence against an oppressive state by paramilitaries such as the IRA. On the other hand, human rights abuses by paramilitaries such as the IRA were used by unionist politicians (and the UK government) to depict these paramilitaries as terrorists and, at the same time, also allowed unionists to question the use of human rights language by republicans and brand it as hypocritical. Second, this chapter highlights how in parallel with the human rights abuses, violence and focus on self-determination, human rights maintained some of its role in the political agenda. This role, as will become apparent, never disappeared and indeed eventually became an indispensable component of the political settlement. This chapter explores how these two strands developed in parallel throughout the period under examination.

Violence and internment: human rights issues

The breakdown in the security situation in Northern Ireland was already referred to in the preceding chapter while alluding to the civil rights marches. The situation deteriorated rapidly in the summer of 1969, especially in the aftermath of the summer marching season. The events of 1969 were especially critical to the emergence of the Provisional IRA within the Northern Ireland landscape. The Provisional IRA came to the fore consequent to the communal violence that ensued after the Battle of the Bogside that, while initially localised in Derry, spread to other locations, especially in Belfast. As violence escalated, the Provisional Irish Republican Army emerged from the existing Irish Republican Army as a defender of the Catholic community against violence from Protestant mobs and security forces. The Official IRA had long been dormant and was accused of failing to defend the Catholic community. The Provisional IRA conversely presented itself and was seen by sections of the Catholic community as their defenders.[1] On the unionist side, the rise of loyalist paramilitaries was, in its turn, presented as defending Northern Ireland against republican violence and against republican attempts at destroying the union between Northern Ireland and the United Kingdom. It is significant that one of the two main loyalist organisations was named the Ulster Defence Association (which was formed in 1971 as a network of loyalist armed groups).[2]

Because of the increase in rioting and other civil disturbances (including the Battle of the Bogside) the UK government deployed its troops in

Northern Ireland. The deployment of the British army was initially well received by the Catholic community as they had little faith in the RUC and thus viewed the British army as preferable to the RUC:

> A broad swathe of Catholic opinion, from the Catholic church and the Nationalist party through to the Independent Organisation accepted the presence of the army. They saw it as necessary, as much for the restoration of law and order and some form of "policing", as for the "defence" of Catholic areas in Derry.[3]

The honeymoon between the British army and the Catholic community did not last long. By the spring of 1970 the situation in Belfast had deteriorated, especially in light of the Ballymurphy riots, while in Derry the policing duties assumed by the army led to clashes with the Catholic community which had continued to protest against the Northern Irish state. The army adopted tough policing methods which further inflamed the already agitated Catholic community.

The early welcome given by the Catholic community to the British army is evident in one of the letters issued by the Campaign for Social Justice on the 28 December 1969. In this letter the CSJ castigated the failure of the Northern Ireland government to protect Catholic residents from attack and stated that "Army units were rushed across from Britain to take over from the Stormont regime the task of restoring law and order, before Catholics were able to venture out again from the shelter of hastily erected barricades."[4] The initial positive reaction to British troops is confirmed by NICRA which, in its 1972 *Dossier on Harassment and Brutality by the British Army in Northern Ireland*, noted that "in 1969, the British army was welcomed into these [Catholic] areas."[5] In 1972 the Sunday Times' Insight Team produced a book focusing on the descent into violence in Northern Ireland. Part of this book, written by investigative journalists of the newspaper, analysed the relationship between the Catholic community and the British army. It confirms the early positive impression made by the army on the Catholic community:

> The Army's relations with the Catholics were, of course, good as 1969 turned into 1970 – though to a large degree this merely reflected the fact that [army] relations with the Protestants were bad. There is some evidence that the Provisionals were unhappy about this fraternization.[6]

It is also suggested that the failure to ban the 1970 Orange Parades and the subsequent Falls Road search and curfew were the turning points in Army–Catholic relations in Northern Ireland. The authors quote a senior civil servant: "It was then that the Army began to be viewed in a different light. Before they had been regarded by the bulk of the Catholic population as protectors. The operation turned things absolutely upside down."[7]

Evidence of the deteriorating relationship may also be adduced from a letter sent to Catholic households by the Commanding Officer of the 2nd Battalion Royal Fusiliers in Belfast. The letter dated 23 December 1971 and signed by Lieutenant Colonel J. C. Reilly attempts to assuage the rising worries and anger of the Catholic community vis-à-vis the British army. It acknowledges that the army's operations "must be both embarrassing and annoying"[8] for the community but at the same time attempts to assure the community that the aim of the operations were "designed to assist in the arrest of individual gangsters who live or operate in your area and that they are not to be intended to be penal afflictions upon your community."[9] It concludes with an assurance that the troops have "firm instructions to be polite and quite impartial".[10] By 1972 the previously quoted NICRA dossier states that the army was

> not accepted as a peacekeeping force and in the people's eyes they have taken the place of the hated Royal Ulster Constabulary and the B. Specials ... even when the army is behaving within the limits of the law, they are seen and behave, like an army of occupation.[11]

This is an important statement since armies of occupation are perceived differently from ordinary forces of law and order to the extent that they are perceived by those who feel subjected to occupation as entities to be resisted rather than entities towards which they feel civil obligations. This also impacts negatively on human rights which depend, to some extent, and, particularly in certain situations, on the normal functioning of the civic space as policed by the forces of law and order. The breakdown of the relationship between the British Army and the minority community was epitomised in the events of Bloody Sunday. One of the key episodes which led to an intensification of the conflict and became part of nationalist iconography of the conflict was Bloody Sunday. The events of Bloody Sunday were long disputed until the 2010 Savile Inquiry Report arguably brought some degree of closure.

The initial facts are not in doubt: around 10,000 people gathered for a civil rights march on Sunday 30 January 1972. The Northern Irish government had decided to allow the march to proceed but not per the route planned by the organisers. The authorities decided that the march would be rerouted through the Catholic areas of Derry only. Because of this decision, the British Army sealed off the original route, which led the organisers to proceed towards the nationalist Bogside area of the city although several marchers decided to continue walking towards an army barricade. At the barricade, there was some rioting with stones thrown at the soldiers who responded with rubber bullets, water cannon and CS gas. The riot was beginning to disperse when soldiers of the 1st Parachute Regiment moved in with a view to arresting the rioters. However, in this context some of these paratroopers opened fire on the crowd, killing 13 men and injuring an equal number, one of whom died some months later. The Army claimed that they had been fired upon first while the leaders of the march and those present strongly refuted this allegation. The Savile Report eventually found that, on balance, the evidence indicated that the Army had fired first and without warning.[12] It also concluded that:

> The firing by soldiers of 1 PARA on Bloody Sunday caused the deaths of 13 people and injury to a similar number, none of whom was posing a threat of causing death or serious injury. What happened on Bloody Sunday strengthened the Provisional IRA, increased nationalist resentment and hostility towards the Army and exacerbated the violent conflict of the years that followed. Bloody Sunday was a tragedy for the bereaved and the wounded, and a catastrophe for the people of Northern Ireland.[13]

In the meantime, in the words of the then UK Prime Minister Edward Heath "as the violence intensified we [the British government] were put under immense pressure from [Northern Ireland's Prime Minister] Faulkner to introduce internment".[14] Heath also realised that such a move would "completely alienate moderate Catholic opinion in the both the north and the south of Ireland" and was concerned that internment would be used as a weapon against republicans in a disproportionate way.[15]

Nevertheless, the UK government consented to the introduction of internment and on 9 August 1971 British troops arrested 337 Catholic men who were suspected of being active in the IRA.

The fact that all the internees belonged to the minority community reinforced the minority's view that the British army was also intent on discriminating against them. Prime Minister Faulkner's assurances that "[t]his is not action taken against any responsible and law abiding section of the community" and that it was "not in any way punitive or indiscriminate" did not persuade the Catholic minority. Increasingly the minority community felt threatened and besieged by security forces which it considered unfair. In this context, an expanding number of Catholics perceived the IRA as their only possible protector and thus both looked to it for support and also entered its ranks.

From a human rights viewpoint internment is a clear breach of the right to liberty and fair trial. Article 9 of the Universal Declaration of Human Rights states that "[n]o one shall be subjected to arbitrary arrest, detention or exile", while Article 10 provides that everyone should have "a fair and public hearing by an independent and impartial tribunal, in the determination of his rights and obligations and of any criminal charge against him". More pertinently to Northern Ireland, the European Convention on Human Rights in Article 5 provides a detailed explanation of the situations where an individual may be arrested or detained. Article 5(1)(c) states that a person may be detained in cases where the detention is a result of:

> the lawful arrest or detention of a person effected for the purpose of bringing him before the competent legal authority of reasonable suspicion of

> having committed an offence or when it is reasonably considered necessary to prevent his committing an offence or fleeing after having done so.

In such a case, the Convention stipulates that anyone who is

> arrested or detained in accordance with the provisions of paragraph 1(c) of this article shall be brought promptly before a judge or other officer authorized by law to exercise judicial power and shall be entitled to trial within a reasonable time or to release pending trial. Release may be conditioned by guarantees to appear for trial.

Thus, internment which consists of detention without trial is a clear breach of the provisions on liberty of person within the Convention. Nevertheless, the same Convention allows states to derogate from certain provisions in cases of emergency. Article 15 allows States to "take measures derogating from its obligations under this Convention to the extent strictly required by the exigencies of the situation" when such States are in a situation of war or otherwise facing a public emergency threatening the life on the nation.

The UK (and at the time the Republic of Ireland) had already resorted to internment in 1957 in an effort to combat the IRA's Border Campaign. Within this context, the UK government in 1957 lodged a notice of derogation from Article 5, which notice was never withdrawn. The notice was thus still applicable when internment was reintroduced in 1971. Within these parameters, the use of internment in 1971 was not in breach of the UK's obligations under the European Convention on Human Rights. This was confirmed by the European Court of Human Rights which also found that it had not been "established that the said derogations exceeded the extent strictly required by the exigencies of the situation, within the meaning of Article 15 para. 1."[16] The Court's decision has been criticised in some quarters as it leaves significant discretion to State Parties to the Convention to decide when an emergency justifies derogation from the rights protected by the Convention and in particular that it lost an opportunity to condemn internment.[17] In particular Professor Brice Dickson commented that the Court "singularly failed to control" effectively the use of internment.[18]

However, one may argue that the fact that a notice of derogation is required to legalise internment implies that it is an objectionable practice from a human rights perspective. This was also implicitly accepted by Prime Minister Faulkner when announcing internment when he said that it "is with understandable reluctance that one uses such powers." It is interesting that in justifying the use of internment its proponents adopted human rights language. Indeed, it was argued that "the action we have now taken is not a policy of repression. We are not acting to suppress freedom, but to allow the overwhelming mass our people to enjoy freedom."[19]

The balance between freedom and security and the use of emergency measures (such as internment) to combat terrorist threats (or other emergencies) have emerged as crucial issues in human rights law post-9/11. In Northern Ireland internment clearly failed to improve the security situation. A serving British army officer pointed out that internment, far from securing a return of law and order, "increased terrorist activity, perhaps boosted IRA recruitment, polarised further the Catholic and Protestant communities and further reduced the ranks of the much-needed Catholic moderates."[20]

It is suggested that apart from the intrinsic objection to internment by those members of the minority community directly affected by the practice, the impact of internment was further exacerbated by the fact that it was almost exclusively directed against the minority community. Thus, to the Catholic community internment constituted further evidence of the discrimination which they had long claimed. The dangers of internment being used disproportionately against the Catholic community were envisaged by some within the British government. Prime Minister Heath "feared, rightly as it turned out, that the authorities in the province would use internment disproportionately as a weapon against Republicans."[21]

The accusation of two-weights, two-measures in the implementation of internment and its (almost) exclusive use against members of the minority community may be proven by referring to previously secret documents. In a document entitled "Arrest Policy for Protestants" prepared by the Commanding Officer of the British army in Northern Ireland it was stated that:

> The policy does not therefore provide for the arrest of Protestants or other non-Provisional terrorists except with the object of bringing a criminal charge. Protestants are not, as the policy stands, arrested with a view to their being made subject to Interim Custody Orders.[22]

In essence, this document proved that internment was, at least initially, only to be directed against Catholics and that Protestants would only be arrested where there was evidence sufficient to the preferring of criminal charges against them. The Northern Irish government recognised the dangers of such a policy in terms of public opinion in the United Kingdom (as well as Europe and the USA) and in terms of validating Catholic claims of discrimination. In fact at a Cabinet meeting of the Northern Irish government on 20 August 1971 – just ten days from the introduction of internment – the Minister of State at the Home Office suggested that "in view of the criticism that the application of detention was one-sided, it might be made known that one or two Protestants were among those arrested for suspected IRA activities."[23] Thus internment in Northern Ireland seemed to offend not only against the freedom from arbitrary arrest but also against norms of anti-discrimination.

From the security point of view internment did not seem to weaken visibly the IRA or to reduce the levels of violence in Northern Ireland. As quoted above some army officers accepted that the effect of internment was to strengthen the IRA within the Catholic community and others have also shared such a sentiment.[24] This view is widely held also in the nationalist/republican community. In his memoirs, Gerry Adams states that "internment had been undertaken to smash the IRA, but, far from succeeding in its aim, it confirmed the IRA in its role and boosted popular support."[25]

The impact of internment on the Catholic community is also attested to in the previously cited *Sunday Times* investigative report published in 1972. The authors assert that there were a number of immediate consequences to the introduction of internment within the Catholic community: (1) heavy sectarian rioting; (2) a strong stream of refugees into the Republic; and (3) a sustained increase in bombings and shootings.[26] They also confirm the view expressed by Gerry Adams when they claim: "The misuse of internment powers became one of the most potent forces driving moderate Catholics away from the middle ground and, in many cases, into the arms of the IRA."[27] The evidence, as shown above and as will be further amplified later, indicates that the introduction of internment was a key moment in shifting the focus of important segments of the Catholic community from civil rights towards resistance to British rule. However, this shift, as will be seen, was neither absolute nor complete. While rights language never disappeared from the political lexicon of Northern Irish politics (particularly with respect to the minority community) it gradually reasserted itself and played an important role in the political process that led to peace.

The British Army's attitude to internment as a method to control violence and enhance security seemed lukewarm. In fact, as late as 4 August 1971 (just five days prior to internment being announced) the UK Home Secretary had indicated to the Northern Ireland Prime Minster that the military authorities were not advocating its introduction: "As I understand it the GOC is not in present circumstances recommending internment on military grounds."[28] If the army was lukewarm about the efficacy of internment to control violence it was right to be so. In the immediate aftermath of internment, a serious escalation of violence occurred in Belfast and Derry. The violence in the years when internment was in force was among the highest of the whole conflict. In fact, 1972 registered the highest number of deaths, 479, of the entire conflict.

Kevin Boyle and Tom Hadden's verdict on the effect of internment is unequivocal: "The result [of internment] was to unite the whole Catholic community in opposition to the Stormont regime and to increase both the flow of recruits to the IRA and the level of terrorist activity."[29] The attitudes to internment within the Catholic community were obviously overwhelmingly negative. Nevertheless, it is worth noting the terms within which internment was opposed by the Catholic community. The calls for an end to internment were widespread, coming particularly from People's Democracy, republican clubs and Sinn Féin, the SDLP, the London-based Anti-Internment League, as well as several smaller groups under various names (including the United Front Against Internment, the People's Assembly of Ardoyne, the Political Hostages Release Committee amongst others). These calls came in different forms, with the SDLP mainly using its newsletter and generally trod a careful step between calling for an end to internment and also an end to violence. In the *SDLP News* of November 1972 the issue of internment was explained in clear human rights terms. This is, once more, a reminder of the continued role of rights language within the Catholic community:

> It may be argued by well-meaning critics that the SDLP resolve over the internment issue is a contradiction of the Party's expressed desire for political discussions. This is not so. On certain issues of fundamental justice, the SDLP will not, indeed cannot, budge.... The crucial point is the right of a citizen to a fair trial. Without that right, there is no basis for the rule of justice in the real sense.[30]

NICRA was very active in denouncing internment both in its NICRA newsletter as well as in numerous posters which it issued in the early 1970s. What is interesting in NICRA's attitude to internment is that it mainly took an accusatory approach based on a comparison of the Northern Ireland state to a Fascist/Nazi state. Upon inception NICRA attempted to stay away from the issue of partition or the legitimacy of the Northern Irish state. The introduction of internment seems to have changed this as it increasingly used Nazi symbolism and language. For example, the NICRA bulletin of 15 January 1972 refers to Brian Faulkner's "Hitlerian colours" and to "Concentration Camp", while its 22 January issue refers to Brian Faulkner as the British government's "local Gauleiter". Furthermore, a 1971 poster issued by NICRA shows the Union flag combined with the swastika. This shift within NICRA seems to mirror the broader developments of this period as outlined in the introduction to this chapter with the border re-emerging as the crucial political question. As further discussed below NICRA continued to use rights language but also moved from a position where it did not comment on the border issue to a position where it adopted a clearly anti-unionist rhetoric.

This is further exemplified by the radicalisation of NICRA against the British and Northern Irish state. This may be seen in the fact that whereas prior to internment it always referred to Northern Ireland it now started referring to the "Six Counties",[31] which in effect constituted non-recognition of the Northern Ireland state and is the term used by republicans. This radicalisation of NICRA's attitude had already emerged as the violence increased prior to the introduction of internment. In a 1970 poster[32] issued by the National Association for Irish Justice and calling for solidarity with NICRA, the NICRA aims were summarised as "1. Civil rights in Ulster now. 2. Free all Irish political prisoners. 3. Britain out of Ireland."[33] In a commentary to this poster it has been suggested that "as violence increased traditional Nationalist concerns [i.e. the border] began to predominate".[34] This poster also illustrates how NICRA was marrying rights language with the border issue calling for both civil rights and for Britain to withdraw from Ireland.

This is not to say that NICRA abandoned its human rights focus. Its literature retained this focus on civil rights with a call for people to join NICRA if they wanted "to release internees, end the Special Powers Act ... Democracy in Northern Ireland ... Freedom of Political Association and Expression ... end the British Reign of Terror".[35] In some cases its appeal married the issue of internment with a direct human rights concern. For example, one of its posters shows a hand clasping barbed wire (a reference to the internees) with a tagline that states "End Injustice, Demand a Bill of Rights Now".[36] This approach by NICRA seemed to combine the two trajectories referred to in the introduction to this chapter. NICRA is both retaining its traditional human rights language while at the same time concerning itself more with the border question and the issue of self-determination. In a sense, this encapsulates the story of human rights in Northern Ireland during the 1970s and early 1980s with the border question or the right to self-determination becoming the major concern while the broader human rights agenda was still being referred to regularly.

Nevertheless, it is surprising that overall the attitudes against internment by the various groups (not just NICRA) were not couched more clearly in human rights language. PD was particularly active in producing anti-internment posters and while it was always more radical and to the left of NICRA, its radicalisation deepened following the introduction of internment. It called for Stormont to be smashed and urged its supporters to "Fight for a Workers' Republic",[37] invited the public to "Join PD and Fight British Imperialism"[38] and, with unmistakeably Marxist rhetoric, it urged the "Workers of the World [to] Unite" and in the same poster made a call to "Free All Irish Political Prisoners".[39] The organisations engaged in advocating the end of internment used various types of imagery and language in their calls. Some attempted to create sympathy with the internees by reflecting on the pain internment caused to their families. For instance, NICRA had one poster with a child asking: "why won't you let daddy come home mister whitelaw?",[40] while a Political Hostages Release Committee poster from 1973 shows a mother and child facing a heavily guarded prison.[41] PD issued Christmas cards in 1971 portraying stylised World War II concentration camps thus re-emphasising the Nazi-like behaviour of the British and Northern Irish governments.

The concept of justice (or its antithesis injustice) also features in a number of anti-internment posters from the early 1970s. NICRA, in a previously cited poster, urges the people to "End Injustice", while a poster produced by the People's Assembly of Ardoyne stated that "The Occupants of this House believe Internment is Unjust. Release Internees Now."[42] In the same vein, an Anti-Internment League 1971 poster poses a question: "Internment without charge or trial in concentration camps: Is this British Justice?"[43] In comparison the posters making direct reference to human rights language are difficult to find. One exception is a poster produced by the United Front Against Internment (one of the numerous groups campaigning against internment) which focused on a particular internee: Mary Kennedy. Mrs. Kennedy's husband had already been interned when she was detained and the poster referred to the fact that the numerous children of the Kennedy's were thus denied both their parents. The poster then refers explicitly to Article 8 of the European Convention on Human Rights and claims that the internment of Mrs Kennedy constitutes a disruption of her family life in breach of Article 8.[44] This explicit reference to the European Convention is interesting as it suggests a degree of public consciousness of the Convention which supports the view that developments in international legal norms assist in expanding local conceptions of fairness and justice. Although Brice Dickson argues that in its early years the Convention was of "greater interest to lawyers than to politicians",[45] there seem to be sporadic references to the Convention which indicate some degree of public awareness.

At this juncture, it is also pertinent to point out that the SDLP also clearly objected to the use of violence by paramilitary organisations. In its proposals to the 1975 Constitutional Convention, the SDLP made this objection clear:

> the S.D.L.P. totally rejects violence as a means of achieving political ends. It has taken an unequivocal stand against all paramilitary organisations in Northern Ireland from the I.R.A. to the U.V.F. These paramilitary organisations are, in the opinion of the S.D.L.P., the bane of Northern Ireland society.[46]

This rejection of violence was reiterated several times by SDLP representatives, including by the SDLP leader John Hume in the House of Commons:

> The SDLP approach was set out before, during and after the election. We fought all corners. In particular, we fought the men of violence. It did not go unnoticed by anybody observing the political scene in Northern Ireland that the party most targeted by the political wing of the IRA was the party that I lead.... I particularly dislike the fact that it decides that the way to unite my country is to kill fellow citizens with whom it disagrees. I do not think that it requires great political intelligence to recognise that that only causes far deeper bitterness and division.[47]

The SDLP did not, however, explicitly use rights language in denouncing violence. Needless to say, unionist politicians also condemned IRA violence from the initial phases of the violent conflict. The penultimate unionist Prime Minister, James Chichester Clarke, argued in August 1969 that republican violence was "a deliberate conspiracy to subvert a democratically elected government."[48] This condemnation of violence by unionist politicians was repeated, inter alia, by Brian Faulkner: "Our aim is to eliminate violence irrespective of its source, we believe this is also the urgent desire of the vast majority of citizens of this country."[49] As already outlined with respect to the SDLP such a condemnation of violence was, however, not couched in human rights terms. The question arises as to why human rights language did not figure more prominently in these public displays of opposition to internment and violence. A number of reasons may be suggested. Nazi and World War II imagery and language may have been regarded as both popular (through history books, fiction and cinema) and shocking and thus a good vehicle to transmit the anti-internment message. Justice was a well known term that was thought to strike a chord with British sentiment. Another possibility is that as a result of the violence the human rights focus was, in some circles, narrowing back on to self-determination and resistance to British rule. Finally, human rights, in comparison with justice, Nazism or children rendered parentless by internment, was a more nebulous and perhaps less direct concept. It may also be significant that human rights were used in relation to a poster focusing on a particular individual rather than in the more generic ones. The net results of internment (from a human rights perspective) may be summarised as follows:

1 breaching the human rights of those subject to it, specifically the right to liberty and freedom from arbitrary arrest and detention;
2 enhancing the activities of an organisation (the IRA) devoted to using violence (including violence against civilians);
3 polarising further community relations;
4 widening irrevocably the breach between the minority community and the security forces. The latter result meant that whole Catholic neighbourhoods entrusted their "policing" to the IRA; and
5 narrowing the range of human rights that groups within the Catholic community sought to mobilise around.

Apart from the issues highlighted above, one may also suggest that the failure of internment led to the establishment of a more complex security-judicial apparatus to deal with terrorist activity. This apparatus, in itself, gave rise to human rights concerns which need to be assessed. Internment was officially discontinued on 5 December 1975. However, before that date numerous alternatives had been put into place within the Northern Ireland justice system. On 24 March 1972, the Northern Ireland Parliament and government were suspended (initially for a period of year) and replaced with direct rule of the province from Westminster. Thus, the British government became directly responsible for all aspects of government in Northern Ireland. The UK Prime Minister in announcing the introduction of direct rule to Northern Ireland highlighted that the reason behind this measure was the Northern Ireland government's refusal to surrender to the UK government de jure and de facto control over law and order in the province.[50]

The UK government's insistence on taking over complete control of law and order in Northern Ireland was intimately linked to internment (and its failure), as is evidenced by the position adopted by the UK government in its discussions with the Northern Ireland government prior to the imposition of direct rule. In a meeting between Mr. Heath and Mr. Faulkner two days prior to the imposition of direct rule, Mr. Heath had explained to Mr. Faulkner that internment had widened the divisions within Northern Ireland. Furthermore, while accepting that the UK government had agreed to internment, it was now in a situation where the UK government had "the responsibility and the blame for what happened as regards internment, but were without real power".[51] Thus it is evident that the introduction of internment and the impact this had on Northern Ireland were very major considerations in the move towards direct rule.

Once direct rule was introduced, the UK government (through the Secretary of State for Northern Ireland) had to deal with two major issues: the situation vis-à-vis law and order and the political situation. The latter issue will be examined in a later section. On the law and order front, the UK government had to deal with the escalating levels of violence as well as find alternatives to large-scale internment. The UK government did not, at this stage, revoke internment but only altered it, as well as introducing other measures to deal with terrorist activity. The main legislation was introduced in 1973 as the Northern Ireland (Emergency Provisions Act), which enacted serious changes to the criminal system in Northern Ireland in terms of the abolition of jury trials for certain criminal offences, rules of evidence, stop-and-search by security officers as well as the creation of new criminal offences such as belonging to certain organisations.

It has been argued that the Act was a manifestation of how "security became the dominant policy consideration".[52] The measures contained in the Act, in effect, created a separate criminal judicial system for persons suspected of committing terrorist acts. Human rights considerations were of limited concern in this context. The Committee on the Administration of Justice, reflecting on the impact of the Act in a "lessons learned" exercise done in the context of the post-September 11 war on terror, stated that:

> In subsequent years, internment fell into disuse but a range of limitations to the principles of due process were introduced: non-jury trials, lower burden of proof, the withdrawal of the right to silence, limited access to lawyers. These measures, when combined with limited oversight of interrogation techniques and allegations of ill-treatment, meant that in the eyes of many, the criminal justice system lost credibility in terms of upholding the rights of the thousands of individuals that came in contact with it.[53]

One may argue that the impact of internment, the emergency act and the ill-treatment of detainees (to be dealt later in this chapter) corroded the trust in the administration of justice on the part of the minority community. This, in itself, was a serious blow to the protection of human rights in Northern Ireland. The rights related to due process, equality before the law and liberty of person are all effected by such a corrosion of trust. Furthermore, by creating proscribed organisations and political offences related to such organisations, emergency legislation such as the 1973 Act (and its successors) politicises the criminal justice system and undermines the non-political role of judges. Internment and the 1973 Act with its attendant changes in the criminal justice system in Northern Ireland polarised the communities and deepened divisions. The political leaders of the majority community viewed both internment and the Act as tools used to protect them against IRA violence and the IRA's long-term goal of dragging them into a united Ireland.

There seems to be little doubt that between 1969 and 1975 violence became an integral part of Northern Ireland. The events of those years including internment, the deployment of British troops for policing duties and the rise in paramilitary violence all assisted in the creation of a culture of violence in Northern Ireland. A 1976 paper circulated to a governmental working party on law and order in Northern Ireland refers to "The Corruption of the Past 6 Years of Violence" and to "the inculcation of violence in the minds of young people."[54] Thus within the relatively short timeframe of five to six years violence had become part and parcel of life in Northern Ireland.

Attitudes to violence within the Catholic community were traditionally divided as between the republican and nationalist attitudes. Republicans largely accepted the physical-force tradition while nationalists renounced violence as a means of achieving desired political objectives. The escalation in violence that followed the introduction of internment seems to have deepened the divide between the two traditions and also shifted some sections of the community from nationalist to republican attitudes to violence.

The deepening of the divisions may be discerned in the language used by the opposing traditions. The SDLP, which continued the Nationalist Party tradition of constitutionalism and non-violence, was fervent in advocating an end to violence. It also linked the ending of internment with the ending of violence. This is clearly stipulated in its 1974 Manifesto entitled *Another Step Forward* where it claimed that SDLP politicians had been at the forefront of the campaign to end internment but were frustrated by the men of violence (i.e. IRA/Sinn Féin):

> They [SDLP MPS] have used all possible peaceful means available to them to bring it [internment] to an end and we suggest that their efforts to end it have been severely frustrated by the continuation of violence.... Violence and men of violence continue to frustrate our efforts to end internment.

The issue of the use of violence was also a cause of friction within the republican movement. The 1971 split between the Official and Provisional Sinn Féin/IRA, while mainly revolving around the question of political ideology (Marxism or socialism) within the party, also touched upon the issue of the role of violence and the armed struggle.[55]

The second aspect relates to the changing attitudes to violence (or the physical force tradition) within the nationalist community which until 1969–1971 was largely anti-violence. While a large majority of the nationalist community remained averse to the use of violence, sections within this community began to accept it as legitimate. This is witnessed by the growing numbers of Catholics joining the IRA – a phenomenon which had already been described – and also a change in the attitude of Catholics who did not join the IRA but came to view their actions as legitimate. An example of the latter is illustrated by the Sunday Times Insight Team who examined the case of a 21 year old Catholic, Kevin Duffy. Following his internment (on very flimsy evidence) and release he stated:

> "I really was a moderate before all this", Duffy said later. "I had no interest in politics and didn't like the methods the IRA used. Living in my house, you saw that Catholics and Protestants could live together peacefully. But everything has changed now." He was not going to rush out and take up a gun, but his attitudes had changed, at least to the extent that he no longer condemned the IRA for its violent methods.[56]

The increasing support for violence may also be gauged from the increasingly violent and militaristic language and imagery present in the posters produced by political parties in the period following 1971. A PD poster from 1974 bears the line "Fight, Don't Vote", with images of rioting in the background.[57] The IRA, naturally, produced numerous posters with military imagery including a poster with the word "Freedom" emerging from the barrel of a gun.[58] This militaristic and violent imagery/language is also evident in what was described as a "Children's Book" by the republican movement. *A Republican ABC* starts with the letter A stating: "A is for Armalite that sends them all running".[59] This language is accompanied by a drawing of a figure standing with the weapon at a street corner.

At the same time, IRA and Sinn Féin attempted to portray their use of violence as an issue of resistance to British imperialism and brutality. Thus, violence is rationalised as a defensive attitude against British aggression. An IRA poster from 1972 states: "***I****rish* ***R****esist* ***A****ggression … Support the Provisionals*".[60] In his abundantly documented and closely argued study of the IRA, Richard English suggests that "defence and anti-imperialist offence were, from early on, interwoven in the IRA's thinking."[61] English also refers to a January 1970 IRA Army Council decision to agree to a three-point plan: defence, retaliation and an attack on British forces that ultimately in their thinking would make "the state ungovernable and … make it more costly for the British to remain than it would be for them to go."[62] The theme of violence as defence is returned to in a much later Sinn Féin poster from 1990 which portrays images of Bobby Sands and Nelson Mandela with a quote from Mandela which includes the words: "Our resort to violence was purely a defensive action."[63] This acceptance of violence is also evident in the language and imagery of the loyalist paramilitary groups who in their turn used the violence of the IRA as their reasoning to resort to violence.[64]

As is evident from the previously quoted SDLP 1974 manifesto, a majority of the Catholic community still supported a non-violent approach. As the violence continued various groups also continued advocating non-violence. NICRA, as a civil rights organisation, did not diverge from its non-violent approach. In the mid-1970s it continued to advocate civil rights as an antidote to violence claiming that what was required in Northern Ireland was "A Bill of Rights to End Violence and Defuse Sectarianism".[65] Perhaps more surprisingly the Official Sinn Féin/IRA which remained active after the 1970 split were by 1975 also distancing themselves from the armed struggle as they took a Marxist attitude stating that "Sectarianism Kills Workers".[66] Groups like the Peace People were also active in promoting non-violence and reconciliation. Perhaps the most explicit rights-based campaign in Northern Ireland during the conflict was the 1976 A Better Life for All Campaign launched by the Northern Ireland committee of the Irish Congress of Trade Unions. Terry Carlin, who was one of the key persons behind the campaign, was clear about its inspiration:

> We based it around the conventions and covenants of the UN on both political and social, economic and cultural rights and the European Convention on Human Rights. I literally read the documents from top to bottom, and distilled what I regard as the six basic principles of right to live, free from violence, intimidation, sectarianism, discrimination, and the other rights are the right to advocate change by peaceful means, the right to adequate housing, health, education and so on.[67]

The above quote confirms that the body of international and regional human rights norms that was developing shaped to some extent political thinking at the time. People involved in the political process, in different scenarios, were being influenced by these developments and hence their political action was also influenced by these norms.

Nevertheless, these campaigns failed to achieve an end to violence which gradually became ingrained in Northern Irish life. The violence was perpetrated through three main entities: the republican paramilitaries, the loyalist paramilitaries and the security forces. Each of the three entities presented reasons for using violence in their activities. The republican paramilitaries (chiefly the Provisional IRA) explained their use of violence initially as protection for the Catholic community against attacks from loyalists and from the British army (violence was expressed as self-defence) and then more explicitly as a means of achieving unification with the Republic. In this latter phase violence was expressed in terms of national liberation and self-determination. Initially – in the more defensive phase – the IRA used violence almost exclusively against the security forces (RUC, B Specials and then the British army). However, it soon resorted to bombing campaigns that killed indiscriminately civilians and security personnel. Instances of bombs with indiscriminate effects are the Bloody Friday bombings (1972) and the Harrods bomb (1983). While the IRA always claimed that it gave adequate warning to the authorities of such bombs, Gerry Adams retrospectively criticised (in a rather muted way) the Bloody Friday bombings:

> It is a moot point whether the IRA operations just stretched the British too far for them to be able to cope with the situation, or whether they deliberately failed to act in relation to two of the bombs, but it is clear the IRA made a mistake in putting out so many bombs, and civilians were killed who certainly should not have been killed. This was the IRA's responsibility and a matter of deep regret.[68]

Loyalist paramilitaries, such as the Ulster Volunteer Force (UVF), explained their use of violence as a means to destroy the IRA and also as a means to ensure that Northern Ireland would remain part of the United Kingdom. Once again, it must be stressed that these loyalist paramilitaries engaged in indiscriminate bombings, such as the McGurk's Bar bomb or the Dublin and Monaghan car-bombings of 1974.

From a human rights perspective, the use of violence against civilians is completely abhorrent, even if, as the IRA claimed, it was acting as a national liberation movement engaged in a war against a colonial power. Violence against civilians is a very grave violation of the laws of war as enshrined in international humanitarian law. The Fourth Geneva Convention of 1949 in Article 3 states that in conflicts of a non-international character, civilians (including members of armed forces who have laid down their arms and those placed hors de combat) are given the following protection:

> To this end the following acts are and shall remain prohibited at any time and in any place whatsoever with respect to the above-mentioned persons:
>
> (a) violence to life and person, in particular murder of all kinds, mutilation, cruel treatment and torture; ....

There is no doubt that the paramilitaries fell short of these international law provisions and humanitarian principles. Each civilian killed, maimed or otherwise injured by paramilitary organisations constitutes a grave breach of humanitarian law and is a serious affront to the concept and practice of human rights.

The security forces, including the British army, were also involved in the use of violence in Northern Ireland. However, the assessment of the use of violence by the army and police force is more problematic in the sense that law-and-order personnel are entitled to use force in specific circumstances. The line between the legitimate use of force for the maintenance of law and order and the use of illegal force may be a difficult one to draw. Nevertheless, whatever the difficulties of ascertaining the line mentioned above, there is no doubt that the British Army and the RUC in Northern Ireland were guilty of using unwarranted violence. The previously quoted Saville Report on Bloody Sunday appointed by the British government in 1998 and reporting in 2010 concluded that "None of the casualties was posing a threat of causing death or serious injury, or indeed was doing anything else that could on any view justify their shooting." UK Prime Minister David Cameron reacted to the findings of Lord Saville by saying: "The conclusions of this report are absolutely clear. There is no doubt. There is nothing equivocal, there are no ambiguities.... What happened on Bloody Sunday was both unjustified and unjustifiable. It was wrong."[69]

Another episode which impacted negatively on the perception of the security forces by the minority in Northern Ireland and on the right to life protected through international human rights law refers to what was termed the shoot-to-kill policy in the early 1980s. This concerned the allegation that a number of suspects were deliberately killed by the police and army without any attempt to arrest them. Three such incidents between November and December 1982 led to the calling of an inquiry headed by the Deputy Chief Constable of Greater Manchester, John Stalker, to investigate the allegations relating to the existence or otherwise of a shoot-to-kill policy. Stalker eventually resigned due to allegations that he was involved with criminals, although he was cleared of all such accusations. The inquiry was then assigned to the Chief Constable of West Yorkshire, Colin Sampson. The report from the inquiry was never made public, although Stalker did publish his findings in a publication.[70] The shoot-to-kill policy was to come to even greater public attention during the Gibraltar killings by the SAS which will be returned to later.

Insofar as the RUC is concerned, the Cameron report – cited in the preceding chapter – while acknowledging the stress under which the RUC was operating and the correct behaviour of the majority of the police officers, had no hesitation in stating that:

> We have to record with regret that our investigations have led us to the unhesitating conclusion that on the night of 4th/5th January a number of policemen were guilty of misconduct which involved assault and battery, malicious damage to property in streets in the predominantly Catholic Bogside area giving reasonable cause for apprehension of personal injury among other innocent inhabitants, and the use of provocative sectarian and political slogans.[71]

The unionist leaders have generally defended unambiguously the actions of the security forces, holding that the security forces were defending law and order and, particularly, the safety of law abiding citizens. They also emphasised the difficult conditions in which the security forces were operating and the IRA attacks which targeted them continuously. Nevertheless, the use of violence by security forces is particularly relevant from a human rights perspective on two counts:

1 the breach of the right to life of the victims;
2 the fact that this breach was perpetrated by agents of the State.

Human rights abuses perpetrated by agents of the state are especially noteworthy as the state is primarily responsible under international law for the protection and promotion of human rights. Furthermore, once state organs start using violence they contribute to the inculcation of a culture of violence in society.

Apart from the use of violence in overt operations, other issues arose vis-à-vis the use of covert force by security forces. The covert use of violence by security forces is of salience with regards to extrajudicial killings and the use of torture or inhuman treatment during the interrogation of detainees. As indicated above this latter issue of torture will be dealt with below. The concept of extrajudicial killings refers to the intentional killing of terrorist suspects who are not in the actual process of committing criminal acts. The European Convention on Human Rights allows state security forces to kill individuals in certain defined circumstances. This can be deduced from the wording of Article 2 which states that:

> Deprivation of life shall not be regarded as inflicted in contravention of this Article when it results from the use of force which is no more than absolutely necessary:
>
> (a) in defence of any person from unlawful violence;
> (b) in order to effect a lawful arrest or to prevent the escape of a person lawfully detained;
> (c) in action lawfully taken for the purpose of quelling a riot or insurrection.

While this wording allows killings in these cases, the use of force that brings about the loss of life has to be "no more than absolutely necessary". A test of absolute necessity has to be overcome by security forces in justifying force that leads to loss of life. In the case of *McCann and Others* v. *United Kingdom*, the European Court of Human Rights stressed the importance of absolute necessity. The case concerned the shooting of three IRA members who were shot dead by the SAS unit of the British army. The SAS had intelligence which led them to believe that the three IRA members were in possession of a remote-control device which was to be used to detonate a car-bomb in Gibraltar. The SAS claimed that their operatives fired to kill the three IRA members in the belief that the latter were about to detonate the car-bomb and thus the killings fell within the test of "absolute necessity". In reality the intelligence proved inaccurate and the men possessed no such detonator at the site where they were killed. Most importantly, the UK government failed to stop the three IRA members from entering Gibraltar when they could have done so. The Court, by a very narrow margin, found that a violation of Article 2 had been committed by the UK government on the following grounds:

> In sum, having regard to the decision not to prevent the suspects from travelling into Gibraltar, to the failure of the authorities to make sufficient allowances for the possibility that their intelligence assessment might, in some respects at least, be erroneous and to the automatic recourse to lethal force when the soldiers opened fire, the Court is not persuaded that the killing of the three terrorists constituted the use of force which was no more than absolutely necessary in defence of persons from unlawful violence within the meaning of Article 2.[72]

While there was disagreement within the Court on whether the facts of the case were such as to pass the test of absolute necessity, the Court was unanimous in finding that the test should be a strict one. This seems to endorse the view that the use of violence by the state should be judged very strictly. It may be argued that such strictness is in keeping with the notion that the State should not resort to the use of violence except in the gravest of circumstances. Finally, this case, which was the first to deal in detail with Article 2, was, as Dickson points out, a critical one for the Court itself and indeed "was a turning point in the Court's own development".[73] As stated in the introduction to this chapter a significant examination of these human rights violations is important insofar as they were a critical contributor to the views held by the two communities towards human rights and towards the other community. For republicans, human rights abuses by state actors were used as a justification of the armed struggle against a state perceived to be oppressive, while for the broader nationalist community it hardened their view that the UK and Northern Irish state actors were prepared to abuse their human rights notwithstanding existing national and international obligations not to do so. This necessarily lessened the legitimacy of the UK state in the view of the nationalist community. From a unionist and UK government perspective the human rights abuses perpetrated by the republican paramilitaries (chiefly the IRA) were a confirmation of their belief that these paramilitaries were in effect terrorist organisations. Such violations also allowed them to portray the IRA as a terrorist organisation, which assisted in the introduction of emergency legislation purportedly to deal with such terrorist activities. The emergency legislation in itself further eroded human rights standards of protection in Northern Ireland and further eroded the trust of the minority community in the state.

Prisoners: rights and status

The issue of internment, discussed in the preceding section, brought to the fore another aspect of human rights practice: the rights of detainees. Internment brought about a huge increase in the number of detained persons in Northern Ireland. During internment and in the period following internment, when arrests for terrorist activity increased dramatically, accusations of torture and ill-treatment in detention centres also increased. The accusations made by members of the minority community focused initially on the ill-treatment of those detained during Operation Demetrius. In his memoirs Gerry Adams claims that those interned where subjected to numerous practices such as beatings around the kidneys, between the legs, on the back and on the back of the legs.[74]

There is now no doubt that ill-treatment did occur, as was established by the European Court of Human Rights in the case of *Ireland* v. *United Kingdom*.[75] In this case the matter was first referred to the European Commission of Human Rights (as was the practice at the time) which found that a number of practices to which detainees were subjected in Northern Ireland constituted torture within the meaning of Article 3 of the Convention.[76] The case was then referred to the Court for a final decision and the Court decided the practices complained of by the applicant while not constituting torture did constitute inhuman treatment which is also prohibited in Article 3. While it is beyond the scope of this study to define the line between torture and inhuman treatment the fact that the British state was found guilty of inhuman treatment reinforces the claim that the protection of human rights in Northern Ireland was seriously deficient and that the state must assume a share of the responsibility for this deficiency. This case also highlights how the issue of internment was also addressed through the European human rights mechanism, which underscores the role that regional norms were playing within the conflict and the political situation more broadly. This links to the earlier point referring to the explicit reference to the ECHR in the previously cited Better Life For All Campaign. The impact of this case on the political situation is also very relevant since, as Dickson has argued, the "ramifications on the European Court's decision … were significant, but perhaps more at the political level than at the human rights level" and "it served to put the Northern Irish conflict on the European, if not the world, legal stage."[77] It is worth noting that this case has re-emerged in recent years as a matter of public debate with claims that the case should be revisited by the UK (and European) courts given that UK Ministers knew that torture was being practiced. In June 2015 leave was granted to the affected men allowing them to seek judicial review of their case by the High Court.[78]

Apart from the matter of torture and inhuman treatment, the arrest and detention of IRA operatives and other paramilitaries gave rise to the issue of the status which such prisoners should have. The UK government upon the introduction of internment decided to assign to the internees a special category status. This was, in part, a reflection of the specific nature of internment and an implicit recognition that the detention of internees was a *sui generis* situation. The decision to award special category status would prove, like the decision to introduce internment, a fateful one.

Once the internees were gradually replaced by prisoners whose arrest was validated by a court of law and who were found guilty of certain offences (mainly offences introduced under the Emergency Provisions Act cited above) the special category status was also extended to such prisoners.

The essential feature of such a status was that it distinguished between those found guilty of crimes of a paramilitary character and "ordinary" criminals who were guilty of regular criminal offences. Such a special status entitled those who obtained it certain privileges such as not wearing prison uniform and free association with other prisoners with the same status. The inference through these distinctions was that detainees who had special category were not criminals and the IRA, in particular, was keen to portray such detainees as political prisoners. This distinction allowed the detainees who had special status to avoid the stigma associated with criminality and instead were perceived in some parts of the nationalist community as brave young men fighting for a political cause. This, in turn, aided the IRA in its efforts to recruit volunteers.

Soon the UK government realised that the award of special category status to prisoners convicted of paramilitary-related offences was aiding the IRA in its efforts to portray itself as a national liberation movement rather than a terrorist organisation. The UK government thus decided to discontinue the award of special category status for prisoners convicted after the 1975 Gardiner Report recommended its discontinuance. This decision resulted in a series of protests by the prisoners denied special status culminating in the 1981 hunger strike, the election of Bobby Sands to the Westminster Parliament and the death of ten hunger strikers (including Bobby Sands).

From a human rights perspective, the issues which are most pertinent to examine in the context of the status of prisoners are the following:

1 Did the prisoners claiming special status have a right to such status under human rights law or international humanitarian law?
2 Were the acts of the prisoners (and their respective paramilitary organisations) in pursuing their claim for special status legitimate from a human rights viewpoint?
3 Were the acts of the British government in dealing with the claims of the prisoners (and the activities pursued by them to achieve such an end) compliant with human right laws and principles?

Insofar as the right to claim special status is concerned, the relevant principles may be deduced from the Universal Declaration of Human Rights, the International Covenant on Civil and Political Rights, the European Convention on Human Rights and the Geneva Convention III of 1948. The Declaration and the European Convention make no reference to such a right to special status. They only prohibit arbitrary arrest and detention while stipulating guarantees of due process. The Covenant is more expansive in this respect. Article 10 stipulates that:

> 1. All persons deprived of their liberty shall be treated with humanity and with respect for the inherent dignity of the human person.
> 2. (a) Accused persons shall, save in exceptional circumstances, be segregated from convicted persons and shall be subject to separate treatment appropriate to their status as unconvicted persons; …

Thus, the only distinction that the Covenant requires is that between accused persons as opposed to convicted persons. Convicted persons only have right to be treated with humanity and respect (a matter that will be relevant in terms of question 3 above) but do not qualify for any special status with reference to the nature of the crimes they are convicted of.

The remaining legal instrument which needs to be examined is the Third Geneva Convention relative to Prisoners of War of 1948. This Convention regulates the treatment of prisoners of war during armed conflict. The Convention regulates, almost exclusively, armed conflict of an international nature. However, it does establish certain rules (in Article 3) applicable to armed conflict of a non-international nature. These rules do not refer to a separate status for detainees as they only refer to the humane treatment of such detainees. The 1977 Additional Protocol I to the Geneva Conventions also covers situations of a non-international character. In this Protocol the question of detainees in circumstances of non-international armed conflicts is dealt with more amply. The Protocol provides for the granting of prisoner-of-war status to combatants. Article 43 defines combatants as

> the armed forces of a Party to a conflict consist of all organized armed forces, groups and units which are under a command responsible to that Party for the conduct of its subordinates, even if that Party is represented by a government or an authority not recognized by an adverse Party. Such armed forces shall be subject to an internal disciplinary system which, inter alia, shall enforce compliance with the rules of international law applicable in armed conflict.

Within this definition of combatant, it is doubtful that members of the IRA would qualify as combatants given that they may not fulfil the condition that they conduct their operations "in compliance with the rules of international law applicable in armed conflict". The UK government certainly believed that the IRA deliberately targeted civilians[79] while the IRA has always denied this.

In any event, Additional Protocol I also provides that:

> 1. Any combatant, as defined in Article 43, who falls into the power of an adverse Party shall be a prisoner of war.
> 2. While all combatants are obliged to comply with the rules of international law applicable in armed conflict, violations of these rules shall not deprive a combatant of his right to be a combatant or, if he falls into the power of an adverse Party, of his right to be a prisoner of war, except as provided in paragraphs 3 and 4.
> 3. In order to promote the protection of the civilian population from the effects of hostilities, combatants are obliged to distinguish themselves from the civilian population while they are engaged in an attack or in a military operation preparatory to an attack. Recognising, however, that there are situations in armed conflicts where, owing to the nature of the hostilities an armed combatant cannot so distinguish himself, he shall retain his status as a combatant, provided that, in such situations, he carries his arms openly:
>
>   (a) during each military engagement, and
>   (b) during such time as he is visible to the adversary while he is engaged in a military deployment preceding the launching of an attack in which he is to participate.
>
>   Acts which comply with the requirements of this paragraph shall not be considered as perfidious within the meaning of Article 37, paragraph 1(c).
> 4. A combatant who falls into the power of an adverse Party while failing to meet the requirements set forth in the second sentence of paragraph 3 shall forfeit his right to be a prisoner of war, but he shall, nevertheless, be given protections equivalent in all respects to those accorded to prisoners of war by the Third Convention and by this Protocol. This protection includes protections equivalent to those accorded to prisoners of war by the Third Convention in the case where such a person is tried and punished for any offences he has committed.

The net effect of the provisions quoted above, in the case of the Northern Ireland context, is that IRA operatives clearly failed the test provided in sub-article 3 above in terms of distinguishing themselves from the civilian population during military operations. Indeed, the success of IRA activities depended on not being distinguishable from the civilian population. Thus, IRA operatives would under sub-article 4 be denied prisoner of war status whereas they would still be entitled to humane treatment.

A further complication arises in this context since the British government never accepted that the violence in Northern Ireland constituted a non-international armed conflict whereas it always classified the IRA as a terrorist organisation. The continuing references to The Troubles as opposed to conflict in British media seemed designed to reinforce the view that the conflict in Northern Ireland did not constitute civil war. This enabled the British government to maintain that the situation in Northern Ireland remained a purely internal affair and also to eschew the possibility of applying the norms of international humanitarian law.

While it appears that prisoners belonging to paramilitary organisations could not avail themselves of the protection granted to prisoners of war in terms of international humanitarian law, other human rights concerns emerge. The position of the British government was essentially that individuals who were convicted of terrorist-related activities under the Emergency Powers Act were to be treated in the same manner as other convicted prisoners.

The prisoners themselves claimed that they were political prisoners and that as such they were entitled to special category status which in effect meant that they claimed five specific demands:

1 to wear their own clothes;
2 to refrain from prison work;
3 to associate freely with one another;
4 to organise recreational facilities and to have one letter, visit and parcel a week;
5 to have lost remission fully restored.[80]

The prisoners themselves claimed that they had a right to special category status and to these specific privileges on the basis that they were imprisoned on the basis of their political beliefs. This is evidenced in the case brought before the European Commission of Human Rights by a group of prisoners in the Maze. One of the complaints made by the prisoners was that they considered themselves as "political prisoners" and thus "should not be subjected to the same prison regime as other prisoners convicted of 'ordinary' criminal offences".[81] This view was unambiguously rejected by the European Commission of Human Rights. The Commission stated that:

> the applicants are seeking to achieve a status of political prisoners which they are not entitled to under national law or the Convention. Furthermore … the Commission does not consider that such an entitlement in the present context may be derived from existing norms of international law.[82]

However, others in Northern Ireland argued that the special category status which was claimed by the prisoners should derive not so much from the fact that these prisoners were political prisoners but rather as a consequence of the legislation under which their convictions were secured. This point was made by the SDLP[83] as well as by the leaders of the Catholic Church in Northern Ireland:

> The authorities refuse to admit that these prisoners are in a different category from the ordinary, yet everything about their trials and family background indicates that they are different. They were sentenced by special courts without juries. The vast majority were convicted on allegedly voluntary confessions obtained in circumstances which are now placed under grave suspicion by the recent report of Amnesty International.[84]

The argument expressed here is based on the special nature of the legislation under which, and through which, a large number of prisoners were arrested and convicted. The Emergency Provisions Act as already mentioned did away with trial by jury, made convictions easier to secure through special rules of evidence, etc. Thus, the argument was that individuals convicted through special legislation merited a special status. The UK government consistently and persistently rejected this view and held that

> what we have here are some 350 prisoners who have been convicted through the criminal courts of some of the most serious offences; who before being sentenced had available all the normal safeguards including the laws of evidence, access to legal representation and the right of appeal – without leave – to a higher court; and who themselves have created conditions of squalor in order to draw attention to their claim to be treated differently from other sentenced prisoners.[85]

While the human rights law at the time did not recognise the right to special category status for individuals convicted through special legislation, the perception amongst a part of the nationalist community was that these convictions were not fairly arrived at. Concern with the special nature of the legislation under which the prisoners were detained, charged and convicted was also evident in smaller groups operating outside the mainstream political parties. The Anarchist Information Group in one of its posters stated the following: "The British Government says that those who oppose them in Northern Ireland are criminals. Yet there is: Special Legislation, Special Holding Powers, Special Interrogations, Special Juryless Courts, Special Prisons. Support the Irish hunger strikers for Special Status."[86] Those sections of the population supporting the prisoners explicitly referred to the humanitarian law concept of prisoners of war.

Expressions of support referred to "Support Irish Prisoners of War",[87] "Prisoners of War Aren't Criminals"[88] and in even more explicit rights-talk: "Irish Nationalist Prisoners are denied all rights as Prisoners of War by the British Government".[89]

This feeling was compounded by the perceived inflexibility of the British government in dealing with the demands of the prisoners. Once special category status was removed, prisoners convicted of offences under the Emergency Provisions Act sought to pressure the British government into acceding to their demands through various protests. The three form of protests adopted successively (and at some points simultaneously) by the protesters were the "blanket protest", the "dirty protest" and the hunger strike. The response to these protests by the British government ultimately increased support for the prisoners within their own community, exacerbated community tensions, worsened the relationship between the minority and the British government and led to grave human rights abuses (including self-inflicted ones).

In particular, the dirty protest and the hunger strike led to self-inflicted human rights abuses for the prisoners who followed them. Commenting on the dirty protest and its effects the European Commission of Human Rights in the previously cited McFeeley case stated that:

> The Commission has no doubt that the above described conditions are "inhuman and degrading" within the meaning ascribed to them under the Convention. However, it must observe that these conditions are self-imposed by the applicants as part of their protest for "special category status".[90]

At the same time the Commission, while finding no breach of the Convention by the UK authorities, also criticised the British government for the "inflexible approach of the State authorities which has been concerned more with punishing offenders than to explore ways of resolving such a serious deadlock".[91] This criticism, which has been described as "a very rare example of a European Convention organ "daring" to give advice as to how best to resolve a difficult domestic issue",[92] also reflected on the failure of the British government to fully appreciate the humanitarian perspective which should have led the authorities to improve certain aspects of the prisoners' plight.

This situation was mirrored (albeit with more tragic consequences) in the hunger strikes of 1980 and 1981. At the end of the 1981 hunger strike ten prisoners had died, community relations deteriorated further and support for the IRA solidified. The success of Sinn Féin in electing Bobby Sands to the UK House of Commons during his hunger strike was an indicator of increasing support for republicanism and also a first step that saw the IRA/Sinn Féin move gradually but ultimately completely from the military to the political scenario. The dual impact of the hunger strike is well described by David McKittrick:

> The crisis plunged the province into one of the worst convulsions it has experienced, putting the population through communal trauma and laying the basis for a deadly cycle of increased violence.... And yet the paradox is that this struggle was to set the IRA and Sinn Féin on an unexpected new path which eventually led to the peace process.[93]

The immediate legacy of the hunger strike was a descent into a spiral of violence that exacerbated the human rights abuses of the right to life and physical integrity. From a long-term perspective the hunger strike also further sowed seeds of distrust and even hatred between the communities in Northern Ireland, which have not yet dissipated and which continue to impact on human rights in the province. And yet the success of Bobby Sands' election to the House of Commons and the huge propaganda victory that it constituted for IRA/Sinn Féin was instrumental in shifting the republican movement from a preponderantly military approach to a political platform that in time was to supplant the military dimension. The republican prisoners held in the H-Blocks at the time of the hunger strike were also turning their attention to electoral politics. A communication from the H6 Block prisoners to the Sinn Féin Ard Fheis proposed nine resolutions to be adopted including: allowing Sinn Féin to contest Dail elections on an absentionist platform, allowing Sinn Féin to participate in local elections in the north and to take up the seats, if elected, as well as the setting up of a youth wing of Sinn Féin.[94] These attempts at politicising the struggle came only five days after the end of the hunger strike and are further proof of the increasing realisation by Sinn Féin and IRA that the military approach alone was failing to achieve the desired results and that politics offered an alternative avenue which should be exploited. Gerry Adams acknowledges that republicanism from the 1950s to the 1970s was averse to politics and that "Sinn Féin was eclipsed by the IRA".[95] He also confirmed that the hunger strike was crucial in creating a mass movement for Sinn Féin through which the party established a strong political platform, which in turn was crucial in formulating a peace policy.[96]

All told, the issue of prisoners' rights and status in the Northern Irish conflict is one which touches upon various human rights and humanitarian law concerns. There is no doubt that numerous detainees in Northern Ireland were subjected to ill-treatment during their interrogations and detention. The 1979 Bennett Report commissioned by the Secretary of State for Northern Ireland highlighted the need to *maintain* vigilance with respect to interrogations in the context of adverse decisions of local and European courts against RUC officers as well as reports by Amnesty International.

There is probably no way of ascertaining the extent of such ill-treatment although its existence is clear. Nevertheless, the fact that ill-treatment occurred in police custody is both condemnable for its intrinsic wrongfulness as well as for increasing the sense of grievance in the minority community. Perceptions, always crucial in Northern Ireland, were once again focused on human rights abuses. The use of violence by state authorities as mentioned in the preceding section further contributed to the creation of a spiral of violence and further loosened the bonds of loyalty (admittedly already weak) between the state and those at the receiving end of such violence as well as their family, friends and community.

The prisoners' protest concerning their status provides similar insights although perhaps in a more complex scenario. In this case the root cause of the protest may, at least partially, be attributed to the UK government's decision to introduce internment and to suspend some of the rights of accused persons according to the Emergency Provisions Act and the Prevention of Terrorism Act. These decisions were technically legal in terms of international law since appropriate notices of derogation were lodged by the UK government. However, derogations from rights are still substantially breaches of rights which are allowed by law for reasons of security and order. As such, the prisoners could attach some validity to their claim that they were not ordinary criminals. Had the UK government used the ordinary laws to secure convictions and maintained the normal fair trial procedures there would have been far less sympathy for the prisoners' claims for special status. As shown more recently in the USA's anti-terror legislation, suspending human rights may seem an attractive option in the short term but it brings with it a spate of problems which may take a long time to overcome. The lessons of Guantanamo Bay bear testimony to this.

The foregoing examination of specific instances of serious human rights violations by state and non-state actors is relevant to this study for a number of reasons. First, abuses by state actors were used to justify violence against an oppressive state by paramilitaries such as the IRA. In fact, the IRA presented itself partially as a defensive institution protecting the minority population against the abuse of their rights by the state. Second, human rights abuses by paramilitary organisations such as the IRA were used by unionist politicians (and the UK government) to portray members of such paramilitary organisations as terrorists. Contemporaneously, the recording of these human rights abuses allowed unionists to question the use of human rights language by republicans which they increasingly resorted to and brand it as hypocritical. Finally, these human rights adjudications illustrate the extent to which political actors were using human rights instrumentally or the extent to which such actors had an incomplete understanding of human rights.

The modification of fair trial rights in Northern Ireland was followed by various prisoners' protests culminating in the 1981 hunger strike. It is impossible to conclude that without such suspension of rights the hunger strike would not have happened but the balance of probability lies in the direction that the suspension of rights rendered the descent into a spiral of human rights abuses more likely. The inflexibility of the UK government in the face of the prisoners' protests aggravated an already tragic situation. However, if one adopts a strictly human-rights focused approach to the prisoners' protests, one must conclude that they also contributed to an erosion of human rights culture in Northern Ireland. Human rights as described in the Universal Declaration of Human Rights are based on "recognition of the inherent dignity" of the human person. This statement found in the Preamble of the Declaration provides us with the underlying values of the Declaration and instructs the reader on how the Declaration should be read. Thus, any attack or affront to human dignity clashes with the values base of human rights.

Furthermore, a strict legal reading of Article 30 of the Declaration would support the view that no individual has a right to engage in any act which would breach any right established in the Declaration. It states that:

> Nothing in this Declaration may be interpreted as implying for any State, group or person any right to engage in any activity or to perform any act aimed at the destruction of any of the rights and freedoms set forth herein.

There appears to be no limitation on this duty which thus is an absolute one. Abusing one's own dignity or rights is thus contrary to the spirit and letter of the Declaration. This seems an inescapable conclusion when one reads the Declaration as it was intended to be read, i.e. as a whole.

It is worth noting that concern with special powers continued to be expressed both in Northern Ireland and in Great Britain throughout the period of the conflict. Special powers continued to be exercised throughout the period of the conflict with the introduction of the Prevention of Terrorism Act in 1974, which was routinely amended until 1989.[97] The Acts which were directed primarily against the IRA and loyalist paramilitary organisations contained numerous provisions concerning proscribed organisations, powers of arrest and detention etc., which were clearly limitations on, or derogations from existing human rights legislation. As time went by it appears that opponents of this legislation made more emphasis on its essentially anti-human rights character. A 1980s poster clamouring for the repeal of the Prevention of Terrorism Act stated clearly that "Its Powers are Draconian, It is an attack on Human Rights".[98] It may be argued that by the 1980s the salience and "marketing-power" of human rights had improved in Northern Ireland and the United Kingdom as a whole, thus making direct references to human rights more desirable. In this context, it is pertinent to note that 1981 saw the establishment of the CAJ as an independent human rights organisation within Northern Ireland. The CAJ would go on to play an important role in the human rights scenario of Northern Ireland in promoting human rights through campaigning, research and lobbying.[99]

It is quite striking that, notwithstanding the widely referred to radicalisation, the descent into violence engendered within both communities (explicitly referred to by the above-quoted Gerry Adams) there survives throughout the 1970s and 1980s a strand of rights-based discourse especially within the nationalist community. Even within republicanism appeals to international human rights law are apparent in, for example, campaigning for prisoners' rights. This use of rights language is partly attributable to the local engagement with issues of rights and discrimination since the 1920s (see Chapter 3) and partly attributable to the growing impact of international, regional and local human rights norms. One ought to note that at the international level the International Convention on the Elimination of All Forms of Racial Discrimination came into force in 1969, the ICCPR and ICESCR (referred to in Chapter 1) came into force in 1976, while the Convention on the Elimination of Discrimination Against Women was adopted in 1979. Clearly the late 1960s and the 1970s were a period of significant movement in international human rights law. At the European level, the ECHR was gradually finding its feet and within Britain the rights-based legislative initiatives of the mid- to late 1960s (such as the abolition of the death penalty, the decriminalisation of homosexual acts and the prohibition of racial discrimination) were also gradually leaving an impact on British society as a whole. Northern Ireland was thus impacted by external human rights influences which, however, built on local traditional concern and engagement with rights which had grown significantly because of the civil rights movement. This impact is evident to the extent that even in the most difficult and violent scenario of the 1970s and early 1980s within Northern Irish political discourse, the language of rights is still distinctly audible.

Human rights in negotiations

Throughout the conflict in Northern Ireland while the violence ebbed and flowed there were constant attempts at political breakthroughs in order to end violence and return the province to the path of normality. These political efforts essentially revolved around the form of government for Northern Ireland and the nature and extent of guarantees to the minority community. An analysis of the positions of the Northern Ireland parties in this context reveals a common commitment to human rights guarantees but also a diversity of views on the content and form of such guarantees.

The imposition of direct rule was viewed by the UK government as a temporary measure and it immediately sought to commence consultations amongst political parties in Northern Ireland with a view to re-establish some form of devolved government in the province.[100] The first attempt to forge an agreement between the parties in Northern Ireland resulted in the Sunningdale Agreement. The negotiations leading to the Sunningdale Agreement included the Secretary of State for Northern Ireland, representatives of the Ulster Unionist Party, the SDLP and the Alliance Party. It is noteworthy that representatives of the more hard-line parties (Sinn Féin, DUP, etc.) were not included. Discussions on the formation of a power-sharing Executive touched upon a variety of issues and disagreements surfaced over numerous issues including allocation of seats on the Executive, Standing Orders and the role of the Council of Ireland. The major disagreements from a human rights point of view related to policing and security arrangements.[101] Overall, there was very limited discussion of human rights issues between the parties at this stage.

The issue of human rights did appear in the Sunningdale Agreement as part of the Tripartite talks between the United Kingdom, the Republic of Ireland and the Northern Ireland parties who were to become members of the power-sharing Executive. Paragraph 11 of the 1973 Tripartite agreement stated that the Council of Ireland "would be invited to consider in what way the principles of the European Convention on Human Rights and Fundamental Freedoms would be expressed in domestic legislation in each part of Ireland". There appeared to have been no major démarche over the inclusion of this provision. The representatives of the SDLP would certainly have not objected to its inclusion given their provenance (they were mainly activists of the civil rights movement). The UUP was also by this stage committed to a Bill of Rights for Northern Ireland as is evidenced by their 1972 manifesto entitled "Towards the Future: A Unionist Blueprint", within which they proposed "the introduction of a precise and comprehensive Bill of Rights".[102] This was in itself a noteworthy shift within unionist political thinking. In Chapter 2 and 3 the resistance to any civil rights legislation by unionist politicians was frequently referred to. By 1972 the UUP was advocating in its own electoral manifesto the adoption of human rights legislation.

Prior to the adoption of the Sunningdale Agreement the Northern Ireland Office published a discussion paper entitled "The Future of Northern Ireland" which, inter alia, summarised the views of the political parties of Northern Ireland on various constitutional issues. According to the Discussion Paper the UUP and the Northern Ireland Labour Party made explicit reference to a Bill of Rights whereas the SDLP's views focused on other issues. This is an interesting fact since, given the SDLP's background in the civil rights movement, one would have expected a Bill of Rights to feature prominently in their proposals. Instead the SDLP proposals focused on a declaration by the UK that it favoured a unified Ireland, constitutional design and devolved government mechanisms. The failure to focus on a Bill of Rights is perplexing. Perhaps an emphasis on British withdrawal and on all-Ireland bodies was intended to appeal to moderate republicans. Human rights may have taken second place when faced with political considerations.

Nevertheless, the paper quoted above stated that "there is a wide body opinion that a Bill of Rights should be enacted in Northern Ireland."[103] Although there was this common commitment in principle, the Discussion Paper also warned that there were problems in terms of "what rights are to be enshrined; whether they should be protected through the Courts or by a body specially set up for that purpose"[104] etc. The acceptance of human rights guarantees, as an essential part of the political process, coupled with different views on the definition of human rights and their enforcement was to become a constant feature of the peace process.

The Sunningdale Agreement and the short-lived power-sharing Executive established therein did not have the time to implement any of the human rights ideas mentioned in the Agreement. Nevertheless, soon after the collapse of Sunningdale, the UK government sought to recommence the political process. In its 1974 Report entitled "The Northern Ireland Constitution", the Northern Ireland Office mooted the idea of an elected assembly with consultative powers that could propose political solutions to the Northern Ireland conflict.[105] Such a body was established under the title of the Northern Ireland Constitutional Convention in 1975. Politically the Convention failed to achieve any progress since the vast majority of the unionist members elected to the Convention coalesced into the United Ulster

Unionist Council (UUUC). The UUUC included the UUP, the DUP and the Vanguard Unionist Party, who all agreed to oppose power-sharing. As such there was no possibility to reach an agreement between them and the representatives of the nationalist community (i.e. the SDLP).

The Report from the Constitutional Convention indeed proposed a return to devolved government based on majority rule which the UK government could not accept as this would imply a return to the same system that had collapsed in 1972.[106] Nevertheless, some degree of agreement was once again registered with respect to human rights. The Report summarised the views of the parties that managed to elect members to the Convention on various issues. On the issue of a Bill of Rights, the UUUC, the SDLP and the Alliance Party of Northern Ireland all agreed that such a Bill would be desirable. However, the views on the content of such a Bill of Rights were far from uniform. In this context, it is useful to examine, albeit briefly, the various proposals made by these parties in respect of the Bill of Rights. Such an examination will demonstrate that while agreement on the principle of a Bill of Rights was present, substantive differences on how to implement such principle in practice existed.

The UUUC pointedly referred to a Bill of Rights and Duties in its proposals to the Convention.[107] The inclusion of duties in the Bill of Rights was according to the UUUC essential for a proper understanding of human rights:

> The objects of such a Bill would be educative as well as legislative and accordingly it is important that the duties of citizens as well as their rights should be spelled out. Rights and duties correspond – the right of one party presupposes a correlative duty imposed upon another. The reference to duties also serves to clarify thinking on civil liberties in times of emergency. Those whose rights may have to be suspended will often have themselves rejected the various duties which must be observed if fundamental legal rights are to be maintained for the benefit of all.[108]

The emphasis on duties was thus intended to reinforce the legitimacy of suspending rights during periods of public emergency. This is clearly in contrast to the views within the nationalist community who portrayed the suspension of rights as a contributory factor to the escalation of conflict and strife. Arguably detention powers used by the authorities were a violation of rights to a fair trial even if they were not in breach of the ECHR, as seems to have been the case. One also notices an interesting (if not perplexing) reference to "those whose rights may have to be suspended" and the explicit statement that they are to blame for the suspension of rights and that somehow such suspension is a form of punishment for their failure to fulfil their duties. There are three elements that are striking in this observation. First, reference to "those whose rights may have to be suspended" implies that suspension of rights only applies to a part of the population. From a legal point of view this is evidently fallacious. The derogation of rights in times of emergency should not be applied selectively. The selective application of such derogations would be in itself an abuse of the derogation in international human rights law. It is true that in the case of Northern Ireland the suspension of the right to a fair trial etc. was aimed at those who committed, or who were accused of having committed, certain crimes as defined in the Emergency Provisions Act (and latterly the Prevention of Terrorism Act). However, these Acts should have been applied impartially and indiscriminately across the board. If they were not, this was in itself an act of discrimination. Furthermore, certain suspensions of rights which are most common in situations of civil strife, such as freedom of association, do not and should not target any specific part of the population. Second, the purpose of allowing derogations to rights in international human rights law is not as a form of retribution but only to allow order to be re-established. Portraying derogations from rights as a form of punishment is unacceptable from a human rights point of view.

One may also discern other difference in the attitude to a Bill of Rights as expressed in the Report of the Constitutional Convention. For example, the SDLP favoured the adoption of the ECHR into domestic law of Northern Ireland. In this context, the SDLP also favoured a strong role for the Courts in enforcing human rights legislation and indeed looked towards the US Supreme Court as a model for the enforcement of a Bill of Rights.[109] On the other hand, the Alliance Party preferred to base a Bill of Rights on the Universal Declaration of Human Rights which it argued should form part of any future Northern Ireland Constitution.[110] The scope of application of such a Bill also attracted different views; while the SDLP and Alliance appeared to favour a Bill that was applicable to Northern Ireland, the UUUC insisted that such a Bill should be of UK-wide application.[111] The UUUC gave numerous reasons for its stand, including the fact that a Bill limited to Northern Ireland could be "interpreted as a statement that only in Northern Ireland was there potential for government abuse of power".

One need not enter into any further details of the proposed Bill since it never saw light of day but, as a final note, the UUUC proposals on the Bill referred specifically to:

- the duty of government to defend its citizens and that derogations in times of emergency constitute a contribution to protecting rights and not a detraction from such rights;
- fair and equitable electoral representation;
- a duty of citizens to abide by the law and respect the rights of others;
- a general limitation on rights for specific purposes and a clear statement that there is no right to engage in acts that aim to destroy any of the principles contained in the Bill.

These issues are very specific, especially in the context of a Bill of Rights, and most of them do not appear in either the ECHR or the Universal Declaration of Human Rights. Once again, as highlighted in the previous chapter, there seemed to be a somewhat partial understanding of human rights principles and law within both communities in Northern Ireland.

While the Constitutional Convention failed to achieve its objectives there was one effective proposal contained in the Convention relating to the establishment of a Standing Advisory Commission on Human Rights[112] which had however already been envisaged in the Northern Ireland Constitution Act 1973.[113] In 1977 this Commission published a report on *The Protection of Human Rights by Law in Northern Ireland*,[114] which is interesting to the extent that it strengthens the point that whereas agreement on the principle of a Bill of Rights was present, differences as to its implementation abounded:

> There is widespread support in Northern Ireland for a Bill of Rights. However, examination of these demands has revealed a wide variety of different approaches and emphases, particularly in relation to the scope and character of the rights and freedoms to be guaranteed and the means by which a Bill of Rights should be enforced.[115]

This statement written in 1977 maintained its validity throughout the conflict and indeed in the post-conflict phase. In fact it describes accurately the difficulties which Northern Ireland encountered in adopting the Bill of Rights envisaged in the 1998 Belfast Agreement that ended the conflict. This matter will be revisited in the subsequent chapters.

The late 1970s and early 1980s did not witness great progress in peace negotiations in Northern Ireland. The UK and Irish governments, faced with a political and military stalemate, attempted to go over the heads of the Northern Irish parties and negotiated the 1985 Anglo-Irish Agreement between themselves without reference to the province's political players. The Agreement established an Anglo-Irish Intergovernmental Conference which entitled the Irish government to propose ideas over certain areas of policy for Northern Ireland. This enraged most unionist opinion in Northern Ireland which resented any role for the Irish government in the province. However, the Irish government in return for this limited consultative role pledged that it accepted the status of Northern Ireland as part of the UK and, more importantly, recognised that any change in the status of Northern Ireland could only come about if a majority of the people of Northern Ireland expressed themselves in favour of such a change. The UK government on its part pledged to give effect to such a change if the majority of the people of Northern Ireland so desired.[116] This was an important statement as it provided the answer to the issue of the right to self-determination in Northern Ireland. In effect this was the answer reiterated in the 1998 Belfast Agreement.

The Anglo-Irish Agreement also referred limitedly to other human rights issues within its provisions. Indeed, the scope of the Intergovernmental Conference in Political Matters was exclusively devoted to rights issues. Article 5(a) of the Agreement states that:

> The Conference shall concern itself with measures to recognise and accommodate the rights and identities of the two traditions in Northern Ireland, to protect human rights and to prevent discrimination. Matters to be considered in this area include … the avoidance of economic and social discrimination and the advantages and disadvantages of a Bill of Rights in Northern Ireland.

This is worthy of note for two reasons. First, human rights concerns remained part of the essential discourse of the Northern Ireland political processes. This is witnessed by the fact that human rights were included as one of the few features of the Anglo-Irish Agreement, which only dealt with five policy issues.[117] Second, the Bill of Rights idea was carried forward in this context. Once again, the Bill did not materialise as a result of the Agreement but its inclusion in this treaty continued to build the case for such a Bill.

All told, these brief reflections on human rights in negotiations during the 1970s and 1980s allow a number of tentative conclusions.

1. Human rights were definitely established as one of the issues that conflict resolution negotiations in Northern Ireland had to include.
2. The majority of unionist politicians moved from a rejection of discrimination legislation and human rights law as impracticable or undesirable from the 1930s to the 1960s[118] to an acceptance of such legislation in the 1970s and 1980s.
3. The concept of a Bill of Rights became a key concept in human rights thinking in Northern Ireland and was reiterated in all political negotiations both within Northern Ireland and in bilateral negotiations between the UK and Northern Ireland.
4. The concept of a Bill of Rights revealed the existence of significant differences in the interpretation of rights and in the determination of their enforcement.
5. These divergences as to Bill of Rights and occasional selectivity in the emphasis on certain rights and/or issues highlight the partial understanding of human rights in the various communities in Northern Ireland as already evidenced in Chapter 3.

Conclusion

This chapter has outlined the developments in human rights matters during the period when violence escalated in Northern Ireland, and also highlighted the role played by human rights in the escalation of violence and the broader political framework. It is evident that the introduction of internment (a human rights breach) directed against the minority community was a pivotal point which catalysed the descent into violence and aided the rise of the IRA. Internment further polarised the communities in Northern Ireland and polarised the communities' perceptions of the security forces in Northern Ireland (both the UK army and the RUC). For the minority community, internment flamed perceptions of Northern Ireland as an illegitimate state[119] that was willing to abuse their human rights through its criminal justice system and security forces. Politically the escalating violence that characterised the introduction of internment also witnessed the end of devolved government for Northern Ireland and the introduction of direct rule.

Another key feature of this period from a human rights perspective was the adoption of the Emergency Provisions Act of 1973 which brought about changes to trial by jury, rules of evidence and stop-and-search rules. These changes to the criminal justice system further corroded the already crumbling trust of the minority community in the criminal justice system. While these changes may have been legal under UK law and under the European Convention on Human Rights (as a result of derogations lodged by the UK government), they nevertheless were understood by the minority as an attack on their human rights and freedoms. Conversely, the majority community perceived internment and the Emergency Provisions Act as measures intended to protect their rights from IRA violence and from being dragged into a united Ireland.

As violence became entrenched in Northern Ireland, the UK army, the RUC, republican paramilitaries (chiefly the IRA) and loyalist paramilitaries all committed acts which constituted grave human rights abuses. Thus, the breaches of human rights pertinent to internment and emergency legislation created a cycle of violence that gave rise to more abuses of human rights and deepened divisions.

The period examined in this chapter was also characterised by the issue of the rights and status of prisoners. The IRA sought through all means to claim prisoner-of-war status or some form of special status for persons convicted of paramilitary-related activities. In particular, it sought to use the principles of international humanitarian law to achieve this aim while at the same time failing repeatedly to abide by some of the most basic rules of international humanitarian law (for example, through attacks which killed civilians). The issue of the prisoners was further complicated by the fact that while the UK government refused to grant special status to these prisoners, the judicial processes through which most of these prisoners were convicted were special. In fact, in the determination of their guilt or otherwise, a number of rights ordinarily available to accused persons were unavailable to these prisoners. Thus, both the IRA and the UK government demonstrated a selective approach to rights issues in this context. Further complicating the issue pertaining to prisoners were the regular accusations of torture and inhuman treatment made against the UK government by republican detainees. The European Court of Human Rights eventually confirmed that inhuman treatment had been meted to republican detainees.

The whole scenario relating to prisoners reached its sad apex with the hunger strikes and the deaths of a number of the hunger strikers. Ultimately, these deaths were self-inflicted human rights abuses which worsened significantly the polarisation and violence in Northern Ireland. Evidently, the history of internment, emergency legislation and inhuman treatment lent immense legitimacy to the hunger strikers for the republican movement and indeed for the broader nationalist community of Northern Ireland. Nevertheless, these deaths also promoted the political path for the republican movement with the steady rise of Sinn Féin as an electoral force. This led to the embryonic peace negotiations and eventually to the peace process of the late 1990s.

Throughout the period examined in this chapter attempts at reaching a political settlement continued with a varying degree of urgency but no prospect of success. However, all the various attempts at a political settlement recognised that a human rights dimension would be a necessary part of any such settlement. This was clear from Sunningdale onwards. Interestingly, during this same period the UUP witnessed a first move in its approach towards human rights issues. In fact in its proposals to the Constitutional Convention it included reference to a Bill of Rights for Northern Ireland. Given its previous attitude to the idea of a Bill of Rights (and to human rights legislation) between the 1920s and the early 1960s[120] this was a notable development. Even so, while human rights were proving to be an unavoidable part of any peace process, differences on the interpretation of such rights were already evident. Finally, it is worth emphasising that despite the violence throughout the period under examination and the ostensible liquidation of the civil rights movement, the period still witnessed a significant consciousness of human rights concerns in Northern Ireland. This is partly a result of the expanding international human rights consciousness accompanied by a growth in international and regional human rights norms.

Within the European context, Dickson is of the view that the European Convention "was very largely irrelevant both to the way the conflict was managed while it was raging and the way it was largely resolved through the Belfast (Good Friday) Agreement of 1998".[121] And yet the Convention did gradually embed itself in European public consciousness as may be seen with reference to the number of applications the European system received. The number of applications rose from 138 in 1955, to 310 in 1965 and then to 466 in 1975. While these numbers do not compare with the thousands of applications that have been received since the end of the Cold War, one has to acknowledge that until 1990 there were less than half the current number of State Parties and the Court operated on a part-time basis until the adoption of Protocols 11 and 14 in the 1990s. In essence, the numbers between 1955 and 1975 indicate a clear expansion of the readiness of the European public to use the Convention (no doubt, as Dickson argues, they were guided by lawyers who became more comfortable and adroit at utilising the Convention).

The evidence provided in this chapter suggests that while the European Convention was not critical to the politics of the period, nor to the way the conflict evolved, it did contribute to a continuing engagement with human rights language and practice within Northern Ireland. The same applies to the growing international human rights corpus of norms and practices which, while not of direct application to Northern Ireland, also provided external reference points, which some of the protagonists of the politics of the period sought to use, often instrumentally, to their advantage. As will become more apparent in the next chapter, human rights language gradually became so predominant in international and European relations that no-one in Northern Ireland could conceivably totally ignore it, or be seen to be openly antagonistic to it. Even within the ambit of this chapter, the growing international respectability of human rights may have helped maintain some focus on rights even as other forces were prevailing.

Notes

1 This point will be returned to later in this chapter. For a detailed explanation on the rise of the Provisional IRA, see Richard English, *Armed Struggle: The History of the IRA* (London: Pan Books, 2003).
2 Ian Wood, *God Guns and Ulster: A History of Loyalist Paramilitaries* (Caxton, 2004).
3 Niall Ó Dochartaigh, *From Civil Rights to Armalites* (Cork: Cork University Press, 1997).
4 Campaign for Social Justice, Letter, 28 December 1969, Northern Ireland Political Collection, Linen Hall Library, Belfast.
5 Northern Ireland Civil Rights Association, *Dossier on Harassment and Brutality by the British Army in Northern Ireland: A Sample of Typical Cases* (Northern Ireland Civil Rights Association, 1972), 1.
6 Sunday Times Insight Team, *Ulster*, Penguin Special (Harmondsworth: Penguin Books, 1972), 197.
7 Ibid., 205.
8 Letter from Lieutenant Colonel J. C. Reilly, Commanding Officer 2nd Battalion, 23 December 1971, Northern Ireland Political Collection, Linen Hall Library, Belfast.
9 Ibid.
10 Ibid.
11 Northern Ireland Civil Rights Association, *Dossier on Harassment and Brutality by the British Army in Northern Ireland*, 1.
12 Principal Conclusions and Overall Assessment of the Bloody Sunday Inquiry, para 3.70, www.gov.uk/government/uploads/system/uploads/attachment_data/file/279167/0030.pdf.
13 Ibid., para 5.5.
14 Edward Heath, *The Course of My Life: The Autobiography of Edward Heath* (London: Hodder Stoughton, 1998).
15 Ibid.
16 Case of *Ireland* v. *United Kingdom* (European Court of Human Rights 1978), Application no. 5310/71.
17 See, for example, Brice Dickson, "The Detention of Suspected Terrorists in Northern Ireland and Great Britain", *University of Richmond Law Review* 43, no. 3 (March 2009): 927. Dickson states that "The fact that the European Court upheld the use of internment is greatly to be regretted."
18 Brice Dickson, *The European Convention on Human Rights and the Conflict in Northern Ireland* (Oxford: Oxford University Press, 2010).

19 Statement by the Prime Minister, Mr Brian Faulkner DL MP (Public Records Office of Northern Ireland, 9 August 1971), PM/5/169/14.
20 Quoted in Desmond Hamill, *Pig in the Middle: The Army in Northern Ireland, 1969–1984* (London: Methuen, 1985).
21 Heath, *The Course of My Life*.
22 Arrest Policy for Protestants (Public Records Office of Northern Ireland, 9 December 1972), CAB/9/G/27/6/5.
23 Conclusions of a Meeting of the Cabinet Held at Stormont Castle (Public Records Office of Northern Ireland, 20 August 1971), CAB/4/1610.
24 Brice Dickson, in "The Detention of Suspected Terrorists in Northern Ireland and Great Britain", states that "Most commentators agree that the use of internment in Northern Ireland was a disaster because it ensured continuous enlistment in the IRA."
25 Gerry Adams, *Before the Dawn: An Autobiography* (Dingle, Ireland: Brandon Books, 1996), 167.
26 Sunday Times Insight Team, *Ulster*, 268.
27 Ibid., 270.
28 Letter from the UK Home Secretary to the Prime Minister of Northern Ireland (Public Records Office of Northern Ireland, 4 August 1971), CAB/9/R/238/6.
29 Kevin Boyle and Tom Hadden, *Ireland: A Positive Proposal* (London: Penguin Books, 1985), 65.
30 "Towards Peace", *SDLP News*, November 1972, 2.
31 See, for example, the 1971 NICRA poster advertising an Anti-Internment Rally. Yvonne Murphy, Leonard, Allan, Gillespie, Gordon and Brown, Kris, eds., *Troubled Images: Posters and Images of the Northern Ireland Conflict from the Linen Hall Library, Belfast* (Belfast: Linen Hall Library, 2001), PP00480.
32 Ibid., PP00470.
33 Ibid.
34 Ibid.
35 *NICRA Bulletin* (Belfast: Northern Ireland Political Collection (NIPC), Linen Hall Library, 11 December 1971).
36 Murphy *et al.*, *Troubled Images*, PP00482.
37 Ibid., PP0563.
38 Ibid., PP03137.
39 Ibid., PP00556.
40 Ibid., PP00518.
41 Ibid., PP01373.
42 Ibid., PP00474.
43 Ibid., PP01243.
44 Ibid., PP01251.
45 Dickson, *The European Court on Human Rights and the Northern Ireland Conflict*.
46 http://cain.ulst.ac.uk/events/convention/nicc75app. 3.htm.
47 http://hansard.millbanksystems.com/commons/1985/jun/26/northern-ireland-act1974#S6CV0081P0_19850626_HOC_292.
48 Statement by J. Chichester-Clark, then Prime Minister of Northern Ireland, (15 August 1969), http://cain.ulst.ac.uk/proni/1969/proni_HA-32-3-1_1969-08-15.pdf.
49 Statement by B. Faulkner, then Prime Minister of Northern Ireland (7 March 1972), http://cain.ulst.ac.uk/proni/1971/proni_HA-32-2-55_1971-08-20.pdf.
50 Statement by the Rt. Hon. Edward Heath to the House of Commons (Public Record Office of Northern Ireland, 24 March 1972), HA/32/2/51.
51 Main Points Made by Mr Heath at Downing Street Meeting on 22 March 1972 about the Northern Ireland Situation (Public Records Office of Northern Ireland, 22 March 1972), CAB/4/1647.

52 John. P. Darby, *Scorpions in a Bottle: Conflicting Cultures in Northern Ireland* (London: Minority Rights Publications, 1997), 85.
53 War on Terror: Lessons from Northern Ireland (Belfast: Committee on the Administration of Justice, 2008), accessed 23 August 2012, www.icj.org/IMG/CAJ_report.pdf, 13.
54 The Threat to Law and Order in Northern Ireland over the Next Few Years, in *The Working Party on Law and Order in Northern Ireland* (Public Records Office of Northern Ireland, 13 February 1976), CENT/1/5/5.
55 English, *Armed Struggle*, 104–8.
56 Sunday Times Insight Team, *Ulster*, 272.
57 Murphy *et al.*, *Troubled Images*, PP00483.
58 Ibid., PP0375.
59 Ibid., PA0018.
60 Ibid., PP00041.
61 English, *Armed Struggle*, 124.
62 Ibid., 125.
63 Murphy *et al.*, *Troubled Images*, PP00462.
64 See, for example, ibid., PP01173, a poster depicting the Union flag and a masked gunman with the Biblical quotation: "Thou shalt smite them, and utterly destroy them; Thou shalt make no covenant with them, nor show mercy unto them."
65 Ibid., PP00492.
66 Ibid., PP02647.
67 Murphy *et al.*, *Troubled Images*, Interview with Terry Carlin.
68 Adams, *Before the Dawn*, 210.
69 Statement by the Rt Hon. David Cameron to the House of Commons, 15 June 2010, www.publications.parliament.uk/pa/cm201011/cmhansrd/cm100615/debtext/100615-0004.htm.
70 For a recent account of this matter, see www.theguardian.com/news/2015/jul/09/northern-ireland-terror-shoot-to-kill, accessed 25 January 2016.
71 The Honourable Lord Cameron, *Cameron Report – Disturbances in Northern Ireland*, para. 177.
72 *McCann and Others* v. *United Kingdom* (Grand Chamber, European Court of Human Rights, 27 September 1995), Application no. 00018984/91, para. 215.
73 Dickson, *The European Court on Human Rights and the Northern Ireland Conflict.*
74 Adams, *Before the Dawn*, 191.
75 Case of *Ireland* v. *United Kingdom* (European Court of Human Rights 18 January 1978), Application no. 5310/71.
76 Article 3 of the European Convention on Human Rights states: "No one shall be subjected to torture or to inhuman or degrading treatment or punishment." Council of Europe, *Convention for the Protection of Human Rights and Fundamental Freedoms as Amended by Protocols No. 11 and No. 14*, Art. 3. For a detailed discussion of this case, refer to Dickson, *The European Court on Human Rights and the Northern Ireland Conflict.*
77 Dickson, *The European Court on Human Rights and the Northern Ireland Conflict.*
78 See www.bbc.com/news/uk-northern-ireland-33008186, accessed 23 January 2016.
79 See Chapter 4.
80 See, inter alia, Northern Ireland Information Service, *Prisoners Rights and Privileges in NI: Statement by Secretary of State* (Public Records Office of Northern Ireland, 4 December 1980), CENT/1/10/25.
81 *McFeeley* v. *United Kingdom* (European Commission of Human Rights, 15 May 1980), Application no. 8317/78, para. 27.
82 Ibid., para. 43.

83 See, for example, SDLP, Executive Committee Statement on Ardoyne Meeting on September 10 and on Conditions in "H Block" (Public Records Office of Northern Ireland, 1978), NIO/12/153.
84 Tomás Ó Fiaich, Statement by the Archbishop of Armagh, Dr Tomas O'Fiaich Concerning His Visit Sunday Last to H-Block at Long Kesh Prison, Northern Ireland (Belfast: Public Records Office of Northern Ireland, 1 August 1978), NIO/12/68.
85 Letter from the Secretary of State for Northern Ireland the Rt Hon. Humphrey Atkins MP to Gerry Fitt MP (Belfast: Public Records Office of Northern Ireland, 29 January 1980), NIO/12/175.
86 Murphy *et al.*, *Troubled Images*, PP02697.
87 Ibid., PP01274.
88 Ibid., PP01249.
89 Ibid., PP01428.
90 *McFeeley* v. *United Kingdom* (European Commission of Human Rights 1980), para. 54.
91 Ibid., para. 64.
92 Dickson, *The European Court on Human Rights and the Northern Ireland Conflict.*
93 McKittrick, David, "Remembering Bobby Sands", *Independent*, 5 May 2006, accessed 25 August 2012, www.independent.co.uk/news/uk/this-britain/remembering-bobby-sands-476884.html.
94 Murphy *et al.*, *Troubled Images*, PA0144.
95 Adams, *Before the Dawn*, 263.
96 Ibid., 318–9.
97 Prevention of Terrorism (Temporary Provisions) Act, 1974; Prevention of Terrorism (Temporary Provisions) Act, 1976; Prevention of Terrorism (Temporary Provisions) Act, 1984; and Prevention of Terrorism (Temporary Provisions) Act, 1989.
98 Murphy *et al.*, *Troubled Images*, PP01766.
99 For more information on the CAJ, see www.caj.org.uk, accessed 24 January 2016.
100 See Statement by the Prime Minister of the United Kingdom Edward Heath to the House of Commons on 24 March 1972 where, in announcing direct rule, he stated that the British government was assuming full and direct responsibility for Northern Ireland "until a political solution to the problems of the Province can be worked out in consultation with all those concerned". Statement by the Rt. Hon. Edward Heath to the House of Commons, 24 March 1972, HA/32/2/51.
101 See Note of Talks between the Secretary of State, the Alliance Party, the Social Democratic and Labour Party and the Ulster Unionist Party (Belfast: Public Record Office of Northern Ireland, 5 October 1973), FIN/30/R/2/A/3; and Note of a Meeting between the Secretary of State, the Alliance Party, the Social Democratic and Labour Party and the Ulster Unionist Party (Belfast: Public Record Office of Northern Ireland, 21 November 1973), FIN/30/R/2/A/3.
102 Ulster Unionist Party Publication, *Towards the Future: A Unionist Blueprint* (Belfast: Ulster Publicity and Research Department, 1972), Part 9.
103 Northern Ireland Office, *The Future of Northern Ireland: A Paper for Discussion* (Belfast: Her Majesty's Stationery Office, 1972), para. 69.
104 Ibid.
105 *The Northern Ireland Constitution* (London: Her Majesty's Stationery Office, 1974).
106 Northern Ireland Office, *Northern Ireland Constitutional Convention Report* (London: Her Majesty's Stationery Office, 1975).
107 Ibid., para. 128.
108 Ibid., para. 131.

109 Ibid., para. 129.
110 Ibid.
111 Ibid., para. 132.
112 Ibid.
113 Section 20, Northern Ireland Constitution Act 1973.
114 Standing Advisory Commission on Human Rights, *The Protection of Human Rights by Law in Northern Ireland* (London: Her Majesty's Stationery Office, 1977).
115 Ibid., para. 8.4.
116 Agreement between the Government of the United Kingdom of Great Britain and Northern Ireland and the Government of the Republic of Ireland, Treaty Series No. 62, 1985, Art. 1.
117 Constitutional status, security matters, human rights issues, legal affairs and cross-border cooperation.
118 See Chapters 2 and 3.
119 This is witnessed by the Fascist imagery referred to earlier in the chapter.
120 See Chapters 2 and 3.
121 Dickson, *The European Court on Human Rights and the Northern Ireland Conflict.*

6 Peace and human rights, 1985–1998

The long thaw

Introduction

This chapter addresses three themes which span the timeframe between the signing of the Anglo-Irish and Good Friday Agreements. The three themes relate to: (1) a number of entrenched human rights challenges in Northern Ireland (and the ways in which they continued to be addressed); (2) the role of human rights concerning conflict resolution negotiations; and (3) the extent to which the conflict resolution efforts in Northern Ireland were more concerned with ending physical violence (negative peace) than with building positive peace (including a deep commitment to and engagement with human rights).

The period under examination spans the immediate aftermath of the hunger strikes and Sinn Féin's increasing electoral activism to the negotiations which led finally to the Peace Agreement of 1998. This period was one characterised by continuing violence, continuing negotiations and increasing hopes for a political settlement. In some ways, this period reflected both continuity and hope for change in Northern Ireland. Continuity was evident in the enduring violence[1] perpetrated by republican and loyalist paramilitaries (and occasionally the security forces of the UK) as well as by a continuing concern with human rights issues which had bedevilled Northern Ireland since the 1920s. These human rights concerns centred, inter alia, on: the use of special powers legislation and problems relating to the administration of justice;[2] religious discrimination (particularly in employment);[3] and the whole area of cultural rights and their expression in terms of the use of flags, emblems and parades.[4]

Hopes for change in the period gradually increased as the 1980s drew to a close and the 1990s dawned. These prospects for change were driven by numerous factors, including the new leadership in both London and Dublin with John Major and Albert Reynolds making sustained efforts at breaking the political deadlock. Other factors included an increasing belief within the republican movement that the political avenue was worth pursuing and a contemporaneous sense of conflict fatigue emerging within the IRA, loyalist paramilitaries and UK security forces.[5] With politics gradually becoming a more feasible and attractive option to all parties, the possibility of ending violence became more real than ever. The 1990s, therefore, witnessed long, arduous and hesitating negotiations which finally led to the 1998 Northern Ireland Peace Agreement. Throughout this period, human rights issues formed part of the discourse that coloured the negotiation process, as was evident in the various official communications that emanated from the UK and Irish governments.[6] While human rights concerns were referred to continuously, they did not in themselves prove to be the primary issues in the negotiations. As accounts of the negotiations demonstrate, the key contentious issues during the negotiations proved to be decommissioning, the scope and functions of North–South bodies and to a lesser extent the exact functioning of power-sharing.[7] Within the main negotiations that led to the Peace Agreement, human rights provisions seem to have been agreed to without too much difficulty bar some disagreement on language rights.

Nevertheless, human rights played an important role in the Peace Agreement as it included numerous provisions directly concerned with human rights. It has been suggested that "The language of rights flows through the Agreement."[8] A question which this chapter will seek to address is why was rights discourse integrated so strongly into the Agreement? Was it because all parties were deeply committed to human rights? Or was it because all parties considered it politically correct to bow towards human rights?

A final consideration in this chapter will refer to the nature of the negotiations and the Peace Agreement as exercises directed towards achieving both negative peace and positive peace. The ending of physical violence was clearly the primary objective of the negotiations and agreement. However, it was acknowledged throughout the negotiation process and in the agreement itself that for the peace agreement to be durable it needed to go beyond negative peace, i.e. an agreement to cease violence. The Agreement in fact refers to "the achievement of reconciliation, tolerance, and mutual trust, and to the protection and vindication of the human rights of all".[9] The human rights clauses of the agreement may thus be viewed both in terms of their contribution to end the violence but more importantly in the context of building positive peace that is durable and sustainable.

The extent to which the Northern Ireland Peace Agreement achieves positive peace will be the main question that will be dealt with in the next chapter. However, the elements of this discussion will be introduced towards the end of this chapter.

Human rights in Northern Ireland 1985–1998: old, familiar problems

The extent to which the old, familiar human rights problems continued to form part of the political discourse in Northern Ireland may be gauged by reference to the number of reports, press releases and statements concerning such problems issued by governmental and non-governmental agencies in the period under review. Between 1984 and 1998 one can identify at least 63 reports and documents dealing with human rights issues, published mainly in Northern Ireland (but also in Great Britain and the USA).[10] Of these 63 documents, 36 deal with issues concerning the administration of justice (mainly policing issues and treatment of detainees). A further 20 documents deal with the equality agenda (mainly as it relates to employment).

In order to explore the extent to which the human rights issues remained stable in the period under examination in this chapter a comparison between the documents in the first four years (1985–1988) and the last four years (1994–1997) of the period may be instructive. For the year 1985, the human rights-related documents identified in the Northern Ireland Political Collection (NIPC) and Conflict Archive on the Internet (CAIN) records were six: (1) a report on alleged torture and ill-treatment by Amnesty International; (2) a report on the protection of minority rights by the CAJ; (3) an academic study of the Diplock Courts and their compliance with fair trial requirements by a Dutch scholar; (4) a consultative paper on police complaints and discipline by the Northern Ireland Office (NIO); (5) a report on minorities in Ireland prepared under the auspices of the Irish Council of Churches; and (6) a research paper on religion and educational qualifications prepared by the Fair Employment Agency.

For the year 1986, no human rights-related material was identified while for 1987 the following five documents were located: (1) a report on fair employment by the Standing Advisory Committee on Human Rights (SACHR); (2) a Policy Studies Institute report on equality and inequality in employment and unemployment; (3) a guide to fair employment for employers issued by the NIO; (4) a study on fair employment by two academics; and (5) an article on identity, youth and sectarianism. While the 1987 documents had a strong bias towards the issue of fairness in employment, the 1988 documents while continuing this trend also focus on issues related to the administration of justice. Thus, we find the following five documents: (1) an Amnesty International report on allegations of ill-treatment; (2) a New York city Bar Association study of criminal justice and human rights in Northern Ireland; (3) a report by Amnesty International on extrajudicial killings and super-grass trials; (4) a further Amnesty International report on ill-treatment; and (5) a study on religion, occupation and employment in the annual report of the Fair Employment Agency. Thus, in this four-year period seven documents focused on issues related to the administration of justice while six related to issues pertaining to employment; two further documents dealt with other human rights matters.

The period from 1994 to 1997 comprises a total of 24 human rights-related documents and reports. The year 1994 is sparsely populated in terms of human rights documents and comprises the following materials: (1) a report on the right to silence and fair trials by the Britain and Ireland Human Rights Centre; (2) a report by the Committee for the Prevention of Torture; and (3) a report by the Independent Commission for Police Complaints. For the year 1995 the materials located are the following: (1) a Queen's University research paper on tackling miscarriages of justice in Northern Ireland, the Republic of Ireland and Great Britain; (2) a Standing Advisory Commission on Human Rights document debating fair employment in Northern Ireland; (3) a study on the treatment of Catholics and Protestants by the security forces; and (4) a Central Community Relations Unit report on fair treatment.

While the years 1994–1995 had a strong focus on issues pertaining to the administration of justice with little attention given to issues relating to the equality in employment agenda, 1996 witnesses a more balanced mix of materials. The 1996 documents may be summarised as follows: (1) a review of fair employment legislation by the SDLP; (2) an employment equality review by the Ulster Unionist Information Institute; (3) a CAJ commentary on a Standing Advisory Commission on Human Rights report on fair employment; (4) a study on public perceptions on fair employment and equality commissioned by the Standing Advisory Commission on Human Rights; (5) a Standing Advisory Commission on Human Rights report on policing of disaffected communities; (6) a discussion paper on fair treatment in Northern Ireland by the Standing Advisory Commission on Human Rights; (7) a parliamentary report presented by the Secretary of State on policing in Northern Ireland; (8) a study on community relations, equality and the future forming part of the fifth report on Social Attitudes in Northern Ireland; (9) a CAJ document on policing in the marching season in the summer of 1996; and (10) Northern Ireland Office revised codes of practice relating to the policing and criminal evidence.

As the pace of negotiations increased and the possibility of resolving the conflict became more immediate the attention to human rights-related issues also increased correspondingly. The focus on the administration of justice and equality (especially with regards to employment) remained a constant. The records for the year 1997 show fewer human rights-related documentation but one ought to bear in mind the fact that the year 1997 was an election year in the UK and therefore attention was focused on the broader political process. Nevertheless the materials for 1997 do not veer away from the general norm: (1) a CAJ report on principles for better policing; (2) a Queen's University analysis on the legal control of marches; (3) a Belgian study on defendants' rights; (4) a Human Rights Watch report on human rights and policing; (5) an overview of the implementation of the Fair Employment legislation in Northern Ireland; (6) a Democratic Dialogue publication on pluralism and parity of esteem; and (7) a CAJ report on policing (with specific reference to policing certain events in the summer of 1997).

Of the 24 human rights-related documents identified for the final four-year period of the 1985–1997 timeframe, eleven relate to the administration of justice, eight to the employment/equality agenda and three to other human rights issues. It is therefore clear that both at the beginning and at the end of the 1985–1997 period, the two major human rights concerns in Northern Ireland remained the administration of justice (i.e. policing and criminal justice) and the equality agenda (especially in terms of employment). What is striking is that these two aspects were also key concerns in the early years of the creation of Northern Ireland.[11]

While this denotes a striking continuity in terms of human rights challenges in Northern Ireland from 1921 to 1997, the extent to which these challenges were being met similarly or differently needs to be explored. In respect of equality in employment, the findings in Chapter 3 concerning the period 1921–1945 pointed towards an acknowledgment that the Catholic population suffered from higher rates of unemployment. At the same time, the Northern Irish government and the unionist politicians in particular sought to minimise the extent of Catholic disadvantage and/or state that such disadvantage was not something that could be legislated about.

This approach changed significantly, especially following the introduction of direct rule and particularly with the introduction of the first fair employment legislation in 1976.[12] In 1987 the Standing Advisory Commission on Human Rights in its *Report on Fair Employment* noted that:

> High unemployment is experienced by both sections of the community but there is a greater degree of disadvantage within the Catholic section of the community. The unemployment rate for male Catholics is two and a half times that for male Protestants. This has shown no improvement in the last decade.[13]

This official acknowledgment that there was "no improvement" in the decade since the introduction of the first fair employment legislation is striking in two respects. First, it underlines the entrenched nature of this human rights issue in Northern Ireland and reinforces the point about continuity. Second, the question as to why no progress was registered arises. Was the lack of progress due to defective legislation, a failure of implementation or were the old unionist politicians who claimed this was not a fit subject for legislation right? The report definitely discards this last option while nodding in the direction of the first two options:

> The Commission considers that factors in the labour market which have contributed to the differential such as discrimination, the chill factor, differential access to information, and the operation of kinship patterns, *can and should be influenced by public policy* [emphasis added].... There needs to be a clear and comprehensive legal framework to ensure that necessary action will be taken if it is not forthcoming voluntarily.... A powerful, respected and effective enforcement body is necessary to achieve widespread change.[14]

The latter part of this quotation seems to imply that the existing legislation was neither clear nor comprehensive and that enforcement mechanisms were lacking. The report also recommends numerous policy measures to ameliorate the situation in terms of fair employment, including the establishment of a legal duty to improve equality of opportunity, the formulation of a declaration of practice for employers with incentives for them to adopt such a declaration, the possibility to pursue strategic investigations, the establishment of a new fair employment body etc. A number of these recommendations were, in fact, adopted in the Fair Employment (Northern Ireland) Act of 1989.[15] Overall it seems that the 1989 Act resulted in a marked improvement in fair employment:

> The composition of the workforce changed significantly in the first decade of monitoring. By the year 2000 the Catholic share of the monitored full-time workforce rose from [34.9 per cent] to [39.6 per cent], an increase of 4.7 percentage points.[16]

All of the above seems to indicate that the UK government was committed and successful in dealing with the equality in employment agenda which had bedevilled Northern Irish society since 1921. The Fair Employment Act of 1989 seems to have proven that legislation could play a part in improving equality in employment and the decades-long Catholic grievance in this respect gradually descended the scale of priorities for the Catholic community. This is not to say that the equality agenda disappeared from the debate in Northern Ireland, as it was a protagonist in the Peace Agreement which established the Equality Commission as well as the Human Rights Commission. Nevertheless, it is clear that during the period 1985–1997 major progress was registered in reducing discrimination against Catholics in the sphere of the labour market. This progress continued in the period 1998–2010.[17]

The problems pertaining to the administration of justice, namely the use of special powers, policing and other criminal justice issues proved to be more complex (or at least more difficult to resolve) than those related to discrimination and employment. As was evident in previous chapters the use of special powers in terms of policing and criminal justice matters was a key feature of the administration of justice in Northern Ireland from 1921 onwards.[18] Lord Colville's 1990 review of the Northern Ireland (Emergency Provisions) Acts of 1978 and 1987, acknowledges the fact that in Northern Ireland the administration of justice has always been problematic:

> It must therefore be conceded that "normality" in the rule of law, as it is enjoyed in the rest of the UK, has never been quite the same in Northern Ireland. I can readily understand why there is a concern about human rights.[19]

The sense of grievance against the police and against the criminal justice system amongst the Catholic community was described by a Northern Irish civil servant as "the most widespread cause of alienation".[20] The reasons for this alienation included the fact that Catholic areas were the targets of more house searches and road checks and also that young Catholics were "more likely to have direct experience of interrogation, surveillance and arrest than others".[21]

The problems in the context of the administration of justice can be subdivided into three: (1) policing of Catholic areas; (2) treatment of republican prisoners arrested under emergency legislation; and (3) the application of the criminal justice system in cases involving alleged terrorist activity. The issue of policing was not solely related to the application of emergency legislation. While emergency legislation gave the police in Northern Ireland wider powers than in other parts of the United Kingdom, this was only part of the problem. The other part of the problem was that the Catholic/nationalist/republican population regarded the police with suspicion at best and at worst with outright antagonism as a police force which was overwhelmingly Protestant and unionist. This is acknowledged by the Patten Report, which in its introductory comments states, inter alia, that:

> The roots of the problem go back to the very foundation of the state. Since 1922 and the establishment of the Royal Ulster Constabulary (in part drawn from the ranks of the old Royal Irish Constabulary), the composition of the police has been disproportionately Protestant and Unionist. This has become much more pronounced during the last 30 violent years.[22]

By the 1980s and 1990s the Northern Ireland police force was widely regarded by the minority community as a force composed largely of the majority community in which they had little representation and over which they had minimal influence.

This situation did not alter to any significant degree during the period examined in this chapter. Nor were there any large-scale efforts to change the structure and composition of the RUC until 1999. That this remained a significant problem is also evidenced by the references to policing in the 1998 Peace Agreement. A whole section entitled Policing and Justice is devoted to these issues and in particular this section states that the parties:

> believe that the agreement provides the opportunity for a new beginning to policing in Northern Ireland with a police service capable of attracting and sustaining support from the community as a whole.

It is clear that in the period being examined the police service in Northern Ireland did not attract the support of the whole community. Change in this sector would have to wait until after the Peace Agreement. The sense of grievance against the police force by the minority community in Northern Ireland was one part of the problem; the other part related to the existence and exercise of the wide powers granted to the police (and other security forces) by the emergency legislation.

Within this period one also witnessed the broadcasting ban of 1988–1994, which merits some attention. In October 1988 the then UK Home Secretary issued a notice in terms of the BBC Licence and Agreement to the BBC and a separate notice to the Independent Broadcasting Authority in terms of the Broadcasting Act 1981 prohibiting the broadcast of direct statements by representatives or supporters of 11 Irish political and military organisations. This so called "broadcasting ban" was criticised by, amongst others, BBC journalists who organised a walk out in protest at this ban.[23] Of particular interest is the legal proceeding instituted by a group of six journalists against the Home Secretary claiming that the ban was a breach of the freedom of expression protected under Article 10 the ECHR.[24] The UK High Court rejected the case made by the journalists in 1989 although the case highlights the increasing attention being paid to the human rights implications of the ECHR.[25]

In the final year covered in this chapter there was also a major legislative development in the field of human rights which has had a strong impact upon human rights protection in the UK as a whole; namely the adoption of the Human Rights Act of 1998. The Act, which came into force throughout the UK in 2000, gives legal effect within the UK to certain rights contained in the ECHR. The Act has been used significantly within Northern Ireland[26] and it also has been used by those opposing the adoption of a Bill of Rights for Northern Ireland to argue that such a Bill of Rights is redundant since the Act came into force.

Human rights in conflict resolution from the Anglo-Irish Agreement to the Frameworks Document

The Anglo-Irish Agreement signed on 15 November 1985 has been the subject of great controversy ever since it was announced. The controversy was especially within the unionist community as the Agreement caused consternation amongst unionist politicians by granting a consultative role to the Republic of Ireland over a range of matters in Northern Ireland. Both the UUP and the DUP condemned the Agreement.[27] For unionists the secrecy of the negotiations between the British and Irish governments added to the perception of betrayal[28] and represented, in their view, a first step towards unification with the Republic. These issues have been widely discussed in academic literature and are beyond the scope of this study. What is of interest in the context of human rights is the extent to which the Agreement engaged with human rights issues and what were, if any, the results of such engagement.

The Preamble to the Agreement refers to the issue of rights in three instances; however, it does so in the context of group rights. The first reference explains the need to continue "efforts to reconcile and to acknowledge the rights of the two major traditions that exist in Ireland". This is done with reference to the constitutional status of Northern Ireland. It then further refers to the necessity for "mutual recognition and acceptance of each other's rights" and finally recognises "the right of each [of the two communities] to pursue its aspirations by peaceful and constitutional means".

Thus, the Preamble sets the scene for a fair degree of ambiguity. There is no reference to widely accepted and reasonably clear human rights norms but rather to the nebulous concept of rights pertaining to the two traditions. Notwithstanding this rather nebulous language, it is worth recording that such language was, in fact, anchored in the normative concept of group rights which, as was demonstrated in Chapter 2, has formed part of the body of international law since the inter-war period. The idea of accommodating different ethnicities through the formal recognition of a group's political and cultural rights developed from the late 1960s with the ICCPR as highlighted in Chapter 2 and by the broader concern with minorities which within the European context reached a climax in the 1990s with the adoption of the Framework Convention on National Minorities. Beyond the explicit right to advocate peacefully for the preferred constitutional status of Northern Ireland there is no clear indication of what the rights of the two traditions might be nor of how the mutual recognition of such rights is to be achieved.

The substantive provisions of the Agreement add some further elements to the rights agenda, specifically in article 5 which deals with the political matters that were brought within the purview of the Intergovernmental Conference. Under the terms of the Agreement the rights issues with which the Conference was to concern itself are: (1) the recognition and accommodation of the rights and identities of the two traditions; (2) the promotion of human rights and prevention of discrimination; (3) changes in the electoral system; (4) the promotion of cultural heritage of both traditions; (5) the use of flags and emblems; and (6) consideration of "some form" of a Bill of Rights for Northern Ireland. The same article also envisages the right of the Irish government to submit proposals vis-à-vis statutory bodies. The bodies explicitly listed in the Agreement are: (1) the Standing Advisory Commission on Human Rights; (2) the Fair Employment Agency; (3) the Equal Opportunities Commission; (4) the Police Authority for Northern Ireland; and (5) the Police Complaints Board. It must be significant that all the bodies specifically mentioned were related to human rights (mainly discrimination) and the administration of justice. This reinforces the argument proposed earlier in this chapter as to the continuing primacy of these two issues within the human rights agenda of Northern Ireland.

In Article 8 of the Agreement the two governments also deal with the administration of justice by first agreeing "on the importance of public confidence in the administration of justice". This seems to imply that there were some concerns in this respect. Article 8 then goes on to explain that the two governments through the Conference would "seek, with the help of advice from experts as appropriate, measures which would give substantial expression to this aim" [of having public confidence in the administration of justice]. The rather strained language used here seems to indicate that there was no great enthusiasm by the British government to allow the Republic even a consultative role within this sphere.

The period following the Agreement saw limited progress in terms of human rights. Violence did not abate and indeed some of the worst atrocities of the conflict took place in the years following the Agreement (the Enniskillen Remembrance Day bomb, the extrajudicial killings in Gibraltar, followed by killings of mourners at the subsequent funeral). Thus security issues continued to dominate the agenda. In 1989 a preliminary review of the working of the Agreement was conducted and its findings published[29] together with a paper published by the Secretary of State of Northern Ireland entitled *Developments since the signing of the Anglo-Irish Agreement*; both documents, naturally, sought to give a positive gloss to the Agreement, citing the repeal of the Flag and Emblems Act and the introduction of fair employment legislation as examples of progress.

All told, it seems that the human rights provisions of the Agreement failed to achieve significant results. Unionists were strenuously opposed to the Agreement and to anything that was connected to it and therefore would not have welcomed any developments in this respect. Nationalists and republicans continued to perceive themselves as being discriminated against in terms of employment and the administration of justice. Nevertheless, the fact that the human rights agenda was included in the Agreement set the tone for subsequent Anglo-Irish peace initiatives which all contained substantive human rights provisions.

It seems that the Agreement also established the model whereby human rights issues were not considered as key aspects of negotiations but were rather subsidiary issues. The key issues of the negotiations (foreshadowing later negotiations) were the nature and extent of the involvement of the Irish government in Northern Irish governance, as well as the acceptance by the Irish government that consent by the majority in Northern Ireland was crucial in determining the constitutional position.[30] The "relegation" of the human rights agenda to a subsidiary role designed to reassure a community may perhaps be seen to constitute an element of continuity throughout the negotiations that eventually led to the Good Friday Agreement of 1998.

In formal terms the step following the Anglo-Irish Agreement was the *Joint Declaration on Peace* (more commonly known as the "Downing Street Declaration") of 15 December 1993. The Declaration by the UK Prime Minister and Irish Taoiseach sought to outline basic tenets of "the development of an agreed framework for peace". It contains 12 paragraphs, of which some express shared commitments and positions while others articulate the respective views of the two governments. References to the human rights agenda in the Declaration are somewhat limited. In paragraph 4 the UK Prime Minister acknowledges that the

> role of the British Government will be to encourage, facilitate and enable the achievement of such agreement over a period through a process of dialogue and cooperation based on full respect for the rights and identities of both traditions in Ireland.

Paragraph 5 which expresses the views of the Irish government refers more explicitly to human rights and is indeed written with a strong dose of human rights language. The Irish government stipulated that the right to self-determination of the people of Northern Ireland must be exercised with reference to the democratically expressed wishes of the majority within Northern Ireland but added that such a right needed to be implemented in a manner

> consistent with justice and equity, respect the democratic dignity and the civil rights and religious liberties of both communities, including: the right of free political thought; the right of freedom and expression of religion; the right to pursue democratically national and political aspirations; the right to seek constitutional change by peaceful and legitimate means; the right to live wherever one chooses without hindrance; the right to equal opportunity in all social and economic activity, regardless of class, creed, sex or colour.

The above-mentioned paragraphs of the Declaration present some interesting developments in terms of how the British and Irish governments were interpreting self-determination and how they linked the right to self-determination to other human rights. Specifically, they clarified that the right to self-determination was to be exercised by the people of Northern Ireland, thus establishing the principle that any change in the constitutional status of Northern Ireland would only be decided by the majority of the people of Northern Ireland. This answered one of the questions which, as highlighted in Chapter 2, the right to self-determination poses: i.e. who is the self? Second, there is an unequivocal qualification of the right to self-determination in that it must be exercised in conjunction and consistently with other human rights. This is in effect an exercise in establishing the interdependence of human rights, which was also referred to in Chapter 2, as a key principle for the interpretation of human rights that has developed within the UN structures since World War II. Once more, the particular situation in Northern Ireland links to broader international and regional human rights arguments.

The other paragraphs deal with various issues, all focusing on the necessity of promoting dialogue and reconciliation between the two communities in Northern Ireland and committing the two governments to continue their work towards this end. Particularly, the two governments sought to encourage the inclusion of as many parties as possible in the political dialogue by assuring all involved that any party that was committed to exclusively peaceful methods and which showed that they abided by the democratic process, would be included "in dialogue in due course between the Governments and the political parties on the way ahead".

Thus, the main impetus of the Downing Street Declaration was that of tempting Sinn Féin and the loyalist parties with paramilitary connections into the formal peace process through their renunciation of violence. In fact,

Gerry Adams acknowledges this when stating that in the immediate aftermath of the Declaration "The media spotlight shifted almost immediately to republicans."[31] John Major was also clear on this subject:

> I have made it clear that if it renounces violence, the way is open to Sinn Féin to join in legitimate constitutional dialogue. That is a political route that it now has no excuse not to follow. That is the opportunity offered by the joint declaration.[32]

Nevertheless, the human rights agenda, especially as drafted by the Irish government in paragraph 5, quoted above, seemed to be a way of assuring unionists that (1) Irish unity could only come about if a majority in Northern Ireland wished it and (2) even if such unity came about their civil, political and religious rights would be protected. Once again, it seems that human rights were useful as an assurance to a suspicious community. This is a point worth highlighting given that rights, even if invoked for instrumental reasons, were gradually becoming an indispensable concept in negotiating a final political settlement, building on an existing tradition of rights language that was being developed significantly in this period. Within the context of the pledges given in the Downing Street Declaration, the Unionist Party stated, that it was "pleased by the pledge given by the Prime Minister that 'The future constitutional position of the people of Northern Ireland is a matter for the people of Northern Ireland to determine and for no one else to determine' ".[33]

The Downing Street Declaration, however limited its contribution to the human rights agenda, was clearly an important step forward in creating the conditions for the political dialogue to enter a new, more intense period of operation. After a cautious response by the IRA and Sinn Féin (accompanied by requests for clarifications, which were, eventually, duly supplied) the IRA famously decided to declare a ceasefire in late August 1994. The IRA ceasefire was immediately followed by a ceasefire from the loyalist paramilitary groups. This was one of the crucial episodes in the tortuous path to the peace process as it opened a window of opportunity for discussions to be held in relative peace.

Within the ceasefire period the British and Irish governments sought to direct the peace process by supplying another building block to the proceedings in the form of the Frameworks Document published on 22 February 1995. The Frameworks Document essentially took stock of the political dialogue to date, summarised the obstacles and set out (once more) the three-strand approach to the peace process based on: (1) relationships and structures within Northern Ireland; (2) North–South relations and institutions; and (3) relations between Ireland as a whole and the United Kingdom (the so-called East–West relationships). Moreover, the Document also distilled the guiding principles which would govern the joint action of both governments in the search for peace:

1 the principle of self-determination, as set out in the Joint Declaration;
2 that the consent of the governed is an essential ingredient for stability in any political arrangement;
3 that agreement must be pursued and established by exclusively democratic, peaceful means, without resort to violence or coercion;
4 that any new political arrangements must be based on full respect for, and protection and expression of, the rights and identities of both traditions in Ireland and even-handedly afford both communities in Northern Ireland parity of esteem and treatment, including equality of opportunity and advantage.

Examining these principles, one notes a fascinating mixture of the sometimes competing interpretations of rights being examined throughout this study, particularly the balance between the right to self-determination and who is entitled to exercise it and the concern with group rights and equality. These principles summarise the key human rights concerns that appear throughout the study.

These principles had already been set out in various forms and in different language both in the Downing Street Declaration as well as in other statements made by both parties. However, the Document amplified the principles and put some flesh on the bones of the eventual agreement in terms of the kind of institutions and structures that could be developed as part of a final deal. From a human rights perspective, the two main principles of interest relate to the right to self-determination and the rights of both communities and traditions to parity of esteem and treatment. Within this perspective, while there were no major new departures, it is useful to record that the Irish government was clearly acknowledging the importance of framing the rights language in a manner that is also attractive to the unionist community. Another matter worth recording is the clearly manifested willingness on both sides to recognise two communities with two traditions both of which required respect. Notwithstanding these advances, one should acknowledge that the issue of the right to self-determination, which was the most delicate and which lay at the root of the conflict, had already been disposed of in the Anglo-Irish Agreement and in the Downing Street Declaration. Consequently, the constitutional status of Northern Ireland would be determined by the majority of the people in Northern Ireland.

The unionist reaction to the Frameworks documents was negative. The Ulster Unionist Party stated that "the documents … are a cunningly contrived snare to enmesh the Ulster people into acquiescing and indeed accelerating the end of the Union and their British identity."[34] The main criticisms centred on the North–South relations and institutions (labelled as "an embryonic all Ireland government"[35]). Peter Robinson, then deputy leader of the DUP, commented that "Mr Major's framework is for an all-Ireland structure with executive power, which will be a precursor to a united Ireland."[36] The unionist objection to the Frameworks Document was clearly based on viewing the North–South dimension as the slippery slope to a united Ireland much in the same vein as the Anglo-Irish Agreement.

More interestingly, from the human rights perspective, were the criticisms emanating from Sinn Féin which included the claim that

> regardless of the promise of equality contained within the Framework document, the British continue to demonstrate bad faith and to procrastinate at every step.... We await meaningful indications of Britain's good faith. There are a whole range of civil and human rights issues which can and must be addressed immediately.[37]

This criticism by Sinn Féin seems to indicate that the republican community wanted to include the human rights agenda within the peace process at a higher level of attention. Gerry Adams explains that this emphasis on human rights was also intended to provide an outline of the kind of policies it would seek to promote in a united Ireland: "We needed to reach out to unionists and to explain what sort of Ireland we envisioned – one that is inclusive, built on equality and justice and human rights."[38] This attempt to focus on human rights issues within the peace process was gathering some momentum in the mid-1990s. This view is encapsulated in a statement by Michael Farrell (the former People's Democracy leader) who in 1995 stated that:

> It is our job to put human rights on the agenda in the peace process. Human rights violations were one, if not the fundamental, reason for the conflict in the first place. So human rights protection must become a central aspect to the solution.[39]

In some ways, this call for greater attention to the human rights agenda was heeded. The political parties in Northern Ireland, to varying degrees, included human rights principles and language in their proposals. The SDLP had, since its founding, given high priority to human rights issues. Its electoral manifestos all highlighted the commitment to human rights and justice. The party was to a large extent a by-product of the civil rights movement and thus it is unsurprising that it has had a consistent engagement with the human rights agenda. This was clearly stated in the SDLP electoral manifesto of 1992: "Central to the SDLP's work in the last twenty-two years has been its determined advocacy of human rights."[40] The same manifesto referred to specific SDLP campaigns including fair employment, emergency powers, inquests, lethal force, plastic bullets, the right to silence, the broadcasting ban and, specifically, the right to life and its abuse by paramilitary organisations. In particular, the following statement bears examination in light of future events:

> The greatest contribution to civil and human rights in Northern Ireland would be an end to the paramilitary campaign. It would result in the

> removal of all troops and armed police from our streets and the ending of all the emergency legislation about which there has been so much complaint.[41]

This focus on the end of paramilitary violence during the conflict is both obvious and natural. The end of paramilitary violence did indeed bring huge improvements in the human rights situation in Northern Ireland. However, it is likewise clear that the human rights agenda needed to be, and needs to be, a broader one. Issues of race, gender, sexual orientation, social exclusion, citizenship and the responsibilities this entails are, inter alia, some of the human rights issues which remained largely unaddressed by the ending of paramilitary violence. In its 1997 electoral manifesto the SDLP, with respect to human rights, moved beyond the twin issues of fair employment and administration of justice. The human rights language adopted in the manifesto seemed to indicate a broader approach to rights holding that "as a social democratic party we endorse social and economic rights, as well as political rights" and arguing that the SDLP would focus on issues of health, education, housing as well as employment.[42]

At this stage, with the likelihood of a fresh impetus to the peace process following the 1997 election, the SDLP also moved to make direct connections between an eventual peace agreement and human rights. In discussing issues of justice and policing in 1997, the SDLP argued that "human rights and justice issues [are] essential elements of our problems in Northern Ireland" and that "the incorporation of a bill of rights must be a key aspect of the agreement."[43]

On the other hand, Sinn Féin's developing electoral strategy also moved clearly into the area of human rights discourse. It was obvious that as a party seeking to tap into the nationalist voting pool it had to engage with the traditional nationalist rallying call of combating discrimination in Northern Ireland. Sinn Féin was clearly trying to position itself as a party which was both republican and strongly committed to human rights and social justice. It sought to wed the constitutional issue and the right to self-determination with equality, social justice and human rights.

In its 1992 manifesto Sinn Féin's approach was limited to a focus on national rights, in particular the right to self-determination, explaining that this right was "the core from which flows the ability to promote, exercise and defend other rights".[44] Conversely, the 1997 manifesto offered a stronger and more varied human rights agenda with references to discrimination, social exclusion and antisocial behaviour, as well as youth, women and policing. Sinn Féin's vision is described, inter alia, as follows:

> A vision of the redistribution of wealth, the well-being of the aged, the advancement of youth, the liberation of women, and the protection of our children. It is a vision that rejects forced emigration and unemployment, the destruction of the environment, culture oppression, sexism and inequality.[45]

The stumbling block against this appealing combination for nationalists was Sinn Féin's continuing support of the physical force tradition and its links to the IRA. The natural come-back to a party espousing both human rights and violence was that such a combination was untenable and indeed hypocritical. It is perhaps not surprising that Sinn Féin made huge electoral gains after it renounced support for violent means and when the IRA effectively decommissioned. At that stage the combination of Irish unity, social justice, equality and human rights (unencumbered by any reference to violence) became an overwhelmingly appealing political proposition for the nationalist and republican community in Northern Ireland.

In the mid-1990s the unionist parties' attitude to the human rights agenda also continued to evolve in a somewhat more serpentine manner. The UUP in this period sought to engage with the human rights agenda by crafting its own human rights discourse, which on the one hand accepted that the human rights agenda was part of the peace process while at the same time clarifying its own views on how to construct and construe such an agenda. Its 1992 electoral manifesto gives an early indication of this development when it stated that "The Ulster Unionist Party seeks a new Bill of Rights which will define specifically the rights and responsibilities of all citizens of the United Kingdom."[46] The reference to responsibilities as well as rights is one indicator of the approach to human rights preferred by the UUP, while the proposal to implement such rights as part of a UK-wide policy (rather than through a specific Northern Irish approach) is also noteworthy. This latter point was, of course, completely consistent with the UUP's philosophy, prevalent at the time under Jim Molyneaux's leadership, of seeking integration with the UK rather than advocating a special status for Northern Ireland. The UUP's approach to human rights, policing and the administration of justice issues were also unsurprisingly different from those of the SDLP (or *multo magis* Sinn Féin). While acknowledging that human error, very occasionally, led to mistakes by the forces of law and order in this field, the UUP claimed that such lapses "should not be used as an excuse for subverting the whole British system of justice which hitherto has been a byword for fairness and impartiality".[47] Once again, the UUP's emphasis is on upholding British standards of justice and fairness rather than in any way departing from them.

The UUP's stance in respect of the human rights agenda had developed further by 1996 as evidenced by its proposals in the 1996 manifesto for the Forum elections. After reiterating the desire to have the European Convention on Human Rights incorporated into UK law it also went a step further by advocating consideration of the models for minority protection developed by the Organisation of Security and Cooperation in Europe (OSCE) and Council of Europe, with a view to their possible adaptation for Northern Ireland.[48] This is an extremely interesting and important point for a number of reasons. The first point is that once again one witnesses the architecture of international or European human rights shaping political behaviour and supplying tools that may be used by Northern Irish politicians. Within this context one can claim that these regional and international human rights frameworks aided in achieving a political settlement. Further points of interest in these UUP proposals are that the UUP showed a willingness to consider specific Northern Irish protection (rather than UK-wide measures) and going beyond a Bill of Rights for individuals into the field of minority rights.

In making this proposal the UUP also makes the highly interesting comment that "there are many [minorities] in this society." This seems to indicate that the UUP is (for whatever reason) proposing a wider view of minorities than the one traditionally considered in Northern Ireland. Equally noteworthy is the statement made by the UUP in this manifesto:

> The UUP attaches great importance to this area of our work, believing that safeguarding of individual and group rights will be a fundamental building block in any agreement that is likely to command widespread acceptance throughout the community.

This is a far cry from the position articulated by the party in earlier periods (as illustrated in Chapters 3 and 4) when it either rejected human rights legislation as unworkable or perceived human rights as a cover for republicanism. This shift in the UUP's position vis-à-vis human rights is certainly of note and may be attributed to the developments in international, regional and national human rights law and policy.[49] Incidentally, the UUP manifesto commitment to human rights quoted above also echoes the position of the SDLP in its own 1997 manifesto. It is evident that by 1997 the two main parties in Northern Irish politics at the time considered the human rights agenda as an integral part of the prospective peace agreement. Both parties also viewed with favour the adoption of a bill of rights albeit they differed as to the scope of such a bill, with the UUP favouring a UK-wide bill (through the incorporation of the European Convention on Human Rights) and the SDLP favouring a bill of rights for Northern Ireland.

The Democratic Unionist Party's approach to human rights was altogether less evident than that of other parties. The primary foci of their policy were the replacement of the Anglo-Irish Agreement and a determined and forceful fight against the IRA. Its 1992 electoral manifesto entitled *Time To Tackle Terrorism* was a clear illustration of this approach. In its anti-terrorism policy, the DUP advocated the proscription of Sinn Féin, stiffer sentences, surprise search and seizure, the introduction of ID cards, the possibility of curfews and of executive detention (internment). Some of these policies would have been perceived by the nationalist/republican community as a further abuse in the administration of justice and human rights.[50] Nevertheless, in a summary of their proposals the party included a bill of rights "safeguarding individual liberties".[51] There was no further elaboration of this proposal.

On the issue of employment, the party also referred to the right to work and the efforts to increase employment opportunities, and it also had its own interpretation of fair employment, i.e. recruitment "based on merit alone".[52] This was a direct attack on the Fair Employment Commission (and its predecessor the Fair Employment Agency) which the DUP claimed were encouraging discrimination against Protestants. Again, one notices all parties referencing fair employment and the right to work but interpreting the same language in very different ways. This differential in the interpretation of human rights language (and policy) is a recurring feature of the human rights landscape in Northern Ireland. The DUP's policy vis-à-vis human rights issues did not develop in the period leading to the 1997 elections. Its 1997 manifesto concentrated on denouncing the Anglo-Irish Agreement, the Downing Street Declaration and the *Framework Documents* while attacking the UUP for colluding with the SDLP. It also emphasised decommissioning for an eventual entry of Sinn Féin into talks and reiterated its policy to defeat rather than contain the IRA.[53] The manifesto did not comment on human rights issues.

The Alliance Party, although having limited electoral support, provides interesting insights into the human rights agenda as it involved itself in a full and constant manner in the human rights debate. For instance, in 1997 it proposed several policies which would eventually become part of the Northern Ireland human rights agenda, including the creation of a bill of rights, the creation of a Department of Justice for Northern Ireland and a fully independent police complaints procedure. Apart from these issues, the Alliance manifesto for 1997 engaged with the rights agenda throughout in terms of education, policing, employment, discrimination and also in terms of the political process. With respect to the latter issue the Alliance Party proposed that any peace agreement had to include a bill of rights as one of four main elements. It held this view on the following basis:

> Whilst every community needs a legal structure for the preservation of individual rights, it is particularly vital in a divided society like Northern Ireland, where there is a history of discrimination and disadvantage. Alliance will insist on the incorporation of a Bill of Rights and a series of other measures to give confidence to all citizens that their rights will be protected.[54]

This statement throws light on the fact that substantial overlap existed on the necessity to include human rights as an integral part of any peace agreement (as seen above both the SDLP and UUP also advocated this in different ways). The language used by the Alliance Party also points to another issue: human rights were viewed as a confidence-building measure which could assuage suspicions on all sides. The thinking here seems to imply that both communities had fears emanating from changes to the status quo and the unknown directions these changes could follow. Human rights were presented as a mechanism whereby the process of change inherent in the peace process would always be accompanied by human rights guarantees that gave a modicum of peace of mind to all concerned. One can summarise the development in the human rights agenda of Northern Irish political parties up to the mid-1990s as follows.

1 The main political parties in Northern Ireland all developed – to varying degrees – their position vis-à-vis human rights. Clearly, no party was presenting itself as objecting to human rights principles in theory.
2 The developments witnessed within the UUP with respect to human rights are especially noticeable given that the party shifted considerably its position in this respect.
3 The specific human rights language used and the policies proposed by the parties showed both areas of agreement, as well as disagreement.
4 The two main parties at the time (UUP and SDLP) both recognised that the eventual peace agreement would need to include a strong human rights dimension.
5 It seems that this commitment to the human rights agenda was also coloured by a view of human rights as a confidence-building instrument which could assist in making the conflicting communities more at ease with the peace process.

These developments illustrated both the positive possibilities which the human rights agenda presented but also signalled the potential difficulties. The possibility of crafting a strong human rights dimension to the peace agreement was clear. The potential of disagreeing on the exact terms of this dimension was also evident. In fact, in the lead up to the 1998 Good Friday Agreement both of these facets would come to light. Therefore, an examination of the human rights aspects of the negotiations that led to the Agreement is certainly useful to understand how the parties viewed human rights in the context of the overall agreement.

Human rights in the Peace Agreement

A detailed examination of the negotiations that led to the Peace Agreement is clearly beyond the scope of this study. However, an exploration is merited of the way human rights issues impacted upon the negotiations and of the ways in which the negotiations addressed human rights issues. The increasing recognition of human rights as an important building block in the final agreement made the inclusion of a human rights dimension under Strands 1 and 2 of the negotiations a sine qua non. The UUP acknowledged the importance of this approach when it stated that the areas of justice and rights "because of their special significance, merit particular attention".[55]

Thus, there was no significant obstacle to including the rights and justice issue on the agenda for negotiations within Strand 1, i.e. how to incorporate the human rights and justice agenda through agreed structures and processes within Northern Ireland. The human rights agenda was also part of Strand 2, i.e. whereby the UK and the Republic of Ireland would adopt themselves certain human rights standards and structures.

Notwithstanding the fact that "*significant consensus*" existed on human rights issues, there was also an acknowledgment, at least within some parties, that the "whole question of human rights, group rights and other justice issues are very sensitive matters in our situation".[56] Given the fact that these were very sensitive matters one expected them to be a matter of some debate during negotiations. However, it seems that human rights issues – except for policing – were not a major topic of contention, debate or even discussion during the negotiations.

If one looks at the main matters of contention during the negotiation, one can identify two main areas of substantial disagreement: the scope of the North–South bodies; and the issue of decommissioning. The then UK Prime Minister Tony Blair, writing in the unionist-leaning newspaper the *News Letter*, just before the talks started in earnest, stated that a number of difficult issues would have to be dealt with during the negotiations and that "the most important of these is decommissioning of paramilitary weapons."[57] This view was reiterated in a joint statement of the Prime Minister and the Taoiseach where they considered "the resolution of the decommissioning issue as an indispensable part of the process of negotiation".[58] This focus on decommissioning is also illustrated by the approach taken during the formal negotiations where the issue of decommissioning was isolated from the other issues and dealt with outside the plenary in a special liaison sub-committee.[59] The importance and difficulty of decommissioning was aptly described by Tony Blair as "a big ball and chain round our legs".[60]

The main actors in the negotiations also bear witness to the fact that the major concerns during the negotiations were not human rights issues and justice. This in part was due to recognition that some of the justice issues (particularly policing and criminal justice matters) could not be dealt with during these negotiations and thus it was agreed that they would be dealt with after the negotiations were completed through specially appointed commissions.[61]

Tony Blair's memoirs give a detailed account of what were the main subjects of disagreement with which he had to deal personally in the final stages of the multi-party negotiations. The subjects were somewhat varied but essentially featured: (1) the nature and composition of the executive that was to govern Northern Ireland, more precisely the extent and nature of power sharing agreements; (2) the North–South bodies; (3) the timing of the release of prisoners serving sentences for violent crimes connected to paramilitary activity; and (4) the extent to which the political process foreseen in the Northern Ireland Assembly and the power-sharing executive would function while the process of decommissioning was not yet completed. There were also two other issues which at different stages late in the process threatened to derail the agreement: the status of Ullans as a language in Northern Ireland; and the closure of Maryfield (the building which hosted the secretariat of the Anglo-Irish Agreement).[62] This account is reinforced by the UK government's chief negotiator in Northern Ireland, Jonathan Powell. Powell states that the biggest stumbling block was the scope and extent of the North–South bodies:

> In essence Trimble's problem was not so much the North/South bodies themselves, as the amount of space given to them in the agreement … the agreement was not deliverable as it stood in the unionist community.… George Mitchell took the same line.[63]

He also argued that success in resolving the issue relating to North–South bodies eased the resolution of the impasse related to the formation of the executive under Strand 1, with the unionists agreeing to a power sharing executive rather than the committee system they had originally proposed.[64] The unionist suspicion of what they termed cross-border bodies stemmed from the Anglo-Irish Agreement which they had objected to so vehemently, precisely because it gave a consultative role to the Republic in certain areas of Northern Irish policy. David Trimble writing in 1999 made this clear:

> It appeared to us that the major obstacles were the failure of the two governments to resolve constitutional differences and what appeared to unionists as the ambition of the Irish government, under the guise of cross-border co-operation to take over a substantial part of the internal government of Northern Ireland.[65]

With the possible exception of the status of Ullans (which can be classified as an issue of cultural right), none of the other make or break issues were connected directly to the human rights dimension of the Agreement. David Trimble when describing all the various human rights aspects of the Good Friday Agreement states unambiguously: "All these matters were not controversial in the Talks themselves, Unionists having been committed to the concept of a judicially enforceable Bill of Rights since the early 1970s."

David Trimble's assertion that the human rights dimension was not a matter of contention because the unionists (and the nationalists) had all agreed to a bill of rights is interesting for two reasons: (1) it seems to reduce the human rights dimension of the talks and agreement to one component thereof, i.e. the bill of rights; this in itself would suggest a somewhat limited understanding of the human rights agenda; and (2) it ignores the different understandings that the parties had of what should be included in the bill of rights (and how the bill would operate in practice). These are the problems which, after the Agreement was signed, the Northern Ireland parties and human rights community spent a decade contending with and which remain to some extent unresolved (as will be explored in the next chapter). The fact that the parties had diverging visions on the bill of rights should have been well known,[66] which renders the lack of disagreement (and serious debate) on this aspect of the Agreement more difficult to comprehend.

One possible explanation is that the parties did not have a real interest in the human rights agenda – although once again one must stress that even when using rights language instrumentally, the rights agenda was still influencing and shaping local politics. Nevertheless, the human rights agenda seems to have been a matter of interest, at least to some of the political parties during the negotiations. The submissions made by the various parties to the talks appear to illustrate this point. Sinn Féin submitted 15 pages of documentation focusing on justice and rights issues covering civil, political, economic, cultural, group and individual rights as well as mechanisms for the implementation of rights.[67] Gerry Adams also stated that the human rights issue "was creating a lot of debate".[68] The Alliance Party in its own submissions stated at the outset that "justice and human rights issues are clearly central to these talks and the success of the agreement reached here",[69] while the Northern Ireland Women's Coalition (which notwithstanding its limited electoral appeal was a proactive party to the talks) also presented detailed submissions on human rights claiming that "issues of justice, fairness and rights have played a key role in both the causes of the conflict in Northern Ireland, and the nature of that conflict itself."[70]

Another possible explanation is that the human rights agenda was not fully understood by the parties to the extent they underestimated the extent of the disagreement between the parties vis-à-vis what they understood human rights to mean in practice. Given the role played by human rights issues throughout the conflict, this seems to be a difficult proposition to maintain. Throughout the study the divergent views on human rights held by the different parties over a period of six decades have been outlined. That these divergences should disappear instantaneously is hardly possible.

A more credible contention is that the parties themselves considered human rights as being of secondary importance and believed that the inclusion of a human rights dimension in the Agreement was merely a window-dressing concern that made everyone look good by bowing towards the altar of human rights. This may be a distinct possibility given the increasingly high-profile enjoyed by human rights within the international community. It has been argued that over the last five decades human rights have "been internationalized, and internationally recognized rights have been routinized"[71] and that "for the foreseeable future, the primary issue about human rights in international relations is not whether we should acknowledge them as fundamental norms. Rather, the primary issue is when and how to implement human rights in specific situations."[72] It is certainly the case that within mainstream European politics in the late twentieth century, any party that was seen to be opposing human rights would be viewed as a pariah. In other words, human rights have become a badge of respectability and civilised behaviour. Thus, no party in Northern Ireland would explicitly oppose human rights or oppose their inclusion in any new dispensation. Nevertheless, they did (and do) disagree vigorously on what human rights mean and how they should be implemented.

One may argue that this interpretation of the approach of the Northern Ireland parties towards the human rights dimension of the Agreement is validated by the Agreement itself. While giving significant space to rights, justice and safeguards, a number of key decisions concerning these aspects were deferred or referred to bodies that would examine the issues in due course. This is evident when one compares the very detailed decisions taken in the Agreement vis-à-vis "Democratic Institutions" and the many but more general decisions taken in the Agreement in respect of "Rights, Safeguards and Equality of Opportunity".

In the section on "Democratic Institutions in Northern Ireland" the provisions on an elected Assembly are extremely detailed, including method of election, allocation of Committee Chairs and selection of Ministers, their oath of office and their code of conduct. The detail is quite impressive, especially as to how decisions would be taken and by whom. Conversely, in the section on "Human Rights", while the parties "affirm" their commitment to a number of rights, the human rights obligations on the UK government are drafted in such terms as "subject to public consultation", and "The new Northern Ireland Human Rights Commission will be invited to consult and to advise" on the scope for adopting a Bill of Rights for Northern Ireland. When it comes to the closely related section on "Policing and Justice", the Agreement provided for "an independent Commission ... [to] be established to make recommendations for future policing arrangements in Northern Ireland".

These referral and deferral mechanisms may be explained partly by the sheer impossibility to deal with detail on every issue in the Agreement itself. However, it could also partly be explained by the fact that while the human rights agenda was given ample space in the Agreement, it was considered subsidiary to other elements. In other words, while "the language of human rights flows through the Agreement",[73] the meaning and thus the impact of such language "on the ground" remained uncertain, subject to interpretation and somewhat disputed. As a result the human rights dimension of the Agreement remains problematic in its implications for the protection of human rights in the UK, Northern Ireland and for the Westminster constitutional system.[74]

One can conclude that, given the history of Northern Ireland since its creation, it was inevitable and indeed indispensable for any Peace Agreement to include a significant human rights component. As shown in Chapters 3 to 5, human rights abuses (whether real or perceived) were a major grievance of the minority community. The SDLP and Sinn Féin would not have assented to the Agreement without such a human rights component to the Agreement. For unionists, human rights were not a key concern and some, at least, within unionism retained a suspicion that human rights were a tool used by the minority to attack or belittle the state. However, such suspicions or reservations were not sufficiently strong to create obstacles to the inclusion of human rights provisions. Human rights, as already described, had become a badge of international respectability and thinking around human rights had also developed within unionism, especially within the UUP. Furthermore, some of the human rights provisions were sufficiently open to interpretation that their inclusion could be accepted by parties with different understandings on human rights. That is not to say that the human rights components were insignificant. As will be demonstrated in the next chapter some of the equality, human rights and related provisions, such as the establishment of Human Rights and Equality Commissions, changes to policing and criminal justice and the enactment of human rights compliant legislation, were of significance and changed Northern Ireland's relationship with human rights.

In the next chapter, the challenges associated with implementing the human rights components of the Agreement will be examined in greater detail with a view to ascertaining what the key obstacles and major successes have been in this respect.

Conclusion

The period examined in this chapter was especially crucial in the development of the human rights agenda for the various political parties in Northern Ireland. It was also a crucial period for the envisioning of human rights agenda in its relationship with the peace process. Most fundamentally, this period also witnessed the adoption of the Peace Agreement with a strong human rights dimension. However, human rights in Northern Ireland itself did not develop radically during the period in question, insofar as the focus on specific human rights themes is concerned. There were some legislative developments with respect to human rights that occurred during this period. These included the Disability Discrimination Act 1995, the Race Relations (NI) Order 1997 and the Fair Employment and Treatment (NI) Order 1998. Overall, the human rights situation remained primarily concerned with issues of equality (especially with respect to employment) and with the twin issues of policing and the criminal justice system (referred to jointly as the administration of justice). Nevertheless, human rights did shape and influence political choices and decisions by the Northern Irish political parties as well as the UK and Irish governments. In this sense, human rights language and the rights agenda became more firmly anchored in the Northern Irish political field. The impact of international, regional and UK rights norms on the Northern Irish political field was very evident in the period under examination. It is not overstating the case to hold that during this period the growing impact of international and regional human rights norms made it virtually impossible to avoid rights language by the parties to the political process.

In terms of the human rights themes addressed, equality in employment and an end to discrimination, which was one of the original human rights complaints of the nationalist community, retained its importance within the public policy concerns of Northern Ireland. In fact, the period examined in this chapter witnessed significant progress in the field of employment equality.

This progress probably marked the beginning of the end of employment discrimination as a major human rights issue for the minority community in Northern Ireland. The same level of progress was not registered in the other key human rights challenge: the administration of justice. Policing and criminal justice issues remained largely intractable matters and a continuing cause of alienation for the minority community. This lack of progress may also explain why the Peace Agreement dealt with these two issues by establishing ad hoc commissions to deal with them.

The Anglo-Irish Agreement which was adopted at the beginning of this period, to some extent, set the stage for the treatment of human rights in peace negotiations and agreements. It referred to the rights of the two traditions in general terms while focusing specifically on equality issues and the administration of justice (thus confirming the primacy of these two issues within the Northern Irish human rights agenda). Overall, human rights appeared as an important, but not vital, component of the Anglo-Irish Agreement. In this sense, it may be regarded as a prototype of the role of human rights in peace negotiations in Northern Ireland.

Another important aspect that developed in this period was the attitude, evident in a number of references in the texts and in public utterances, of viewing human rights as guarantees for the "other community". Thus, human rights could be seen as an assurance for nationalists and republicans to persuade them to accept devolved government, while human rights guarantees could also be presented by republicans as guarantees for unionists in a united Ireland. In this context, Sinn Féin was especially ardent in using human rights language to present its vision of a united Ireland.

In this period, one notices an evolution in the engagement with human rights by all the major political parties in Northern Ireland. The SDLP, naturally, continued to advocate human rights as strongly as ever with an emphasis on a Bill of Rights for Northern Ireland. Sinn Féin engaged much more broadly with the human rights agenda than it had done before (when it had focused mainly on self-determination). Nevertheless, its continued support for the IRA remained an obstacle to its human rights agenda. The UUP also witnessed a substantial engagement with the human rights agenda in this period. While becoming more engaged with human rights it also emphasised British notions of rights, fairness and justice. In practice the UUP made suggestions to incorporate the European Convention in domestic law and to adopt Council of Europe and OSCE standards of protection for minorities. The idea of human rights as guarantees is relevant in this context as well. Finally, the DUP witnessed the least development in its attitude to the human rights agenda but nevertheless saw limited progress through its commitment to a Bill of Rights.

The 1990s witnessed development for all main parties in their attitude to human rights with broad agreement on the need for human rights protection in Northern Ireland. However, disagreements on the details of the form, extent and detail of human rights protection were also evident between the parties. Overall, these developments set the stage for a strong human rights dimension in the Peace Agreement. It is also worth noting that in 1995 the Dayton Peace Accords were signed leading to a resolution of the Bosnian conflict. The Accords had a significant human rights component with the establishment of a Commission on Human Rights, composed of a Human Rights Ombudsman and a Human Rights Chamber being one of the elements of the Accords. Furthermore, there was also a commitment by the parties to the Accord to allow full access into Bosnia and Herzegovina of international human rights institutions and agencies.[75] This significant human rights component further evidences the growing role of human rights in conflict resolution processes which may also have had an impact on the eventual contents of the Northern Irish Peace Agreement.

Given this context, it is not surprising that during the negotiations that led to the Peace Agreement there were no major obstacles to a strong human rights component in the Agreement. The major obstacles to reach consensus in the Peace Agreements related to decommissioning of weapons, the detail of power-sharing, the extent of North–South bodies and the early release of prisoners. Nevertheless, given the subsequent history of some of the human rights provisions of the Agreement, the question of why there was no major discussion of the human rights agenda is an open one. In this context, the fact that by the 1990s human rights had become an international badge of respectability may be of some importance. To ensure such respectability all parties may have felt the need to agree to the inclusion of a strong human rights component to the Agreement without too much discussion. Ultimately, the most important decisions vis-à-vis human rights in the Agreement were either referred or deferred to subsequent discussions and fora. Given these referral and deferral mechanisms the parties may not have felt the need to engage with the detail of the human rights component of the Agreement. A political solution and the political/security elements of the Agreement were clearly considered more immediately vital than detailed consideration of human rights issues. The consequences of this are discussed in the next chapter.

The discussion above clarifies how the political parties' attitudes towards human rights shifted in the period discussed in this chapter. The other matter which the study deals with relates to how consciousness of human rights shaped political behaviour. Within this latter context, the chapter has revealed noteworthy developments. It is evident that the architecture of international and European human rights shaped to a certain extent political behaviour and also supplied tools that were used by Northern Irish politicians in different ways. Furthermore, one notes that the developing regional and international human rights framework aided in achieving a political settlement by providing a globally accepted framework in which the various parties (for differing reasons) could anchor the settlement. Globally accepted human rights norms also provided several widely accepted criteria that facilitated acceptance of the political settlement. This chapter also highlighted that rights, even when invoked for instrumental reasons, were gradually becoming an indispensable concept in negotiating a final political settlement. Building on a tradition of rights, which as highlighted in Chapter 3, was of a longer standing in Northern Ireland than normally acknowledged, the parties used the expanding international and regional human rights norms to shape a political settlement.

Notes

1 According to the Colville Report of 1990 (cited below, note 2), the number of conflict-related deaths was 54 in 1985, 61 in 1986, 93 in 1987 and 1988 and 62 in 1989. The number of conflict-related injuries was 916 in 1985, 1,450 in 1986, 1,130 in 1987, 1,047 in 1988 and 959 in 1989.
2 In this context this chapter will refer to the Review of the Northern Ireland (Emergency Provisions) Acts 1978 and 1987 chaired by the Viscount Colville of Culross QC and published by HMSO in 1990 (referred to as the Colville Report). The Viscount Colville of Culross, QC, *Review of the Northern Ireland (Emergency Provisions) Acts 1978 and 1987* (London: Her Majesty's Stationery Office, 1990).
3 The Standing Advisory Commission on Human Rights, *Report on Religious and Political Discrimination and Equality of Opportunity in Northern Ireland* (London: Her Majesty's Stationery Office, 1987) is evidence of the continuing challenges in this field.
4 The Drumcree standoffs in 1995 and 1996 exemplified the continuing significance of parades in the Northern Ireland conflict.
5 In his memoirs, Douglas Hurd recounts that following a visit to Northern Ireland in 1978 he had already formed the view, as a result of discussions with security forces, that the IRA could not be beaten permanently. See Douglas Hurd, *Memoirs* (London: Abacus, 2004), 277. This view was reinforced during his period as Secretary of State for Northern Ireland between 1984 and 1985. Ibid., 334.
6 The 1993 Downing Street Declaration and the 1995 Frameworks Document are two examples. John Major and Albert Reynolds, *Joint Declaration on Peace: The Downing Street Declaration*; and The British and Irish Governments, *The Framework Documents*, 22 February 1995.
7 See, for example, the accounts of the negotiation in George John Mitchell, *Making Peace* (Oakland: University of California Press, 2000); Jonathan Powell, *Great Hatred, Little Room: Making Peace in Northern Ireland* (London: Vintage Books London, 2009); and Tony Blair, *A Journey: My Political Life* (London: Hutchinson, 2010).
8 Colin Harvey, "Building Bridges? Protecting Human Rights in Northern Ireland", *Human Rights Law Review* 1, no. 2 (2001), 244.
9 The Northern Ireland Peace Agreement, Declaration of Support, para. 2.
10 These reports and documents were identified in the Northern Ireland Political Collection of the Linen Hall Library, Belfast and in the CAIN Ulster.
11 See Chapter 2 where the focus on discrimination in employment and the operation of the Special Powers Act are discussed at length.
12 Fair Employment (Northern Ireland) Act, 1976.
13 Standing Advisory Commission on Human Rights, Religious and Political Discrimination and Equality of Opportunity in Northern Ireland, *Report on Fair Employment*, Presented to Parliament by the Secretary of State for Northern Ireland. The Standing Advisory Commission on Human Rights, *Report on Religious and Political Discrimination and Equality of Opportunity in Northern Ireland*, para. 15.2.
14 Ibid., paras 15.3, 15.13 and 15.14.
15 For a review of the impact of the 1989 Act, see Raymond T. Russell, *Fair Employment in Northern Ireland: The Decades of Change (1990–2010)* (Northern Ireland

Assembly, Research and Information Service, 10 August 2012), accessed 15 August 2012, www.niassembly.gov.uk/Documents/RaISe/Publications/2012/general/12112.pdf.

16 Ibid., 4.

17 Ibid.

18 See Chapters 2, 3 and 4.

19 Viscount Colville of Culross, *Review of the Northern Ireland (Emergency Provisions) Acts 1978 and 1987*, para. 1.4.

20 Dr. Maurice Hayes to Sir Ewart Bell, Confidential Minute, 8 February 1982, Northern Ireland Political Collection, Linen Hall Library, Belfast.

21 Ibid.

22 Independent Commission on Policing in Northern Ireland, *A New Beginning: Policing in Northern Ireland: The Report of the Independent Commission on Policing in Northern Ireland* ("Patten Report", Belfast, 9 September 1999), accessed 8 July 2014, http://cain.ulst.ac.uk/issues/police/patten/patten99.pdf, para. 1.3.

23 See http://news.bbc.co.uk/2/hi/4409447.stm, accessed 24 January 2016.

24 *R* v. *Home Secretary*, 139 New L.J.R., 1229 (Div Cit).

25 www.nytimes.com/1989/05/27/world/london-broadcasting-ban-on-ulster-militants-upheld.html.

26 Brice Dickson, "The Impact of the Human Rights Act in Northern Ireland", in *Judges, Transition and Human Rights*, ed. John Morison, Kieran McEvoy and Gordon Anthony (Oxford: Oxford University Press, 2007).

27 The 15 unionist MPs in the House of Commons resigned their seats in December 1985 in protest against the Agreement. On 3 March a 24-hour strike against the Agreement was held in Northern Ireland. The leader of the UUP led a legal challenge against the Agreement which however failed (see Ex-parte Molyneaux, *Weekly Law Reports*, 331 (1986)).

28 In his memoirs, Douglas Hurd, Secretary of State for Northern Ireland during most of the negotiations leading to the Agreement, states that the secrecy of the negotiations "built up a huge grievance amongst the unionists". Hurd, *Memoirs*, 340.

29 *Review of the Working of the Conference*, 24 May 1989, Northern Ireland Political Collection, Linen Hall Library, Belfast.

30 Hurd, *Memoirs*, 336.

31 Gerry Adams, *Hope and History: Making Peace in Ireland* (London: Brandon, 2003), 148.

32 House of Commons, *Ireland (Joint Declaration)*, 15 December 1993, col. 1073, www.publications.parliament.uk/pa/cm199394/cmhansrd/1993-12-15/Debate-1.html.

33 Ulster Unionist Parliamentary Party, *Briefing Note on the Downing Street Declaration of the 15th December 1993*, 15 December 1993, Northern Ireland Political Collection, Linen Hall Library, Belfast.

34 Ulster Unionist Party, Response to Frameworks for the Future, 10 March 1995, Northern Ireland Political Collection, Linen Hall Library, Belfast.

35 Ibid.

36 Peter Robinson, "Dagger in a Friend's Hand", *Independent*, 24 February 1995.

37 *Initial Discussion of "A New Framework for Agreement": Sinn Féin Submission to the Forum for Peace and Reconciliation*, 5 May 1995.

38 Adams, *Hope and History*, 127.

39 Britain and Ireland Human Rights Centre, *Human Rights: A Framework for Peace* (London: Britain and Ireland Human Rights Centre, 21 January 1995), 11.

40 SDLP, *A New North, a New Ireland, a New Europe*, 1992.

41 Ibid.

42 SDLP, *Real Leadership, Real Peace: Westminster General Election Manifesto*, 1997, 1.

43 Ibid., 15.

44 Sinn Féin, *Towards a Lasting Peace in Ireland*, 1992, 4.
45 Sinn Féin, *A New Opportunity for Peace: Manifesto*, 1997, 3.
46 Ulster Unionist Party, *The People's Choice: Manifesto General Election*, 9 April 1992, 3.
47 Ibid., 5.
48 Ulster Unionist Party, *Building Your Future Within the Union: Manifesto Forum Election*, 1996.
49 This is confirmed by Mr Dermott Nesbitt who cited particularly the impact of the Council of Europe Framework Convention on National Minorities of 1995. Mr Dermot Nesbitt, Interview with former UUP MLA (Member of the Legislative Assembly) and spokesperson on human rights, 15 April 2014.
50 Ulster Democratic Union Party, *Time to Tackle Terrorism 1992: Election Manifesto*, 1992, 1–2.
51 Ibid., 3.
52 Ibid., 5.
53 Democratic Unionist Party, DUP Manifesto, *Democracy – Not Dublin Rule*, 1997.
54 The Alliance Party of Northern Ireland, *Agenda for Change: The Alliance Manifesto*, 1 May 1997, 5.
55 Ulster Unionist Party, *Pathways to Peace within the Union*, 4 March 1997.
56 Ibid.
57 The Rt Hon. Tony Blair MP, "All Have to Make Compromises", *News Letter*, 13 September 1997, 5.
58 Joint Statement of the Prime Minister and the Taoiseach, 15 September 1997.
59 *Procedural Motion, All-Party Negotiations Background Documents*, 24 September 1997. (Documents given to all participants in the Multi-Party Talks, Belfast, Northern Ireland Office, October 1997).
60 Blair, *A Journey*, 163.
61 Gerry Adams stated that "In our view policing and criminal justice were not problems we could resolve in this negotiation." Adams, *Hope and History*, 345.
62 For a full version of the account of the negotiations as viewed by the then UK Prime Minister, see Blair, *A Journey*, 167–75.
63 Powell, *Great Hatred, Little Room*, 92–3.
64 Ibid., 98.
65 David Trimble, "The Belfast Agreement", *Fordham International Law Journal* 22, no. 4 (1999), accessed 31 October 2013, www.davidtrimble.org/speeches_toraiseup13.htm.
66 The fact of the disagreement around the nature and scope of a bill of rights for Northern Ireland should have been known to the parties at least since 1985 when the Campaign for the Administration of Justice published a report entitled *Ways of Protecting Minority Rights in Northern Ireland*. In the report the different views held by all the political parties (except for Sinn Féin) on the possibility of adopting a bill of rights for Northern Ireland were set out. See Committee on the Administration of Justice, *Ways of Protecting Minority Rights in Northern Ireland*, vol. 7, June 1985.
67 Sinn Féin, Peace in Ireland: For a Future as Equals, Justice Issues, Rights and Safeguards. A Sinn Féin Submission to Strands One and Two of the Peace Talks, 10 November 1997.
68 Adams, *Hope and History*, 347.
69 The Alliance Party, *The Alliance Party Submissions to the Multi-Party Talks*, December 1997.
70 Northern Ireland Women's Coalition, Strand 1 Submission, Justice, Rights and Safeguards, December 1997.
71 David P. Forsythe, *Human Rights in International Relations* (Cambridge University Press, 2000), 5.

72 Ibid., 12.
73 Harvey, "Building Bridges?", 244.
74 This point is made by Alice Donald, Philip Leach and Andrew Puddephatt, *Developing a Bill of Rights for the United Kingdom*, Research Report 51 (Equality and Human Rights Commission, 2010).
75 See Annex 6 of the Dayton Accords, www.state.gov/p/eur/rls/or/dayton, accessed 23 January 2016.

7 Human rights in Northern Ireland, 1999–2014

An unfulfilled agenda?

Introduction

The previous chapter examined the extent to which human rights played a part in the negotiations leading to the Peace Agreement and the scope of the human rights provisions within the Agreement. The prominence of human rights and equality issues in the Agreement is clear and gave rise to considerable expectations that human rights would become better protected in Northern Ireland. It was expected that in some ways Northern Ireland would become a "model" in terms of human rights protection in post-conflict societies.[1] This chapter explores whether the promise of better human rights protection in Northern Ireland has been achieved in the decade since the Agreement and the reasons for such an achievement or lack thereof.

The questions mentioned above are important ones in order to understand the degree to which the human rights components of the Agreement were important to the political parties in Northern Ireland and the extent of the parties' commitment to human rights. This is directly related to the hypothesis referred to in Chapter 6, that conflict resolution efforts in Northern Ireland have focused more with ending physical violence than with building positive human relations within a society (including a deep commitment to and engagement with human rights).[2]

The following matters are examined in this chapter: (1) the recurring human rights themes in Northern Ireland and whether the Agreement led to their resolution; (2) whether the specific human rights provisions envisaged within the Agreement have been fully implemented; and (3) whether the overall protection and promotion of human rights in Northern Ireland can be viewed as successful in terms of building the positive peace referred to in Chapter 6.

It is clear that since 1998 there have been an abundance of legislative and policy measures within Northern Ireland which have a direct relevance to human rights. The two most obvious legislative measures with a direct impact on the protection and promotion of human rights in Northern Ireland are the Northern Ireland Act 1998 (and its subsequent amendments), which in Part VII focuses on human rights, and the UK-wide Human Rights Act of 1998 which also applies to Northern Ireland. In terms of policy initiatives and instruments, the Human Rights Commission and the Equality Commission were created through this Act and their work in the field of human rights and equality has been significant, albeit not without criticism. In particular, the Human Rights Commission's lengthy and, so far, unsuccessful attempt at reaching agreement on a Bill of Rights for Northern Ireland has caused debate and controversy. The Patten Report on policing in Northern Ireland and its subsequent implementation also have significant relevance from a human rights perspective with, inter alia, the creation of the PSNI and the Policing Board. The code of conduct on policing adopted in 2008 is of special salience in this respect with a strong emphasis on human rights. With reference to justice issues, there was an important development when justice matters were devolved to the Assembly and a Ministry of Justice was created within the Executive in 2010. Less successful has been the attempt by Northern Ireland to deal with the legacy of conflict. The 2009 Report of the Consultative Group on the Past chaired by Lord Eames and Denis Bradley was met by significant criticism upon its publication, while the talks chaired by Richard Haass intended to deal with the legacy of the conflict in a comprehensive manner failed to reach agreement. At the end of December 2014, the Stormont House Agreement was adopted, which included provisions related to legacy issues. This, however, requires an implementation process. Whether the legacy provisions are eventually implemented remains an open question. While a number of the legacy issues are not directly linked to human rights matters, others (such as the granting of immunities and the vexed issue of parades) do have a human rights dimension. Even a cursory glance at the human rights scenario post-1998 reveals a high level of activity, progress in some matters while other matters have failed to progress to any significant degree. This chapter will present a balance sheet of the broad human rights situation in Northern Ireland in the aftermath of the Peace Agreement, registering the human rights issues where legal and policy progress has been achieved and identifying those human rights issues where the status quo has prevailed.

Northern Ireland's recurring human rights challenges: finally resolved?

The recurring human rights issues referred to throughout this study have revolved around two main areas: (1) equality and discrimination and (2) the administration of justice and policing. A third critical human rights dimension emerged during the conflict from the start of the Troubles: killings by state security forces and by republican and loyalist paramilitaries. These killings, as discussed in Chapter 5, breached the most basic human right of all: the right to life. It is, therefore, important to assess the extent to which the 1998 Peace Agreement achieved its (arguably) most important human rights and general objective: an ending to the killings.

The number of conflict-related deaths in Northern Ireland between 1969 and 1998, according to the Sutton Index, was 3,483.[3] From 1999 to 2010, the number of deaths associated with the conflict was 85, while there is some doubt whether all of these were, in fact, related to the conflict. The total of 85 for this 11-year period is less than the number of deaths registered in the single year of 1993 when 88 conflict-related deaths occurred. It is also worth noting that for the five-year period 2006 to 2010 the total number of deaths was nine. This constitutes clear evidence that the situation in Northern Ireland with respect to the most basic human right, the right to life has improved very significantly. In fact, based on these statistics, a simple, but clear and unequivocal, first assessment can be made in terms of the human rights balance sheet for post-Peace Agreement Northern Ireland: abuses of the right to life, by state and non-state actors, have decreased to a very large degree. Former UUP human rights spokesman, Dermot Nesbitt, acknowledged the nature of this progress when saying: "we are a much better place than we were. There is stability and we are not going back to war."[4]

It is also important to note that the objective of ending the killings may have obfuscated the need to investigate fully and, possibly bring prosecutions, with respect to conflict-related killings. The issue of investigating conflict-related deaths and disappearances has three dimensions: killings by British security forces; killings by loyalist paramilitaries aided covertly by British forces or agents (the issue of collusion); and the disappearances and killings committed by paramilitary organisations. The Peace Agreement did not deal explicitly with this issue, bar some references to the rights of victims. The failure to deal with this issue has become an important and delicate matter, which is part of that dimension known as the legacy of the conflict. The investigations of historic human rights abuses will be further discussed in the section on human rights and legacy issues. From a human rights perspective, this is a critical matter since if historic abuses of the right to life remain unacknowledged (and unresolved), the right to life itself remains insecure.

Equality and non-discrimination after the Agreement

The origins of the dispute around discrimination and equality in Northern Ireland were outlined in Chapter 3. Discrimination remained a "live" issue in Northern Ireland throughout the decades, with housing and employment being the two areas where such discrimination was perceived most potently by the minority community. As a result of the reforms of the 1960s and 1970s discrimination in housing gradually diminished as a matter of controversy and debate. Conversely, the debate around discrimination in employment never dissipated from the Northern Irish political sphere. More broadly, the issue of equality and equality of opportunity remained firmly within the political discourse of the nationalist and republican community. Writing in 2005 Gerry Adams said: "Nationalists in the Six Counties continue to experience bigotry from the unionist and British Establishment."[5]

As a result, the Peace Agreement placed considerable emphasis on equality. In their Declaration of Support the parties to the Agreement acknowledged that equality (together with partnership and mutual respect) was "the basis of relationships within Northern Ireland". The Agreement also establishes an Equality Commission "to monitor a statutory obligation to promote equality of opportunity in specified areas and parity of esteem between the two main communities, and to investigate individual complaints against public bodies". This commitment to equality is further strengthened through a Ministerial Pledge of Office which, inter alia, requires Ministers "to serve all the people of Northern Ireland equally, and to act in accordance with the general obligations on government to promote equality and prevent discrimination". It seems clear that the memories of discrimination felt by the nationalist community loomed large over the language used in the Agreement.

This deep-seated concern with equality and non-discrimination is particularly evident in the Human Rights and Safeguards section of the Agreement where the UK government bound itself to establish a statutory duty to promote equality on all public authorities. This statutory duty was given effect by Section 75 of the 1998 Northern Ireland Act, while Section 76 rendered illegal discrimination by public authorities.[6] The same 1998 Act also established the Equality Commission as envisaged in the Agreement. Thus, from a formal, legislative point of view the main equality provisions articulated in the Agreement have been enacted. This is significant progress but does not answer the broader question of whether discrimination has been overcome and whether equality is being achieved. In order to implement this duty Schedule 9 of the 1998 Act also requires public authorities to develop equality schemes, which detail how they propose to fulfil the duties imposed by Section 75 in relation to their relevant functions. The importance of the equality and non-discrimination provisions within the Northern Ireland Act cannot be discounted. It has been suggested that the

> duty to promote equality of opportunity in the Northern Ireland Act 1998 is one of the most significant human rights developments in Northern Ireland over the past thirty years.... The new duty is nothing less than an attempt to make equality issues central to the whole range of public policy debates.[7]

Section 75 articulates the duty of promoting equality of opportunity not only between the unionist and nationalist communities or the Protestant and Catholic communities but within a much wider ambit. The categories between which equality is to be promoted of course includes political opinion and religious beliefs, but also extends to racial groups, marital status, sexual orientation, gender and disability among others. The legislation clearly extends its scope beyond the traditional unionist/nationalist or Protestant/Catholic paradigm. Yet, there still seems to be some limitations to such a comprehensive understanding of equality and non-discrimination. Paul Nolan writing in 2014 argued that:

> The Northern Ireland interpretation of inequality is less concerned with the gap between rich and poor. The term is understood mainly in terms of what is sometimes referred to as "horizontal equality", that is the relationship between the two blocs, Catholic and Protestant.[8]

Once again, the salience of group rights is highlighted. The group rights are understood in terms of the national/ethnic/religious minority rights framework described in Chapter 2 and, as noted, constituted a recurring theme throughout this study. The extent to which this limited view of equality and non-discrimination impacts on the current equality scenario in Northern Ireland is of crucial importance to the success or otherwise of the equality agenda.

Apart from the statutory duty to promote equality, the most important legislative/policy initiative that emerged from the Peace Agreement from the equality perspective was the establishment of the Equality Commission.

Equality and non-discrimination: the current situation

The situation described in Chapters 3 and 4 in terms of discrimination vis-à-vis the nationalist community in Northern Ireland no longer exists. In terms of employment and housing the situation for the nationalist community has improved significantly. Memories of discrimination persist and a sense of historical grievance lingers. Catriona Ruane, Sinn Féin MLA at Stormont, articulated the situation as follows:

> We are living in an area where there is deep anti-nationalism, anti-Irishness. People will dress it up as anything they like but our flag, our language, our culture are still not given the status they deserve. Now the equality is on the agenda in a way that it was never on the agenda before.[9]

This statement is interesting in terms of underlining the historical sense of grievance by referring to the deep anti-nationalism and also by referring how equality was never given enough attention before. However, it also acknowledges the progress since 1998 in having equality as a key component of the political and legislative agenda. The references to culture, language and flags also seem to indicate a shift in the kind of equality now being pursued: not employment and housing but rather cultural equality.

The reality on the ground for the nationalist community is clearly not comparable to the period 1920–1970. The fact that nationalist politicians are ministers in government probably also has a beneficial effect in terms of perception. And yet, challenges remain. Unemployment remains somewhat higher in the nationalist community[10] while the unionist politicians have expressed discomfort at what they see as discrimination against their community.[11] This is especially relevant in terms of state agencies and the voluntary sector which, unionists claim, under-represents them. Even more worrying in terms of equality issues are the rising social and income inequalities within the unionist community. Former UUP human rights spokesperson and Stormont Minister Dermot Nesbitt stated that social inequalities within both of the main communities needed more attention.[12] The Community Relations Council's *Peace Monitoring Report* of March 2014 by Paul Nolan validates this view. One of the ten key findings in this report stated bluntly:

> 6. Failure lies in wait for young working-class Protestant males
>
> The educational under-achievement of a section of socially disadvantaged Protestant males is a seedbed for trouble. Using the standard measure of five "good" GCSEs, Protestant boys with free-school-meal entitlement achieve less than any of the other main social groups in Northern Ireland and hover near the very bottom when compared with groups in England. By contrast, Catholic girls from Northern Ireland not on free-school-meal entitlement vie with the Chinese students at the top of the tree of educational attainment in England. The latest analysis by religion of the Labour Force Survey found that 24 per cent of Protestants aged 16 to 24 were unemployed, compared with 17 per cent of their Catholic counterparts.[13]

The analysis by Nolan clearly establishes that working-class boys have especially low equality of opportunity and suffer disproportionately from social inequalities. This is an aspect of equality and non-discrimination that goes beyond the traditional focus of unionist/nationalist equality.

Equality and discrimination continue to be seen primarily through the lens of the conflict: unionist versus nationalist. This is problematic as discrimination and inequality within any society have a more diverse complexion than the minority versus majority paradigm. As evidenced above, there are serious issues of inequality within the majority unionist community.

It has been suggested that Northern Ireland

> should be looking at how to deal with social inequalities whether you are Protestant, Catholic or dissenter.... There are social inequalities on all sides and that is where policy should focus on. Yet, we still somehow focus on unionist/nationalist issues.[14]

This sentiment is also echoed by the first Chief Commissioner of the Northern Ireland Human Rights Commission, who also feels that other aspects of equality "have suffered because of the focus on political and religious discrimination" and that Northern Ireland has "also got much more serious problems of income inequality".[15]

The limitations of the unionist/nationalist paradigm, in terms of equality and non-discrimination, which have been inculcated as a result of the conflict, become apparent in terms of the new minorities that have arisen in Northern Ireland. The numbers of eastern European, Asian and Muslim persons living in Northern Ireland increased dramatically since the end of the conflict.[16]

This reality has brought with it new minorities who fall outside the unionist versus nationalist paradigm. Another aspect of equality legislation which still lags behind in Northern Ireland when compared to the rest of the United Kingdom and Ireland relates to discrimination based on sexual orientation. Unlike Ireland or the rest of the United Kingdom, Northern Ireland does not allow same-sex marriages. It can be said that the focus on equality between nationalists and unionists has dominated the discourse of equality and non-discrimination in Northern Ireland for so long that it has been difficult to move away from it.

Referring back to the relationship between community relations and equality one notes challenges within this context as well. Community relations remain problematic not only between unionists and nationalists but also increasingly vis-à-vis immigrant communities from eastern Europe, Asia and the Muslim world. The serious and recurring attacks on Romanian communities in Belfast in 2009 are one example of this problem.[17] Other examples of this are attacks on the Chinese community in 2004[18] and the surge in attacks on ethnic minorities in early 2014.[19] A further indication of the problems with discrimination, violence and community relations in Northern Ireland is the situation that arose in 2014 with the First Minister Peter Robinson appearing to support anti-Muslim comments by a Protestant pastor.[20] In the ensuing furore Alliance MLA Anna Lo (who is of Chinese descent) stated that she wanted to quit politics as a result of racist abuse and also considered leaving Northern Ireland as she did not feel safe in Northern Ireland.[21]

A balance sheet of equality and non-discrimination

The policy achievements in the field of equality since the Agreement have been significant. Section 75 of the Northern Ireland Act setting the statutory equality duty on all public authorities is a huge step forward in the context of the history of Northern Ireland. In Chapters 3 and 4 the extent of the demand for such legislation by the nationalist community was clearly illustrated. The unionist resistance to such statutory standards on equality was equally clearly demonstrated. The fact that Section 75 was enacted is in itself a measure of progress. The same applies to the Equality Commission. Its existence has served to assure nationalists that they are not second-class citizens in Northern Ireland. Conversely, the unionist community has demonstrated some wariness around the equality bodies since they view them as skewed against them: if more jobs go to nationalists there will be fewer jobs for unionists. This was evident in the unionist dislike of the 50/50 recruitment in the PSNI (which will be referred to later).

This wariness is also linked to the inequalities emerging within communities. The statistics cited above in respect of working-class unionists and their aspirations and opportunities is a serious reminder of the gravity of their situation. The equality agenda has clearly not worked for them. The equality agenda has also failed to work in respect of ethnic minorities in Northern Ireland who have been at the receiving end of hate crimes as illustrated above. Racism and xenophobia are, together with social inequalities, the major challenges which the equality agenda has to deal with at the present juncture.

The reasons for these problems are difficult to attribute with absolute certainty. Nevertheless, it appears evident that the traditional focus on equality between the two main communities in Northern Ireland has left intra-community equality issues and the fight against racism with insufficient attention. Thus, the conflict agenda has to some extent limited a more comprehensive understanding of equality and inequality.

The administration of justice and policing

The issue of policing and justice is another contentious issue which stretches back to the years of the formation of Northern Ireland. In the previous chapters the various grievances of the nationalist community against the Royal Ulster Constabulary and against the implementation of the various special/emergency laws were examined together with the unionist responses to these grievances. Given the progress registered from the 1970s onwards in terms of equality in employment and housing, the issue of policing and the administration of justice remained as the most long-standing human rights challenge in Northern Ireland. As seen in the previous chapter the 1998 Agreement acknowledged the importance of policing and justice issues in the section on "Rights, Safeguards and Equality of Opportunity" with its promise of "a new beginning to policing in Northern Ireland".[22]

The task of charting this new beginning in policing was entrusted to the Independent Commission for Policing in Northern Ireland, chaired by Lord Patten and referred to as the Patten Commission. In its report the Patten Commission emphasised the central role of human rights in its deliberations. Indeed, one of the five key tests applied by the Commission to any proposed change was: "Does it protect and vindicate the human rights and human dignity of all?"[23] Furthermore, a whole chapter of the report (Chapter 4) was devoted to examining human rights aspects of policing. The Report made it clear that it would make human rights a central element of the proposed reforms:

> It is a central proposition of this report that the fundamental purpose of policing should be, in the words of the Agreement, the protection and vindication of the human rights of all. Our consultations showed clear agreement across the communities in Northern Ireland that people want the police to protect their human rights from infringement by others, and to respect their human rights in the exercise of that duty.[24]

In the subsequent sections the legal and policy measures that have been enacted in Northern Ireland in the field of policing and justice will be assessed.

Legal and policy measures

The Patten Report made numerous recommendations in terms of a new beginning for policing. The key recommendations in terms of human rights were the adoption of an oath of office for all police officers which has a strong human rights component; the adoption of a new Code of Ethics firmly based on human rights law; a strong emphasis on human rights training for all police officers, as well as oversight of the police's human rights compliance by a new Policing Board. The emphasis on human rights training was put forward in forceful terms:

> We also recommend, as a matter of priority, that all members of the police service should be instructed in the implications for policing of the Human Rights Act 1998, and the wider context of the European Convention on Human Rights and the Universal Declaration of Human Rights.[25]

The proposals relating to the Policing Board were especially critical in terms of its composition and functions. As illustrated in previous chapters, one of the key criticisms of the RUC was that it was not representative of both communities in Northern Ireland but was instead overwhelmingly composed by individuals coming from the unionist community. The Patten Report recommended that the Policing Board be fully representative of all the political parties who are elected at Stormont as well as of the broader civil society. The Board's functions would also include the appointment of the senior police officers which would give some comfort to all sectors of the community that these posts would be broadly reflective of the community as a whole. Another key function of the Board, as proposed by the Patten Report, was that of ensuring accountability of the police force. This related to another major grievance of the nationalist community, especially salient during the conflict, that the RUC was not sufficiently accountable for errors committed by its officers. The Patten Report made numerous recommendations, some of which are beyond the scope of this study; however, it is worth noting that proposals on all of these issues were made: community policing and the importance of partnership; the reduction of the role of the army as the security situation improved; the impact of emergency legislation on policing; public order policing with special emphasis on parades; the phasing-out and replacement of plastic bullets; the composition of the force; and the change of the name and symbols of the force. It is also important to note that independently of the Peace Agreement and the Patten Commission, the Secretary of State for Northern Ireland had appointed Dr Maurice Hayes to conduct a review of the police complaints system in Northern Ireland. Dr Hayes reported in 1997 and an Office of the Police Ombudsman for Northern Ireland was established in 1998 through the Police (Northern Ireland) Act of that year. The establishment of an independent police complaints procedure was an important step in the field of policing and met one of the demands that the CAJ had campaigned for over many years.[26]

A number of recommendations made in the Patten Report were brought into force via the Police (Northern Ireland) Act 2000 as amended by the Police (Northern Ireland) Act 2003. The 2000 Act, inter alia, renamed the police force as the Police Service of Northern Ireland (PSNI) and created the Northern Ireland Policing Board with many of the functions suggested in the Patten Report, including ensuring the accountability of the PSNI in terms of compliance with the 1998 Human Rights Act. The 2000 Act also provided for the adoption of a code of ethics by the Policing Board, which again was linked to the 1998 Human Rights Act.

Section 46 of the 2000 Police Act provided, as a temporary measure, that half of the new recruits within the PSNI will be of a Roman Catholic background. This measure was intended to achieve a better reflection of the community within the ranks of the PSNI over a period of time and to resolve the historical under-representation of the Catholic community within the police force. However, this measure was viewed as fundamentally unfair by many Protestants since qualified Protestants who, based on merit alone would have been able to join the PSNI, were unable to do so due to the operation of the 50/50 mechanism which required a Catholic to be recruited for every non-Catholic. This system was described as "one of the bitterest pills they [unionists] had to swallow".[27] Mechanisms such as the 50/50 recruitment or any other quotas may be legitimately criticised for being fundamentally unfair and unjust. However, it is worth recalling that, for various reasons (including IRA targeting of Catholic officers), the RUC never had more than 8 per cent of its force made up of Catholics. This clearly had to change, if the police service was to be representative of the community as a whole and if it was to gain acceptance by the nationalist population. In effect, therefore, "something difficult and radical had to be done to change the composition"[28] of the police service. In 1993 the number of perceived Roman Catholic RUC officers stood at 7 per cent of the total.[29] The percentage of PSNI officers perceived to be Roman Catholic in 2014 stood at 30 per cent.[30] It is therefore evident that the concerted effort to render the composition of Northern Ireland's police service more reflective of the community itself was met with a significant degree of success.

The extent to which the PSNI is today accepted by a very large part of the population of Northern Ireland is testament to the fact that the measure was effective. It is interesting to note that, according to a Policing Board survey in January 2014,[31] 68 per cent of respondents thought the PSNI was doing a very or fairly good job in their area. The percentage of Protestants satisfied with the PSNI performance in their area stood at 65 per cent which interestingly was the same percentage of Catholics who thought likewise. Comparing the percentages for 2014 with those for 2010, one notes that the percentage of satisfied Catholics rose by 8 per cent (from 57 per cent to 65 per cent). The increasing levels of satisfaction are also evident in statistics (also issued by the Policing Board) which rate public satisfaction with the PSNI's work in Northern Ireland as a whole. In 2010 the percentage of Catholics who thought the PSNI was performing fairly or very well in Northern Ireland (as opposed to just in their locality) stood at 62 per cent while the Protestant figure stood at 73 per cent. In 2014 the Protestant figure had remained stable at 73 per cent while the Catholic figure had increased to 70 per cent. It is clear that the attempt to increase the confidence of the Catholic community in Northern Ireland's policing is registering reasonable success.

The statistics on crime reporting are also interesting in this respect. The "Experience of Crime Findings", from the 2013/14 *Northern Ireland Crime Survey*, show that all comparable violent crime reporting in Northern Ireland was higher percentage-wise than the statistics for England and Wales. This might indicate at least a comparable level of trust for the police services in Northern Ireland as for England and Wales.

The impact of the human rights agenda on the new beginning for policing is perhaps best captured in the attestation that all police offers are required to make in terms of Section 38 of the 2000 Act:

> I hereby do solemnly and sincerely and truly declare and affirm that I will faithfully discharge the duties of the office of constable, with fairness, integrity, diligence and impartiality, upholding fundamental human rights and according equal respect to all individuals and their traditions and beliefs; and that while I continue to hold the said office I will to the best of my skill and knowledge discharge all the duties thereof according to law.[32]

The role of human rights as a guarantee of fairness, equality and respect of human dignity is clearly intended to assuage any nationalist fears that the PSNI may revert to what they consider the shortcomings of the RUC. This attempt at instilling a human rights ethos within the PSNI was not welcomed by everyone. At the outset, some unionists considered that "the police was being emasculated through, what they viewed, as woolly human rights policing" although "broadly speaking unionism has come to terms with the new dispensation in policing".[33]

One of the key aspects of the 2000 Act was the requirement on the Policing Board to adopt a code of ethics for the PSNI. The Policing Board adopted the *Code of Ethics* in 2003 (revised in 2008) as the disciplinary code for all police officers. In his Foreword to the 2008 version of the code, the then Chairman of the Policing Board described the Code as "one of the success stories in advancing the human rights agenda in the PSNI".[34] The *Code of Ethics* is steeped in the language of human rights and pays particular attention to compliance with the 1998 Human Rights Act and the European Convention on Human Rights. A member of the Policing Board has defined the code as being "heavily rooted in human rights standards".[35] This is also confirmed when one compares the Preamble of the Northern Ireland PSNI *Code of Ethics* with the Preamble of the *Code of Practice for the Principles and Standards of Professional Behaviour for the Policing Profession of England and Wales*.[36] The PSNI Code's Preamble has five references to the term "human rights" whereas there are none in the English and Welsh equivalent. The relevance of Preambles is that they provide an interpretative framework for legal, quasi-legal and policy documents. Thus, the PSNI Code clearly provides a stronger human rights framework of interpretation than the English and Welsh Code.

Without going into the many detailed provisions of the *Code of Ethics*, reference to the first principle enshrined in it (Article 1.1) serves to demonstrate how human rights standards have taken a key role in policing. Every police officer, in carrying out his/her duties, is obliged to "obey and uphold the law, protect human dignity and uphold the human rights and fundamental freedoms of all persons as enshrined in the Human Rights Act 1998, the European Convention on Human Rights and other relevant human rights instruments".[37]

The Code was distributed to every police officer, who was required to sign that they had received, read and understood the Code. In retrospect, the Code of Ethics is viewed largely positively by police officers as a tool that was relevant to their job and indeed helped them carry out their duties.[38]

The positive changes brought forward in the field of policing are acknowledged even by Sinn Féin politicians who for so long were the most critical voices in terms of policing in Northern Ireland. Catriona Ruane, for example, cited the Policing Board as one area where progress has been registered in terms of the human rights situation.[39] This success is also evidenced by the levels of satisfaction with the PSNI cited above.

Apart from the issue of policing, the Agreement also referred to the criminal justice system. The legacy of the conflict in terms of criminal justice was such that the nationalist community was (as in the case of policing) loath to accept the Northern Irish justice system as fair and impartial. The fact that this was a problematic issue was acknowledged in the Agreement[40] which inter alia emphasised that the criminal justice system needed to "deliver a fair and impartial system of justice to the community" and "have the confidence of all parts of the community".

In this context of a need to change perceptions (and in some cases also reality) the Agreement provided for "a wide ranging review of criminal justice (other than policing and those aspects of the system relating to emergency legislation)". The Criminal Justice Review Group was formed in 1998 and submitted its (voluminous) report in March 2000. The Report dealt with the criminal justice system comprehensively from issues of appointments to judicial office, the role of the prosecution, juvenile justice, sentencing and prisons to victims and witnesses. From the perspective of this study, what is most interesting is the primacy which the report gave to human rights issues. It is fair to say that the report not only contained a chapter devoted to human rights matters but also mainstreamed human rights principles throughout. The Report states unambiguously "that human rights are central to the criminal justice system"[41] and it demonstrates commitment to this principle throughout. Each chapter includes a human rights background section which examines the relevant human rights principles and rules for each matter being investigated. This clearly validates the commitment to a human rights-based process.

A number of the recommendations contained in the Review Group Report were implemented through the Justice (Northern Ireland) Act of 2002 and the Justice (Northern Ireland) Act of 2004. The latter Act provided for the Attorney General to have the power to issue guidelines to criminal justice organisations "on the exercise of their functions in a manner consistent with international human rights standards relevant to the criminal justice system".[42] The provisions of this section have been used, since the devolution of justice matters to the Northern Ireland Assembly and the concomitant appointment of an Attorney General for Northern Ireland, to provide human rights guidance to the Northern Ireland Prison Service,[43] Forensic Service Northern Ireland,[44] the Public Prosecution Service[45] and the State Pathologist's Department.[46]

In terms of ensuring that the criminal justice system is accepted by the community as a whole to be representative of all the traditions in Northern Ireland, the 2004 Act also provides that the commission entrusted with the appointment of judicial offices is reflective of the community in Northern Ireland and that while the actual appointments are to be made only on the basis of merit the commission is obliged to follow a programme of action that "is designed to secure, so far as it is reasonably practicable to do so, that appointments to listed judicial offices are such that those holding such offices are reflective of the community in Northern Ireland". As in the case of the reforms to recruitment in the PSNI the need to ensure that the nationalist community develop an allegiance to the criminal justice system is a crucial component of the peace process. The efforts to create this sense of allegiance (or at least acceptance) amongst the nationalist community integrates the equality agenda with the policing and criminal justice systems, which had been especially suspect elements of the Northern Irish state insofar as the nationalist community was concerned. Human rights (including equality) thus became essential components of securing a change in the perceptions and approach of the nationalist community towards the Northern Ireland state.

Another key aspect of the policing and justice element was defined by the Agreement as the "normalisation of security arrangements and practices". This referred, inter alia, to the "removal of emergency powers in Northern Ireland". If general policing and criminal justice were considered by the nationalist community to be biased against them, the attitude of the nationalists towards the special or emergency laws was even more critical. As evidenced in previous chapters the nationalist community considered the various emergency laws adopted in Northern Ireland from 1922 onwards as being particularly targeted against them.[47] Thus, the repeal of the remaining Northern Ireland emergency laws was a critical demand of the nationalist political parties. This demand has not been fully met given that a number of special powers such as the possibility of criminal trials without a jury in specific circumstances still exist.[48]

In the context of anti-terrorism legislation, the Terrorism Act 2000 is also relevant since it established special legislation on a UK-wide basis. While the Terrorism Act 2000 contained anti-terrorism provisions which were criticised from a human rights perspective (for example the very wide stop and search powers), the Act by not targeting specifically Northern Ireland was better received by the nationalist community. In effect the Terrorism Act 2000 (and the spate of other anti-terrorism legislation adopted on a UK-wide basis post-September 11, 2001) signified the return to a degree of "normal" security arrangements for Northern Ireland, thus partially fulfilling the promise of the Agreement. From a purely human rights perspective the anti-terrorism legislation that has proliferated in the UK since 2001 is certainly regressive. Courts in the UK and the European Court of Human Rights have found certain provisions in anti-terror laws to be in breach of the Human Rights Act 1998 and the European Convention on Human Rights.[49] While from a Northern Ireland vantage point there has been a distinct perceptual progress with respect to emergency laws, substantially, there still exist emergency laws with dubious human rights compliance that are effectively applicable to Northern Ireland as part of the UK.

A balance sheet for justice and policing

The changes brought about in the fields of policing (and justice) in Northern Ireland have been significant and have enjoyed considerable success. The first indicator of the success is the extent to which the previously maligned (by nationalists) RUC was transformed into a police service which enjoys the confidence of the vast majority of the population of Northern Ireland. This is certainly a welcome improvement, although it is salutary to recall that satisfaction with the PSNI remains at lower levels within the Catholic community as evidenced in the Policing Board surveys quoted above. The surveys show that there has been improvement but that further efforts are required. The overall satisfaction ratings of the PSNI (i.e. of the community as a whole) stand at 71 per cent, which compare well with London where overall the Metropolitan Police scored 67 per cent of Londoners being satisfied with the police's performance as at November 2013.[50] If compared to Scotland, another devolved administration, its 2012–2013 statistics show that "61% thought the police were doing a good or excellent job in their area, while 29% thought they were doing a fair job".[51] The total percentage of those who give an overall positive judgment of policing in Scotland is 90 per cent. Hence, comparison with Scotland demonstrates there is still room for improvement in Northern Ireland.

The acceptance by Sinn Féin of membership in the Policing Board is one clear example of the progress that has been registered in this domain but there are other, less public examples.[52] Notwithstanding the broad success achieved in this respect, "there are some republican and loyalist areas where there are still huge confidence issues and perceptions of bias and political policing."[53] Most of these difficulties involve cultural issues like flags, parades and legacy issues. An example of this problem with legacy issues relates to the policing of historic human rights abuses. The arrest of Gerry Adams in April 2014 was a difficult moment for the PSNI and the peace process in general. Martin McGuniness' remark that Sinn Féin could review its support of policing if Gerry Adams was prosecuted for the McConville murder is a stark reminder of the difficulties that still exist.[54] Such remarks hinting at dark forces within the PSNI are dangerous and could undo at least some of the work that over the past decade has brought to Northern Ireland a more normal policing structure. The link between policing and legacy issues dealt with, unsuccessfully, in the Haass talks will be further examined later in this chapter.

The mainstreaming of human rights within the PSNI is also a hugely welcome development. The PSNI has through its Code of Ethics a sound, human rights-based code that assists and guides police officers in the exercise of their duties. The success of the human rights standards in guiding police officers in difficult cases is testimony to the progress made:

> [I]n some instances the PSNI had to deal with very sensitive situations with the danger of lives being lost; we policed those situations in a human rights compliant way without any loss of life. The fact that nothing happened and people were kept safe and perhaps arrests were made rather than lethal force being deployed is tremendously important. It's essential that our actions and decisions are compliant with human rights standards. I think human rights have been important also in other areas such as policing parades or other sensitive issues such as child abuse or sexual offenders. I think human rights have been incredibly important for policing in Northern Ireland.[55]

This is a testament to the success of the reform in the sector of policing and the role human rights have played in this reform. Within this context, it has been suggested that there has been "a revolution in the way in which Northern Ireland is policed".[56]

Progress has also been evident with the administration of justice both in terms of the human rights standards introduced as well as with the normalisation of the security arrangements with the withdrawal of the British army from Northern Ireland's streets. The progress in terms of the emergency legislation has been perceptual rather than substantive. While ad hoc emergency or anti-terrorism laws for Northern Ireland have been repealed, other UK-wide laws have been adopted which fall foul of human rights standards.

Human rights and a Bill of Rights for Northern Ireland

Together with the Equality Commission, the other main body established under the auspices of the Agreement was the Human Rights Commission for Northern Ireland. The establishment of the Human Rights Commission was a milestone in the human rights history of Northern Ireland. The Agreement established the scope of the mandate of the Commission to include the following:

> [K]eeping under review the adequacy and effectiveness of laws and practices, making recommendations to Government as necessary; providing information and promoting awareness of human rights; considering draft legislation referred to them by the new Assembly; and, in appropriate cases, bringing court proceedings or providing assistance to individuals doing so.

Furthermore, the Agreement also provided that the Commission would be

> invited to consult and to advise on the scope for defining, in Westminster legislation, rights supplementary to those in the European Convention on Human Rights, to reflect the particular circumstances of Northern Ireland, drawing as appropriate on international instruments and experience. These additional rights to reflect the principles of mutual respect for the identity and ethos of both communities and parity of esteem, and – taken together with the ECHR – to constitute a Bill of Rights for Northern Ireland.

One may discern two main components of the Commission's mandate: (1) a general mandate to improve the human rights situation in Northern Ireland through the provision of advice to government and through raising awareness around human rights; and (2) a more specific task to advise on the possibility of legislating for a Bill of Rights for Northern Ireland. This latter mandate has created considerable debate and controversy within Northern Ireland and arguably took a large part of the Commission's time and energy in its first decade of operation. The discussion around the Bill of Rights process also deserves particular attention because it threw in clear relief some of the key differences in how human rights are understood by the major political parties in Northern Ireland.

The Human Rights Commission: its work to improve the human rights situation

The Northern Ireland Human Rights Commission was, like the Equality Commission, established through the 1998 Northern Ireland Act. Section 68 of the Act provides for the establishment of the Commission, while section

69 outlines its statutory functions. In terms of the more general functions of the Commission the Act refers to the following:

1 review the adequacy and effectiveness in Northern Ireland of law and practice relating to the protection of human rights;
2 advise the Secretary of State and the Executive Committee of the Assembly of legislative and other measures which ought to be taken to protect human rights whenever requested or whenever the Commission deems it appropriate to do so;
3 advise the Assembly whether a Bill is compatible with human rights, whenever requested or whenever the Commission deems it appropriate to do so;
4 give assistance to individuals who have commenced (or wish to commence) proceedings involving law or practice relating to the protection of human rights in Northern Ireland in accordance with the Act; and
5 promote understanding and awareness of the importance of human rights in Northern Ireland; and for this purpose it may undertake, commission or provide financial or other assistance for research or educational activities.

A brief examination of the functions of the Commission establishes that the Commission has wide functions in terms of the promotion and protection of human rights in Northern Ireland. This can be seen in the fact that the Commission is, in effect, entitled to provide advice on any matter relating to human rights in Northern Ireland whenever it deems it appropriate. The Commission is not limited in its scope of giving advice (both to the Secretary of State and to the devolved institutions). It can provide advice on the effectiveness of human rights law and practice; on the human rights compatibility of Bills; and on legislative (or other) measures for the better protection of human rights that it considers appropriate. Furthermore, it can provide such advice whether or not requested by the Secretary of State and the devolved institutions. In terms of the function of advising government, the Commission has been advising and commenting to Government regularly on human rights issues and on the human rights implications of governmental policies. In 2013 the Commission published 19 pieces of advice addressed to government and up to October 2014 it had published another 19 pieces of advice related to government law and policy. This, given the staff and budget available to the Commission, is a solid record of achievement.

The Commission may also assist individuals involved in court proceedings that concern human rights law and practice. Finally, it also has an educational role with respect to the promotion of human rights in Northern Ireland. In the early years of the Commission this particular function provided the context of one of the most controversial initiatives the Commission has entertained. This concerned the Holy Cross dispute, in which one of the parents of the school children affected decided to bring a case against the police, claiming that the police's actions were inadequate to secure their right to be free from inhuman and degrading treatment. The Commission's case-law committee decided to support the parents' case and this caused significant controversy. The controversy impacted the Commission internally where the then Chief Commissioner appeared to disagree with the case-law Committee's decision, a fact that became public knowledge when a letter written by the Chief Commissioner to the then Chief Constable was made public during legal proceedings.[57]

The Commission was eventually also criticised for intervening in the House of Lords judgment, with two of the Law Lords criticising the Commission for intervening in the proceedings without adding anything to what was already argued by the appellants.[58] All told, the Commission's involvement in the Holy Cross dispute was unfortunate in many ways. In the aftermath of the dispute, the Commission agreed to new rules for the taking of decisions relating to case-work.[59] The current policy is spelled out in the Commission's website:

> The Commission is focusing its attention on the needs of those who are most vulnerable and marginalised. This includes persons with disabilities, children in the care of or detained by the state, prisoners, ethnic minorities (including Travellers), persons in need of health and social care and those suffering deprivation. We will consider taking up your case only if it directly relates to human rights and falls within one of these areas of priority.[60]

The extent to which the Commission has effectively pursued the agenda set out in the Northern Ireland Act is a matter of debate. In the early years of the Commission a number of Commissioners resigned on various grounds. Two of the resigning Commissioners, Inez McCormack and Christine Bell, cited lack of powers and resources and also ineffectiveness.[61] Furthermore, in 2003 Patrick Yu resigned from the Commission, citing his disappointment with the draft provisions for the protection of ethnic minorities in the Bill of Rights for Northern Ireland, while Christopher McGimpsey resigned in order to stand for election to the Northern Ireland Assembly. Frank McGuinness and Patricia Kelly withdrew from the Commission as from September 2003.[62] It is certain that the early years of the Commission were difficult ones in a number of respects. The Holy Cross issue and the resignation of a number of Commissioners are evidence of these difficulties. This, however, is hardly surprising. Establishing a national human rights institution is a complex endeavour in every circumstance. Such an endeavour is more difficult in a much divided society which has just exited from a period of protracted violent conflict.

It may be argued that the Commission devoted too much attention to the Bill of Rights process to the detriment of its other functions. The priority assigned to the Bill of Rights process was acknowledged in the 2001 Report of the Commission where it stated clearly that "Work on the Bill of Rights was prioritised by Commissioners as the main focus for Commission resources, both human and financial, during the year."[63] This is further evidenced by the Chief Executive's 2001 summary of the main work of the Commission in the year 2000–2001 which indicates that the Bill of Rights process featured significantly in its early work. She highlighted the following achievements for the period:

> The production of our first Annual Report and Strategic Plan; the computerising of the accounts; the Bill of Rights consultation process and associated publications; the Bill of Rights Working Groups; the visit of Justice Arthur Chaskalson, President of the Constitutional Court in South Africa; the development of an Equality Scheme for the Commission; the two-year Review and the refurbishment of and move to new offices.[64]

The view that the Bill of Rights deflected from the other functions of the Commission is refuted by the Commission's first Chief Commissioner:

> [The Commission] got some additional funding to help with the Bill of Rights work, which allowed one or two staff to specialise in that area, particularly on training and outreach activities. Plus, we were able to integrate some of the Bill of Rights work into our other work – e.g. when raising human rights awareness, commenting on new draft policies and laws, or making submissions to treaty monitoring bodies. The Bill of Rights work also helped to raise the profile of the Commission amongst NGOs and political parties.[65]

The outreach and educational functions envisaged in the 1998 Act were, in fact, strongly tied in with the Bill of Rights process. In the 2000–2001 period the Commission focused on two main educational priorities: (1) providing education resources and training on human rights to ensure widespread participation in the Bill of Rights consultation process; and (2) promoting awareness of human rights education among educationalists in the formal and informal sectors. Given that the Commission was statutorily obliged to consult within the Bill of Rights process it was natural that it should link the process with the educational/awareness raising dimension of its work. In terms of human resources and funding this was a sensible decision. Whether this decision limited the Commission's educational scope in its early years is a moot point.

The Commission in its investigation and research work focused primarily on the investigation of deaths, the situation in places of detention with particular emphasis on women and children. This is a natural choice of themes given the history of the conflict in Northern Ireland. However, the Commission also started reflecting the changing nature of Northern Ireland with an increasing focus on investigative and research work around the issues of migration, asylum and race.[66] Thus, one notes both a reflection of Northern Ireland's particular circumstances and history but also of the changing nature of Northern Ireland and the human rights challenges which it faces.

This was acknowledged by the then Chief Commissioner Monica McWilliams who, in her Foreword to the Commission's 2010 *Annual Report*, stated that the changing focus of the Commission's work, with particular reference to immigration issues, "shows how far we have come since the Commission's establishment in 1999 when so much of our attention at the time focused on the legacy of the past".[67] It is positive that the Commission has given sustained attention to issues relating to migration and asylum in Northern Ireland over the past years. In the Summer 2006 NIHRC Newsletter, it was stated that

> increasingly in its work, the Northern Ireland Human Rights Commission is seeing how it is non-citizens of the UK and Ireland living in Northern Ireland that are among the most vulnerable groups in our society, whether they be migrants or asylum seekers.[68]

This claim is backed up by a number of initiatives undertaken by the Commission in recent years in the field of immigration and asylum. In 2009, for example, the Commission published two reports dealing with this matter: *No Home From Home*,[69] which dealt with non-UK nationals and destitution, and *Our Hidden Borders*, which examines legal and policy measures pertaining to "the detention of perceived offenders of immigration law and asylum seekers".[70] Another instance of this focus is found in the Commission's *Shadow Report* addressed to the Committee on the Rights of the Child, where the Commission paid particular attention to the situation of children asylum seekers.[71]

Another specific focus of the Commission in recent years has been children, particularly children in detention. In 2002 the Commission published *In Our Care: Promoting the Rights of Children in Custody*, which provided an overview and analysis of the legal and policy context and also recommendations for improving both contexts.[72] An update report, *Still in Our Care: Protecting Children's Rights in Custody in Northern Ireland*, was published in 2006 which highlighted areas of progress, but also areas where more needed to be done.

More recently, the Commission has been responding to the economic downturn that commenced in 2008 and which has had a severe impact on the UK as a whole in the period 2010 onwards. In fact the 2013–2016 Strategic Plan of the Commission has identified three pillars upon which the Commission is to work. The third pillar refers to:

> Protecting Human Rights in a Time of Austerity. Economic recession and austerity measures have led to unemployment and budget cuts that impact deeply on the enjoyment of human rights, including the right to

> an adequate standard of living. While those who are already at a disadvantage suffer the most, it has to be recognised that recession impacts on the human rights of all the people of Northern Ireland.[73]

This is evidence of the Commission's effort not only to focus on traditional human rights issues related to the conflict but also to respond to the changing realities faced by the people of Northern Ireland in their daily life. In the Commission's Annual Statement for 2012 the Chief Commissioner reiterated that due to the economic crisis "one issue that has emerged as a high priority for the Commission is that of how to address the scourge of poverty".[74]

The initiatives pertaining to immigrants, asylum seekers and those worse hit by the economic crisis indicates that the Commission has developed a clear policy of focusing its efforts on protecting the human rights of the most vulnerable in society. This particular attention towards the most vulnerable was also indicated in the then Chief Commissioner's Foreword to the Annual Report of 2011–2012 where he stated that the Commission would be

> addressing the situation of the most vulnerable – evidenced, for instance by the publication of the investigation of the human rights situation of older persons in nursing homes, as well as our continued attention to the human rights of persons held in detention.[75]

All of this demonstrates that the Commission has developed a clear strategy focusing on legacy issues but also on the rights of the most vulnerable. This is a defensible and sensible approach given Northern Ireland's history and its current realities.

A matter which necessarily impacted on the Commission's performance of its functions related to the budget and powers made available to the Commission. The Commission from the outset claimed it required more funding to carry out its functions. In the introduction to its first annual report the Commission stated:

> At every meeting with the Secretary of State the Chief Commissioner has stressed that he believes the Commission is under-funded. The Commission continues to seek to demonstrate that it could achieve a lot more if only it were supplied with greater resources.[76]

Relations with both the UK government and the devolved government also may have taken a toll on the Commission's performance. One view on the UK government's approach to the Commission was that it was never really interested in the work of the Commission and gradually began to look upon the Commission as an irritant, while the Commission's 2002 negative comments on the impending invasion of Iraq further alienated the government.[77] In his introduction to the 2004 *Annual Report* the then Chief Commissioner stated bluntly that the

> Commission, in short, has been extremely disappointed at the way in which the Government has treated the Commission as a "political" institution, rather than as a completely independent body whose sole concern is the promotion and protection of human rights.[78]

The relations between the Commission and the devolved institutions were more nuanced, with unionist politicians being sceptical of the Commission's approach, especially in terms of the Bill of Rights process.[79] With respect to its powers the Commission had long requested further powers of investigation which initially it did not possess. This demand was also made by the UK Parliament's Joint Committee on Human Rights in a 2003 report.[80] This demand was met in 2007 with the enactment of the Justice and Security (Northern Ireland) Act, which granted the Commission additional powers to enter places of detention and to compel individuals and agencies to give evidence and produce documents.

The emphasis on a Bill of Rights

Apart from the general functions assigned to the Commission, the Agreement also articulated a specific function for the Commission in advising on the scope for the adoption of a Bill of Rights for Northern Ireland. This specific function was given a statutory basis in section 69 of the 1998 Act.

The Bill of Rights process turned out to be laborious, lengthy and eventually futile in terms of facilitating the adoption of a Bill of Rights for Northern Ireland. The reasons for the laboriousness, length and failure may all be attributed to the differing vision of human rights between unionist and nationalist political parties. This divergence, as shall be seen, related both to differences on the concept of human rights in general as well as to differences on the specificities of the Bill of Rights in particular.

The main difference between unionist and nationalist views of a Bill of Rights for Northern Ireland was primarily expressed in terms of the extent to which the two sides wished to anchor the Bill in the terms of the particular circumstances of Northern Ireland, i.e. the conflict. The Agreement stated that any such Bill was to include:

> rights supplementary to those in the European Convention on Human Rights, to *reflect the particular circumstances of Northern Ireland*, drawing as appropriate on international instruments and experience.
>
> These additional rights to reflect the principles of mutual respect for the identity and ethos of both communities and parity of esteem.[81]

The unionist parties insisted on a restrictive interpretation of the phrase "the particular circumstances of Northern Ireland", whereas the nationalist parties (and most NGOs) wanted a wide interpretation of the same phrase.[82] This in turn meant a polarisation between those arguing for a maximalist Bill of Rights for Northern Ireland that included every possible human right and those arguing for a minimalist Bill of Rights that included only those rights which were not already present within the ECHR and which reflected the particular circumstances of Northern Ireland narrowly defined. For unionists, the "particular circumstances of Northern Ireland" related clearly only to the conflict itself, narrowly understood, whereas for the nationalists the "particular circumstances" included any aspects that could be related to the conflict. A key example of this difference may be seen in the approach towards socioeconomic rights as described by the Chairperson of the Bill of Rights Forum:

> The view of nationalists and NGOs was that Northern Ireland was historically economically depressed and that the years of conflict had both economic causes (in the economic and other inequalities between the two main communities) and economic consequences for Northern Ireland today. In particular, they say the conflict had causes and consequences related to economic disadvantage. Therefore, in this view dealing with economic and social rights was squarely part of the "particular circumstances of Northern Ireland". But the unionists defined the "particular circumstances of Northern Ireland" as only directly related to direct and immediate factors relating to the conflict. So, parading and the display of unionist banners would be a "particular circumstance" but unemployment, poor living conditions and poor education and health were not.[83]

This view is corroborated by representatives of the parties themselves. Dermot Nesbitt, who served as human rights spokesperson for the UUP and eventually also served as a Minister in the Executive expressed the unionist view very clearly when he argued that the Agreement clearly mandated the Commission to advise on rights additional to the European Convention on Human Rights and that such rights were to reflect the particular circumstances of Northern Ireland in terms of identity, ethos and parity of esteem of the two communities. This mandate was, in his view, stretched beyond breaking point by the Human Rights Commission under Brice Dickson and Monica McWilliams, which viewed the Bill of Rights process as an opportunity to have a comprehensive Bill of Rights with everything in it including children's rights, health rights and environmental rights.[84] Jonathan Bell MLA, a former member of the Human Rights Commission, made similar points insofar as the DUP is concerned:

> We wanted a strategic, high-level Bill of Rights particular to the circumstances of Northern Ireland. What was produced was a wish-list by the various sectoral groups; a wish-list of what everybody wanted with no cognisance of how to balance all of it.[85]

Conversely, the view of the nationalist political parties (and of most NGOs) was that the Bill of Rights process was an opportunity to achieve a comprehensive human rights settlement in Northern Ireland. Sinn Féin's Catriona Ruane argued that "as a society emerging out of conflict in the north (and in the south) we need comprehensive legislation".[86] The NGOs with whom the Commission consulted took a very strong line that the Bill of Rights should be as comprehensive as possible and were described as having a dogmatic and uncompromising approach to this issue. It has been suggested that they seemed to want all or nothing – and so in the end they got nothing.[87]

The Bill of Rights process involved initial consultations by the Commission with civil society (including the political parties) as a result of which the Commission eventually published a first consultation document to which organisations in Northern Ireland as well as the public were invited to react. The first consultation document was published by the Commission in 2001.[88] The draft was criticised by human rights NGOs as not going far enough[89] while unionists criticised it for going too far. The process was then resumed with further successive consultations by the Commission which culminated in a decision to establish a Bill of Rights Forum as a structure through which all the interested parties could discuss in detail and in a structured manner the Bill of Rights. The Forum was eventually established in 2008 under the chairmanship of Professor Chris Sidoti from Australia. The Forum failed to achieve consensus on the Bill of Rights, although Chris Sidoti considered the (Bill of Rights) exercise useful in two aspects: (1) in producing a clear report on the positions of the various parties (political parties and NGOs) with respect to each element of the proposed Bill of Rights; and (2) in providing a space where for a period of a year representatives of all the key players discussed human rights together.[90] The latter was something which had never happened in Northern Ireland (and has not happened since).

The Forum did, in fact, bring into clear relief the key differences between the parties in terms of the Bill of Rights. These differences may be summarised as follows:

1 differences relating to the inclusion of specific rights;
2 differences relating to the inclusion of rights already provided for in the Human Rights Act 1998;
3 differences relating to the definition of the particular circumstances of Northern Ireland.

The first set of differences relates to the inclusion of specific rights, mainly socioeconomic ones, within the Bill of Rights. While the human rights NGOs and the nationalist parties supported their inclusion and indeed were vociferous in support of such inclusion, the unionist parties were unequivocally against. The UUP's official position on this is clear:

> We are firmly of the opinion that socio-economic rights should not be included in any Bill of Rights ... establishing legally enforceable socio-economic rights and effectively drawing the courts into resource allocation decisions is also not a set of circumstances which the Ulster Unionist Party views as acceptable and indeed this runs contrary to the Party's fundamental belief in democratic process; courts are not elected to take such decisions.[91]

This view is echoed by the DUP who argue that focusing on socioeconomic rights is not progress in terms of human rights but rather the opposite, as it could tie down the human rights agenda to the social policy of the day and it was also objectionable in that it could "tie down the block grant we receive by saying we must divide the grant this way or that particular way. For us that's impinging on the realm of politics."[92]

In terms of the divergences relating to the inclusion of rights already provided for in the 1998 UK Human Rights Act, this was particularly interesting since it expressed within it the fundamental ideological difference between unionists and nationalists. The unionists wanted to rely primarily on the UK-wide Act since it underscored Northern Ireland's position as an integral part of the UK. An example of this stand may be seen in the position of the DUP and UUP on including provisions related to the right to life within the Bill of Rights. Within the Forum both parties rejected the inclusion of the right to life on the grounds that section 2 of the Human Rights Act "sufficiently protects the right to life".[93] The unionists would only countenance a Bill of Rights which did not duplicate any provision already in the Human Rights Act except insofar as such a provision was clearly providing for a particular circumstance of Northern Ireland. The UUP commented that it was "unacceptable that one part of the United Kingdom could have a differing set of rights to another as this undermines the institutional integrity of that state".[94] This view is broadly confirmed by Jonathan Bell who argued that "it is impossible to justify that if you live in Belfast you should be entitled to a better standard of healthcare than if you lived in Birmingham."[95] Moreover, in relation to whether the Human Rights Act 1998 is broadly sufficient for the protection of human rights in Northern Ireland, Jonathan Bell responded: "I remain to be convinced that there is need for extra human rights legislation that is currently not available in Northern Ireland."[96] Conversely, the nationalists wanted to include within the Bill rights which were already provided for in the Human Rights Act "with an implied subtext that they did not recognise the application of the UK Act to Northern Ireland".[97]

The nationalist view articulated by Catriona Ruane is that they "do not agree with those who say that the Human Rights Act and other ad hoc legislation are sufficient".[98] They are clear that they "want to see a Bill of Rights for the north and an All-Ireland Charter of Rights".[99] The reference to the All-Ireland Charter of Rights[100] is a further indication of the ideological differences referred to above which relate to the nationalist conception of

Northern Ireland as part of Ireland and the unionist conception of Northern Ireland as an integral component of the United Kingdom. The border, therefore, played a role even in discussions around the Bill of Rights.

Reference has already been made to the divergences relating to the definition of what constitute the particular circumstances of Northern Ireland in the context of the Bill of Rights. In its final report the Forum stated that it "was unable to come to a single view on the issues, most notably on an understanding of what constituted 'the particular circumstances of Northern Ireland'."[101] For unionists there are

> some really particular circumstances: we do have many victims and survivors and we have a mental health legacy that should be looked at … one of the biggest legacy issues from the conflict has been the lack of horizontal human rights between citizen and citizen because for some human rights are very much the state's obligation towards the citizen.[102]

This latter issue of horizontal human rights related to a broader difference in the interpretation of human rights between unionists and nationalists which will be examined later.

The unionist view was summed up by the UUP in its response to the Commission's final draft of 2008:

> It is the view of the Ulster Unionist Party that the subsequent drafting of a comprehensive Bill of Rights by the NIHRC (presented in December 2008) was not part of the Belfast Agreement and we broadly supported the NIO consultation document "The Bill of Rights for Northern Ireland: Next Steps" which set out a robust rejection of the NIHRC proposals. We also reached the conclusion that the NIHRC could play no further constructive part in the debate around a Bill of Rights given the position which they adopted.[103]

On the nationalist side, there was an insistence on a comprehensive Bill of Rights with a very generous interpretation of what constituted the particular circumstances of Northern Ireland. In its submissions to the Forum, Sinn Féin made it clear it believed in "a comprehensive and inclusive Bill of Rights".[104] The SDLP likewise sought "a progressive and comprehensive Bill of Rights" and argued for a Bill that would have a "broad scope [which] includes a wide range of relevant social and economic issues".[105]

Ultimately, the Forum could only bring out the (numerous) differences between the main political parties in terms of the Bill of Rights. It did so clearly and comprehensively. Once the Forum's *Final Report* was submitted to the Commission the Commission had to decide on its final advice to the Secretary of State. The Commission's final advice, issued on 10 December 2008, also failed to command unanimous consensus within the Commission. Two of the Commissioners (Jonathan Bell and Daphne Trimble) objected to the advice on the grounds illustrated above, that the advice was going beyond the scope of the Agreement, specifically in its interpretation of the particular circumstances of Northern Ireland.[106]

In the final analysis, the UK government had the responsibility to decide how and whether to proceed with legislating for a Bill of Rights. The Agreement clearly established that a Bill of Rights for Northern Ireland was a matter for Westminster legislation. In this context, the UK government through the Northern Ireland Office responded to the Commission's advice in November 2009 with a consultation paper entitled *A Bill of Rights for Northern Ireland: Next Steps*. In effect, the paper sought to limit the scope of the Bill of Rights and moved away from the comprehensive approach adopted by the Commission in its final advice. In fact, the paper suggested that the range of issues that should be dealt with in the Bill of Rights include equality, representation and participation in public life; identity, culture and language; sectarianism and segregation; victims and the legacy of the conflict; and criminal justice".[107] Notable absences from this list are socioeconomic rights and other thematic rights such as children's rights or the rights of older people.

Since 2010 the focus on a Bill of Rights for Northern Ireland has not been as sharp. This may be attributable to a number of reasons. It has been suggested that at a time of austerity the Bill of Rights was not a priority even for nationalist parties in terms of "the list of issues confronting them at a time of austerity when they have to consider issues like closing down schools, etc. It is not viewed as a priority at this moment in time."[108] There has also been a lack of enthusiasm for the Bill of Rights project from Westminster since the change of government in 2010. It has been suggested that the failure to achieve a Bill of Rights by 2010 is due to the fact that the whole process

> has lost momentum and it lost momentum because the Bill of Rights had been dragged on for such a long time that by the time the UK government had the opportunity to consider any Bill of Rights it had come to the election and then a government came along which has no commitment to the process.[109]

The Conservative–Liberal Democrat coalition has, in the view of some, "no interest in Ireland" except when something arises that might jeopardise the peace process.[110] With the Conservative Party in the UK discussing the possibility of repealing or amending the Human Rights Act, the likelihood of the UK government taking the lead in the Bill of Rights process was certainly minimal. This renders the possibility of progress on the Bill of Rights more remote.

In the view of a former Secretary of State for Northern Ireland, progress can only be made if the British and Irish governments "take an initiative to bring people together in dealing with the issue" and that the process "definitely needs the two governments (UK and Ireland) to work with the political parties to get an agreement".[111] The Chairperson of the Bill of Rights Forum took a similar view that an initiative is required in order to bring the parties together and that imposes a deadline on them to reach agreement:

> The UK government needs to say: at the end of this period of 12 months we will legislate a Bill of Rights for Northern Ireland. The Northern Ireland parties have 12 months to negotiate its content and if they fail we will legislate anyway.[112]

What is certainly beyond dispute is that 14 years from the Agreement, which envisaged a Bill of Rights for Northern Ireland, the people of Northern Ireland are still without such a Bill. This is certainly an unfinished business in terms of the Agreement.

A balance sheet of the Human Rights Commission and the Bill of Rights process

The creation of the Human Rights Commission through the Northern Ireland Act of 1998 not only fulfilled a requirement of the Agreement but also helped give shape and structure to the commitment towards human rights articulated therein. The powers of the Commission initially were not fully compliant with the UN Paris Principles on National Human Rights Institutions[113] although as from 2011 the Commission is considered to be fully compliant with the Principles. This, in itself, is evidence of a commitment to the Commission and to independent and effective human rights protection and promotion.

The work of the Commission has, naturally, not been without its criticisms. During the Holy Cross dispute the decision by the Commission to support a court case by one of the parents of the schoolgirls drew criticism from outside the Commission as well as fuelling divisions within it. The already cited resignations and withdrawals from the Commission were also indicators of significant divisions within the Commission. More broadly, the Commission also failed to present unanimous advice to the Secretary of State with respect to the Bill of Rights. The fact that the two dissenting Commissioners were from a unionist background rendered the fracture an uncomfortable one. The already existing perception that the human rights agenda is a nationalist issue (as evidenced in previous chapters) was probably confirmed as a result.

The Northern Ireland Human Rights Commission has attracted a considerable amount of criticism, particularly in its early years.[114] In attempting to evaluate the work of the Commission one must acknowledge that the Commission was established in a community which was not only deeply divided, but also with polarised views on human rights themselves which were coloured by decades of conflict. The early years of the Commission were years when the political institutions at Stormont were mostly suspended. As confirmed by one of the holders of the office of Secretary of State at the time, the work of the Commission was not a priority for the UK government.[115] Re-establishing the devolved institutions were the main priority until 2007 when the St Andrew's Agreement was signed. The Commission was also mandated by the Belfast Agreement with the task of producing advice on the Bill of Rights.

The Bill of Rights process cannot be viewed to have been a success in terms of achieving what it set out to do, i.e. adopt a Bill of Rights for Northern Ireland. There is no doubt, however, that the process did increase public awareness of, and interest in, human rights in Northern Ireland.[116] As Chris Sidoti has remarked, the Bill of Rights Forum provided a space where the political parties and civil society could discuss human rights in a structured manner. There had been and was no other place where this could occur.

The Forum's Report is also useful as a framework that describes the positions of the parties in respect of each element of the proposed Bill. On the negative side, the process confirmed the different views of the interpretation of human rights by the political parties. Nationalist focus on state abuses as opposed to unionist focus on human rights abuses by individuals is one example of this division. The desire to include socioeconomic rights by nationalists and the refusal to include such rights by unionists is another example. In essence though the process was further evidence of how human rights in Northern Ireland remain understood within the ambit of the conflict and of their political position, or as Chris Sidoti explained that the parties "interpreted human rights within the framework of their ideological cause and as a result human rights became part of the ideological struggle".[117]

This specific task of drafting advice on a Bill of Rights seems to have been the major preoccupation of the Commission in its early years. The Bill of Rights process was a very long and fraught one. The difficulties in producing this advice are probably not attributable to the shortcomings of the Commission but rather to entrenched attitudes towards human rights in Northern Ireland. It can be argued that the Commission's role should have been to move the parties away from such entrenched attitudes. However, within the Commission itself commissioners had different views on human rights which were not easily bridged.[118] In sum, it appears that the Commission's early years were very difficult ones due to a number of reasons:

1 a lack of resources (including sufficient powers), support and interest from the UK government (which was focusing on reviving the moribund devolved institutions);
2 the intrinsic difficulties of establishing an institution in a divided community;
3 the entrenched attitudes towards human rights both in the society at large and within the Commission; and
4 a focus on the Bill of Rights process which was a specific duty of the Commission in terms of the Belfast Agreement but which proved to be an albatross around the Commission's neck.

Nevertheless, the overall assessment of the Commission has to bear in mind that a degree of political stability was only achieved within Northern Ireland (with a functioning Assembly and Executive) post-2007. Prior to this date, the Commission operated in a situation of political instability and uncertainty. This cannot have helped the Commission's work. The current strategy adopted by the Commission, with a focus on both legacy issues and the rights of the most vulnerable offers a clear direction which may bear fruit as the Commission consolidates its role within Northern Ireland.

Human rights and legacy issues

> The passage of time – and the passing of those with information to share and wounds to salve – will also deprive Northern Ireland of the chance to learn as much as possible about its history while there is still time to do so. This loss would compound the social and emotional costs of our prolonged conflict.[119]

A human rights perspective on this matter brings to the fore the issue of historic human rights abuses which remain unresolved. This has, in some families and some communities, allowed a sense of grievance to fester in the same way in which the discrimination of the 1920s to 1960s created a feeling of grievance amongst the nationalist community. The 1972 killing of Jean McConville and the disappearance of her body by the IRA is one example of how historic human rights abuses have returned to haunt the peace process in Northern Ireland. The deprivation of the right to life of so many by security forces and paramilitary organisations has led to a sense of unfairness and injustice being prolonged and engrained in both communities.

It has also led to evidence of further disagreements between different parties to the conflict as to what actions constitute human rights violations and what actions do not. Essentially the disagreement revolves around the matter whether human rights violations may only be committed by the state or whether non-state actors may also commit human rights violations. Sinn Féin has traditionally argued that only the state and state agencies may commit human rights violations while actions by non-state actors are a matter for criminal law to deal with. This was also a debate in the broader community. The first Chair of the Human Rights Commission (HRC) recounts how early on in the history of the HRC there was a debate on whether the Commission should deal with punishment beatings on teenagers conducted by paramilitary organisations: "We had a big discussion about this and we could not reach agreement that this was an appropriate matter for the Commission to deal with. There was a strong minority who insisted that this was not a state issue."[120] For the unionist community, who suffered mainly as a result of attacks by paramilitary organisations, this is an intolerable approach and has, it is suggested, played a role in how the unionist community has developed a wary approach towards human rights. This sentiment has been expressed as follows:

> If you look at the situation in Bosnia and Rwanda you see a lot of emphasis on the human rights abuses of non-state actors while here there has not been such an emphasis. I think that causes a huge amount of resentment from the victims of IRA terrorism for example. These were the same people who were clamouring that if arrested you had a right to a phone call within 2 hours and yet they were taking people away, torturing them and shooting them in the head. At times these were juveniles: kids of 14, 15, 16. There was no trial, no lawyer, no phone call.[121]

Conversely, Sinn Féin's position remained that there needs to be "a particular focus on states because they signed particular conventions, they are the most powerful actors."[122] While international human rights law is moving towards a clear rule that establishes international obligations on non-state actors for violations of human rights,[123] international criminal law already recognises (and has done so since the Nuremberg Trials) that individuals (irrespective of their status as agents of the state or not) are liable under international law for certain acts including gross violations of human rights. Notwithstanding any arguments based on international law, it seems clear that the whole basis of the human rights movement is founded on an acknowledgment that individuals (and groups) of individuals are responsible for the promotion and protection of human rights. Irrespective of issues of legal liability for breaches of human rights by non-state actors, there is no doubt that individuals or groups of individuals who kill and maim other individuals are through their actions breaching the human rights of their victims.

The Universal Declaration of Human Rights refers to the role of the individual in promoting human rights. The idea that rights may be breached by individuals is also acknowledged in Article 17 of the European Convention on Human Rights:

> Nothing in this Convention may be interpreted as implying for any State, group or person any right to engage in any activity or perform any act aimed at the destruction of any of the rights and freedoms set forth herein.

Even more emphatically, Article 7 of the Statute of the International Criminal Court establishes that killings, enforced disappearances and torture (amongst other types of conduct) amount to crimes against humanity and that such crimes subsist whether committed in consequence of a state or organisational policy. Therefore, it is not only state-sponsored conduct that qualifies as a crime against humanity but also conduct sponsored by a non-state organisation.

As highlighted above, the issue of historical killings which remained unresolved has been a matter of dispute and unease within Northern Ireland both in terms of allegations of extrajudicial killings by security forces, allegations of collusion and paramilitary killings. The Peace Agreement provided for the early release of prisoners but not for amnesties for persons who committed offences which remained unresolved at the time of the Agreement. Thus, the Agreement did not provide for a mechanism to deal with historical human rights abuses by state security forces or paramilitary organisations. This vacuum led to a number of developments within Northern Ireland.

Before the Agreement was signed a number of cases concerning allegations of collusion by state security forces with loyalist paramilitaries were submitted to the European Court of Human Rights. The cases, known collectively as the McKerr Cases, led the UK government to take steps in the sphere of unresolved conflict-related killings. In 2001 the European Court delivered judgment in the McKerr case where it found the government of the UK to have been in breach of its obligations under Article 2 of the Convention (right to life) by not providing an adequate and effective investigation to protect the right to life.[124] The Court delivered similar judgments in the other cases concerning conflict-related killings, including the case of the killing of lawyer Pat Finucane.[125] This latter case was the last judgment to be delivered in this series of judgments in 2003.

Consequent to this series of judgments delivered by the European Court of Human Rights, the UK government announced, inter alia, the setting up of the Historical Enquiries Team (HET) with the remit to investigate conflict-related killings and where appropriate refer for prosecution such persons suspected of having been involved in such killings. This measure was intended to fulfil the UK government's obligation under Article 2 of the European Convention on Human Rights. The fact that the HET was set up as a reactive measure following the European Court's judgments demonstrates that during negotiations not enough attention was paid to the matter of breaches of the right to life and its attendant need for truth and closure.

The HET was not intended to reinvestigate in detail all conflict-related deaths but was designed to "provide a thorough and independent reappraisal of unresolved cases, with the aim of identifying and exploring any evidential opportunities that exist". It was only if fresh evidence was identified during the HET review process that "the investigation of the death will proceed and where there is credible evidence available reports will be forwarded to the Public Prosecution Service with a view to prosecution."[126] This in itself fails to fulfil the criteria required by the European Court of Human Rights that breaches of the right to life should all be investigated promptly, effectively, independently and transparently.[127]

Apart from the legal points mentioned above, an inspection of the HET by Her Majesty's Inspector of Constabulary identified a number of shortcomings, including: confusion with respect to the HET's terms of reference; insufficient involvement of families concerned; the lack of a public communication strategy; and a lack of a single complaints procedure. These shortcomings are of particular concern in view of the impact they have on one of the key objectives of the HET: bringing a measure of resolution to those affected by the deaths. The issue of bringing resolution to the families of those killed or disappeared is an issue which has clearly not been dealt with comprehensively or even appropriately in Northern Ireland. The criticisms levelled at the HET in the Her Majesty's Inspector of Constabulary (HMIC) Inspection revealed "a level of mistrust in the way that the HET is carrying out its work".[128] Northern Ireland has evidently failed to identify a procedure for dealing with historic human rights abuses which commands the very high levels of public confidence required to deal with such a delicate problem. This problem is exacerbated by the fact that in September 2014 it was announced that the HET would be disbanded as a result of the budgetary cuts.[129] The Stormont House Agreement adopted on 23 December 2014 provided for the setting up of a Historical Investigations Unit to replace the HET.[130] Such a unit is not yet operative at the end of 2014 and will in all likelihood require many months to become operational. The PSNI, however, established a Legacy Issues Branch to continue with historical investigations. The success or otherwise of these units remains to be seen. Within Northern Ireland there is still considerable anger about unresolved killings: both amongst nationalists complaining of collusion[131] as well as by the families of victims of paramilitary organisations. In this latter case, there has been anger over the "on the runs" controversy[132] especially when IRA suspects who allegedly committed murder received letters from the UK government which implied an assurance that they were no longer facing prosecution.[133]

The complexity and intractability of this whole issue of truth, amnesty and prosecution was also evident in the furore created when the UK government introduced the Northern Ireland (Offences) Bill in November 2005. The Bill would have seen conflict-related offences tried in Special Tribunals with persons sentenced by such Tribunal being released on license. Eventually the then Secretary of State withdrew the Bill after the second reading due to the strong opposition in Northern Ireland to the scheme. A similar furore ensued in November 2013 when the Northern Ireland Attorney General suggested that there should be an end to conflict-related prosecutions.[134] The regular uproars created by attempts to deal with the matters of historical human rights abuses (especially killings) demonstrate the complexity and sensitivity of the issue.

Ultimately, under international law and according to the McKerr cases, the UK government is still responsible to fulfil its obligations under Article 2 of the European Convention. More importantly, Northern Ireland still needs to find a way to bring a measure of closure to the bereaved. These requirements may need a more comprehensive and holistic approach than the ones adopted so far.[135]

The conflict in Northern Ireland has left a difficult and, so far unresolved, legacy of dispute on other issues which have some connection to the human rights and equality agenda. The issues of parades and flags are arguably the two most dividing issues between nationalists and unionists in Northern Ireland today. It is no coincidence that the Haass Talks intended to identify a way forward focused on flags and parades as two of the key issues in the agenda: "Difficulties surrounding parades and protests, flags and emblems, and the past are symptoms of much deeper divisions."[136]

It is necessary to state at the outset that the issues of flags and parades are not issues which fall easily into the human rights and equality agenda. Early on in its existence the Northern Ireland Human Rights Commission sought to contribute to the debate around these issues. In doing so it acknowledged the limitations of human rights in resolving these issues: "Human rights legislation will not provide easy solutions to political and community relations problems. However, human rights legilsation should make a contribution to providing structures within which disputes can be justly resolved."[137] The Commission emphasised human rights legislation in its approach. It may be suggested that in the resolution of these issues a human rights ethos or culture which emphasises common humanity and empathy may be even more conducive to resolving such issues. A human rights perspective may be useful in suggesting responses to these issues but ultimately these two issues must also be resolved with reference to ideas of reconciliation, the promotion of good relations and a commitment to a shared future. This study is not intended to deal comprehensively with the issues of flags or parades but will instead focus on examining what these two issues reveal in terms of the understanding of human rights in Northern Ireland.

Parading does bring to the fore of the debate the rights to freedom of assembly and association and to freedom of expression, two of the traditional rights found in the Universal Declaration of Human Rights, the International Covenant on Civil and Political Rights and the European Convention on Human Rights. The unionist community, particularly those individuals who are members of the Orange Order, claim vociferously these rights in respect of their traditional parades. These rights, however, even in the formulation adopted in the European Convention, are not absolute.

Both Article 10 (freedom of expression) and 11 (freedom of assembly) of the European Convention contain legitimate limitations on these rights. In particular, they can be limited by public authorities for the protection of public safety, the prevention of crime or disorder and the protection of the rights and freedoms of others. These are general limitations which apply in all contexts. The proposed Haass Agreement suggested that, further to these limitations, there should be consideration for "Northern Ireland's unique history and characteristics. This requires that the tradition of parading, protesting, and assembling be conducted in a way that contributes to the goal of building a shared and open society."

Another way of putting it from a human rights perspective, is to look not just at the letter but also at the spirit of human rights. An insistence by Orangemen that they have a right to freedom of expression and assembly countered by an insistence by nationalist neighbourhoods that in terms of the Peace Agreement they have a "right to freedom from sectarian harassment" is not conducive to any resolution. The Haass proposals suggested that "Restraint and generosity in the exercise of the freedom of expression, assembly, and association, as well as fulfilment of the associated responsibilities, can advance this goal."[138] The Universal Declaration of Human Rights makes a similar point. Article 1 states: "All human beings are born free and equal in dignity and rights. They are endowed with reason and conscience and should act towards one another in a spirit of brotherhood." The spirit of brotherhood or solidarity seems to be notably absent from both sides in the parading dispute who insist on "their rights". Article 29 of the Declaration also makes reference to the duty to consider "the general welfare in a democratic society" in the enjoyment of our human rights. In Northern Ireland, the general welfare seems to be all too often set aside in favour of very rigid positions in how rights are interpreted and understood.

The issue of flags is also a deeply emotive and divisive one. Together with parading it has caused some of the most serious public disorders since the Agreement in 1998. In Chapters 3 and 4 reference was made to the issue of flags in Northern Ireland, with the Union flag and the Irish tricolour being symbols of the divergent views on self-determination for unionists and nationalists respectively. The nationalists viewed, and some still view, the Union flag as a symbol of the discrimination they consider they endured since the creation of Northern Ireland in 1921. Nationalists further cemented this view of the Union flag during the conflict, as they swiftly changed their perception of the British Army from protectors to oppressors of their community as described in Chapter 5. On the opposite front, unionists view the Union flag as the ultimate symbol of their belonging to the United Kingdom.

The Haass proposals admitted that after considering numerous options on how to deal with the issue of flags on official buildings and sites it failed to achieve a consensus. Nationalists, for example, considered the taking down of the Union flag from Belfast City Hall (except for designated days) as an "equality measure".[139] The many hundreds who protested in December 2012 against this decision (in some instances violently) clearly considered it an attack on their identity. In the words of Ian Paisley Jr., the removal of the flag was "an attack on the symbol of Britishness" and a "symbolic removal of our national identity".[140] Once again the two main communities use the language of rights in order to buttress their position. In both cases, there seems to be a lack of awareness of the rights and perceptions of others. Given the history of the conflict in Northern Ireland and the sensitive nature of flags and symbols the political parties failed to demonstrate a degree of leadership in moving the agenda forward.

Instead, they sought either to explain (and some would argue justify) the ensuing violence or condemn the violence outright without examining their own actions from which the violence ensued. Human rights do not provide a neat answer to the flags issue although it offers a framework within which decisions may be taken. A comprehensive understanding of human rights would have suggested that rights need to be balanced against each other and interpreted generously and in a spirit of solidarity. Such an understanding would also require leaders to use their positions to avoid violence in all circumstances. The Stormont House Agreement, which materialised in the last week of the period covered in this chapter, does make specific reference to the need to construct a comprehensive framework to deal with the past. Human rights are included as part of that framework, but are not the only component that is mentioned:

> As part of the transition to long-term peace and stability the participants agree that an approach to dealing with the past is necessary which respects the following principles:
>
> - promoting reconciliation;
> - upholding the rule of law;
> - acknowledging and addressing the suffering of victims and survivors;
> - facilitating the pursuit of justice and information recovery;
> - is human rights compliant; and
> - is balanced, proportionate, transparent, fair and equitable.

One should also avoid a unique focus on the legalistic aspects of human rights in dealing with these issues and focus equally on the core values that underpin human rights law, i.e. the value of universality so often cited as a bedrock of human rights. This value of universality is based on the concept of common humanity and brotherhood. Such an approach may be of some value in dealing with the past and in moving towards a shared future. The principles highlighted by the Stormont House Agreement quoted above, particularly balance and proportionality are very important ones in this context.

A balance sheet for legacy issues

The mere fact of the failure of the Haass talks are a clear indicator that progress in this field has been, at best, limited. The success or otherwise of the Stormont House Agreement remains a very open question which will be answered in the coming years. Certainly, within the timeframe covered in this chapter (1998–2014) legacy issues remained problematic. The worse incidents of violence and unrest in Northern Ireland have involved flags and parades, while the most serious challenge to the policing service has come from the investigation of historic human rights abuses, particularly the Gerry Adams arrest. This illustrates the lack of progress made in this respect. Northern Ireland is not unique in this respect. In Rwanda, Yugoslavia, Chile and South Africa to name a few conflict zones, legacy issues have proved difficult to contend with. However, unlike any of these countries, Northern Ireland has still not decided how to deal with its past. Moreover, unlike Rwandans, former Yugoslavs, Chileans and South Africans, the people of Northern Ireland remain in fundamental disagreement about their national identity and their long-term political future. No answer or decision will be perfect, although the current situation where no answers are provided and no decisions are taken is probably an untenable situation: "The pain of the past is not going to be healed by the passage of time alone."[141] It has been suggested that "the biggest challenge [faced by Northern Ireland] is to deal with the legacy issues and that is the bedrock if we are to succeed."[142] A human rights framework applied to legacy issues will not be a panacea. For instance, a human rights perspective on historic abuses would suggest judicial processes that may inflame the situation further and which may cause a rupture in the political process. There has not been a serious dynamic towards a Truth and Reconciliation Commission either.

A 2004 Northern Ireland Life and Times Survey on public support for the establishment of a truth commission revealed that 50 per cent of those interviewed thought that such a commission was important against those (28 per cent) who did not. It also showed that Catholics were more likely than Protestants to think that a truth commission was important for Northern Ireland (58 per cent as opposed to 44 per cent). Overall, the survey showed that there was significant but not overwhelming support for a truth commission, with people showing scepticism on the degree to which such a commission would be successful, with statistically significant numbers expressing their preference for alternative ways of dealing with the past.[143] A report published by the Healing Through Remembering organisation also examined the attitudes of political parties towards a truth commission and it is evident that unionist parties are very sceptical about such a commission while the SDLP and Sinn Féin are significantly more favourably inclined.[144] Once again, the dividing line between the two communities has made progress on this matter very problematic. As highlighted in the preceding section this matter of truth and reconciliation remains particularly elusive. In a few cases the HET made progress and there have been grass roots and community-based attempts at dealing with truth and reconciliation, such as the Healing Through Remembering project. Nevertheless, issues of truth and reconciliation have not been dealt with satisfactorily in Northern Ireland either from a human rights perspective[145] or a peace-building one.[146]

The Report of the Consultative Group on the Past had recommended the establishment of a Legacy Commission which would have combined "processes of reconciliation, justice and information recovery" with the "overarching objective of promoting peace and stability in Northern Ireland."[147] This never materialised. In fact, the recommendations contained in the Report have been largely shelved so far. This is a further indication that legacy issues have yet to be dealt with in a structured and substantive manner. Although human rights do not feature prominently in the Group's Report, they did constitute one of the guiding principles which the Group adopted to guide their work:

> A new approach to dealing with the past is required. But it must be shaped in a way which recognises the rights and responsibilities defined by the European Convention on Human Rights (ECHR) and the

> decisions of both the domestic and international courts. Alongside the legal rights of the individual, a society has the right to live peaceably and create a better future for all.[148]

This, in one sense, confirms the attempt outlined in the Agreement to mainstream human rights through all the new structures and institutions created in Northern Ireland. However, in another sense, it also reads somewhat stiffly as a nod in the direction of human rights without exploring in greater detail what a human rights framework can contribute to reconciliation. This is especially relevant in the context of the need to create good relationships as a prerequisite to reconciliation and a shared future.[149] Human rights are too often understood in Northern Ireland (as elsewhere) as being legalistic standards to be met in a formal way. As Mary Robinson has pointed out, human rights understood as fairness are essential in creating the right relationships between individuals and within society.[150] This view is echoed by the first Chairperson of the Northern Ireland Human Rights Commission: "human rights are basically values for a better society. And I remember I once said that we [the Human Rights Commission] could have been called something like A Fairer and Better Society Commission rather than the Human Rights Commission."[151] Such an understanding of human rights could have contributed more and better to Northern Ireland's reflection on its past and how to deal with it.

A post-script: political developments in 2015

Political life in Northern Ireland during 2015 was significantly dominated by two issues: the tortuous pathway to the implementation of the Stormont House Agreement and the reaction to the murder of Kevin McGuigan (a former IRA member) on the streets of Belfast in August 2015. Both issues challenged the stability and existence of the Northern Irish institutions.

The Stormont House Agreement referred to earlier dealt with a broad array of issues including flags and parades as well as budgetary and welfare reform. The implementation of the budgetary and welfare reform was derailed in March 2015 when Sinn Féin rejected the welfare reforms which were in the process of being enacted. This caused an impasse which threatened the stability of the Executive.

The PSNI's appraisal that the murder of Kevin McGuigan involved elements of the IRA raised doubts on the extent to which the IRA had fully decommissioned. This caused serious ructions in Northern Irish politics with the UUP deciding to withdraw its only member from the Executive as a reaction to this event. The DUP also withdrew its ministers but using procedures which enabled the Executive to survive until the impasse was resolved.

The DUP and Sinn Féin eventually agreed to a deal intended to resolve both disputes. The deal provided for the setting up of a commission to monitor the state of paramilitarism and charged with producing annual reports on the state of paramilitarism in Northern Ireland. Under the same deal the

PSNI was to receive additional funding while a cross-border task force was created to deter cross-border criminality through the coordination of police, customs and security agencies on both sides of the Irish border.

The agreement also dealt with the budgetary issues which had dogged Northern Irish politics for the previous 12 months. A one-off payment of £500 million was allocated to the Northern Ireland Assembly from the UK government intended to provide for some of the legacy issues in Northern Ireland, including the dismantling of the so-called "peace walls". Welfare reform was handed back to the UK thus enabling the Northern Ireland parties to avoid responsibility for any cuts that were implemented.

The deal was also important for what it left unresolved: most significantly the issue of how to deal with the legacy of the conflict including victims' issues. This exclusion was criticised by victims' organisations in Northern Ireland while the then First Minister defended the deal on the basis that it stabilised the Northern Irish political institutions. This could be interpreted as evidence that the realm of high politics was taking precedence over victims' rights because the political parties remained unable to take a broad and comprehensive approach to the human rights agenda in Northern Ireland. The omission was also criticised by the NIHRC's Chief Commissioner Les Allamby in his Foreword to the 2015 *Annual Report* of the NIHRC. He stated that:

> The failure to reach agreement on dealing with the legacy of the past and bring forward legislation and further details of the institutions outlined in the Stormont House Agreement is disappointing. Victims and survivors are getting older and investigations and justice becomes more difficult to achieve as time passes.

The planned reductions in welfare spending which are impacting the UK will also have significant repercussions on Northern Ireland. The extent to which these cuts will be applied with due regard to socioeconomic rights remains to be seen.

However, some human rights progress was registered in 2015. Examples of such progress include the areas of domestic violence and human trafficking. The amendments introduced by the Justice Act (NI) 2015, provide for several new provisions intended to ameliorate the protection available to victims. Inter alia the Act provides "for the implementation of Domestic Violence Protection Notices and Orders in Northern Ireland and the additional offence of 'Causing or allowing a child or vulnerable adult to suffer serious physical harm'". In the field of human trafficking the Assembly adopted the Human Trafficking and Exploitation (Criminal Justice and Support for Victims) Act (Northern Ireland) which establishes human trafficking offences and provides for the care and protection of victims in Northern Ireland. These are signs that, to some extent, the human rights agenda continues to maintain its place in the Northern Irish political space.

Conclusion

The success of the Agreement in human rights terms can be described as huge if one places the developments of 1998 onwards in the context of 30 years of violent conflict and 80 years of societal conflict within Northern Ireland. On the other hand, if one assesses the degree to which developments in human rights have met the hope engendered by the Agreement that Northern Ireland would become a model and an "instructive case" in human rights protection, then the assessment is mixed.

The end of the killings that characterised Northern Ireland for 30 years in itself qualifies as huge progress in human rights terms. The right to life is, after all, a prerequisite for the enjoyment of all other rights. The end of petty forms of discrimination against the nationalist community also features as significant progress within the human rights and equality agenda. This progress has been promoted and buttressed by statutory measures and structures that have become an important part of the legal and policy landscape of Northern Ireland. The reforms in policing and the criminal justice systems have been particularly impressive and it can be argued that the PSNI reforms with their strong human rights ethos could serve as a model for other jurisdictions emerging from conflict. Furthermore, punishment beatings by paramilitary organisations or other vigilante type groups have diminished significantly, in part as a result of the changes in policing. The creation of the Human Rights Commission and its work in promoting human rights in Northern Ireland is also to be commended. The existence of national human rights commissions is strongly advocated by the UN and in this respect Northern Ireland is broadly in line with international best practice, although the Commission does not have all of the powers which such best practice requires.[152] The requirement that all legislation be proofed against the Human Rights Act is evidently an important step as a guarantee of fairness. These factors are all positive, factual evidence of progress in Northern Ireland. In the context of 30 years of violent conflict and 80 years of sociopolitical division on a grand scale, the progress is even more impressive.

Nevertheless, when one compares the great expectations for human rights that the Agreement fomented the assessment is less optimistic. The failure to agree and legislate for a Bill of Rights is a crucial indicator of the failure to turn Northern Ireland into a model for human rights protection. The fact that the political leaders of Northern Ireland cannot, as yet, agree on a set of rights for the protection of everyone must be an indication of how far Northern Ireland still is from being an instructive case for human rights protection. This failure also illustrates how human rights in Northern Ireland remain mediated through the conflict (as well as the legacy of the conflict) and the ideas engendered by the conflict around human rights. The extent to which the past has not been dealt with effectively (or in any other way) continues to impact negatively on human rights in Northern Ireland as is clear by the tension and occasional violence around flags and parades.

The human rights agenda has also suffered from a failure by the political elites to give it sufficient attention and focus. As Paul Murphy pointed out in the crucial post-Agreement years the main political drive was the establishment of the institutions and the successive efforts to reignite the institutions after their suspension. In effect, the key objective of the main actors was saving the Agreement. In this period, human rights were not a political priority.[153] Once the institutions looked secure in the post-St Andrew's Agreement[154] phase, normalisation of the political landscape gradually took hold. This normalisation seems to have had the effect of dissipating the energy required for bold steps in the human rights arena. The British and Irish governments adopted a "do not rock the boat" approach, as can be seen by the failure of both governments to push the Bill of Rights debate to a conclusion. Normalisation, in effect, resulted in the normalisation of human rights as an appendix to the political process (as is the case in most countries) rather than the mainstreaming of human rights as a vital part of the political process as was the promise of the Belfast Agreement. This negative evaluation must be balanced by the facts that both political traditions still use the language of rights extensively and that there have been significant attempts – only partially successful – to institutionalise a human rights culture. Finally, one must also bear in mind that as this study shows, the levels of engagement with rights in the Northern Irish political debate have remained reasonably high. Such engagement is also part of a rights culture. This engagement reflects the relatively high interest in rights in Northern Ireland, which as shown throughout this study precedes the civil rights movement and has expanded consistently, reflecting the expanding role of human rights norms at the international and regional level.

Notes

1 Colin Harvey, "Building Bridges? Protecting Human Rights in Northern Ireland", *Human Rights Law Review* 1, no. 2 (2001), 243–64.
2 See Introduction to Chapter 5.
3 See Malcolm Sutton, *Sutton Index of Deaths*, accessed 6 July 2014, http://cain.ulst.ac.uk/sutton/.
4 Mr Dermot Nesbitt, Interview with former UUP MLA and spokesperson on human rights, 15 April 2014.
5 Gerry Adams, *The New Ireland: A Vision for the Future* (Dublin: Brandon Books, 2005), 44.
6 It is worth noting that section 76 of the Northern Ireland Act 1998 can be traced back to provisions in the Government of Ireland Act 1920 and then the Northern Ireland Constitution Act 1973.
7 McCrudden, Christopher, "The Equality of Opportunity Duty in the Northern Ireland Act 1998: An Analysis", in *Equality and Human Rights: Their Role in Peace Building: The Equality Provisions of the Good Friday Agreement and the NI Act* (Belfast: Unison, 1999), 11, includes proceedings of a conference held on 2 December 1998.
8 Paul Nolan, *Northern Ireland Peace Monitoring Report*, March 2014.
9 Ms. Catriona Ruane MLA, Interview with Sinn Féin Chief Whip at the Northern Ireland Assembly, 15 April 2014.

10 Office of the First Minister and Deputy First Minister, *Labour Force Survey 2012 Religion Report*, Press release (Northern Ireland Executive, 29 January 2014), accessed 8 July 2014, www.northernireland.gov.uk/newsofmdfm-290114-labour-force-survey.
11 See, for example, comments by DUP MP and MLA Gregory Campbell in "Protestant Workers 'Face Discrimination'", *BBC*, 16 March 2004, Northern Ireland, http://news.bbc.co.uk/2/hi/uk_news/northern_ireland/3515210.stm.
12 Mr Dermot Nesbitt, Interview with former UUP MLA and spokesperson on human rights, 15 April 2014.
13 Paul Nolan, *Northern Ireland Peace Monitoring Report*.
14 Ibid.
15 Professor Brice Dickson, Interview with former Chairperson of the Northern Ireland Human Rights Commission, 24 February 2014.
16 According to the 2011 census 1.8 per cent (32,400) of the usually resident population of Northern Ireland belonged to minority ethnic groups in 2011, more than double the proportion in 2001 (0.8 per cent). Northern Ireland Statistics and Research Agency, *Census 2011: Key Statistics for Northern Ireland*, 11 December 2012, accessed 8 July 2014, www.nisra.gov.uk/Census/key_stats_bulletin_2011.pdf.
17 See for example, "Northern Ireland: Further Racist Attack against Romanians in Belfast", *Telegraph*, 18 June 2009, accessed 8 July 2014, www.telegraph.co.uk/news/uknews/law-and-order/5565531/NorthernIreland-further-racist-attack-against-Romanians-in-Belfast.html.
18 See Angelique Chrisafis, "Racist War of the Loyalist Street Gangs", *Guardian*, 10 January 2004, accessed 8 July 2014, www.theguardian.com/uk/2004/jan/10/northernireland.race.
19 See Chris Kilpatrick, "Two Racist Attacks Every Day in Northern Ireland's Race-Hate Crime Surge", *Belfast Telegraph*, 21 April 2014, accessed 8 July 2014, www.belfasttelegraph.co.uk/news/northern-ireland/tworacist-attacks-every-day-in-northern-irelands-racehate-crime-surge-30202329.html.
20 Liam Clarke, Rebecca Black and Claire Cromie, "Muslim Rant Preacher: First Minister Peter Robinson Moves to Defuse Islam Row", *Belfast Telegraph*, 29 May 2014, accessed 8 July 2014, www.belfasttelegraph.co.uk/news/northern-ireland/muslim-rant-preacher-first-minister-peter-robinson-moves-to-defuse-islam-row-30312816.html.
21 John Mulgrew, "Anna Lo 'to Quit Politics' due to Ongoing Racist Abuse by Loyalists", *Belfast Telegraph*, 29 May 2014, accessed 8 July 2014, www.belfasttelegraph.co.uk/news/northern-ireland/anna-lo-to-quit-politics-due-to-ongoing-racist-abuse-by-loyalists-30314364.html.
22 The Northern Ireland Peace Agreement.
23 Independent Commission on Policing in Northern Ireland, *A New Beginning*, 6.
24 Ibid.
25 Ibid., 95.
26 See http://cain.ulst.ac.uk/othelem/organ/caj/caj_20110616_oponi.pdf, accessed 24 January 2016.
27 Ms. Judith Gillespie CBE OBE, Interview with former Deputy Chief Commissioner, PSNI, 31 July 2014.
28 Ibid.
29 David Mckittrick, "Catholics Make up 7% of RUC", *Independent*, 28 January 1993, accessed 8 July 2014, www.independent.co.uk/news/uk/catholics-make-up-7-of-ruc-1481268.html.
30 Police Service of Northern Ireland, "Workforce Composition Figures", 16 February 2015, accessed 8 July 2014, www.psni.police.uk/index/updates/updates_statistics/updates_workforce_composition_figures.htm.

31 Northern Ireland Policing Board, "Public Perceptions of the Police, PCSPs and the Northern Ireland Policing Board Survey", www.nipolicingboard.org.uk/sites/nipb/files/media-files/omnibus-survey-january-2014.pdf
32 Police (Northern Ireland) Act 2000, S. 38(1), accessed 8 June 2014, www.legislation.gov.uk/ukpga/2000/32/section/38.
33 Ms. Judith Gillespie CBE OBE, Interview with former Deputy Chief Commissioner, PSNI, 31 July 2014.
34 Northern Ireland Policing Board and The Police Service of Northern Ireland, *Police Service of Northern Ireland Code of Ethics 2008* (Belfast, 2008), 2, accessed 8 June 2014, www.nipolicingboard.org.uk/final_code_of_ethics-2.pdf.
35 Professor Brice Dickson, Interview with former Chairperson of the Northern Ireland Human Rights Commission, 24 February 2014.
36 *A Code of Practice for the Principles and Standards of Professional Behaviour for the Policing Profession of England and Wales*, accessed 17 June 2015, www.college.police.uk/What-wedo/Ethics/Documents/Code_of_Ethics.pdf.
37 Northern Ireland Policing Board and The Police Service of Northern Ireland, *Police Service of Northern Ireland Code of Ethics 2008*, 8.
38 Ms. Judith Gillespie CBE OBE, Interview with former Deputy Chief Commissioner, PSNI, 31 July 2014.
39 Ms. Catriona Ruane MLA, Interview with Sinn Féin Chief Whip at the Northern Ireland Assembly, 15 April 2014.
40 The divided attitudes towards the criminal justice system in Northern Ireland are also acknowledged in the Criminal Justice Review Group Report which, in its Introduction, refers to these differences:

> Some thought that it had served Northern Ireland well, in the face of the considerable challenges posed by the security.... Others, however, felt differently and expressed strong views about what they believed to be bias against particular parts of the community and failure adequately to safeguard human rights.
>
> Criminal Justice Review Group, *Review of the Criminal Justice System in Northern Ireland*, March 2000, 6–7, accessed 19 August 2014, http://cain.ulst.ac.uk/issues/law/cjr/chap1.pdf

41 Ibid., 25.
42 Justice (Northern Ireland) Act, 2004, Section 8.
43 See John F. Larkin, *Human Rights Guidance for the Northern Ireland Prison Service: Prison Order and Discipline*, Guidance by the Attorney General for Northern Ireland pursuant to Section 8 of the Justice (Northern Ireland) Act 2004, 10 April 2014, accessed 20 October 2014, www.attorneygeneralni.gov.uk/human_rights_guidance_for_the_northern_ireland_prison_service_on_prison_order_and_discipline.pdf.119kb.
44 See John F. Larkin, *Human Rights Guidance for Forensic Science Northern Ireland*, Guidance by the Attorney General for Northern Ireland pursuant to Section 8 of the Justice (Northern Ireland) Act 2004, 8 May 2013, accessed 20 October 2014, www.dojni.gov.uk/index/fsni/fsni-publications/attorney-general-guidance-for-fsni.pdf.
45 See John F. Larkin, *Human Rights Guidance for the Public Prosecution Service*, Guidance by the Attorney General for Northern Ireland pursuant to Section 8 of the Justice (Northern Ireland) Act 2004, 21 March 2014, accessed 20 October 2014, www.attorneygeneralni.gov.uk/human_rights_guidance_for_the_public_prosecution_service__pdf_133kb_.
46 See John F. Larkin, *Human Rights Guidance for the State Pathologist's Department*, Guidance by the Attorney General for Northern Ireland pursuant to Section 8 of the Justice (Northern Ireland) Act 2004, 8 May 2013, accessed 21 October 2014, www.attorneygeneralni.gov.uk/spd_pdf_website.pdf.

47 See Chapter 2.
48 See sections 1–9 of the Justice and Security (Northern Ireland) Act 2007.
49 See, for example, Case of *Gillan and Quiton* v. *United Kingdom* (European Court of Human Rights, 12 January 2010), Application no. 4158/05 where the European Court of Human Rights held that section 44 of the Terrorism Act 2000 was incompatible with the European Convention. See further *A and Others* v. *Secretary of State for the Home Department* (United Kingdom House of Lords 2004) UKHL 56, wherein the House of Lords declared the incompatibilty of section 23 of the Anti-terrorism, Crime and Security Act 2001 with the European Convention on Human Rights. The case concerned the indefinite detention without trial of foreign detainees. In another case In Re MB[2006] EWHC 1000 (Admin) (12 April 2006), Section 3 of the Prevention of Terrorism Act 2005 was held to be incompatible with the Human Rights Act 1998. See Mr Justice Sullivan, Re MB (England and Wales High Court (Administrative Court) 2006), EWHC 1000 (Admin).
50 Metropolitan Police, *Surveys in the MPS: Londoners' Views Count*, November 2013, www.met.police.uk/about/performance/documents/LVC_Quarter_2_13_14.pdf. acc.
51 The Scottish Government, *Scottish Crime and Justice Survey 2012–13*, 3 July 2014, www.scotland.gov.uk/Publications/2014/03/9823/10.
52 In an interview with former Deputy Chief Commissioner of the PSNI Judith Gillespie CBE OBE, Ms Gillespie recounts a police meeting in a staunchly republican area which was held with the agreement of the local population notwithstanding a threat of a bomb scare (which the police were sure was not genuine).
53 Ms. Judith Gillespie CBE OBE, Interview with former Deputy Chief Commissioner, PSNI, 31 July 2014.
54 "Gerry Adams Arrest: Police Get Another Two Days to Question Sinn Féin President over Jean McConville's Murder", *Belfast Telegraph*, 3 May 2014, accessed 20 July 2014, www.belfasttelegraph.co.uk/news/northern-ireland/gerry-adams-arrest-police-get-another-two-days-toquestion-sinn-Féin-president-over-jean-mcconvilles-murder-30239798.html.
55 Ms. Judith Gillespie CBE OBE, Interview with former Deputy Chief Commissioner, PSNI, 31 July 2014.
56 Professor Brice Dickson, Interview with former Chairperson of the Northern Ireland Human Rights Commission, 24 February 2014.
57 "Rights Head Admits Dispute 'Flaws'", *BBC*, 23 July 2003, accessed 22 October 2014, http://news.bbc.co.uk/2/hi/uk_news/northern_ireland/3088615.stm.
58 In re E (a child) (AP) (Appellant) (Northern Ireland) (House of Lords, 12 November 2008), UKHL 66.
59 "Rights Head Admits Dispute 'Flaws'".
60 Northern Ireland Human Rights Commission, "Advice for You", accessed 24 October 2014, www.nihrc.org/advice-for-you.
61 "Human Rights Members Resign", *BBC*, 9 September 2002, accessed 22 October 2014, http://news.bbc.co.uk/2/hi/uk_news/northern_ireland/2247268.stm.
62 Northern Ireland Human Rights Commission, *Annual Report 2004*, accessed 17 July 2014, www.nihrc.org/documents/nihrc-general/corporate-reports-plans/annual-report-financial-accounts-2004lores.pdf, 9.
63 Northern Ireland Human Rights Commission, *Annual Report 2001*, December 2001, accessed 16 July 2014, www.nihrc.org/documents/nihrc-general/corporate-reports-plans/annual-report-financial-accounts-2000-2001lores.pdf, 19.
64 Ibid., 15.
65 Professor Brice Dickson, Interview with former Chairperson of the Northern Ireland Human Rights Commission, 24 February 2014.

66 Information on the Commission's investigative and research work is available in the Annual Reports of the Human Rights Commission.
67 Northern Ireland Human Rights Commission, *Annual Report and Accounts 2010–2011*, 7, accessed 22 October 2014, www.gov.uk/government/uploads/system/uploads/attachment_data/file/247208/1455.pdf.
68 Northern Ireland Human Rights Commission, *NIHRC Review*, no. 2 (Summer 2006), 2.
69 Roisin Devlin and Sorcha McKenna, *No Home from Home: Homelessness for People with No or Limited Access to Public Funds* (Belfast: Northern Ireland Human Rights Commission, September 2009).
70 Nazia Latif and Agnieszka Martynowicz, *Our Hidden Borders: The UK Border Agency's Powers of Detention* (Belfast: Northern Ireland Human Rights Commission, April 2009).
71 Northern Ireland Human Rights Commission, *Submission to the United Nations' Committee on the Rights of the Child: Shadow Report on the Third and Fourth Periodic Reports of the United Kingdom of Great Britain and Northern Ireland* (Belfast, May 2008), accessed 24 October 2014, www.qub.ac.uk/research-centres/advancing-childrens-rights/Filestore/Filetoupload,403611,en.pdf.
72 Ursula Kilkelly, *In Our Care: Promoting the Rights of Children in Custody* (Belfast: Northern Ireland Human Rights Commission, March 2002).
73 Northern Ireland Human Rights Commission, "Priorities and Plans", accessed 24 October 2014, www.nihrc.org/about-us/what-we-do/priorities-plans.
74 Northern Ireland Human Rights Commission, *The 2012 Annual Statement: Human Rights in Northern Ireland* (Belfast, 2012), accessed 24 October 2014, www.nihrc.org/uploads/publications/HRC_Annual_Statement_2012.pdf.
75 Northern Ireland Human Rights Commission, *Annual Report and Accounts 2011–2012*, 7, accessed 24 October 2014, www.gov.uk/government/uploads/system/uploads/attachment_data/file/246547/0490.pdf.
76 Northern Ireland Human Rights Commission, *The First Annual Report of the Northern Ireland Human Rights Commission, 1999–2000* (Belfast, 2000), 7, accessed 16 July 2014, www.nihrc.org/documents/nihrc-general/corporate-reports-plans/annual-report-financial-accounts-1999-2000lores.pdf.
77 Ibid.
78 Northern Ireland Human Rights Commission, *Annual Report 2004*, 7.
79 Professor Brice Dickson, Interview with former Chairperson of the Northern Ireland Human Rights Commission, 24 February 2014. The unionist politicians' scepticism in this respect will be analysed further in the subsequent section.
80 House of Lords House of Commons, Joint Committee on Human Rights, *Work of the Northern Ireland Human Rights Commission*, Session 2002–2003 (London: The Stationery Office, 15 July 2003), accessed 26 October 2014, www.publications.parliament.uk/pa/jt200203/jtselect/jtrights/132/132.pdf.
81 The Northern Ireland Peace Agreement.
82 Professor Chris Sidoti, Interview with the Chairperson of the Bill of Rights Forum, 16 April 2014.
83 Ibid.
84 Mr Dermot Nesbitt, Interview with former UUP MLA and spokesperson on human rights, 15 April 2014.
85 Mr Jonathan Bell MLA, Interview with Junior Minister in the Office of the First Minister and Deputy First Minister, 17 April 2014.
86 Ms. Catriona Ruane MLA, Interview with Sinn Féin Chief Whip at the Northern Ireland Assembly, 15 April 2014.
87 Professor Chris Sidoti, Interview with the Chairperson of the Bill of Rights Forum, 16 April 2014.

88 A full explanation of the various stages of the Bill of Rights process can be found at Northern Ireland Human Rights Commission, *A Bill of Rights for Northern Ireland: Advice to the Secretary of State for Northern Ireland* (Belfast: Northern Ireland Human Rights Commission, 10 December 2008), 10–13, accessed 22 July 2014, www.nihrc.org/documents/bill%20of%20rights/bill-of-rights-for-northern-ireland-advice-to-secretary-state2008.pdf.

89 Professor Brice Dickson, Interview with former Chairperson of the Northern Ireland Human Rights Commission, 24 February 2014.

90 Ibid.

91 Ulster Unionist Party, *Ulster Unionist Party Position on a Bill of Rights*, accessed 21 July 2014, http://uup.org/assets/images/featured/Ulster%20Unionist%20Party%20Position%20on%20a%20Bill%20of%20Rights.pdf.

92 Ms. Emma Little, Interview with the Special Advisor to the First Minister, 17 April 2014.

93 Bill of Rights Forum, *Final Report: Recommendations to the Northern Ireland Human Rights Commission on a Bill of Rights for Northern Ireland* (Belfast, 31 March 2008), 38, accessed 23 July 2014, http://cain.ulst.ac.uk/issues/law/bor/borf310308_report.pdf.

94 Ulster Unionist Party, *Ulster Unionist Party Position on a Bill of Rights.*

95 Mr Jonathan Bell MLA, Interview with Junior Minister in the Office of the First Minister and Deputy First Minister, 17 April 2014.

96 Ibid.

97 Professor Chris Sidoti, Interview with the Chairperson of the Bill of Rights Forum, 16 April 2014.

98 Ms. Catriona Ruane MLA, Interview with Sinn Féin Chief Whip at the Northern Ireland Assembly, 15 April 2014.

99 Ibid.

100 One of the human rights desiderata in the Peace Agreement is that the Joint Committee of the Northern Ireland Human Rights Commission and the Irish Human Rights Commission (now the Irish Human Rights and Equality Commission) consider the possibility of adopting a human rights charter that would protect the rights of all persons living on the island of Ireland as a whole. The Agreement states:

> It is envisaged that there would be a joint committee of representatives of the two Human Rights Commissions, North and South, as a forum for consideration of human rights issues in the island of Ireland. The joint committee will consider, among other matters, the possibility of establishing a charter, open to signature by all democratic political parties, reflecting and endorsing agreed measures for the protection of the fundamental rights of everyone living in the island of Ireland.

101 Bill of Rights Forum, *Final Report*, 11.

102 Ms. Emma Little, Interview with the Special Advisor to the First Minister, 17 April 2014.

103 Ulster Unionist Party, *Ulster Unionist Party Position on a Bill of Rights.*

104 Bill of Rights Forum, *Final Report*, 27.

105 Ibid.

106 Mr Jonathan Bell MLA, Interview with Junior Minister in the Office of the First Minister and Deputy First Minister, 17 April 2014.

107 Northern Ireland Office, *A Bill of Rights for Northern Ireland: Next Steps*, Consultation Paper (30 November 2009), 7, accessed 23 July 2014, http://cain.ulst.ac.uk/issues/law/bor/nio301109bor.pdf.

108 The Rt Hon. Paul Murphy MP, Interview with the former Secretary of State for Northern Ireland, 25 February 2014.

109 Professor Chris Sidoti, Interview with the Chairperson of the Bill of Rights Forum, 16 April 2014.
110 Ms. Catriona Ruane MLA, Interview with Sinn Féin Chief Whip at the Northern Ireland Assembly, 15 April 2014.
111 The Rt Hon. Paul Murphy MP, Interview with the former Secretary of State for Northern Ireland, 25 February 2014.
112 Professor Chris Sidoti, Interview with the Chairperson of the Bill of Rights Forum, 16 April 2014.
113 The Paris Principles were adopted by the UN General Assembly: see United Nations General Assembly, *National Institutions for the Promotion and Protection of Human Rights*, A/RES/48/134, 1993, accessed 19 July 2014, www.un.org/documents/ga/res/48/a48r134.htm. The status of the Commission as fully compliant with the Paris Principles can be viewed here: International Coordinating Committee of National Institutions for the Promotion and Protection of Human Rights (ICC), "Chart of the Status of National Institutions Accredited by the International Coordinating Committee of National Institutions for the Promotion and Protection of Human Rights", 28 January 2014, accessed 19 July 2014, www.ohchr.org/Documents/Countries/NHRI/Chart_Status_NIs.pdf.
114 See, for example, the extended critique provided to the UK Parliament's Joint Committee on Human Rights by the former Commissioners Christine Bell and Inez McCormack: Joint Committee on Human Rights, "Memorandum from Professor Christine Bell and Dr Inez McCormack, Former Commissioners of the NIHRC", 15 July 2003, accessed 19 July 2014, www.publications.parliament.uk/pa/jt200203/jtselect/jtrights/132/132we05.htm.
115 The Rt Hon. Paul Murphy MP, Interview with the former Secretary of State for Northern Ireland, 25 February 2014.
116 This can be seen in the opinion polls conducted by the Commission during the process.
117 Professor Chris Sidoti, Interview with the Chairperson of the Bill of Rights Forum, 16 April 2014.
118 For example, on one occasion the Commission could not agree whether to issue a statement concerning a punishment beating since Commission members had diverging views on whether this was a human rights issue. Professor Brice Dickson, Interview with former Chairperson of the Northern Ireland Human Rights Commission, 24 February 2014.
119 Northern Ireland Executive, *Proposed Agreement: An Agreement among the Parties of the Northern Ireland Executive on Parades, Select Commemorations, and Related Protests; Flags and Emblems; and Contending with the Past*, 31 December 2013, accessed 8 June 2014, www.northernireland.gov.uk/haass.pdf.
120 Professor Brice Dickson, Interview with former Chairperson of the Northern Ireland Human Rights Commission, 24 February 2014.
121 Ms. Emma Little, Interview with the Special Advisor to the First Minister, 17 April 2014.
122 Ms. Catriona Ruane MLA, Interview with Sinn Féin Chief Whip at the Northern Ireland Assembly, 15 April 2014.
123 See United Nations General Assembly, *Declaration on the Right and Responsibility of Individuals, Groups and Organs of Society to Promote and Protect Universally Recognized Human Rights and Fundamental Freedoms, United Nations General Assembly Resolution*, 53/144, 9 December 1998, accessed 20 July 2014, www.ohchr.org/EN/ProfessionalInterest/Pages/RightAndResponsibility.aspx, in respect of situations of conflict. See also Andrew Clapham, "Human Rights Obligations of Non-State Actors in Conflict Situations", *International Review of the Red Cross* 88, no. 863 (September 2006), accessed 20 July 2014, www.icrc.org/eng/assets/files/other/irrc_863_clapham.pdf.

124 Case of *McKerr* v. *United Kingdom* (European Court of Human Rights, 4 May 2001), Application 28883/95.

125 Case of *Finucane* v. *United Kingdom* (European Court of Human Rights, 1 July 2003), Application no. 53743/09.

126 Information provided to the Committee of Ministers of the Council of Europe quoted in HMIC, *Inspection of the Police Service of Northern Ireland Historical Enquiries Team*, 2013, accessed 14 October 2014, www.justiceinspectorates.gov.uk/hmic/media/inspection-of-the-police-service-of-northern-ireland-historical-enquiries-team-20130703.pdf.

127 Kieran McEvoy and Louise Mallinder, *Truth, Amnesty and Prosecutions: Models for Dealing with the Past*, 3 December 2013, 3, accessed 14 October 2014, www.patfinucanecentre.org/truth/McEvoy%20&%20Mallinder%20Models%20on%20Truth%20Amnesty%20 &%20Prosecution%203%20Dec%202013.pdf.

128 HMIC, *Inspection of the Police Service of Northern Ireland Historical Enquiries Team*, 60.

129 Claire Cromie, "PSNI Cuts 300 Jobs and Axes Historical Enquiries Team", *Belfast Telegraph*, 30 September 2014, accessed 14 October 2014, www.belfasttelegraph.co.uk/news/northern-ireland/psni-cuts-300-jobsand-axes-historical-enquiries-team-30626460.html.

130 www.gov.uk/government/uploads/system/uploads/attachment_data/file/390672/Stormont_House_Agreeme nt.pdf, accessed 18 January 2015.

131 See, for example, the legal bid against the UK government being announced in 2014 by 32 affected families: "Legal Bid over Murders 'Collusion'", *Belfast Telegraph*, 11 April 2014, accessed 14 October 2014, www.belfasttelegraph.co.uk/news/local-national/northern-ireland/legal-bid-over-murders-collusion-30177197.html; or the Loughlinisland families anger at the findings of the Police Ombudsman in 2011: Adrian Rutherford, "Loughinisland Families 'Angry and Disgusted' at Report Findings", *Belfast Telegraph*, 25 June 2011, accessed 14 October 2014, www.belfasttelegraph.co.uk/news/northern-ireland/loughinisland-families-angry-and-disgusted-at-report-findings-28630458.html.

132 The Peace Agreement provided that any person convicted of paramilitary crimes was eligible for early release. This provision did not include persons suspected of such crimes, nor did it include individuals who had been charged or convicted but who had escaped from custody (these were referred to as "on the runs"). Following the signing of the Peace Agreement, the matter of how to deal with the "on the runs" remained an open question. Negotiations continued after the signing of the agreement between Sinn Féin and the UK government on how to deal with the "on the runs". During the committal proceedings of John Downey, who was accused of bombings that killed four British soldiers, it emerged that the accused had received a letter from the Northern Ireland Office assuring him he was not wanted by the PSNI. The presiding judge decided that such a letter meant that the trial could not proceed. This case laid bare the fact that such letters had been issued to a number of "on the runs".

133 See, for instance, the comments by Shelly Gilfillan, niece of IRA murder victim Lexie Cummings: "I am very disappointed that the victims have not been given something to give a little hope to perhaps giving closure to some of these murders." "On the Runs: Reaction to Secret Fugitive Letters Report", *BBC News*, 17 July 2014, accessed 14 October 2014, www.bbc.com/news/uk-northern-ireland-28340830.

134 "Victims Condemn Northern Ireland Troubles Prosecutions Call", *BBC News*, 20 November 2013, accessed 15 October 2014, www.bbc.com/news/uk-northern-ireland-25021286.

135 On the matter of models for truth recovery, amnesties and prosecution of historical abuses, see McEvoy and Mallinder, *Truth, Amnesty and Prosecutions*.

136 Northern Ireland Executive, *Proposed Agreement: An Agreement among the Parties of the Northern Ireland Executive on Parades, Select Commemorations, and Related Protests; Flags and Emblems; and Contending with the Past.*
137 Michael Hamilton, Neil Jarman and Dominic Bryan, *Parades, Protests and Policing: A Human Rights Framework* (Belfast: Northern Ireland Human Rights Commission, March 2001), v.
138 Ibid.
139 Ms. Catriona Ruane MLA, Interview with Sinn Féin Chief Whip at the Northern Ireland Assembly, 15 April 2014.
140 Stephen Sackur, "Flag Removal 'Attack on Identity' – Democratic Unionist MP, Ian Paisley Jr", Interview, *HARDTalk* (*BBC World News*, 10 April 2013), accessed 14 July 2014, www.bbc.co.uk/programmes/p017jc7g.
141 FT View, "Facing the Past in Northern Ireland", *Financial Times*, 2 May 2014, 6.
142 Ms. Judith Gillespie CBE OBE, Interview with former Deputy Chief Commissioner, PSNI, 31 July 2014.
143 Patricia Lundy and Mark McGovern, "A Truth Commission for Northern Ireland?", *Research Update* 46 (October 2006), accessed 14 October 2014, www.ark.ac.uk/publications/updates/update46.pdf.
144 Kieran McEvoy, *Dealing with the Past? An Overview of Legal and Political Approaches Relating to the Conflict in and about Northern Ireland* (Healing Through Remembering, 2013), accessed 15 October 2014, www.healingthroughremembering.org/images/uploads/HTR_Dealing_with_the_Past__Legal_and_Political_Approaches_Report.pdf.
145 In terms of the right to life and the European Convention on Human Rights Article 2 implications.
146 In terms of building confidence between the communities, providing closure for victims and promoting reconciliation within Northern Ireland.
147 Consultative Group on the Past, *Report of the Consultative Group on the Past*, 23 January 2009, accessed 14 October 2014, http://cain.ulst.ac.uk/victims/docs/consultative_group/cgp_230109_report.pdf.
148 Ibid., 50.
149 Ibid.
150 Mary Robinson, *Equality and Human Rights: Their Role in Peace Building*, Speech at the Stormont Hotel, December 1998, quoted in Committee on the Administration of Justice, *CAJ's Submission to the UK Bill of Rights.*
151 Professor Brice Dickson, Interview with former Chairperson of the Northern Ireland Human Rights Commission, 24 February 2014.
152 This best practice is epitomised in what are termed the "Paris Principles on National Human Rights Institutions": see United Nations General Assembly, "National Institutions for the Promotion and Protection of Human Rights".
153 The Rt Hon. Paul Murphy MP, Interview with the former Secretary of State for Northern Ireland, 25 February 2014.
154 The St Andrew's Agreement is an agreement signed by the governments of the United Kingdom and Ireland as well as the Northern Irish political parties. Inter alia the agreement Sinn Féin agreed to support the PSNI and the Northern Irish court system while the DUP agreed to enter into power sharing with Sinn Féin. The St Andrew's Agreement led to the restoration of devolved government in Northern Ireland.

8 Conclusion

Introduction

This study sought to answer the question of the extent to which, and ways in which, human rights influenced the Northern Ireland conflict. The study also examined the related question as to how the conflict in Northern Ireland influenced the understanding of human rights within Northern Ireland with specific reference to the two main political traditions (i.e. unionism and nationalism). These two related questions were examined from the creation of the Northern Ireland state in 1921 until 2014. The timeframe is particularly salient given that human rights issues are usually examined in relation to the Northern Irish conflict in the context of the civil rights period. This study examined the effects of human rights on the conflict, as well as the impact of the conflict on human rights, throughout the pre-violent conflict phase, the violent conflict phase and the post-violent conflict phase. This broader discussion of the relationship between human rights and conflict in Northern Ireland is part of the originality of this study.

Insofar as the term "human rights" is concerned the definition of human rights was taken to be the one found in the Universal Declaration of Human Rights (as well as related international human rights law treaties and the European Convention on Human Rights). The study adopted a chronological approach in answering the questions listed above. This concluding chapter summarises the main findings of the study chronologically and then proceeds to answer the key questions posed by the study based on these findings.

Human rights and their evolution on the international plane

Northern Ireland was born in the early 1920s when Woodrow Wilson's call for the self-determination of peoples was at the cutting edge of international politics. The call for self-determination, as highlighted in Chapter 2, had a significant influence on the redrawing of European borders in the aftermath of World War I. The period following the Great War saw two main developments in the sphere of the fledgling movement to bring the protection of rights within the international ambit: both related to the assertion of group rights.

The rise of self-determination was the first such development, intended to provide ethnic and national groups the right to determine their own political future. This was particularly relevant with the dissolution of the multi-ethnic Ottoman and Austro-Hungarian Empires. The second development concerned the rise of minority rights, with the international community seeking to provide protection to ethnic minorities in states where such minorities existed. The two developments were interdependent given that the right of self-determination, as exercised within the European continent, created a host of new states with ethnic minorities within them. Therefore, the right of self-determination for the majority community had to be tempered with minority protection. The minorities regime described in Chapter 2 was an example of this approach to managing the challenges brought about by self-determination in Europe.

In terms of the development of human rights within the international community it is evident that World War II was a defining moment and marks the emergence of the protection of individual, as opposed to group rights, in international law. Whereas the inter-war period saw the emergence of self-determination and minority rights, the post-war period witnessed the emergence of the protection of individual rights. This development occurred at a number of levels: internationally, the adoption of the UDHR in 1948 was the first and fundamental step in the rise of human rights. This step was followed by other international and regional developments. With the process of decolonisation, inspired by the right to self-determination, underway from the 1950s onwards, newly independent states often adopted the standards of the UDHR in their constitutions. Meanwhile, in Europe, the Council of Europe adopted the ECHR which was also inspired, as its Preamble declares, by the UDHR.

The rise of the human rights movement, beyond the legal and political domains, had to await the 1960s which witnessed a period when, mainly across the USA and Europe, the generation born during or immediately after World War II utilised the concept of human rights and non-discrimination as a rallying-call and mobilising factor to challenge governmental (and in some cases religious) authority. The US civil rights movement (which started in the second half of the 1950s but reached its climax in the 1960s) was an early example of this. In 1961 Amnesty International was established in London as a prototype of the non-governmental human rights organisations that spread thick and (quite) fast in the following years. The 1968 student-led protests in France, Italy, Germany and elsewhere are further examples of this process, with their emphasis on economic and social rights. The Prague Spring of 1968 witnessed the attempt to discard authoritarianism in favour of civil and political liberties. The Northern Ireland civil rights movement, as seen in Chapter 4, also falls within this period. Moreover, it was also inspired by the human rights movement. These various movements were not pursuing an identical agenda. In some ways, they were unconnected or even pursuing opposing agendas. The Parisian protests of 1968 challenged western European models of democracy while the Prague Spring challenged the eastern European (predominantly Soviet) ideas of political leadership. The UK-based Anti-Apartheid Movement, founded in 1959, intensified its action following the 1961 Sharpeville Massacre. The US civil rights movement struggled to end discrimination against the black population whereas the Northern Ireland CRM sought to end discrimination against nationalists. On the other hand, Amnesty International was established in London as an organisation seeking to ensure freedom for political prisoners around the world. What they had in common was an inspiration derived, to a greater or lesser degree, from the language of human rights and freedoms. Thus, human rights became both an idea that inspired political action, as well as a tool used to justify political action.

The power of the idea of human rights as a mobilising force was also evident in the 1980s with the campaigns to topple dictatorships in Latin America, eastern Europe and South Africa. In this period, democracy and human rights were increasingly seen as twin concepts that were interdependent and mutually reinforcing. Charter 77 in Czechoslovakia, Solidarność in Poland, the African National Congress in South Africa and the Catholic Church's La Vicaria de Solidaridad[1] in Chile, for example, were all inspired, at least partially, by human rights principles and adopted human rights discourse. By the end of the decade most of the dictatorships in Europe, Latin America and South Africa had either fallen or were on the way to fall. The inspirational idea of human rights and its mobilising power played some part in these developments.

It is also worth pointing out that from the 1960s onwards there was a continuing process of codification of human rights norms in international law through successive human rights treaties both at the global and regional level.[2] This further enhanced the role of human rights in international, regional and local political spheres. These legislative developments were also accompanied by an increase in the number of human rights structures at the international, regional and domestic levels with judicial, quasi-judicial, advisory or awareness-raising mandates. Examples of these include the establishment of the UN Office of the High Commissioner for Human Rights in the wake of the 1993 Vienna World Conference on Human Rights, the International Criminal Court adopted in 1998, the African Court of Human and People's Rights which also came into being in 1998, as well as various national human rights institutions which were established throughout the 1990s and thereafter.[3]

These developments meant that the post-Cold War period witnessed the coming of age of human rights within the international community. In this period, human rights became a badge of international and domestic respectability.[4] Consequently, international organisations, regional organisations, individual states and political parties within states, had to engage with, and often adopt, human rights discourse and frameworks. The rise of human rights in the international, regional and domestic spheres and the multiplication of laws, declarations, structures and institutions devoted to human rights also had another consequence. It has been argued that the conception of human rights found in the UDHR was never intended to "produce completely uniform practices" but its architects "expected that its fertile principles could be brought to life in a legitimate variety of ways".[5] This tendency to interpret human rights in various ways has increased with the multiplication of human rights laws, structures and principles and was, in fact, sanctioned at the 1993 Vienna UN World Conference on Human Rights. The growth of human rights bodies and courts has also had the inevitable consequence of supplying numerous decisions and interpretations of specific rights. In other words, the very success of the idea of human rights has encouraged "many different kinds of music to be played on the document's [UDHR] thirty strings".[6]

The early years in Northern Ireland

Chapter 3 established that the history of the Northern Irish state illustrates how human rights were inextricably linked with the question of the border and the right to self-determination from the creation of the state. The fact that the question of self-determination featured prominently in the early years of the formation of the Northern Irish state resulted from the partition of Northern Ireland but also coincided with the post-World War I international concern with self-determination. Thus, Northern Ireland's concern with self-determination was shaped by the broader international currents and debates.

Effectively, what happened in the early years of the formation of the state was that the two main communities developed the perception that their rights could only be safeguarded if their constitutional status was tied to the UK or the Irish Free State respectively. For unionists, the civil and religious rights they associated with the UK could only be guaranteed by remaining part of the UK. They considered that the Irish Free State would deny their civil and religious rights, a perception that would be fuelled later with De Valera's strong conservative, Catholic policies. Conversely, nationalists felt they could only be safeguarded from discrimination by becoming part of the Irish Free State. The perception was strengthened by the discrimination suffered by Catholics in the years following the formation of the Northern Irish state with respect to issues such as employment, housing and the electoral system.

The first 20 years of the Northern Irish state witnessed two parallel developments: (1) the strengthening of nationalist perceptions that their rights could not be guaranteed while remaining part of the UK, since unionists in Northern Ireland were actively undermining their rights by practising discrimination; and (2) the hardening of unionist attitudes in believing that nationalists were actively undermining the state through various means including by claiming discrimination. These two developments led to nationalists believing that unionism was inimical to their human rights while unionists believed that the concept of rights and discrimination were being instrumentalised by nationalists in their quest to delegitimise the Northern Irish state. In this period the respective attitudes to human rights formed within the two communities. Nationalists, perceiving a tide of discrimination against them, began to develop an idea of rights as antidote to discrimination. Conversely, unionists began to view the language of rights and discrimination as an attack on the legitimacy of the state. Moreover, discrimination (whether actual or perceived) established itself as a source of grievance for the nationalist community. This sense of grievance against abuse and discrimination would expedite the move from a non-violent to a violent conflict.

Ironically, the period discussed in Chapter 3 also covers the timeframe within which socioeconomic rights in Northern Ireland improved as a result of the policies advanced by the UK administration after 1945, which included the adoption of the welfare state. It is worth noting that the post-war phase also witnessed the acceptance of socioeconomic rights as part and parcel of the conception of human rights. This is demonstrated by the adoption of the UDHR, which included a strong socioeconomic rights component. In particular, the improvement in educational standards eventually led to an improvement in the human rights awareness and in the mobilising power of the minority community. This was clearly evidenced with the role of the educated, nationalist, middle class within the civil rights movement. This rise in human rights awareness on the part of the minority community was also aided by the rise of human rights globally with the adoption of the UDHR and related international human rights instruments. These factors influenced the rise of the civil rights movement in Northern Ireland which was a pivotal period for both the developments of human rights in Northern Ireland and the eventual descent into a spiral of violent conflict.

The civil rights era

As shown in Chapter 4, the rise of the civil rights movement was due to a multiplicity of factors, including the increasing educational opportunities and aspirations within the minority community, as well as the rise of human rights at the international level. However, both of these factors alone, without a strong sense of discrimination within the nationalist community, would not have given rise to the movement. Although the movement included, at least in its earlier phases, some liberal unionists, there is no doubt that the driving force behind the movement was found within the minority community. The linkages between the movement and the developments described in Chapter 3 are therefore clear.

The movement is a pivotal point for Northern Ireland, both from a conflict point of view as well as from a human rights perspective. From a human rights perspective, the movement brought human rights to centre stage in Northern Ireland. Rights language became, for the first time, deeply engrained in the media and in public discourse more generally. In this period, the activities of the civil rights movement also helped to bring Northern Ireland to a wider international attention for the first time. The movement, however, focused primarily on a limited number of human rights concerns, which were of primary interest to the nationalist community, and it failed to articulate a broader, and more comprehensive, human rights agenda.

Political parties had to respond to the movement and they did so by developing four broad responses: the approach adopted by O'Neill-style unionists which viewed human rights as a way of assimilating nationalists; the approach adopted by hard-line unionists such as William Craig, which viewed human rights as a threat to continuing the constitutional link with the UK; the approach of the nationalist leadership, which viewed human rights as a relief from discrimination; and the attitude of the republican leadership, which viewed human rights as a weapon in the struggle to unite Ireland. These different approaches to human rights were the result of different conceptions of human rights, with moderate unionists conceiving of human rights as an assimilative instrument granted by the state to citizens to encourage them to behave better. This conception relied to an extent on a conception of human rights as privileges granted by the state. For nationalists, human rights were an instrument through which their socioeconomic and political situation could be ameliorated. This latter conception of human rights was also linked to the idea of social justice. For republicans, human rights were conceived as claims through which the state could be belittled and destabilised. Thus, human rights are viewed as a revolutionary concept to conduct the political battle. Finally, the hard-line unionists viewed the revolutionary, destabilising conception of human rights as a tool used by Catholics to impinge on their historical acquisition of civil and religious liberties. Their conception of human rights was very much linked with the Protestant idea of civil and religious liberty of the Glorious Revolution, as opposed to what they viewed as Roman Catholic dogmatic obscurantism.

From the point of view of the conflict, the civil rights period resulted in a descent into violence as the marches and protests, which characterised the movement, met with violent responses from some unionist groups and, on some occasions, from the security forces. Hence, the civil rights movement, and human rights more generally, became linked to violence through the reactions which the movement engendered. Conversely, even violent movements continued to be shaped by the legacy of the civil rights movement, in their use of rights-based appeals and rights-based language, as was apparent later in the conflict within the context of the hunger strikes.

From internment to the hunger strikes

This link between human rights and violence was to become more apparent in the period following the civil rights movement, as the abuse of human rights in the form of internment became a key trigger for a deeper escalation of violence. In a sense, the introduction of internment was a final nail in the civil rights movement's coffin. Internment, as a human rights abuse, had numerous consequences: (1) it hardened even further nationalist perceptions of an unfair state which abused their most fundamental rights; (2) it widened significantly the breach between the security forces and the minority community; and (3) it fuelled violence by serving as a recruiting agent for the IRA.

The descent into ever more violent conflict that emerged from the civil rights period and the subsequent decision to introduce internment led to a further erosion of human rights. This was particularly apparent through the 1973 Emergency Provisions Act, which introduced limitations to a number of human rights-related issues, in particular, policing and judicial matters. The emergency legislation was viewed by unionists as necessary to guarantee their rights, while it was viewed by the minority community as a further repressive measure intended to limit their rights. This further underlined the widening discrepancy between the two communities, in the interpretation of what human rights are and how they should be guaranteed.

What emerges from this period is that there developed an increasing selectivity in applying and claiming human rights. At the same time, there was a continuing and growing invocation by everyone of the developing body of international and regional human rights norms. This selectivity is particularly evident when one considers the prisoner's protests, eventual hunger strikes and associated violence. The IRA claimed that the republican prisoners were prisoners of war according to international humanitarian law and yet the IRA itself breached the most fundamental rules of international humanitarian law by killing civilians. On the other hand, the UK government claimed that under human rights law the prisoners had no right to a special status while ignoring the fact that most of the convictions of such prisoners had been secured under emergency legislation which limited the rights of the accused. In this period, the UK government was very active in defining the conflict in terms of a fight against terrorism, downplaying the political context. As Prime Minister, Margaret Thatcher portrayed the conflict in Northern Ireland as a straight fight between the state and armed terrorists who were intent on attacking it.

Mrs Thatcher's biography demonstrates her concern with the IRA's success both within the nationalist community and internationally in "giving a romantic respectability to terrorism that belies its sordid realities".[7] Furthermore, the then Prime Minister stated that her policies vis-à-vis Northern Ireland were "always determined by whatever [she considered] at a particular time would bring greater security". This approach lent force to the propensity to deny rights to individuals who committed terrorist-related offences.

The hunger strikes were another pivotal episode in the history of Northern Ireland. They culminated with a number of terrible deaths which shook Northern Ireland, the UK and the Republic of Ireland. These deaths also brought the situation in Northern Ireland to significant attention worldwide. The hunger strikes and deaths constituted human rights abuses (being both inhuman and degrading treatment as well as a breach of the right to life) but they were effectively self-inflicted human rights abuses. Nevertheless, they occurred in a specific context for which the UK government (and previous Northern Irish governments) were, in large part, responsible. The context was one in which the minority community felt discriminated against over a long period of time and also felt their human rights abused by the government through special laws and measures. At the same time, as already noted, the UK government was also responsible for the introduction of the welfare state (especially the educational reforms) which was an important factor in prompting a more ambitious human rights agenda within the minority community in Northern Ireland.

The human rights situation in Northern Ireland, especially in terms of the right to life, was affected very adversely by the hunger strikes. In the aftermath, violence deepened and widened and Northern Ireland went through one of its worst convulsions. Nevertheless, the political avenue, opened by the election of Bobby Sands as a Sinn Féin MP, proved the start of a political engagement which would eventually lead to the peace process. Once again, a series of human rights abuses proved to be a game-changer in the political life of Northern Ireland. As argued in Chapter 6, the hunger strikes also helped to recast the conflict within the mainland UK and also internationally. Within the mainland UK, as well as internationally, the deaths of the hunger strikers increased sympathy for the republican cause. The conflict was recast, at least in some minds, as a struggle about ideals for which individuals were willing to give up their life. Using the "ultimate sacrifice" as a tool to advertise a cause and to obtain rights also evokes historical association with other struggles. For instance, it recalls the struggle for women's suffrage with the hunger strikes adopted by the suffragettes and Emily Davison's suicide by throwing herself in the way of the King's horse at the Epsom Derby.

While the political path to a negotiated peace took a very long time to come to fruition, the situation in Northern Ireland vis-à-vis human rights did not stall completely. Prior to its suspension, the Northern Irish government had already dealt with the discriminatory nature of the electoral system. The UK government, under direct rule, introduced various measures intended to deal with discrimination in employment. However, policing and the criminal justice system remained intractable issues, with continuing suspension of human rights laws being justified according to the UK government by the continuation of the violent conflict. This further strengthened the perception amongst nationalists that the UK government was willing to ignore human rights when it suited their purposes. At the same time, political reforms signalled that other rights might be conceded if sufficient pressure could be mobilised. It is also worth noting that in this period the conflict became internationalised to a significant degree: this was particularly the case with respect to the USA. American interest (which would later transform into American involvement) increased in the 1970s, so that by the close of the decade President Carter had issued a declaration urging the UK and Irish governments to cooperate to reach a solution to the conflict (1977) and a declaration calling for an international commission on human rights in

Northern Ireland (1978). The Irish American community, led by such figures as Tip O'Neill, Daniel Patrick Moynihan and Ted Kennedy (citing his own position in favour of human rights), exerted significant pressure on the President to act on Northern Ireland.[8]

From the Anglo-Irish Agreement to the Peace Agreement

Notwithstanding the lack of progress in human rights terms in the field of the administration of justice, progress was registered in the relationship between human rights and the main political parties of Northern Ireland. In the late 1980s and early 1990s, the SDLP continued its strong emphasis on human rights but Sinn Féin also witnessed a greater engagement with human rights issues, as did the UUP which, by this time, also started advocating the adoption of a Bill of Rights, a step which it had objected to for a long time.

This broader engagement with human rights issues was also evident in the negotiations between the UK government and the Irish government. The Anglo-Irish Agreement contained both generic human rights references as well as more specific rights provisions (focusing on justice and equality). All the subsequent Anglo-Irish documents referred, to a greater or lesser degree, to human rights issues. The gradual mainstreaming of human rights within Anglo-Irish negotiations and also within the Northern Irish political parties is witness to the growing relevance of human rights as part of the political discourse in Northern Ireland, Ireland and the UK. This relevance can be explained, at least partially, by the developments in the international arena where, particularly after the end of the Cold War, human rights achieved a special status in the international community. Within Europe, the end of the Cold War was of special salience in human rights terms. The end of the Cold war paved the way for the eastern European states to join the Council of Europe and become parties to the European Convention on Human Rights. This transformed the Convention from a human rights mechanism for western Europe into a human rights instrument that held sway over Europe as a whole. In a way, human rights became a badge of respectability and civilised behaviour. References to human rights became inevitable both in the international and the domestic scenarios.

This inevitability of human rights explains, to some extent, the fact that there were no substantial obstacles to the inclusion of a strong human rights dimension in the Peace Agreement. Moreover, the study has highlighted that the inclusion of human rights language in the peace negotiations and in the Peace Agreement itself has been indispensable in securing the end of the violent conflict. This process was aided by the existence of local historically entrenched discourses of human rights (although differing discourses within the respective communities) which ensured a degree of engagement with human rights language.

The absence of strong objections to the inclusion of a human rights agenda was also aided by the fact that human rights, while important considerations, were not the main concern of the parties to the Agreement during negotiations. It is clear that for the UK and Irish governments, resolving the political and security situations constituted their overriding interests. Likewise, the Northern Irish political parties were mainly concerned with matters such as the mechanics of power sharing, the extent and powers of the North/South bodies and the issue of decommissioning of paramilitary weapons.

The lack of substantial obstacles to the inclusion of human rights is also explained by the fact that the some of the key human rights components included in the Agreement necessitated further discussion and agreement. Thus, several human rights commitments undertaken were, in fact, undertakings to refer or defer such matters to other fora or bodies. This allowed the parties to agree to the human rights dimension knowing that substantive decisions on these matters would be taken at a later stage. Finally, the human rights agenda which was agreed to allowed the various parties to believe they could interpret human rights in a manner which suited their ideas. This interpretative quandary became especially evident in the context of the Bill of Rights debate. Such developments were further evidence of a tendency towards selective applications, and self-serving interpretations, of human rights that are evident in the history of Northern Ireland and which have been highlighted throughout this study.

The post-Agreement phase

This is not to deny that the Peace Agreement brought real progress in human rights terms for Northern Ireland. Most fundamentally, the Agreement ended an almost 30-year-old cycle of violence which breached the most fundamental of all rights: the right to life. The developments in police reform ushered in by the Patten Report which was envisaged in the Agreement resolved (to a large degree) a key human rights concern which had existed since the formation of the Northern Irish state. Furthermore, the establishment of the Human Rights Commission and the Equality Commission created two statutory bodies that, not without difficulties and in different ways, contributed to the mainstreaming of human rights in Northern Ireland. The requirement that all Stormont legislation be proofed against the UK Human Rights Act and the European Convention on Human Rights was also an important step in ensuring that laws are not only human rights compliant but are seen to be so. In a society like Northern Ireland, where perceptions have shaped strongly the human rights agenda, this is a significant step.

However, for all this progress, one cannot help conclude that human rights have not reached the apex of maturation that the Peace Agreement seemed to portend. Fifteen years after the Agreement, human rights in Northern Ireland are still mediated through the lens of the conflict. To a significant extent, human rights are still viewed through the prism of the ideas on rights engendered by the conflict. This means that the two main communities still understand human rights, to a significant extent, within the context of the Northern Ireland conflict. As evidenced throughout this study, human rights have been part and parcel of the Northern Ireland conflict and, perhaps understandably, the two main communities are facing difficulties in untying human rights from the conflict. Effectively, this means that the two communities still understand human rights as part of the ideological struggle between unionism and nationalism. This is most evident in the failure to enact the Bill of Rights: not so much, or not only, in the failure to enact the Bill, but perhaps more importantly in the debates that occurred around the Bill. The debates around the Bill demonstrated the extent to which political parties, in the previously cited words of the Chair of the Bill of Rights Forum, "interpreted human rights within the framework of their ideological cause and that therefore human rights were part of the ideological struggle".

In the view of the Chair of the Forum, Professor Chris Sidoti, this point was clearly demonstrated in the work of the Bill of Rights Forum. The unionist position within the Forum was that a Bill of Right for Northern Ireland was not necessary, given that human rights legislation in the form of the Human Rights Act, applicable to the UK as a whole, already existed. Unionists wished to rely on the UK-wide Human Rights Act and certainly did not wish to duplicate any provision of it in Northern Ireland law except for any particularisation that related to the particular circumstances of Northern Ireland very strictly defined. This was part of the broader ideological perspective of unionism. On the other hand, Professor Sidoti noted that the approach taken by nationalists was that they wanted a Bill of Rights for Northern Ireland, with an implied subtext that they did not recognise the application of the UK Act to Northern Ireland because the UK was the occupying power.[9]

On the negative side of the ledger, one cannot help but note the fact that human rights have not really become central to the political life of Northern Ireland. In the crucial post-Agreement phase, both the UK and Irish governments gave priority to saving the Agreement from the various insidious obstacles it faced. Once a degree of normalisation was achieved after the St Andrew's Agreement, the two governments did not want to rock the boat of normalisation while the main political parties in Northern Ireland focused on the practicalities of power-sharing and devolved government. There was no impetus to bring human rights to the centre of political attention. Thus, normalisation became the normalisation of human rights as an issue of secondary importance.

How did human rights influence the conflict in Northern Ireland?

Human rights violations were both an underlying cause as well as an immediate cause of the violent conflict. This study has shown that human rights issues, although initially couched in the language of equality and discrimination, have had a longer-standing impact on the conflict than usually acknowledged. As evidenced in Chapter 1, existing literature on the Northern

Ireland conflict tends to centre on the civil rights period as the focus for human rights in Northern Ireland. Chapter 3 highlighted that these issues arose, as points of contrast and tension between the two main communities, in parallel with the creation of the state. Furthermore, Chapters 3 to 5 clearly established that the minority community developed a strong sense of grievance based on their experience of discrimination which provided a context for the descent into violence. This longer-term perspective on the role of human rights in influencing the conflict both establishes that the human rights dissensions and grievances had deep roots in the minority community. It also proves that Northern Ireland developed an autochthonous sense of equality, rights and discrimination. This provided a context upon which the developments in human rights on the international, regional and national levels could be grafted and, to some extent, grounded.

Within this context, Chapter 3 demonstrated that the issues of discrimination and inequality constituted underlying causes of the violent conflict that would eventually emerge. The structural violence perceived by the minority community made the descent into violent conflict more likely.

Furthermore, Chapters 4 and 5 demonstrated that the breach of the right to freedom and to physical integrity were an immediate and direct cause of the descent into violence. Moreover, a further critical role of human rights was the provision of a conceptual framework within which the minority community could express its grievances both domestically and internationally. The existence of such a human rights framework also prompted the expression of such grievances. Moreover, the expression of such grievances within a rights framework contributed at certain points in time to fuelling the conflict (most evidently in the civil rights movement phase).

In Chapter 5 the documented human rights abuses played an important role in the conflict by exacerbating the conflict on both sides. The human rights abuses committed by UK or Northern Irish governmental entities were used as justification for violence by republican paramilitaries. Such abuses were also used by republican and, in some cases nationalist, politicians to campaign against the continued UK presence in Northern Ireland. Such abuses also contributed to hardening anti-UK and anti-unionist sentiments amongst the minority community. Conversely, the human rights abuses committed by republican paramilitaries hardened attitudes amongst the unionist community and complicated the conflict resolution process.

The connections between human rights and the violent conflict had the consequence of making the human rights dimension a necessary component of the peace process. Throughout the continuation of the conflict, an acknowledgment of the importance of human rights for the conflict resolution process was apparent through legislative and policy measures undertaken by the UK government that were intended to improve standards related to equality and non-discrimination.

Chapter 6 showed clearly that human rights played a role throughout the various negotiations. Clearly, human rights always formed part of the possible solution to the conflict. While human rights were not the main contentious points during the negotiations, they were an indispensable part of the negotiations from the beginning. Thus, while human rights were not critical in the negotiations that led to the Peace Agreement, they were an important and indispensable part of them. Partially, this was because human rights issues (including issues of inequality, discrimination) had formed part of the political discourse of Northern Ireland since the creation of the state.

The growing tide of international human rights law and increasing international recognition of human rights standards also played a role in shaping the UK (and Irish) governments' actions, as well as the policies pursued by the political parties in Northern Ireland. Thus, the twin forces of (1) the particular history of Northern Ireland (in terms of discrimination, rights and conflict), coupled with (2) the international dynamics related to the growth of global human rights, rendered human rights an important element of the conflict-resolution process.

Within this context, it is also important to note that the various Northern Ireland political parties were also impacted by the growing human rights movement. The SDLP was born out of the civil rights period and thus from the outset declared itself to be committed to human rights issues. However, even other Northern Ireland political parties gradually developed a stronger human rights emphasis. Sinn Féin, as highlighted in this study, sought to present its political struggle within a human rights framework as it witnessed the potential mobilising force of rights language. This became less difficult to argue once Sinn Féin renounced violence and entered the political mainstream. The Ulster Unionist Party also developed its position vis-à-vis human rights quite significantly. Chapter 6 highlighted this shift. The impact of human rights on the Democratic Unionist Party is less evident, although one still notes that the DUP has its own views of human rights which are essentially tied to a British conception of liberty and security of person.

The inclusion of a considerable human rights agenda in the Peace Agreement raised expectations that human rights promotion and protection in Northern Ireland would become a model for other jurisdictions and shape significantly Northern Ireland's post-conflict phase. To some extent the expectation that human rights would influence the post-conflict phase was fulfilled in certain areas. The end of the violent conflict dramatically improved the human rights situation in terms of the right to life. The establishment of independent statutory bodies charged with promoting human rights and equality enhanced Northern Ireland's human rights structural framework while the reforms in policing and the criminal justice system addressed two of the longest-standing and seemingly intractable aspects of Northern Ireland's human rights challenges. The human rights agenda has impacted very considerably on the new policing system in Northern Ireland. As demonstrated in Chapter 7, this change has been a very significant one for the people and politics of Northern Ireland. A widely accepted policing service, grounded in a human rights ethos, has to a great extent resolved one of the most fundamental problems faced by Northern Ireland since the creation of the state. The changes to the criminal justice system have also led to the elimination of ad hoc emergency legislation specific to Northern Ireland. Moreover, various legislative changes brought about since 2002 (as seen in Chapter 7) have improved the Northern Ireland criminal justice system, with provisions designed to enhance human rights and equality. Furthermore, the political action of Northern Ireland's executive and assembly was limited by the requirement that any legislation enacted by the Assembly be proofed against the Human Rights Act and the European Convention on Human Rights. These steps are clear evidence of the continuing influence of human rights on Northern Ireland's post-conflict political landscape.

In other aspects, human rights have not influenced Northern Ireland as much as its history may have suggested. Northern Ireland's human rights agenda has been dominated by the conflict, and human rights issues not directly related to the conflict (such as issues of racism, educational opportunities for the working class and socioeconomic rights more generally) have not developed significantly in Northern Ireland. Consequently, the extent to which these issues have impacted on Northern Ireland's political life is more limited. The reasons for this are directly related to the question of how the conflict in Northern Ireland influenced the understanding and practice of human rights.

How did the Northern Ireland conflict influence human rights?

Human rights are still broadly understood by the two main political traditions in terms of the conflict or, to put it another way, human rights continue to be mediated through the lens of the conflict. This can be attributed to several factors.

As demonstrated in Chapter 3, ideas around rights and discrimination started developing within the Northern Irish political system in unfavourable circumstances. Even before the formation of the Northern Irish state, the perception existed within each community that their rights could only be guaranteed by the constitutional association with the UK or Ireland respectively. Moreover, upon the formation of the state, claims of discrimination and inequality by the minority community were considered by the majority unionist community as attempts to delegitimise the nascent state and as a tool through which nationalists conducted a partisan political campaign. The references to discrimination and inequality were viewed as a "constant attempt to undermine the state or belittle the state … [it] was seen as an attempt to deny the legitimacy of NI and its own government within the UK."[10]

On the other side, nationalists perceived the Northern Irish state as being *ab initio* intent on discriminating against them. Thus, human rights abuses became associated in the minds of nationalists with Protestant, unionist rule: such abuses were perceived as tools through which the majority sought to control, restrain and punish the minority. In effect, the conflict between the two communities in Northern Ireland resulted in the idea of rights and equality being shaped in two ways: (1) the exercise of self-determination was considered as a precondition for the protection of their respective rights by the two communities; and (2) the minority community perceived the abuse of human rights as a tool of repression while the majority community perceived claims of human rights abuses as a tool for destabilising the state.

This particularised conception of discrimination and inequality, and eventually of human rights, runs throughout the history of the Northern Irish state. The civil rights movement essentially consolidated this view within both communities. The civil rights period was in some ways a missed opportunity because it reiterated the particularised understanding of human rights within Northern Ireland and failed to broaden its conception.

The 1960s were, in various ways, an era when human rights came into their own within the international community. It was an era of reform and progressive politics in many parts of the world. Human rights treaties like the International Covenant on Civil and Political Rights and the International Covenant on Economic, Social and Cultural Rights were adopted in 1966 (which together with the Universal Declaration formed the International Bill of Rights). The landmark Convention on the Elimination of Racial Discrimination was adopted in the same year. Amnesty International was founded in 1961, while in the USA the civil rights movement shook the country and essentially changed the USA profoundly with a significant number of non-African Americans actively or silently supporting this cause.

However, as described in Chapter 4, the civil rights movement in Northern Ireland while inspired by some of these developments, remained an essentially nationalist movement. It focused on a limited number of requests, which while legitimate failed to inspire any great numbers of unionists. Furthermore, the involvement in the movement of republicans was used by unionist politicians to substantiate their view that the movement was a front for the IRA. In effect, the civil rights movement was politically complex: it included middle-class nationalists (some of whom would later proceed to form the SDLP); republicans who had associations with Sinn Féin; and young left-wing intellectuals who formed the nucleus of the People's Democracy. Gradually, as the Movement encountered greater violent responses to its campaign, the influence of the middle-class constituency within the Movement declined, while those who favoured more confrontation and, possibly, destabilisation became more influential in deciding the Movement's direction. The unionist politicians' attitudes towards the civil rights movement veered between suspicion and abhorrence and the view that human rights was something "done" by nationalists and republicans and therefore "not done" by unionists became cemented in the minds of unionists.

This zero-sum game attitude towards human rights in Northern Ireland became further entrenched during the conflict itself. For nationalists, the introduction of internment, the use of torture or inhuman and degrading treatment, the suspension of certain civil liberties, as well as the use of lethal force by state security forces, confirmed their view that the Northern Irish state was inimical to their human rights. This also shaped the nationalist and republican view that human rights abuses were essentially committed by the state and only the state could be held accountable for human rights abuses. As witnessed in the preceding chapter, this attitude towards human rights remained ingrained within some republican and nationalist mindsets.

With respect to the unionist community, the period of violent conflict reinforced their view that the ultimate aim of human rights language adopted by nationalists and republicans was the destruction of the Northern Irish state. The use of human rights laws by IRA operatives to defend themselves during legal proceedings further alienated unionists from the human rights agenda:

> These same people (IRA operatives who had committed serious crimes) were taking the British government to court for their human rights being infringed and that led to a lot of people being very concerned about the human rights agenda: that it was being taken by terrorists to allow them to do further terrorism.[11]

Even the negotiations leading to the peace process witnessed this duality of attitude by the two communities towards human rights. For nationalists, human rights were regarded as an essential component of the peace agreement as guarantees of protection from unionists discriminating against nationalists. According to Catriona Ruane, Sinn Féin "knew and understood that if you don't have a Human Rights Commission, an Equality Commission and strong equality legislation you would just go back to the way things were before where nationalists and republicans were discriminated against."[12] This was reflected during the negotiations and resulted in the nationalists/republicans being "much more concerned with those [human rights] issues" during the talks.[13]

Reference has been made to unionists' approach to the human rights agenda as part of the peace agreement,[14] which was somewhat antagonistic. It has been suggested that

> because unionists felt human rights were to their detriment or that somehow this is "owned" by nationalists; somehow they felt nationalists were always championing human rights from the civil rights movement for example. Therefore, human rights were regarded as something for nationalists and thus the argument was in the minds of many unionists that if this is for nationalists it cannot be for unionists.[15]

The UUP human rights spokesperson at the time of the negotiations, Dermot Nesbitt, was according to the then Minister of State at the NIO Paul Murphy actively involved in the negotiations on human rights issues but "had very particular ideas on human rights which were rather different"[16] to those of the nationalists and republicans. Nesbitt's views on human rights were very much tied to the Council of Europe Framework Convention for the Protection of National Minorities of 1995. In Nesbitt's view the Convention is an important legal instrument from the point of view of unionism, since it requires the acceptance of the existing borders of a state with a series of human rights guarantees for minorities. Thus, in a parallel to the nationalist and republican community viewing human rights as a guarantee for them, the view espoused by Nesbitt views human rights protection in the form of the Framework Convention as a guarantee for unionism. Although this is not specifically explicated by unionist representatives, this approach to human rights as guarantees for minorities could also allay fears for unionists should they constitute a minority in future constitutional dispensations or demographic developments.

All of the above underlines the extent to which human rights in Northern Ireland have been understood, practiced and interpreted within a conflict-based prism: be it the conflict over the constitutional status of Northern Ireland, the conflict around discrimination and equality or the violent conflict of the 1970s, 1980s and early 1990s.

This has ensured that human rights, rather than being understood in their totality and within the context of the values upon which human rights are based, are instead understood within a very particular (sometimes partisan) context. This view is confirmed, in the sphere of policing, by the PSNI Assistant Chief Commissioner Will Kerr: "sometimes around contentious issues some partisan perspectives on human rights are taken by both sides."[17]

The extent to which human rights in Northern Ireland have been influenced by the conflict and how this is having a profound impact on the development of human rights law and discourse in the post-conflict phase became most evident in the Bill of Rights debate. The terms of reference for drafting the Bill of Rights, articulated in the Agreement and in the Northern Ireland Act of 1998, gave official sanction to a particularised understanding of human rights. The proposed Bill of Rights was to be drafted with reference to the "particular circumstances of Northern Ireland". This language may have provided a hostage to fortune as these "particular circumstances" are at the heart of the disagreement between the two main communities. These circumstances, i.e. the conflict, are understood very differently by nationalists and unionists. It was therefore inevitable that tying the Bill of Rights to these particular circumstances was in effect tantamount to sanctioning a divergent interpretation of what should be contained in the Bill. In the introduction to Chapter 3 it was argued that in Northern Ireland there are many histories and interpretations of history. These differing interpretations are even more acute insofar as the years of the conflict are concerned. Since such fundamental disagreement exists as to the nature and development of the conflict it was inevitable that producing a Bill of Rights that reflected the circumstances of the conflict was not conducive to creating a shared understanding of human rights within Northern Ireland.

The Bill of Rights debate was an important opportunity for Northern Ireland to reflect upon, debate and, hopefully, agree on basic human rights principles and on why human rights are important for everyone within Northern Ireland. By tying the debate to the circumstances of the conflict, the opportunity was somewhat squandered. Instead of encouraging all sides to move away from the partisanship and politics of conflict that had coloured human rights throughout Northern Ireland's history, the Bill of Rights process was dominated by the conflict and its legacy.

In a society emerging out of violent conflict it is impossible to expect that such a conflict will not play a role in a debate on human rights. Nevertheless, the decision to tie the debate so strongly to the conflict made such a role so overwhelming that it pushed to the side some of the more universal and fundamental aspects of human rights. It also allowed the conflict to continue to colour to a very large extent the debate on human rights within Northern Ireland.

In the previous chapter, the extent to which human rights in Northern Ireland continue to be understood and read in terms of the conflict was highlighted, as were some of the repercussions of such a limited reading. The growth of xenophobia and racism, the paucity of opportunities for working-class people and the partisan exploitation of human rights in the case of contentious parades are examples of how the limited, conflict-coloured understanding of human rights impacts on the daily lives of the people of Northern Ireland.

The inherent difficulty of extricating human rights from the conflict in Northern Ireland has already been alluded to. Nevertheless, measures to lessen the extent to which the conflict continues to colour human rights in Northern Ireland may be taken. The Universal Declaration of Human Rights, as pointed out in Chapter 2, was drafted and adopted in a post-conflict scenario. While the conflict certainly played a role as a catalyst and a context for its adoption, the Declaration goes beyond the confines of conflict and encompasses universal values applicable to any society. It features a wide range of rights and is underpinned by key values such as equality, justice, peace and brotherhood. It is suggested that the human rights agenda in Northern Ireland (including the Bill of Rights) should also be reconstructed around this generous and universal understanding of human rights. Assistant Chief Commissioner Will Kerr concurred with this view:

> I fundamentally agree … on this, the need to interpret human rights in a spirit of brotherhood for example … we certainly need to look at where human rights are coming from, their provenance and their values as you were saying.[18]

This transformation in the approach towards human rights requires political leaders to acknowledge that change is required; that continuing to understand and view human rights through the lens of Northern Irish conflict is damaging the people of Northern Ireland in ways already cited. Apart from a change of attitude and perspective, specific measures need to be undertaken with respect to the two main communities.

Throughout this study the extent of the wariness (and at times downright antagonism) of the unionist leadership and community towards the human rights agenda has been evident. This matter needs to be addressed as a priority by the Human Rights Commission and the broader human rights non-governmental community as well as by the Northern Irish Executive. The idea that human rights constitute a zero-sum game should be challenged and eventually overcome. Overcoming decades of wary suspicion towards human rights is clearly an extremely difficult task. However, without dealing with this matter and without creating a more positive engagement with human rights by the unionist community, the human rights agenda of the peace process will remain unfulfilled.

Insofar as the nationalist and republican community is concerned, their contribution towards creating a more positive engagement with human rights by unionists should not be underestimated. Reaching out to unionists within the human rights context means interpreting human rights in a spirit of solidarity and not in an over-legalistic manner. An appreciation of where the unionist community is coming from in terms of human rights may be useful in creating a shared understanding of human rights. The nationalist and republican community may also reflect on the need to consider the responsibilities individuals have in upholding human rights. As witnessed in previous chapters, the traditional approach of many in the nationalist and republican folds has been to view human rights abuses as being the sole responsibility of the state. Acknowledging that non-state actors also have responsibilities for upholding human rights could be an important step in creating a fuller and more comprehensive understanding of human rights. Incidentally, such an acknowledgement could also serve to create the conditions for the republican leadership to admit that the IRA did commit human rights abuses. Such an admission could go some way in reaching out to unionists in terms of human rights.

Final observations

Finally, it is worth stating that the approach adopted in this study has revealed several perspectives on the relationship between human rights and conflict in Northern Ireland. Answering the two questions posed in this study using a human rights framework of analysis has provided a number of conclusions.

In the first place, a human rights framework demonstrates that the Northern Ireland conflict was shaped, at some points, very significantly, by human rights issues. It demonstrates that the conflict was also about who owns and defines human rights and that this has been the case for a longer period than hitherto accepted. Moreover, a human rights framework assists in interpreting, or in interpreting differently, some of the key episodes of the conflict.

Examples of such episodes are the political developments of the early years of the state, the civil rights movement, the hunger strikes and the Peace Agreement itself.

In the context of the above issue of interpretation, a human rights framework is also relevant to provide value judgments, based on human rights principles, about some of the key decisions taken by the main actors. For example, the introduction of internment, the hunger strikes, and the resort to terrorist acts by state and non-state actors, are all amenable to adjudication from a human rights view point. While other studies consider and judge, or even excuse, such decisions via political, socioeconomic or military frameworks, this study judges them by reference to international human rights standards. By doing so, one can provide some answers as to the behaviour of the various political and military actors in some specific cases with reference to internationally accepted standards.

A further conclusion is that human rights began to be used – albeit instrumentally – by the parties to the conflict in the 1970s and 1980s and such use also shaped the conflict. The consideration of how even in the 1970s and 1980s human rights retained a voice in the Northern Irish political landscape is also a matter not previously examined extensively in academic literature. Within this context, it also emerged that even an instrumental use of human rights contributes to building a lexicon of human rights that provides the ground for constructing useful institutions and to achieve reforms in sectors such as policing. The human rights framework also explains, at least partially, some of the politics of Northern Ireland today. The adoption by Sinn Féin of a significant human rights agenda is one example.

Furthermore, the analysis of the relationship between human rights and conflict in Northern Ireland explains the root causes of the main human rights issues faced by Northern Ireland today (for example the rise in racism and xenophobia, the lack of opportunity for working-class unionists, the inability to agree a Bill of Rights for Northern Ireland). This is a relevant explanation that may assist in understanding better the rationale behind some of the human rights deficiencies in Northern Ireland today. Such an understanding may play a role in responding to such deficiencies.

The analysis provided in this study also explains why Northern Ireland today has a police service with a strong human rights ethos, why it has not one, but two, bodies dealing with Human Rights and Equality, why Northern Ireland has some of the most elaborate human rights proofing mechanism for its legislation, and also why Northern Ireland's leaders have largely failed to deal with human rights abuses of the past.

A further conclusion sustained in this study is that whereas human rights issues and language framed much of the politics of Northern Ireland, it became clear early on that there were very divergent views on what human rights are; and what their implications might be for different parties in Northern Ireland. The human rights framework also proves clearly that human rights remained largely the preserve of the nationalist movement and were initially eschewed by unionists and only reluctantly engaged with by them later on. Within this context, it is also important to underline that while human rights are given considerable space in the Peace Agreement, having such an agreement rooted in a human rights framework poses certain problems. Such problems arise for both the UK and Republic of Ireland governments, as well as for the main political parties that at various times find some of the human rights norms inconvenient.

The adoption of a human rights framework to study the conflict shows that the growth of international human rights norms and architecture, emanating from outside Northern Ireland, influenced events internally and impacted on how the UK and Irish governments had to respond as they did, e.g. special courts, the hunger strike, use of torture etc. This framework reminds us of the importance of international norms, opinion and pressure both directly, through courts such as the European Court of Human Rights, as well as more indirectly through the impact of the growing stature of human rights. This made the adoption of human rights discourse and norms a sine qua non of "polite" society in the international arena.

Overall, this study has demonstrated that human rights have impacted on the conflict significantly, not so much by influencing its nature but by initially providing a sense of grievance to the minority community, upon which the descent into violent conflict partially depended. Human rights also influenced the content of the Peace Agreement although the human rights components of the Agreement were not serious stumbling blocks in the negotiations and played a marginal role in the latter phases of the peace talks. Nevertheless, the Agreement had to contain significant human rights provisions if it was to be accepted by the minority community. The inclusion of considerable human rights components in the Agreement, without major negotiating obstacles, also indicated that the various parties had by the 1990s become used to the idea that human rights would have to form part of the Agreement. This was both because of the Northern Irish human rights history (as portrayed in this study) and because of the international and regional rise of human rights, which impacted on Northern Ireland (as it did on other parts of the world). This study also contributes a, hopefully, useful addition to the literature on the relationship between human rights and conflict by providing a sustained examination of the role played by human rights before, during and after violent conflict.

Notes

1 It is worth noting that the Catholic Church itself had also moved to adopt human rights language in its teachings. See, for example, the Encyclical, Pope John Paul II, *Sollicitudo Rei Socialis*, 1987, para. 15, accessed 9 March 2015, http://w2.vatican.va/content/john-paul-ii/en/encyclicals/documents/hf_jp-ii_enc_30121987_sollicitudo-reisocialis.html.

2 The main human rights treaties adopted since the 1960s are listed here, OHCHR, "The Core International Human Rights Instruments and Their Monitoring Bodies", 2014, www.ohchr.org/EN/ProfessionalInterest/Pages/CoreInstruments.aspx.

3 The growth of national human rights institutions is also attributable to the 1991 Paris Principles on National Human Rights Institutions which were formally endorsed by the UN General Assembly in its Resolution 48/134 of 1993. United Nations General Assembly, *National Institutions for the Promotion and Protection of Human Rights*.
4 See Chapter 6.
5 Mary Ann Glendon, *A World Made New: Eleanor Roosevelt and the Universal Declaration of Human Rights* (New York: Random House, 2001), 230.
6 Ibid.
7 Margaret Thatcher, *The Downing Street Years* (London: HarperCollins, 1993).
8 Burton I. Kauffman, *The Carter Years* (Facts on File, USA), 105.
9 Interview with Professor Chris Sidoti, Interview with the Chairperson of the Bill of Rights Forum, 16 April 2014.
10 Mr Jonathan Bell MLA, Interview with Junior Minister in the Office of the First Minister and Deputy First Minister, 17 April 2014.
11 Mr Jonathan Bell MLA, Interview with Junior Minister in the Office of the First Minister and Deputy First Minister, 17 April 2014.
12 Ms. Catriona Ruane MLA, Interview with Sinn Féin Chief Whip at the Northern Ireland Assembly, 15 April 2014.
13 The Rt Hon. Paul Murphy MP, Interview with the former Secretary of State for Northern Ireland, 25 February 2014.
14 See Chapter 7.
15 Mr Dermot Nesbitt, Interview with former UUP MLA and spokesperson on human rights, 15 April 2014.
16 The Rt Hon. Paul Murphy MP, Interview with the former Secretary of State for Northern Ireland, 25 February 2014.
17 Mr. Will Kerr, Interview with PSNI Assistant Chief Commissioner, 28 August 2014.
18 Mr. Will Kerr, Interview with PSNI Assistant Chief Commissioner, 28 August 2014.

Bibliography

Primary documentation

Acts

Fair Employment (Northern Ireland) Act, 1976.
Civil Authorities (Special Powers) Act (Northern Ireland), 1922.
Justice (Northern Ireland) Act, 2004.
Police (Northern Ireland) Act, 2000.
Prevention of Terrorism (Temporary Provisions) Act, 1974.
Prevention of Terrorism (Temporary Provisions) Act, 1976.
Prevention of Terrorism (Temporary Provisions) Act, 1984.
Prevention of Terrorism (Temporary Provisions) Act, 1989.

Agreements

Agreement between the Government of the United Kingdom of Great Britain and Northern Ireland and the Government of the Republic of Ireland. Treaty Series No. 62, 1985.
The Northern Ireland Peace Agreement.
The Sunningdale Agreement, 1973.

Cases

A and Others v. *Secretary of State for the Home Department* (United Kingdom House of Lords 2004).
Ex-parte Molyneaux, Weekly Law Reports (1986).
Finucane v. *United Kingdom* (European Court of Human Rights 2003).
Gillan and Quiton v. *United Kingdom* (European Court of Human Rights 2010).
Ireland v. *United Kingdom* (European Court of Human Rights 1978).
McCann and Others v. *United Kingdom* (European Court of Human Rights 1995).
McFeeley v. *United Kingdom* (European Commission of Human Rights 1980).
McKerr v. *United Kingdom* (European Court of Human Rights 2001).
Minority School in Albania, Advisory Opinion 26 (Permanent Court of International Justice 1935).
Re E (a child) (AP) (Appellant) (Northern Ireland) (House of Lords 2008).
Re MB (England and Wales High Court (Administrative Court) 2006).
Re Secession of Quebec [1998] 2 SCR 217 (Supreme Court of Canada 1998).

Constitution

The Northern Ireland Constitution. London: Her Majesty's Stationery Office, 1974.

Conventions

American Convention on Human Rights, 1969.
Council of Europe. *Convention for the Protection of Human Rights and Fundamental Freedoms as Amended by Protocols No. 11 and No. 14*, 1950.

Declarations

House of Commons. *Ireland (Joint Declaration)*, 15 December 1993. www.publications.parliament.uk/pa/cm199394/cmhansrd/1993-12-15/Debate-1.html.
International Conference on Human Rights. *Proclamation of Teheran, Final Act of the International Conference on Human Rights. U.N. Doc. A/CONF. 32/41*. Vol. 3, 1968. www1.umn.edu/humanrts/instree/l2ptichr.htm.
Major, John, and Reynolds, Albert. *Joint Declaration on Peace: The Downing Street Declaration*, 15 December 1993.
The British and Irish Governments. *The Framework Documents*, 22 February 1995.
United Nations General Assembly. *Declaration on the Right and Responsibility of Individuals, Groups and Organs of Society to Promote and Protect Universally Recognized Human Rights and Fundamental Freedoms. United Nations General Assembly Resolution*. 53/144, 1998. Accessed 20 July 2014, www.ohchr.org/EN/ProfessionalInterest/Pages/RightAndResponsibility.aspx.
United Nations General Assembly. *The Universal Declaration of Human Rights*, 1948.
United Nations World Conference on Human Rights. *Vienna Declaration and Programme of Action*, A/Conf.157/23 (25 June 1993). Accessed 15 June 2014, www.ohchr.org/EN/ProfessionalInterest/Pages/Vienna.aspx.
Vienna Declaration and Programme of Action. A/Conf.157/23 (12 June 1993). Accessed 12 October 2014, www.ohchr.org/EN/ProfessionalInterest/Pages/Vienna.aspx.
Wilson, Woodrow. *President Wilson's Fourteen Points*, 1918. Accessed 24 January 2012, http://wwi.lib.byu.edu/index.php/President_Wilson's_Fourteen_Points.

Dossier

Northern Ireland Civil Rights Association. *Dossier on Harassment and Brutality by the British Army in Northern Ireland: A Sample of Typical Cases*. Northern Ireland Civil Rights Association, 1972.

Encyclical

Pope John Paul II. *Sollicitudo Rei Socialis*, 1987. Accessed 9 March 2015, http://w2.vatican.va/content/john-paul-ii/en/encyclicals/documents/hf_jp-ii_enc_30121987_sollicitudo-rei-socialis.html.

General communications

Campaign for Social Justice. "Letter", 28 December 1969. Northern Ireland Political Collection. Linen Hall Library, Belfast.

Communication to Civil Rights Association Members from Mrs Brid Rodgers, John Donaghy and Conn McCluskey, 1 February 1970.
Hayes, Dr. Maurice. Letter to Sir Ewart Bell. "Confidential Minute", 8 February 1982. Northern Ireland Political Collection. Linen Hall Library, Belfast.
Letter from Lieutenant Colonel J. C. Reilly, Commanding Officer 2nd Battalion, 23 December 1971. Northern Ireland Political Collection. Linen Hall Library, Belfast.
Letter from Captain Terence O'Neill to Sir Knox Cunningham. Public Records Office of Northern Ireland, 13 March 1968.
Letter from the Secretary of State for Northern Ireland the Rt. Hon. Humphrey Atkins MP to Gerry Fitt MP. Belfast: Public Records Office of Northern Ireland, 29 January 1980.
Letter from the UK Home Secretary to the Prime Minister of Northern Ireland. Belfast: Public Records Office of Northern Ireland, 4 August 1971.
Ó'Fiaich, Tomás. *Statement by the Archbishop of Armagh, Dr Tomas O'Fiaich Concerning His Visit Sunday Last to H-Block at Long Kesh Prison, Northern Ireland*. Belfast: Public Records Office of Northern Ireland, 1 August 1978.
Speaker unknown. "Speech", 21 December 1968. Northern Ireland Political Collection. Linen Hall Library, Belfast, P1063.

General reports and studies

Bill of Rights Forum. *Final Report – Recommendations to the Northern Ireland Human Rights Commission on a Bill of Rights for Northern Ireland*. Belfast: Bill of Rights Forum, 31 March 2008. Accessed 23 July 2014, http://cain.ulst.ac.uk/issues/law/bor/borf310308_report.pdf.
Britain and Ireland Human Rights Centre. *Human Rights: A Framework for Peace*. London: Britain and Ireland Human Rights Centre, 1995.
Committee on the Administration of Justice. *CAJ's Submission to the UK Bill of Rights Commission – Discussion Paper: "Do We Need a UK Bill of Rights?"*, November 2011. Accessed 24 August 2014, www.caj.org.uk/files/2011/11/15/S367_CAJs_submission_to_the_UK_Bill_of_Rights_Commission,_Nov_2011.pdf.
Committee on the Administration of Justice. *Ways of Protecting Minority Rights in Northern Ireland*. Vol. 7, 1985.
Consultative Group on the Past. *Report of the Consultative Group on the Past*, 23 January 2009. Accessed 14 October 2014, http://cain.ulst.ac.uk/victims/docs/consultative_group/cgp_230109_report.pdf.
Criminal Justice Review Group. *Review of the Criminal Justice System in Northern Ireland*, 2000. Accessed 19 August 2014, http://cain.ulst.ac.uk/issues/law/cjr/chap1.pdf.
Devlin, Roisin, and McKenna, Sorcha. *No Home from Home: Homelessness for People with No or Limited Access to Public Funds*. Belfast: Northern Ireland Human Rights Commission, September 2009.
Dickson, Brice, ed. *The CAJ. Handbook Civil Liberties in Northern Ireland*. 2nd edn. The Committee on the Administration of Justice, 1993.
Donald, Alice, Leach, Philip and Puddephatt, Andrew. *Developing a Bill of Rights for the United Kingdom*. Research Report 51. Equality and Human Rights Commission, 2010.
Gogarty, Frank. *Speech by Dr. Frank Gogarty, Chairman of NICRA to the First National Conference of the National Association for Irish Justice*. New York: City Center, November 1969.

Hamilton, Michael, Jarman, Neil and Bryan, Dominic. *Parades, Protests and Policing: A Human Rights Framework*. Belfast: Northern Ireland Human Rights Commission, March 2001.

Higgins, Rosalyn. *International Law and the Avoidance, Containment and Resolution of Disputes*. General Course on Public International Law. Recueil Des Cours, Vol. 230. The Hague: Martinus Nijhoff, 1991.

HMIC. *Inspection of the Police Service of Northern Ireland Historical Enquiries Team*, 2013. Accessed 14 October 2014, www.justiceinspectorates.gov.uk/hmic/media/inspection-of-the-police-service-of-northern-ireland-historical-enquiries-team-20130703.pdf.

Independent Commission on Policing in Northern Ireland. *A New Beginning: Policing in Northern Ireland – The Report of the Independent Commission on Policing in Northern Ireland*. Belfast: Independent Commission on Policing in Northern Ireland, 9 September 1999. Accessed 8 July 2014, http://cain.ulst.ac.uk/issues/police/patten/patten99.pdf.

Initial Discussion of "A New Framework for Agreement": Sinn Féin Submission to the Forum for Peace and Reconciliation, 5 May 1995.

International Coordinating Committee of National Institutions for the Promotion and Protection of Human Rights (ICC). "Chart of the Status of National Institutions Accredited by the International Coordinating Committee of National Institutions for the Promotion and Protection of Human Rights", 28 January 2014. Accessed 19 July 2014, www.ohchr.org/Documents/Countries/NHRI/Chart_Status_NIs.pdf.

Kilkelly, Ursula. *In Our Care: Promoting the Rights of Children in Custody*. Belfast: Northern Ireland Human Rights Commission, March 2002.

Larkin, John F. *Human Rights Guidance for Forensic Science Northern Ireland*. Guidance by the Attorney General for Northern Ireland pursuant to Section 8 of the Justice (Northern Ireland) Act 2004, 8 May 2013. www.dojni.gov.uk/index/fsni/fsni-publications/attorney-generalwww.dojni.gov.uk/index/fsni/fsni-publications/attorney-general-guidance-for-fsni.pdfguidance-for-fsni.pdf.

Larkin, John F. *Human Rights Guidance for the Northern Ireland Prison Service – Prison Order and Discipline*. Guidance by the Attorney General for Northern Ireland pursuant to Section 8 of the Justice (Northern Ireland) Act 2004, 10 April 2014. www.attorneygeneralni.gov.uk/human_rights_guidance_for_the_northern_ireland_prison_ service_on_prison_order_and_discipline.pdf.119kb.

Larkin, John F. *Human Rights Guidance for the Public Prosecution Service*. Guidance by the Attorney General for Northern Ireland pursuant to Section 8 of the Justice (Northern Ireland) Act 2004, 21 March 2014. Accessed 20 October 2014, www.attorneygeneralni.gov.uk/human_rights_guidance_for_the_public_prosecution_service__pdf_133kb_.

Larkin, John F. *Human Rights Guidance for the State Pathologist's Department*. Guidance by the Attorney General for Northern Ireland pursuant to Section 8 of the Justice (Northern Ireland) Act 2004, 8 May 2013. Accessed 21 October 2014, www.attorneygeneralni.gov.uk/spd_pdf_website.pdf.

Latif, Nazia, and Martynowicz, Agnieszka. *Our Hidden Borders: The UK Border Agency's Powers of Detention*. Belfast: Northern Ireland Human Rights Commission, April 2009.

McEvoy, Kieran and Mallinder, Louise. *Truth, Amnesty and Prosecutions: Models for Dealing with the Past*, 3 December 2013. Accessed 14 October 2014, www.patfinucanecentre.org/truth/McEvoy%20&%20Mallinder%20Models%20on% 20Truth%20Amnesty%20&%20Prosecution%203%20Dec%202013.pdf.

Metropolitan Police. *Surveys in the MPS: Londoners' Views Count*, November 2013. www.met.police.uk/about/performance/documents/LVC_Quarter_2_13_14.pdf.

National Council for Civil Liberties. *Report of a Commission of Inquiry Appointed to Examine the Purpose and Effect of the Civil Authorities (Special Powers) Acts (Northern Ireland) 1922 and 1933*. London: NCCL, 1972.

NICRA. "Proposals for Peace, Democracy and Community Relations". NICRA, Belfast, March 1973. Accessed 18 February 2012, http://cain.ulst.ac.uk/events/crights/nicra/nicra73.htm.

NICRA Bulletin, 1971.

Nolan, Paul. *Northern Ireland Peace Monitoring Report*. Community Relations Council, March 2014.

Northern Ireland Human Rights Commission. *A Bill of Rights for Northern Ireland: Advice to the Secretary of State for Northern Ireland*. Belfast: Northern Ireland Human Rights Commission, 10 December 2008. Accessed 22 July 2014, www.nihrc.org/documents/bill%20of%20rights/bill-of-rights-for-northern-ireland-advice-to-secretary-state-2008.pdf.

Northern Ireland Human Rights Commission. *Annual Report 2001*. Accessed 16 July 2014, www.nihrc.org/documents/nihrc-general/corporate-reports-plans/annual-report-financial-accounts-2000-2001-lores.pdf.

Northern Ireland Human Rights Commission. *Annual Report 2004*. Accessed 17 July 2014, www.nihrc.org/documents/nihrc-general/corporate-reports-plans/annual-report-financial-accounts-2004-lores.pdf.

Northern Ireland Human Rights Commission. *Annual Report and Accounts 2010–2011*. Accessed 22 October 2014, www.gov.uk/government/uploads/system/uploads/attachment_data/file/247208/1455.pdf.

Northern Ireland Human Rights Commission. *Annual Report and Accounts 2011–2012*. Accessed 22 October 2014, www.gov.uk/government/uploads/system/uploads/attachment_data/file/246547/0490.pdf.

Northern Ireland Human Rights Commission. *NIHRC Review*, no. 2 (Summer 2006).

Northern Ireland Human Rights Commission. *Submission to the United Nations' Committee on the Rights of the Child: Shadow Report on the Third and Fourth Periodic Reports of the United Kingdom of Great Britain and Northern Ireland*. Belfast: Northern Ireland Human Rights Commission, May 2008. Accessed 24 October 2014, www.qub.ac.uk/research-centres/advancing-childrenswww.qub.ac.uk/research-centres/advancing-childrens-rights/Filestore/Filetoupload,403611,en.pdfrights/Filestore/Filetoupload,403611,en.pdf.

Northern Ireland Human Rights Commission. *The 2012 Annual Statement: Human Rights in Northern Ireland*. Belfast: Northern Ireland Human Rights Commission, 2012. Accessed 24 October 2014, www.nihrc.org/uploads/publications/HRC_Annual_Statement_2012.pdf.

Northern Ireland Human Rights Commission. *The First Annual Report of the Northern Ireland Human Rights Commission, 1999–2000*. Belfast: Northern Ireland Human Rights Commission, 2000. Accessed 16 July 2014, www.nihrc.org/documents/nihrc-general/corporate-reports-plans/annual-report-financial-accounts-1999-2000-lores.pdf.

Northern Ireland Policing Board and The Police Service of Northern Ireland. *Police Service of Northern Ireland Code of Ethics 2008*. Belfast: Northern Ireland Policing Board, 2008. Accessed 8 June 2014, www.nipolicingboard.org.uk/final_code_of_ethics-2.pdf.

Northern Ireland Statistics and Research Agency. *Census 2011: Key Statistics for Northern Ireland*, 11 December 2012. Accessed 8 July 2014, www.nisra.gov.uk/Census/key_stats_bulletin_2011.pdf.

Northern Ireland Women's Coalition. "Strand 1 Submission, Justice, Rights and Safeguards", December 1997.

Russell, Raymond T. *Fair Employment in Northern Ireland: The Decades of Change (1990–2010)*. Northern Ireland Assembly, Research and Information Service, 10 August 2012. Accessed 15 August 2012, www.niassembly.gov.uk/Documents/RaISe/Publications/2012/general/12112.pdf.

SDLP. *Executive Committee Statement on Ardoyne Meeting on September 10 and on Conditions in "H Block"*. Public Records Office of Northern Ireland, 1978.

Sinn Féin. "Peace in Ireland: For a Future as Equals, Justice Issues, Rights and Safeguards. A Sinn Féin Submission to Strands One and Two of the Peace Talks", 10 November 1997.

Sinn Féin. *Towards a Lasting Peace in Ireland*, 1992.

The Alliance Party. *The Alliance Party Submissions to the Multi-Party Talks*, 1997.

The Campaign for Social Justice in Northern Ireland. *Northern Ireland: The Plain Truth*. 2nd edn. CAB/9/B/300/3. Castlefields, Dungannon, 1969.

The Campaign for Social Justice in Northern Ireland. "Northern Ireland: Why Justice Cannot Be Done", 1964. Accessed 9 February 2012, http://cain.ulst.ac.uk/events/crights/pdfs/csj85.pdf.

The Social Democratic and Labour Party. "Towards a New Ireland: Proposals by the Social Democratic and Labour Party". The Social Democratic and Labour Party, 1972. Accessed 18 February 2012, http://cain.ulst.ac.uk/events/crights/sdlp1972.htm.

Ulster Unionist Parliamentary Party. *Briefing Note on the Downing Street Declaration of the 15th December 1993*, 15 December 1993. Northern Ireland Political Collection. Linen Hall Library, Belfast.

Ulster Unionist Party. *Pathways to Peace within the Union*, 1997.

Ulster Unionist Party. "Response to Frameworks for the Future", 10 March 1995. Northern Ireland Political Collection. Linen Hall Library, Belfast.

Ulster Unionist Party. *Ulster Unionist Party Position on a Bill of Rights*. Accessed 21 July 2014, http://uup.org/assets/images/featured/Ulster%20Unionist%20Party%20Position%20on%20 a%20Bill%20of%20Rights.pdf.

Ulster Unionist Party Publication. *Towards the Future: A Unionist Blueprint*. Belfast: Ulster Publicity and Research Department, 1972.

War on Terror: Lessons from Northern Ireland. Belfast: Committee on the Administration of Justice, 2008. www.icj.org/IMG/CAJ_report.pdf.

Government reports, declarations and memoranda

Arrest Policy for Protestants. Public Records Office of Northern Ireland, 9 December 1972.

Captain Terence O'Neill. *Television Broadcast by Captain Terence O'Neill, Prime Minister of Northern Ireland BBC (Northern Ireland) and Ulster Television*. Public Records Office of Northern Ireland, 9 December 1968.

Great Britain Parliament. *Formation of the Ulster Defence Regiment*. Belfast: Her Majesty's Stationery Office, November 1969.

House of Lords House of Commons, Joint Committee on Human Rights. *Work of the Northern Ireland Human Rights Commission*. Session 2002–2003. London: The

Stationery Office, 15 July 2003. Accessed 26 October 2014, www.publications.parliament.uk/pa/jt200203/jtselect/jtrights/132/132.pdf.
Joint Committee on Human Rights. *Memorandum from Professor Christine Bell and Dr Inez McCormack, Former Commissioners of the NIHRC*, 15 July 2003. Accessed 19 July 2014, www.publications.parliament.uk/pa/jt200203/jtselect/jtrights/132/132we05.htm#.
"Joint Statement of the Prime Minister and the Taoiseach", 15 September 1997.
List of Principal Meetings and Other Events Connected with the Free Presbyterian Church during the Month of September 1968. Public Records Office of Northern Ireland, 1968.
List of Principal Meetings and Other Events Connected with the Paisleyite Movement during the Month of October 1968. Public Records Office of Northern Ireland, 1968.
Main Points Made by Mr Heath at Downing Street Meeting on 22 March 1972 about the Northern Ireland Situation. Public Records Office of Northern Ireland, 22 March 1972.
Northern Ireland Executive. "Proposed Agreement: An Agreement among the Parties of the Northern Ireland Executive on Parades, Select Commemorations, and Related Protests; Flags and Emblems; and Contending with the Past", 31 December 2013. Accessed 8 June 2014, www.northernireland.gov.uk/haass.pdf.
Northern Ireland Information Service. *Prisoners Rights and Privileges in NI: Statement by Secretary of State*. Public Records Office of Northern Ireland, 4 December 1980.
Northern Ireland Office. *A Bill of Rights for Northern Ireland: Next Steps*. Consultation Paper, 30 November 2009. Accessed 23 July 2014, http://cain.ulst.ac.uk/issues/law/bor/nio301109bor.pdf.
Northern Ireland Office. *Northern Ireland Constitutional Convention Report*. London: Her Majesty's Stationery Office, 1975.
Northern Ireland Office. *The Future of Northern Ireland: A Paper for Discussion*. Belfast: Her Majesty's Stationery Office, 1972.
Note of a Meeting between the Secretary of State, the Alliance Party, the Social Democratic and Labour Party and the Ulster Unionist Party. Belfast: Public Record Office of Northern Ireland, 21 November 1973.
Note of Talks between the Secretary of State, the Alliance Party, the Social Democratic and Labour Party and the Ulster Unionist Party. Belfast: Public Record Office of Northern Ireland, 5 October 1973.
Office of the First Minister and Deputy First Minister. *Labour Force Survey 2012 Religion Report*. Press release. Northern Ireland Executive, 29 January 2014. Accessed 8 July 2014, www.northernireland.gov.uk/news-ofmdfm-290114-labour-force-survey.
Procedural Motion. All-Party Negotiations Background Documents, 1997.
Public Records Office, Northern Ireland. *Conclusions of a Meeting of the Cabinet Held at Stormont Castle*, 5 October 1968.
Public Records Office, Northern Ireland. *Conclusions of a Meeting of the Cabinet Held at Stormont Castle*, 14 October 1968.
Public Records Office, Northern Ireland. *Conclusions of a Meeting of the Cabinet Held at Stormont Castle*, 7 November 1968.
Public Records Office, Northern Ireland. *Conclusions of a Meeting of the Cabinet Held at Stormont Castle*, 20 November 1968.
Public Records Office, Northern Ireland. *Conclusions of a Meeting of the Cabinet Held at Stormont Castle*, 15 January 1969.
Public Records Office, Northern Ireland. *Meeting at 10 Downing Street*, 4 November 1968.
Public Records Office, Northern Ireland. *Memorandum by the Prime Minister*, 14 October 1968.

Public Records Office of Northern Ireland. *Conclusions of a Meeting of the Cabinet Held at Stormont Castle*, 20 August 1971.

Review of the Working of the Conference, 24 May 1989. Northern Ireland Political Collection. Linen Hall Library, Belfast.

Standing Advisory Commission on Human Rights. *The Protection of Human Rights by Law in Northern Ireland*. London: Her Majesty's Stationery Office, 1977.

Statement by the Prime Minister, Mr Brian Faulkner DL MP. Public Records Office of Northern Ireland, 9 August 1971.

Statement by the Rt Hon. Edward Heath to the House of Commons. Public Record Office of Northern Ireland, 24 March 1972.

The Honourable Lord Cameron. *Cameron Report – Disturbances in Northern Ireland*. Belfast: Her Majesty's Stationery Office, September 1969.

The Standing Advisory Commission on Human Rights. *Report on Religious and Political Discrimination and Equality of Opportunity in Northern Ireland*. London: Her Majesty's Stationery Office, 1987.

"The Threat to Law and Order in Northern Ireland over the Next Few Years." In *The Working Party on Law and Order in Northern Ireland*. Public Records Office of Northern Ireland, 1976. The Viscount Colville of Culross, Q.C. *Review of the Northern Ireland (Emergency Provisions) Acts 1978 and 1987*. London: Her Majesty's Stationery Office, 1990.

International charter

African Charter of Human and Peoples' Rights, 1981.

Interviews

Mr Dermot Nesbitt. Interview with former UUP MLA and spokesperson on human rights, 15 April 2014.

Mr Jonathan Bell MLA. Interview with Junior Minister in the Office of the First Minister and Deputy First Minister, 17 April 2014.

Mr. Will Kerr. Interview with PSNI Assistant Chief Commissioner, 28 August 2014.

Ms. Catriona Ruane MLA. Interview with Sinn Féin Chief Whip at the Northern Ireland Assembly, 15 April 2014.

Ms. Emma Little. Interview with the Special Advisor to the First Minister, 17 April 2014.

Ms. Judith Gillespie CBE OBE. Interview with former Deputy Chief Commissioner, PSNI, 31 July 2014.

Professor Brice Dickson. Interview with former Chairperson of the Northern Ireland Human Rights Commission, 24 February 2014.

Professor Chris Sidoti. Interview with the Chairperson of the Bill of Rights Forum, 16 April 2014.

The Rt Hon. Paul Murphy MP. Interview with the former Secretary of State for Northern Ireland, 25 February 2014.

Manifestos

Campaign Newsletter. Vol. 4. Castlefields, Dungannon: Campaign For Social Justice in Northern Ireland, 1967.

Campaign Newsletter. Vol. 8. Castlefields, Dungannon: Campaign For Social Justice in Northern Ireland, 1968.

Campaign Newsletter. Vol. 11. Castlefields, Dungannon: Campaign For Social Justice in Northern Ireland, 1970.
December 1968; towards a Programme of Campaign for 1969, 1969.
Democratic Unionist Party: DUP Manifesto. *Democracy – Not Dublin Rule*, 1997.
People's Democracy. *Peoples Democracy: What It Stands For, Its Attitudes*, 1972.
SDLP. *A New North, a New Ireland, a New Europe*, 1992.
SDLP. *Real Leadership, Real Peace: Westminster General Election Manifesto*, 1997.
Sinn Féin. *A New Opportunity for Peace: Manifesto*, 1997.
The Alliance Party of Northern Ireland. *Agenda for Change: The Alliance Manifesto*, 1997.
Ulster Democratic Union Party. *Time to Tackle Terrorism 1992: Election Manifesto*, 1992.
Ulster Unionist Party. *Building Your Future Within the Union: Manifesto Forum Election*, 1996.
Ulster Unionist Party. *The People's Choice: Manifesto General Election*, 1992.

Newspaper articles

"400,000 Students Back North's CR Movement". *Irish News*, 30 November 1968.
BBC News. "On the Runs: Reaction to Secret Fugitive Letters Report". *BBC News*, 17 July 2014. Accessed 14 October 2014, www.bbc.com/news/uk-northern-ireland-28340830.
BBC News. "Victims Condemn Northern Ireland Troubles Prosecutions Call". *BBC News*, 20 November 2013. Accessed 15 October 2014, www.bbc.com/news/uk-northern-ireland-25021286.
Blair, Tony. "All Have to Make Compromises". *News Letter*, 13 September 1997.
Chrisafis, Angelique. "Racist War of the Loyalist Street Gangs". *Guardian*, 10 January 2004. Accessed 8 July 2014, www.theguardian.com/uk/2004/jan/10/northern ireland.race.
Clarke, Liam, Black, Rebecca and Cromie, Claire. "Muslim Rant Preacher: First Minister Peter Robinson Moves to Defuse Islam Row". *Belfast Telegraph*, 29 May 2014. Accessed 8 July 2014, www.belfasttelegraph.co.uk/news/northern-ireland/muslim-rant-preacher-first-minister-peter-robinson-moves-to-defuse-islam-row-30312816.html.
Cromie, Claire. "PSNI Cuts 300 Jobs and Axes Historical Enquiries Team". *Belfast Telegraph*, 30 September 2014. Accessed 14 October 2014, www.belfasttelegraph.co.uk/news/northern-ireland/psni-cuts-300-jobs-and-axes-historical-enquiries-team-30626460.html.
FT View. "Facing the Past in Northern Ireland". *Financial Times*, 2 May 2014.
"Gerry Adams Arrest: Police Get Another Two Days to Question Sinn Féin President over Jean McConville's Murder". *Belfast Telegraph*, 3 May 2014. Accessed 20 July 2014, www.belfasttelegraph.co.uk/news/northern-ireland/gerry-adams-arrest-police-get-another-two-days-to-question-sinn-fein-president-over-jean-mcconvilles-murder-30239798.html.
"How the Russians See Us". *Belfast Telegraph*, 22 January 1969.
"Human Rights Members Resign". *BBC*, 9 September 2002. Accessed 22 October 2014, http://news.bbc.co.uk/2/hi/uk_news/northern_ireland/2247268.stm.
"Interview with Kenneth Bloomfield". *BBC Radio Ulster*, 7 December 2007.
"Interview with Terence O'Neill". *Belfast Telegraph*, 10 May 1969.
Irish Weekly, 29 May 1965.

Kilpatrick, Chris. "Two Racist Attacks Every Day in Northern Ireland's Race-Hate Crime Surge". *Belfast Telegraph*, 21 April 2014. Accessed 8 July 2014, www.belfasttelegraph.co.uk/news/northern-ireland/two-racist-attacks-every-day-in-northern-irelands-racehate-crime-surge-30202329.html.

"Legal Bid over Murders 'Collusion'". *Belfast Telegraph*, 11 April 2014. Accessed 14 October 2014, www.belfasttelegraph.co.uk/news/northern-ireland/legal-bid-over-murders-collusion-30177197.html.

"Le Monde Asks How Long Can Britain Stay Aloof?". *Irish News*, 14 January 1969.

McKittrick, David. "Catholics Make up 7% of RUC". *Independent*, 28 January 1993. Accessed 8 July 2014, www.independent.co.uk/news/uk/catholics-make-up-7-of-ruc-1481268.html.

McKittrick, David. "Remembering Bobby Sands". *Independent*, 5 May 2006. Accessed 25 August 2012, www.independent.co.uk/news/uk/this-britain/remembering-bobby-sands-476884.html.

McSparran, James. "Reformers and Reforms". *Irish News*, 29 January 1969.

Mulgrew, John. "Anna Lo 'to Quit Politics' due to Ongoing Racist Abuse by Loyalists". *Belfast Telegraph*, 29 May 2014. Accessed 8 July 2014, www.belfasttelegraph.co.uk/news/northern-ireland/anna-lo-to-quit-politics-due-to-ongoing-racist-abuse-by-loyalists-30314364.html.

"Northern Ireland: Further Racist Attack against Romanians in Belfast". *Telegraph*, 18 June 2009. Accessed 8 July 2014, www.telegraph.co.uk/news/uknews/law-and-order/5565531/Northern-Ireland-further-racist-attack-against-Romanians-in-Belfast.html.

"Offences of Genocide in North". *Irish News*, 5 March 1969.

OHCHR. "The Core International Human Rights Instruments and Their Monitoring Bodies", 2014. www.ohchr.org/EN/ProfessionalInterest/Pages/CoreInstruments.aspx.

"Protestant Workers 'Face Discrimination'". *BBC*, 16 March 2004, sec. Northern Ireland. http://news.bbc.co.uk/2/hi/uk_news/northern_ireland/3515210.stm.

"Rights: Baptist Pledges Support". *Belfast Telegraph*, 21 November 1968.

"Rights Head Admits Dispute 'Flaws'". *BBC*, 23 July 2003. Accessed 22 October 2014, http://news.bbc.co.uk/2/hi/uk_news/northern_ireland/3088615.stm.

Robinson, Peter. "Dagger in a Friend's Hand". *Independent*, 24 February 1995.

Rutherford, Adrian. "Loughinisland Families 'Angry and Disgusted' at Report Findings". *Belfast Telegraph*, 25 June 2011. www.belfasttelegraph.co.uk/news/northern-ireland/loughinisland-families-angry-and-disgusted-at-report-findings-28630458.html.

Sackur, Stephen. "Flag Removal 'Attack on Identity' with Democratic Unionist MP, Ian Paisley Jr". Interview. *HARDTalk. BBC World News*, 10 April 2013. Accessed 14 July 2014, www.bbc.co.uk/programmes/p017jc7g.

"Social Justice March in England". *Belfast Telegraph*, 7 December 1968.

"Sorrow Over NI: Vatican Newspaper". *The Irish Times*, 8 January 1969.

"Towards Peace". *SDLP News*, November 1972.

"US Sees Mirror in Ulster". *Belfast Telegraph*, 8 January 1969.

Parliamentary debates

Northern Ireland House of Commons. *The Parliamentary Debates: Official Report*, 14 March 1922. http://stormontpapers.ahds.ac.uk/stormontpapers/pageview.html?volumeno=2&pageno=.

Northern Ireland House of Commons. *The Parliamentary Debates: Official Report*, 15 March 1922. http://stormontpapers.ahds.ac.uk/stormontpapers/pageview.html?volumeno=2&pageno=29.

Northern Ireland House of Commons. *The Parliamentary Debates: Official Report*, 21 March 1922. http://stormontpapers.ahds.ac.uk/stormontpapers/pageview.html?volumeno=2&pageno=85.

Northern Ireland House of Commons. *The Parliamentary Debates: Official Report*, 22 April 1926. http://stormontpapers.ahds.ac.uk/stormontpapers/pageview.html?volumeno=7&pageno=671.

Northern Ireland House of Commons. *The Parliamentary Debates: Official Report*, 5 April 1927. http://stormontpapers.ahds.ac.uk/stormontpapers/pageview.html?volumeno=8&pageno=597.

Northern Ireland House of Commons. *The Parliamentary Debates: Official Report*, 3 May 1927. http://stormontpapers.ahds.ac.uk/stormontpapers/pageview.html?volumeno=8&pageno=1033.

Northern Ireland House of Commons. *The Parliamentary Debates: Official Report*, 25 October 1927. http://stormontpapers.ahds.ac.uk/stormontpapers/pageview.html?volumeno=8&pageno=2239.

Northern Ireland House of Commons. *The Parliamentary Debates: Official Report*, 7 October 1952. http://stormontpapers.ahds.ac.uk/stormontpapers/pageview.html?volumeno=36&pageno=1301.

Northern Ireland House of Commons. *The Parliamentary Debates: Official Report*, 30 March 1954. http://stormontpapers.ahds.ac.uk/stormontpapers/pageview.html?volumeno=38&pageno=1541.

Northern Ireland House of Commons. *The Parliamentary Debates: Official Report*, 5 February 1957. http://stormontpapers.ahds.ac.uk/stormontpapers/pageview.html?volumeno=41&pageno=1.

Northern Ireland House of Commons. *The Parliamentary Debates: Official Report*, 5 June 1957. http://stormontpapers.ahds.ac.uk/stormontpapers/pageview.html?volumeno=41&pageno=1.

Northern Ireland House of Commons. *The Parliamentary Debates: Official Report*, 2 April 1958. http://stormontpapers.ahds.ac.uk/stormontpapers/pageview.html?volumeno=42&pageno=43.

Northern Ireland House of Commons. *The Parliamentary Debates: Official Report*, 7 May 1958. http://stormontpapers.ahds.ac.uk/stormontpapers/pageview.html?volumeno=42&pageno=561.

Northern Ireland House of Commons. *The Parliamentary Debates: Official Report*, 16 June 1959. http://stormontpapers.ahds.ac.uk/stormontpapers/pageview.html?volumeno=44&pageno=1900#f wd-44–1805.

Northern Ireland House of Commons. *The Parliamentary Debates: Official Report*, 15 March 1960. http://stormontpapers.ahds.ac.uk/stormontpapers/pageview.html?volumeno=46&pageno=713.

Northern Ireland House of Commons. *The Parliamentary Debates: Official Report*, 8 June 1960. http://stormontpapers.ahds.ac.uk/stormontpapers/pageview.html?volumeno=46&pageno=1847.

Northern Ireland House of Commons. *The Parliamentary Debates: Official Report*, 22 October 1963. http://stormontpapers.ahds.ac.uk/stormontpapers/pageview.html?volumeno=55&pageno=1.

Northern Ireland House of Commons. *The Parliamentary Debates: Official Report*, 23 October 1963. http://stormontpapers.ahds.ac.uk/stormontpapers/pageview.html?volumeno=55&pageno=45.

Northern Ireland House of Commons. *The Parliamentary Debates: Official Report*, 27 February 1964. http://stormontpapers.ahds.ac.uk/stormontpapers/pageview.html?volumeno=56&pageno=1281.

Northern Ireland House of Commons. *The Parliamentary Debates: Official Report*, 3 March 1964. http://stormontpapers.ahds.ac.uk/stormontpapers/pageview.html?volumeno=56&pageno=1359.

Northern Ireland House of Commons. *The Parliamentary Debates: Official Report*, 12 May 1964. http://stormontpapers.ahds.ac.uk/stormontpapers/pageview.html?volumeno=57&pageno=791.

Northern Ireland House of Commons. *The Parliamentary Debates: Official Report*, 16 June 1964. http://stormontpapers.ahds.ac.uk/stormontpapers/pageview.html?volumeno=57&pageno=1963.

Northern Ireland House of Commons. *The Parliamentary Debates: Official Report*, 5 November 1969. http://stormontpapers.ahds.ac.uk/stormontpapers/pageview.html?volumeno=74&pageno=951.

Northern Ireland House of Commons. *The Parliamentary Debates: Official Report*, 20 May 1970. http://stormontpapers.ahds.ac.uk/stormontpapers/pageview.html?volumeno=76&pageno=559.

Theses

Hope, Ann. *From Civil Rights to Guerrilla War: The Northern Ireland Civil Rights Association's Struggle for Democracy 1969–1972*. Labour Studies Diploma Thesis, Ruskin College, 1976.

Nolan, James T. *The Status of the Catholic Minority in Northern Ireland 1920–1939*. Unpublished Doctoral Thesis, Fordham University, 1953.

Treaties

Anglo-Irish Treaty, 1921.

International Bill of Human Rights. 217. Vol. III, 1948.

International Covenant on Civil and Political Rights, 1966.

International Covenant on Economic, Social and Cultural Rights, 1966.

United Nations documents

Capotorti, Francesco. *Study on the Rights of Persons Belonging to Ethnic, Religious and Linguistic Minorities*. Geneva: UN Center for Human Rights, n.d.

UN General Assembly Resolution. Vol. 1541, 1960.

United Nations General Assembly. *National Institutions for the Promotion and Protection of Human Rights*. A/RES/48/134, 1993. Accessed 19 July 2014, www.un.org/documents/ga/res/48/a48r134.htm.

United Nations General Assembly. *Principles Which Should Guide Members in Determining Whether or Not an Obligation Exists to Transmit the Information Called for under Article 73E of the Charter of the United Nations. United Nations General Assembly Resolution*. Vol. 1541, 1960. www.ohchr.org/EN/ProfessionalInterest/Pages/RightAndResponsibility.aspx.

Secondary documentation

Books

Adams, Gerry. *Before the Dawn: An Autobiography*. Dingle, Ireland: Brandon Books, 1996.
Adams, Gerry. *Hope and History: Making Peace in Ireland*. London: Brandon, 2003.
Adams, Gerry. *The New Ireland: A Vision for the Future*. Dublin: Brandon Books, 2005.
Aristotle. *Politics*. Translated by T. A. Sinclair. Harmondsworth: Penguin Books, 1983.
Barritt, Denis P. and Carter, Charles F. *The Northern Ireland Problem: A Study in Group Relations*. 2nd edn. New York: Oxford University Press, 1972.
Bell, Christine. *Peace Agreements and Human Rights*. Oxford: Oxford University Press, 2000.
Bell, J. Bowyer. *The Irish Troubles: A Generation of Violence 1967–1992*. New York: St. Martin's Press, 1993.
Bew, Paul. *Ireland: The Politics of Enmity 1789–2006*. Oxford: Oxford University Press, 2007.
Bew, Paul, Gibbon, Peter and Patterson, Henry. *Northern Ireland 1921–2001: Political Forces and Social Classes*. London: Serif, 2001.
Blair, Tony. *A Journey: My Political Life*. London: Hutchinson, 2010.
Boyle, Kevin and Tom Hadden. *Ireland: A Positive Proposal*. Harmondsworth: Penguin Books, 1985.
Brownlie, Ian. *Principles of Public International Law*. 5th edn. Oxford: Oxford University Press, 1998.
Cassese, Antonio. *International Law*. 2nd edn. Oxford: Oxford University Press, 2005.
Claude, Richard P. and Weston, Burns H. *Human Rights in the World Community*. 2nd edn. Philadelphia: University of Pennsylvania Press, 1992.
Cochrane, Feargal. *Northern Ireland: The Reluctant Peace*. New Haven: Yale University Press, 2013.
O'Brien, Conor Cruise. *States of Ireland*. London: Hutchinson, 1972.
Crawford, James R. *The Creation of States in International Law*. 2nd edn. Oxford: Oxford University Press, 2007.
Darby, John P. *Scorpions in a Bottle: Conflicting Cultures in Northern Ireland*. London: Minority Rights Publications, 1997.
Dickson, Brice. *The European Convention on Human Rights and the Conflict in Northern Ireland*. New York: Oxford University Press, 2012.
Dudley Edwards, Ruth. *The Faithful Tribe: An Intimate Portrait of the Loyal Institutions*. London: Harper Collins, 1999.
Elliott, Sydney. *Northern Ireland Parliamentary Election Results, 1921–72*. Chichester: Political Reference Publications, 1973.
English, Richard. *Armed Struggle: The History of the IRA*. London: Pan Books, 2004.
Falk, Richard A. *Human Rights Horizons*. London: Routledge, 2000.
Forsythe, David P. *Human Rights in International Relations*. Cambridge: Cambridge University Press, 2000.
Franck, Thomas M. *Fairness in International Law and Institutions*. Cambridge: Clarendon Press, 1998.
Gallagher, Frank. *The Invisible Island: The Story of the Partition of Ireland*. London: Victor Gollancz, 1957.
Glendon, Mary Ann. *A World Made New: Eleanor Roosevelt and the Universal Declaration of Human Rights*. New York: Random House, 2001.

Hamill, Desmond. *Pig in the Middle: The Army in Northern Ireland, 1969–1984.* London: Methuen, 1985.

Harvey, Colin J., ed. *Human Rights, Equality and Democratic Renewal in Northern Ireland.* Oxford: Hart Publishing, 2001.

Heaney, Seamus. *The Cure at Troy: A Version of Sophocles' Philoctetes.* New York: Farrar, Straus and Giroux, 1991.

Heath, Edward. *The Course of My Life: The Autobiography of Edward Heath.* London: Hodder Stoughton, 1998.

Held, David. *Models of Democracy.* 2nd edn. Cambridge: Polity Press, 1996.

Hurd, Douglas. *Memoirs.* London: Abacus, 2004.

Ishay, Micheline R. *The History of Human Rights: From Ancient Times to the Globalization Era.* Oakland: University of California Press, 2008.

Lee, Joseph J. *Ireland 1912–1985: Politics and Society.* Cambridge: Cambridge University Press, 1989.

Lijphart, Arend. *Patterns of Democracy.* New Haven: Yale University Press, 1999.

McCluskey, Conn. *Up off Their Knees: A Commentary on the Civil Rights Movement in Northern Ireland.* Conn McCluskey and Associates, 1989.

McEvoy, Kieran. *Dealing with the Past? An Overview of Legal and Political Approaches Relating to the Conflict in and about Northern Ireland.* Healing Through Remembering, 2013. Accessed 15 October 2014, www.healingthroughremembering.org/images/uploads/HTR_Dealing_with_the_Past _-_Legal_and_Political_Approaches_Report.pdf.

McGarry, John and O'Leary, Brendan. *Explaining Northern Ireland: Broken Images.* Oxford and Massachusetts: Blackwell Publishers, 1995.

McKay, Susan. *Bear in Mind These Dead.* London: Faber & Faber, 2008.

McKittrick, David and David McVea. *Making Sense of the Troubles: The Story of the Conflict in Northern Ireland.* Chicago: New Amsterdam Books, 2002.

Mitchell, George John. *Making Peace.* Oakland: University of California Press, 2000.

Murphy, Yvonne, Leonard, Allan, Gillespie, Gordon and Brown, Kris, eds. *Troubled Images: Posters and Images of the Northern Ireland Conflict from the Linen Hall Library, Belfast.* Belfast: Linen Hall Library, 2001.

Northern Ireland Civil Rights Association. *"We Shall Overcome" … The History of the Struggle for Civil Rights in Northern Ireland 1968–1978.* Belfast: Northern Ireland Civil Rights Association, 1978.

O'Connell, Rory, Nolan, Aoife, Harvey, Colin, Dutschke, Mira and Rooney, Eoin *Applying an International Human Rights Framework to State Budget Allocations: Rights and Resources.* London: Routledge, 2014.

Ó Dochartaigh, Niall. *From Civil Rights to Armalites.* Cork: Cork University Press, 1997.

Pomerance, Michla. *Self-Determination in Law and Practice: The New Doctrine in the United Nations.* The Hague: Martinus Nijhoff Publishers, 1982.

Powell, Jonathan. *Great Hatred, Little Room: Making Peace in Northern Ireland.* London: Vintage Books, 2009.

Purdie, Bob. *Politics in the Streets: The Origins of the Civil Rights Movement in Northern Ireland.* Belfast: Blackstaff Press, 1990.

Robertson, Geoffrey. *Crimes against Humanity: The Struggle for Global Justice.* Harmondsworth: Penguin Books, 2006.

Sandel, Michael, ed. *Justice: A Reader.* New York: Oxford University Press, 2007.

Summers, James. *Peoples and International Law: How Nationalism and Self-Determination Shape a Contemporary Law of Nations.* The Hague: Martinus Nijhoff Publishers, 2007.

Sunday Times Insight Team. *Ulster.* Penguin Special. Harmondsworth: Penguin Books Ltd, 1972.

Thatcher, Margaret. *The Downing Street Years*. London: HarperCollins, 1993.
Thornberry, Patrick. *International Law and the Rights of Minorities*. Oxford: Clarendon Press, 1991.
Whyte, John Henry. *Interpreting Northern Ireland*. Oxford: Clarendon Press, 1990.
Wilson, Harold. *A Personal Record: The Labour Government, 1964–1970*. New York: Little, Brown, 1971.

Book chapters

Aughey, Arthur. "The 1998 Agreement: Unionist Responses". In *A Farewell to Arms? From "Long War" to Long Peace*, edited by Michael Cox, Adrian Guelke and Fiona Stephen. Manchester: Manchester University Press, 2000.
Guelke, Adrian. "The United States and the Peace Process". In *The Northern Ireland Question: The Peace Process and the Belfast Agreement*, edited by Brian Barton and Patrick J. Roche. London: Palgrave Macmillan, 2009.
McCrudden, Christopher. "The Equality of Opportunity Duty in the Northern Ireland Act 1998: An Analysis". In *Equality and Human Rights: Their Role in Peace Building: The Equality Provisions of the Good Friday Agreement and the NI Act*, 11–23. Belfast: Unison, 1999.
Mensargh, Martin. "The Background to the Irish Peace Process". In *A Farewell to Arms? From "Long War" to Long Peace*, edited by Michael Cox, Adrian Guelke and Fiona Stephen, Manchester: Manchester University Press, 2000.
O'Dowd, Liam. "Shaping and Reshaping the Orange State: An Introductory Analysis". In *Northern Ireland: Between Civil Rights and Civil War*, by Liam O'Dowd, Bill Rolston and Mike Tomlinson. CSE Books, 1980.
Parlevliet, Michelle. "Icebergs and the Impossible: Human Rights and Conflict Resolution in Post-settlement Peace Building". In *Human Rights and Conflict Resolution in Context*, edited by Eileen F. Babbett and Ellen L. Lutz. New York: Syracuse University Press, 2009.
Shannon, Catherine B. "From House Rights to Civil Rights 1936–1968". In *The Field Day Anthology of Irish Writing*, edited by Angela Bourke. Cork: Cork University Press, 2002.
Whyte, John. "How Much Discrimination Was There under the Unionist Regime, 1921–68?" In *Contemporary Irish Studies*, edited by Tom Gallagher and James O'Connell. Manchester: Manchester University Press, 1983.

Journal articles

Birrell, Derek. "Relative Deprivation as a Factor in Conflict in Northern Ireland". *The Sociological Review* 20, no. 3 (1 August 1972): 317–43.
Burton, John W. "Conflict Resolution: The Human Dimension". *International Journal of Peace Studies* 3, no. 1 (January 1998). Accessed 15 June 2014, www.gmu.edu/programs/icar/ijps/vol. 3_1/burton.htm.
Clapham, Andrew. "Human Rights Obligations of Non-State Actors in Conflict Situations". *International Review of the Red Cross* 88, no. 863 (September 2006). Accessed 20 July 2014, www.icrc.org/eng/assets/files/other/irrc_863_clapham.pdf.
Dickson, Brice. "The Detention of Suspected Terrorists in Northern Ireland and Great Britain". *University of Richmond Law Review* 43, no. 3 (March 2009): 927.

Donohue, Laura K. "Regulating Northern Ireland: The Special Powers Acts, 1922–1972". *The Historical Journal* 41, no. 4 (1998): 1089–120.
Éamonn Ó Ciardha, and Micheál Ó Siochrú. "A Laboratory for Empire". *History Today* 17, no. 6 (December 2009).
Feeney, Vincent E. "Westminster and the Early Civil Rights Struggle in Northern Ireland". *Eire Ireland* 11, no. 4 (1976).
Galtung, Johan. "Violence, Peace, and Peace Research". *Journal of Peace Research* 6, no. 3 (1 January 1969): 167–91.
Guelke, Adrian. "The USA and the Northern Ireland Peace Process". *Ethnopolitics* 4, no. 4 (November 2012): 424–38.
Harvey, Colin. and Schwartz, Alex. "Designing a Bill of Rights for Northern Ireland". *Northern Ireland Legal Quarterly* 60, no. 2 (2009): 181–99.
Harvey, Colin. "Building Bridges? Protecting Human Rights in Northern Ireland". *Human Rights Law Review* 1, no. 2 (2001): 243–64.
Harvey, Colin. "The Implementation of a Bill of Rights in Northern Ireland". *Northern Ireland Legal Quarterly* 51, nos 3/4 (2001): 342.
Kovalcheck, Kassian A. "Catholic Grievances in Northern Ireland: Appraisal and Judgment". *The British Journal of Sociology* 38, no. 1 (March 1987): 77–87.
Lijphart, Arend. "Constitutional Design for Divided Societies". *Journal of Democracy* 15, no. 2 (April 2004): 93–109.
Lundy, Patricia, and McGovern, Mark. "A Truth Commission for Northern Ireland?" *Research Update* 46 (October 2006). Accessed 14 October 2014, www.ark.ac.uk/publications/updates/update46.pdf.
Mitchell, Christopher. "Beyond Resolution: What Does Conflict Transformation Actually Transform?", *Peace and Conflict Studies* 9, no. 1 (May 2002).
Morgan, Michael. "Post-War Social Change and the Catholic Community in Northern Ireland". *Studies: An Irish Quarterly Review* 77, no. 308 (December 1988): 422–33.
Mulholland, Marc. "Assimilation versus Segregation: Unionist Strategy in the 1960s". *Twentieth Century British History* 11, no. 3 (2000): 284–307.
Trimble, David. "The Belfast Agreement". *Fordham International Law Journal* 22, no. 4 (1999). Accessed 31 October 2013, www.davidtrimble.org/speeches_toraiseup13.htm.
Xu, Xiaobing, and Wilson, George. "On Conflict of Human Rights". *Pierce Law Review* 5, no. 1 (December 2006).

Web articles

Department of Peace and Conflict Research, Uppsala University. "Definition of Armed Conflict", n.d., www.pcr.uu.se/research/ucdp/definitions/definition_of_armed_conflict.
International Labour Organization. "Conventions", 2012. Accessed 24 January 2012, www.ilo.org/dyn/normlex/en/f?p=NORMLEXPUB:12000:0::NO:::.
Melaugh, Martin. "'The Troubles' – Suggested Reading", 1 November 2007. http://cain.ulst.ac.uk/bibdbs/bibliography/index.html.
Northern Ireland Human Rights Commission. "Advice for You". Accessed 24 October 2014, www.nihrc.org/advice-for-you.
Northern Ireland Human Rights Commission. "Priorities and Plans". Accessed 24 October 2014, www.nihrc.org/about-us/whatwww.nihrc.org/about-us/what-we-do/priorities-planswe-do/priorities-plans.

Police Service of Northern Ireland. "Workforce Composition Figures", 16 February 2015. Accessed 8 July 2014, www.psni.police.uk/index/updates/updates_statistics/updates_workforce_compositio n_figures.htm.

Sutton, Malcolm. *Sutton Index of Deaths*. Accessed 6 July 2014, http://cain.ulst.ac.uk/sutton.

The Scottish Government. "Scottish Crime and Justice Survey 2012–13", 3 July 2014. www.scotland.gov.uk/Publications/2014/03/9823/10.

Index

Note: NI = Northern Ireland; HR = human rights; 'n' denotes chapter notes.

For Product Safety Concerns and Information please contact our EU representative GPSR@taylorandfrancis.com
Taylor & Francis Verlag GmbH, Kaufingerstraße 24, 80331 München, Germany

www.ingramcontent.com/pod-product-compliance
Ingram Content Group UK Ltd.
Pitfield, Milton Keynes, MK11 3LW, UK
UKHW020014200926
475702UK00014B/1889